ORALITY:
THE QUEST FOR MEANINGS

ORALITY:
THE QUEST FOR MEANINGS

Zothanchhingi Khiangte

PARTRIDGE

To order additional copies of this book, contact
Partridge India
000 800 10062 62
orders.india@partridgepublishing.com

www.partridgepublishing.com/india

Contents

Foreword

*O*rality: *the Quest for Meaning* offers a range of diverse approaches on orality. The collection provides a comprehensive introduction into the study of oral traditions, offered by scholars of eminence from diverse fields, cultures and regions. I am happy with the initiative taken by Dr. Zothanchhingi Khiangte in producing this volume. I am sure this kind of laudable work will enrich not only the academia but the society as a whole, for most of the works in this volume deal with issues which are prevalent and relevant in our society giving valuable insights pertinent to the understanding of these issues. Among such issues is the practice of witch hunting which unfortunately remains a social menace in Assam. There are also some less glaring issues of sexual discrimination in the patriarchal set-up of which the society can be made aware of through academic discourses. I feel that this collection is especially meaningful for the region since most cultures of Northeast India are oral cultures and research in this field needs to be promoted. I am glad that the international seminar on Orality, of which this volume is an outcome could act as an important platform to generate significant discourses from eminent scholars across the world, which I am sure will go a long way in the promotion of further research in this field of study.

Ravi Shankar Borgoyary
Director
Higher Education, BTC.

Acknowledgements

This book is an outcome of the international seminar on Orality organized by the Department of English, Bodoland University. Therefore, I owe special thanks to the BTC, especially Mr. Khampa Borgoyary, the Deputy Chief of Bodoland Territorial Council without whose immense support the seminar would not have been possible to organize. I am grateful to the university authorities for their support.

My particular thanks to the Partridge Publishers who have always been courteous and kind enough to publish this volume.

Preface

From the ancient to the contemporary, philosophers and thinkers have undertaken the task of, borrowing K.C Baral's phrase, 'meaning-making', with each school of thought trying to improvise upon the precedent. However, these quests still remain inconclusive and the search for meanings that lurk beneath the apparent will continue. The academia has been engaged in varied interpretations and re-interpretations of literature that has been produced over the centuries. In spite of the fact that writing is a relatively recent invention with most cultures recording their experiences, history, traditions, proverbs and beliefs through oral traditions which are remembered and passed on through generations, it was not until the last century that the academic obsession to the 'written text' could be peeled off and veered towards the 'oral'. The new surge of interest in non-western cultures, spurred by post-colonial studies, has also necessitated the renewed study of the unwritten verbal art of the people across the world. The study reveals a diverse worldview different from the western conception of the 'universal' and offers us alternative ontological theories.

The re-discovery of oral traditions, Miles Foley has claimed, is "an achievement of the twentieth century" (*Teaching Oral Traditions*: 1998) and with this 're-discovery' comes a spectrum of genres poised to unearth a host of meanings contained in oral traditions. According to Ulo Valk, the quest for meaning emerged as a significant trend in folkloristics in the 1970s, represented by Alan Dundes, Lauri Honko, Bengt Holbek, Lutz Röhrich, and others ('The

Quest for Meaning in Folklore and Belief Narrative Studies'). Valk's critical analysis, in this volume, on the genre of belief narratives offers us the dialectics of belief systems.

The twentieth century has witnessed the development of several theories by which literary works can be approached and these theories have been applied to the study of oral traditions as well. A wide range of approaches have been employed to the study of orality— the more "mechanical" Finnish historic-geographic method and the age-area hypothesis which focused on documenting the spread of a tale, resulting in the Aarne and Thompson's *Types of Folktale* and Thompson's *Motif –Index of Folk Literature*, followed by cultural approaches which lay emphasis on oral tradition as an information system that encoded cultural meaning and served the needs of the members of the society; some prefer to use the structural approach which examines oral literature as revealing the underlying, universal structure of the human mind. According to Claude Levi-Strauss, human beings perceive the world in binary opposites such as night-day, man-woman, dark-light and so forth and aspects of culture provide symbolic means to bridge or mediate these opposites which are structurally embedded at a deep, cognitive level of the human mind. But this approach is rejected as arbitrary intellectual approach by other approaches which stress on the importance of the "native's point of view" within a specific culture and stress upon this 'local' context which is ignored by the universality of Strauss's approach. And there is also the psychoanalytic approach, according to which, oral tradition serves as a symbolic projection of unconscious desires. These approaches are again followed by the postmodern approaches like the ethnopoetics, which lays stress to not only the text but the context with all the elements of performance like gestures, laughter, sighs etc thus encapsulating the living performances into the text. For ethnopoetic theorists like Dennis Tedlock, the prosaic narratives become poetry. According to him, documenting or translating a text must necessarily encapsulate the living performance. With the ethnopoetic approach, the sole focus on the text is shifted to the context and all the elements of performance. John Zemke in his paper "Tradition, Language and Continuity: Endangered Languages and Oral Traditions"(Keynote address at the International Seminar on "Orality: Quest for meaning" at Bodoland University, Kokrajhar, 26-27th May 2016) examines the question as to whether the significance of oral traditions lies in their 'content' or in their 'rhetorical power', 'the idea that their meaningfulness arises from their rhythms of linguistic patterning, independent of and indifferent to semantic content'.

However, the limitations of western approaches have to be recognized when it comes to the study of the non-western cultures since these theoretical constructs, as Ulo Valk cautions, may act as 'ideological baggage' which 'might obscure our vision' if we do not have 'alternatives' and it is this need for an 'alternative… outside the western paradigm' which Baral emphasises in his paper "Orality: the Quest for Meaning". (Plenary Lecture at the International Seminar on "Orality: Quest for meaning" at Bodoland University, Kokrajhar, 26-27th May 2016)

Oral traditions have been approached from different perspectives to deal with issues like identity politics, gender, race, class, ethnicity, ecology etc. Northeast Indian writers such as Desmond Kharmawphlang see the folk as preservers of traditional wisdom and culture and turn to the village elders to gather the remnants of the quaint past. Many feminist writers, including Esther Syiem, Temsula Ao, and Margaret Ch. Zama re-read oral narratives of their cultures to deconstruct "male paradigms" and thereby reconstruct models which are more expressive of women's emotions and experiences. Though writing for a long time had primarily been a male domain, in orality we find a number of women's expressive voices. For example, in the oral poetry of the Mizos, a number of early folk songs are named after women composers, one among whom was said to have been buried alive by the village authorities because they feared that she would not leave any song for posterity to compose. We also find the female presence in lullabies and love songs. The antiphonal Assamese and Bodo songs of Assam sung during festivals like Bihu and Bwisagu offer a wide spectrum of subtle female vocabulary, expressing their concerns and anxieties in a jocular fashion. In many cultures, songs become the forms of expressions of women, who are often been dominated, silenced and marginalized by men. We find a continuum of this trend in the writings of women poets.

This volume contains diverse approaches on oral narratives, which include analyses on the representations of female characters in oral narratives. Maria Palleiro's study, by examining the representations of the fairy tale character of Little Red Riding Hood in different socio-cultural contexts, explores the 'rhetoric of female corporality' in Argentinian context. Again, S. Dkhar's and Rashmi Narzary's essays offer interpretations of culture from a gender perspective.

When we talk of orality and writing, it is pertinent to note that as far as conducting cultural affairs goes, even in the last few years of the millennium, the greater part of the world's population still conducts most of its cultural affairs without writing. And in the case of most societies of the Northeast India, the customary laws still exist in an oral form though a few have been codified.

It is interesting to note that the epistemic understanding of Northeast India is usually derived through the scanty writings that one finds on the region through anthropological works or colonial reports which offer more or less distorted views on the region and its people and which often promote negative connotations. However the oral narratives offer a different understanding of the region. Oral traditions play an undeniable role in establishing the identity of a tribe by giving an insight into the tribe's history. In the native sense, the oral myths and narratives are history though incidents may not be factually accurate and they may qualify as history because they are what a culture considers as truth. They are, in the words of Arnold Krupat, "public knowledge of the past— public in the sense of being culturally shared" (*Red Matters*: 2002) In the same vein, Jan Vansina has also said that among the peoples without writing, oral tradition forms the main available source for the reconstruction of the past (*Oral Tradition*: 1972). In this volume, an eminent historian from Northeast India Salam Irene redefines historiography focusing on the significance of the 'oral' in the 'writing' of native history thereby reaffirming the possibilities of alternatives. And this possibility provokes further discourse in the line of Michel de Certeau's famous proclamation that history is not a faithful record, not 'truth' because it is writing and all writing as praxis is already a colonization of a terrain not its own (Certeau, *The Writing of History*). This further leads us to question the politics and poetics of historiography.

The subtle nuances, the rhythmic arrangement of lines, the deliberate pauses, onomatopoetic devices, the formulaic system, etc of their poetry, the various dance forms with various allusions to nature, the intricate patterns of their attire and many other elements involved in the verbal art of these non-literate societies offer a cosmology and worldviews of a people who have remained secluded and excluded for a long time. It is only by the turn of this new millennium that the region has witnessed some of its native writers experimenting with writing. But considering the fact that this phenomenon is comparatively new with hardly enough written literature to fill an entire shelf of a library, it might be dangerous if not misleading to focus exclusively on the written literary text as the unrivaled paragon of literary art.

Besides the realization and the consequent preservation of knowledge, the study of oral traditions has led to a better understanding of those cultures who have not otherwise found adequate representation in the written literature of the modern world.

_____ Zothanchhingi Khiangte
Editor

Tradition, Language and Continuity: Endangered Languages and Oral Traditions

John Zemke

The election of tradition, language, and continuity as themes for reflection ensures that one has arrived last to the topics and is indebted to the scholars and thinkers whose writings have advanced key insights into these concepts. Their writings shape and color what I may reasonably claim to have to say about the meanings and functions that triad of social phenomena. The first, tradition, commonly and un-reflexively is thought to name a phenomenon whose meaning is straightforward and unproblematic, but which, upon closer scrutiny, turns out to cloak a problematic semantic enigma, and counts as an example of words that parse the world in unempirical ways. The second term, language, is the distinctive feature of humankind, a communicative strategy developed some 100,000 to 50,000 years ago. Continuity is a problem for mathematicians and philosophers, and I restrict my remarks about it to the areas of tradition, identity, and language.

The anthropologist Clifford Geertz observed that culture constitutes a body of instructions a society develops to guide its members. Culture orients the individual offering a chart for navigating life in its quotidian and extraordinary dimensions. Culture is "background knowledge or assumptions governing the conduct of everyday affairs" (Goodenough, 1957, quoted in Gumperz,

758). Culture is an intellectual commons that all members of a community draw upon in building a future (O Giollain, 24). Geertz cautioned that the failure to correctly read and internalize cultural instructions would condemn an individual to social alienation and a society to dystopia. Geertz's analysis is apposite to developing an understanding of the pathology that characterizes many oral traditions today, and perhaps, for formulating measures to restore their relevance in communities where they currently are dying.

Some scholars, for instance Henry Glassie, argue that culture and tradition are synonyms, that the two words refer to one and the same phenomenon, which can also be called folklore. Historically, a substantial body of cultural, traditional or folklore instructions was conveyed by word of mouth from one generation to the next. Human societies universally devised complex narratives—myths, epics, legends, tales, and songs— as well as other forms — proverbs, riddles, medical healing charms, weather lore, and knowledge of flora and fauna— traditions transmitted orally. Some narratives represent human plights and model strategies for overcoming adversity, situating oneself properly in the time and place of experience, and fulfilling one's social roles. From a narrative perspective, then, language is a basic matrix of culture and creates culture. According to the psychologist Jerome Brunner, there must be in human society "a local capacity for accruing stories into a diachronic structure that permits continuity to construct a history, a tradition, or a legal system" ("The Narrative Construction of Reality," 10). Narrative, Brunner claims, "represents and constitutes reality" (4) and is able to "hold uncanniness rather than resolve it" (16).

Those narrative genres may be called "Oral Traditions," though the term has raised legitimate objections about its analytic value. Ruth Finnegan's criticism comes to mind. And there is, too, an ontological question, do oral traditions need necessarily transmit intelligible content or is what gives them meaning their rhetorical power? Here the idea is that their meaningfulness arises from their rhythms of linguistic patterning, independent of and indifferent to semantic content, such is Pascal Boyer's argument.

Returning to Geertz's prescription of social and cultural, what is underway socially when the empirical circumstances that the individual experiences no longer conforms with the horizon of expectations the larger society formerly contemplated, and for which it developed a body of instructions? When the usefulness of cultural instructions for negotiating everyday reality has lapsed, a kind of pervasive cognitive dissonance takes hold of the individual and the society as a whole. Profound shifts, geographical dislocations, and social displacements in the developed and developing worlds have produced what the anthropological linguist John J. Gumperz characterizes in the following terms (785):

> "One of the most important and least understood effects of post-industrial society is the profound change it has caused in the nature of interpersonal relationships. Whether through peaceful migration, disaster, war, or revolution, people everywhere are leaving their small local communities to settle in new, complex, and often uncontrollable settings. [...] Whatever their cause, the end effect is everywhere the same: a radical alteration in interaction patterns causing changes in everyday routine and requiring new modes of communication."

Gumperz's insight goes directly to the status of oral traditions in the present and their future viability. The Eurocentric and Romantic view that writing creates a new kind of mentality simply encodes the cultural chauvinism of 19th century European elites' claim to embody the pinnacle of human intelligence and cultural achievement, a position that insists on the reality of a difference in mental cognition that separates the literate from the illiterate. The linguist Roy Harris, has demonstrated that this claim of lettered-unlettered dichotomy is false and obscures a realistic understanding of how writing does restructure thought. Harris argues that all new technologies restructure thought and cognition, for instance, the advent of the abacus more deeply affected human thought than the invention of writing, and the advent of the camera even more than the abacus. What writing does, according to Harris, is to create "autoglottic inquiry," that is to say, writing introduces a "conceptual gap between sentence and utterance" and this gap is the locus for the creation of an "autoglottic space," which make logic and dialectic possible (104). This space presupposes the validity of "unsponsored speech," words that are detached from the speaker, allowing for decontextualized words (104), speech divorced from the face-to-face presence of interlocutors. The authority to speak, and responsibility to tradition for the accuracy and validity of the utterances pronounced, is usurped by writing and made available for evaluation independently of the speaker's intentions (105).

Oral traditions are a class of speech, a hyponymy of language, consisting of specialized registers distinct from everyday speech, which differ from language to language and genre to genre. This distinctive feature of oral traditions has been corroborated by multiple studies in anthropology, folkloristics, philology, ethnography of speech, and performance studies.

Tradition

Tradition is a problematic term. Max Radin concluded that it possesses a:

> "primary characteristic of vagueness, remoteness of source, and wider ramification to make it seem peculiarly strong to those who have recourse to it and peculiarly weak to those who mean to reject it" (1935:67). Max Weber identified tradition as one of three "ideal types" of authority, a complementary of rational authority and charismatic authority (Finnegan, 67). Ruth Finnegan has characterized three essential qualities of tradition: (i) it has multiple meanings as both a process and a product; (ii) though it is a neutral term, its emotive sense is linked to power, academic, political or moral; and, finally, (iii) in all its definitions there are three recurring themes: (a) unwritten or oral transmission (b) something handed down and old, and (c) a set of valued beliefs and practices (Finnegan, 67).

Traditions are not eternal super-organic entities they exist by virtue of human agency, and are advanced through time by dint of a performer's volition. For the traditional performer this creative action is "a job that must be done" and to do it properly requires taking responsibility for the enacted tradition, keeping faith with the past and the future in the present. Tradition need not have a quality of deep historical time, though it often can, rather it must necessarily possess two essential qualities: value and significance for the individuals who lay claim to it.

The sociologist Edward Shils refers to "the ineluctability of tradition" in all human thinking and action, tangible and intangible, written and oral, even in science itself (147). Traditions are ubiquitous despite Western philosophical antipathy towards them since the Enlightenment. Cartesian reason holds that only that what is universal, unalterable, and eternal is true knowledge (Isaiah Berlin, quoted in O'Giollain, 35). The inheritors of the Enlightenment viewed "tradition" as an instrument of oppression and advocated benign neglect of traditions or their outright destruction (Honko, 131).

Lauri Honko, represented tradition as a set of potentials, active and inactive, connected with a group, stored in the human mind and subject to irrevocable loss because of loss of social function (133). Professor Honko emphasized that tradition denotes a "cultural potential or resource, not the actual culture of the group" (133), and he linked "identity" to specific focalizing markers such as language, music, dance, costume, ritual, and so forth, emblems that bear "a symbolic meaning" and are imbued with "an air of sacredness" (133). He devised a model to illustrate "the translation of tradition into culture into identity" (134). In this model, "tradition" forms part of a dynamic force of self-creation, a set of cultural resources for "the preservation of identity" (142).

Now, the word *tradition* derives from the Latin *traditio*, "handing over" or "delivering," and refers to a *mode* of transferring ownership in Roman property law, the intentional hand-to-hand transfer of property or a symbol of it (Noyes, "Tradition," 239). Tradition implies a reciprocal relationship involving individuals, one having the conscious intention to receive something and another having the conscious intention of delivering that thing. Yet, what is delivered and received by the participants in an oral tradition is not a physical entity but a symbolic expression of identity. Traditions, like identities, move along social networks and, according to Linda Dègh, flow through "conduits of like minded individuals" (quoted in Noyes, "Tradition," 238) linking material and immaterial forms within human relationships (245).

Performances of traditional verbal art may be seen as "texts" possessing formal, thematic, and pragmatic properties that make them *"memorable, repeatable*, and thus *sharable* and *durable*. Reiteration of the texts gives them a social currency and locates them on a "temporal continuum of inter-textually related cognate texts, a *"tradition"* (Bauman, "The Philology of the Vernacular," 31). Another way of understanding *tradition* is to regard it as an *interpretive process*, which is both continuous and discontinuous. Since all cultures are in a constant state of change, something that is in an objective sense temporally "new" may be endowed with the *symbolic value of the traditional* (Hander and Linnekin, 273), since social life is "always symbolically constructed, never naturally given" (281). The category of tradition is, then, "an assigned meaning, an arbitrary symbolic designation, not an objective quality" (285). The idea is straightforward: the continuity of the present with the past is always constructed in the present through a symbolic process that makes continuity from discontinuity (287). Along these same lines, Dell Hymes summarized tradition "as a process that involves continual recreation" (quoted in Handler and Linnekin, 287), one that continuously produces and contains mulitforms. Early in the 20th century, the noted Spanish philologist Ramón Menéndez Pidal articulated this insight with the lapidary phrase: "traditions live in variants."

Identity

"Identity" is derived from the Latin *idem*, meaning 'the same'. Yet sameness arises only in opposition to differences, there is no self without the other, no group A without group B. Allan Dundes illustrates the point citing Margaret Mead's classic question, "how do you define a man if you don't mention a woman, and how do you define a woman if you don't mention a man?" (Dundes, 149). Identity is, however, not a single mode, but involves multiple modes: the individual takes on and performs different social identities according to the requirements of circumstance. Identity simultaneously connotes the sharing of common characteristics with others (150), selfsameness, as well as opposition to others, singularity. A common set of symbolic and emblematic traditions announce to others who one is. For an ethnic minority, the dynamic interplay between majority and minority freights the experience of opposition more heavily on the minority. The principal means by which individuals and groups assert identity is through folklore. Psychiatrists, sociologists, and folklorists share the judgment that one's identity emerges from the stories one tells about oneself or one's community, and that each recounted incident corroborates the uniqueness of the individual and crafts a badge of group membership (Abrahams, "Identity" 201).

Identity, then, may be seen as a performance. Ervin Goffman has described how individuals and groups stage themselves to audiences to foreground. Dorothy Noyes argues that "performances make community real through *repetition, formalization*, and *consensus* ("Group," 468). Indeed, any individual utterance can be considered an "act of identity," yet collective identity is generally a reactive response to external oppression. Common action, i.e., acting in common, makes community (468), and community identity exists in its collective performances, those that evince consensus, "feeling together," a feature of the locus of the imagined community. The demise of any traditional practice, according to John McDowell, coincides with the disappearance of the imagined community (quoted in Noyes, "Group," 465).

Identity is a "persistent cultural system" that foregrounds how individuals participate in culture. It brings into play a set of identity symbols, "a sort of storage mechanism for human experience, a means for organizing the accumulating experience of people" (Spicer, 796), in other words, a tradition. The sociologist Edward Spicer holds that identity is comprised of a set of symbols and their meanings, of spheres of participation, of shared understandings and sentiments regarding those symbols, and of networks of social relations that maintain those meanings (798). Though the ability to speak a language is not the sole necessary condition for identifying with a group, without it the individual's "participation in the moral sphere is hardly imaginable" (799). Persistent cultural systems such as identity operate by means of "an oppositional process involving the interactions of individuals in environments," and are characterized by larger organizations that engender "a high degree of internal solidarity," and motivate individuals to continue participating in the kinds of experiences that are "'stored' in the identity system in symbolic form" (799), in other words, traditions.

Language

In what follows, when I mention language I am alluding to oral traditions.

Language is a primary index, or symbol, or register of identity, as the linguist R. M.W. Dixon noted, "a language is the emblem of its speakers" (quoted in Crystal, *Language Death*, 40). Upon learning that the linguist Stephen Morey had documented the repertoires of speakers of Tai languages in Assam, India, the Venerable Phra Preng Pathassaro volunteered: "When we study language, we study the heritage of human thought" (Morey, 1). Similarly, Michael Krauss characterizes language as "a supreme achievement of a uniquely human collective genius, as divine and endlessly a mystery as a living organism" (8). Each idiom possesses a unique rhythm, a unique worldview, and poses an epistemology. Generations of speakers endeavor to persuade, deceive, explain, protect, and in so doing create intricate systems that represent humankind's most fundamental achievement, without which, none of the others could be begun (Evans, 2). Ralph Waldo Emerson referred to languages as "the archives of history" ("The Poet" 1884, quoted in Crystal, 41). They are simultaneously repositories of cultural knowledge, symbols of social identity, and vehicles for personal and political interaction. Within the mosaic of unique visions that human languages present, the forms of talk, the categorization of objects, colors, events, and the ways relationships to others are expressed, as well as deictic conceptions of time and space, and of how something is known to the speaker manifest multiple differences. All these properties of language constitute a "resource for the discovery of shared social knowledge (Gumperz, 786). Wilhelm von Humboldt perceived that each language offers a distinct vantage point on the world, and carries with it the legacy of a people's attempts to grasp reality, one that results from the constant interplay between *energeia*, the activity of speech, and *ergon*, the product of speech (Evans, 36).

The proposition that language structures speakers' perceptions of reality is associated with Edward Sapir and his student Benjamin Whorf, who claimed that "grammatical structure directly reflects a native speakers conception of the universe around him" (quoted in Gumperz, 787). The Spanish philosopher José Ortega y Gasset devised a thought experiment to illustrate how the comparison of languages reveals difference: Superimpose the templates of two different languages: their points of coincidence and divergence, what each declares or silences, as well as their respective preferences. This illustration suggests that all languages possess markers of individuality that are in some respect unique. The comparison further implies similar singularities will hold true for different oral traditions and their performances.

Languages operate with systems of phonology, lexicon, syntax, and prosodic features, in other words, diction, content, and context. And Diction matters. Susan Jamison's superb illustration of how it matters is codified in the Goldilocks Principle. For mother-tongue English speakers the word "porridge" immediately conjures a particular narrative space that its synonym, "oatmeal," does not. So too, the unremarkable question, "Who has been sleeping in my bed?" gives instant access to that same narrative space. Joshua Katz refers to a similar phenomenon in Indo-European epics, when diction is eliminated "what appears to be the same stories show up again and again" (47). These examples illustrate the importance of register in oral traditions.

The matter of a word's place or register is mirrored by the question of the word in a place. Discourse always arises in an immediate here and now. The translator Franz Paepcke emphasizes that: "every text is embedded in a situation which is not itself language" but, rather, a cultural, social or economic space in and from which the text speaks to us (quoted in Snelling-Hornby, 33). Charles Fillmore distinguishes formal propositional knowledge from experiential knowledge, which exists as memories, and avers that: "comprehending a text involves mentally creating a world whose properties depend on the individual interpreter's private experience" ("Scenes-and-Frames Semantics," 61). Focusing attention on performance allows a fuller appreciation that the meaning of folklore is discernible in its performance (Lindhal, 264). Every folklore utterance unfolds in an immediate social context: "in continuity with traditional knowledge and understanding" (265).

Epic is sung rather than recited, performed as a song rather than spoken as poetry (Reichl, 163). Performance involves a performer, an audience, rhythm, diction, content, and temporal and physical circumstances. The aesthetic differences between experiencing performance of a ballad or epic and reading a text is one of kind not of degree (177-78). Entextualization, the transformation of a performance into a text, flattens or eliminates key dimensions of the performance Karl Reichl questions whether it is even possible to adequately document an epic performance (156-59).

Folkloristics has concerned itself with describing the "context" of an expressive form (Abello et al., 69). Indeed, setting and performance are considered part and parcel of the conveyed message (Rubel and Rosman, 12). A folklore performance is a total social event. All discourse is situated in a time and place (Snelling-Hornby, 165). Even the time of a performance can affect meaning (Ben-Amos 1983, 287). And meaning is embedded in a situation that is itself not solely language but also cultural, economic, and social. Context determines whether a proposition is an *explicature* or an *implicature,* and this determination is always culturally specific (Ernst-August Gutt, quoted in Snelling-Hornby, 73). Mina Skafte Jensen has argued convincingly that certain common traits link genres, a special register of style and language, a feeling of shared values, the entertainment power of narrative, characteristics that are: "all based on the event of performance" (49). No cultural expression can be performed outside a frame-of-reference and all such communication is always subject to the generic conventions of a specific society. "Tellers always tell tales," observes Ulrich Marzolph, and tales unfold in the reality of a narrative situation in which performers embrace the improvisation, variability, and creativity sanctioned by the art of story telling ("'Folktale', 'Tale-Type'" 221). From Marzolph's perspective, "tales always convey ideas related to specific cultural contexts" (*id.*).

Carl Lindhal observes that different iterations of a constant plot shape may mean very different things, that is to say, a stable plot pattern does not vouchsafe stable meaning but "a change in pattern almost certainly signals a major shift in signification" (267).

Myths and epics are highly specific to a particular culture or cultural area (Jason, 2000). Heda Jason advocates istudying a culture's oral traditions with an eye to identifying their endemic genres: "the genres of a culture [...], form a system ordered along several axes" (2000, 36), and genre is specific to particular cultural areas (2000, 137). Jason advocates the development of analytic schemes keyed to specific cultures, even if the scheme itself is, ultimately, arbitrary. That genre is cultural not universal has been forcefully advanced by Ben-Amos (1992, 5), who observes that what history and literature might consider "a fact" is determined by the interests of a particular researcher, citing Max Webber's dictum: "There is no absolutely "objective" scientific analysis of culture" (Webber 1949, 72; quoted *ibid.*, 12). Standard European narrative categories are scholarly inventions—Myth, Edmund Leach reported, is not a phenomenon that ethnographers encounter in the field (1982, 3; quoted in Dundes 1968, xvii).

Oral Tradition Research

John Miles Foley argued that there is not one "oral tradition" or "OT composition." Different societies, different languages with their unique prosodies and their mythic repositories, he insisted, configure different oral traditions. OT research examines process of change, interplay between genres, interactions between performer and audience, performance conventions, and interpretation, questions that lend themselves best to fieldwork, rather than archival research (Finnegan, "Tradition, But What and For Whom," 116). Oral Tradition research investigates specifics as well as generalities, and understands traditional forms not as distinctive things nor age-old products of the past but, rather, as researchable in living practice (121).

From its beginnings, folkloristics treated orality as a touchstone, with "oral" acting as the characterizing adjective in compounds such as "oral tradition," "oral poetry," or "oral literature," all synonymous with the term "folklore" (32). According to Diarmuid O Giollain, folkloristics arises in the "dialogue between universalism and particularism," what Johann Gottfried von Herder averred was the: "incommensurability of the values of different cultures and societies" (35).

Roman Jakobson and Prague structuralists identified *parallelism* and a special relationship of *langue* and *parole* as distinctive featuresof oral traditions. The enduring contribution of Albert Lord and Milman Parry's Formulaic Theory is the validation of tradition as a "multiform," existing in varied realizations rather than as decaying forms of a single UR-text. Lord and Parry's work brought to the forefront the role of individual creativity "in the act of performance," freedom within generic constraints of poetic system and the contextual constraints of the performance arena" (Bauman, 33). Ethnopoetic studies are concerned with the *internal organization* of oral texts (Noyes, "Tradition," 237-38). The locus of oral traditions (at least for riddles) is "not the local community but social networks", according to the findings of Honorio Velasco, (Velasco, cited in Noyes, "Tradition," 254). Linda Dègh's reported a similar finding locating tradition in "conduits of like minded individuals." Dense networks tends to be multiplex, repositories of conservative vernacular culture characterized by interaction, solidarity, social control, and integrity in sufficiently robust to resist external pressure to conform with dominant norms (Noyes, "Group," 458).

Philology examines the social and temporal circulation of texts. Richard Bauman posits that it is the iteration and reiteration of texts that gives them social currency. Time operates on the collective catalogue of folkloristic texts. Successive iterations of a text through time produce variant forms, multiforms, cognate texts that are related to each other and cohere in a *"tradition"* (31). Bauman emphasizes the dynamic tension between textual persistence or continuity—tradition, and textual change—variation or creativity: "one or another vector (tradition or change) and one or another set of textual properties (formal, thematic, pragmatic) may be foregrounded, but always in [...] relation to the others" (32).

Lauri Honko hypothesized that the performers of oral traditions possess a mental text, one that holds an overall sense of its structure, and intuit a picture of the text as a whole. To ensure transmission of a text oral performers use sophisticated linguistic techniques. Oral texts are performed by declamation, chanting, and singing. Sequences are elaborated and incorporate repetitive motifs, figures of speech, patterns of verbal elaboration, e.g., praising, boasting, abusing, formulaic hyperbole, digressions, and other linguistic devices, elements of the grammar and registers of oral genres and performances. And a master performer's knowledge of plot and discourse may bulk to encyclopedic proportion, including detailed catalogues of gods or kings, accounts of victories and defeats, stories of legends and heroes, details of recipes and remedies, all of which offer insights into social structures, mythology, and folklore (Crystal, *Language Death*, 43)

One of the central threads running through John Miles Foley's work was to promote study of the world's traditional verbal arts, genres that were, or still are, ignored or dismissed by academic departments unable or unwilling to countenance their, complexity, intricacy, and sophistication. He worked tirelessly to educate the reading public to the "complexity and worth of literatures which non-literate people transmitted" (Jacobs, 2). He subscribed to Melville Jacob's judgment, "no sociocultural heritage is simple. No people is simple-minded" (2). The verbal arts of indigenous peoples merit serious attention and study.

The author of the foreward to Desmond Kharmawphalang's *Khasi Folktales and Songs* laments the fact that the traditional verbal arts of tribal peoples in India are "conventionally perceived as a mere anthropological curiosities, at best a source for oral history" (ii); one has only to read a *Khasi* tale or song to appreciate how wrong convention can be:

> *Thuk thuk* the strings sound
> the poet keeps on singing
> The *marynthing* and the *maryngod*
> the spinning loom chimes in tune
> the old deaf woman chews betel
> till her heart becomes rusty.

Endangered Languages

From the confluence of tradition, culture, identity, and language in oral traditions I want to introduce the topic of endangered languages because language is the common vehicle of their creation, expression, and continuity. There is a basic analogy between how biological systems and climatic conditions affect a biosphere and how linguistic systems and social and economic forces affect an ethnosphere, and particularly how they affect the logosphere, the term Michael Krauss' coined to refer to the totality of the realm of the world's words, the languages they inhabit, and the links between them (Evans, *Dying Words*, ix). The analogy is of interest because oral traditions have for millennia formed an integral part of the human logosphere. Just as loss of diversity in a biosphere augurs poorly for the diversity of the flora and fauna that comprise it—greater biological homogeneity precipitates ecological instability and results in a precarious situation for the diversity of species—so too, loss of diversity in the logosphere portends an existential threat to the he diversity of humanity's oral traditions.

The biologist Jared Diamond notes that the phrase 'the tragic loss of diversity' usually refers to loss of biodiversity, but an equally tragic loss of diversity is the extinction of languages: "Language is the most complex and distinctive product of the human mind. Possession of language is our most important distinguishing feature" (1). Each language is the focus of its speakers' culture, the vehicle for their expression. Thousands of languages have disappeared throughout history, yet today languages are disappearing at an alarming rate, overwhelmed by the tsunami of American consumerism and globalization that is contributes to the domination of fewer languages in government, business, entertainment and the internet. Though some 6,000 languages are spoken today, by the end of the 21st century they may be reduced to just 200. The large-scale eclipse of languages is fulfilling Margaret Mead's prophecy of a time sooner rather than later when "human imagination is to be narrowed to just a few modalities of thought, there is no memory of the fact that there were other possibilities." This is a matter of deep concern and the main question I want to explore. Everything I have to offer derives from the writings of scholars who have systematically examined this question. The subject bears repeating.

The annals of the catastrophe that befell American indigenous peoples reveal how European and European-American colonialists persecuted them, organized their genocide by means of disease, war, and the wholesale extermination of the animals that provided their food, clothing, tools, and spiritual guidance, and endeavored to eradicate the culture of those left alive, denying them the use of their mother tongue alienating them from their traditional knowledge. In North America today, most native languages are on the verge of extinction. Even Navajo with about 100,000 speakers is at risk, many if not most Navajo children now speak only English. How Indian languages disappeared is no secret. European settlers devoted themselves to exterminating, subjugating, expelling or acculturating Indian peoples. Once the population was subjugated, the national government determined to "civilize" Indian children by sending them to boarding schools, to speak English only. Only in 1967 did the U.S. federal government reverse its complete ban on school instruction in any Indian language; only in 1990 were funds found to foster Native American Language studies (Diamond, 5). Today many Indians in the U.S. and Canada are caught up in poverty, alienation, heath crises and personal tragedy. For North American Indians, as for people everywhere, their language is the vehicle of their culture.

My point is not to dwell on wholly justifiable denunciation of crimes against humanity— crimes that in the guise of poverty and despair, continue to be perpetrated on a daily basis on tribal reservations across North America— but, instead, to invoke a counter argument to the Folkloristic criticism of the "salvage" or "graveyard" trope. The salvage trope ironizes the insistent pleading voiced since the early 19th century that one or another tradition teeters precipitously on the verge of extinction, yet the folklorist fails to recognize that the tradition in question never quite slips over the precipice into the abyss of oblivion and succumbs to Modernity. The salvage trope criticism has its place, but it is, nevertheless, no less true, and arguably more compelling, to recognize that when a language becomes extinct, whatever portion of its linguistic repertoire that remained undocumented at the point of death is permanently unrecoverable.

In the preface to his *Reversing Language Shift*, Joshua Fishman, the pioneer of endangered language scholarship, writes: "Today, the worldwide process of globalization of the economy, communication and entertainment media [...] and consumerism as a way of life threatens to sweep away everything locally authentic, and different." (). The rapid endangerment and death of many minority languages across the world is a matter of concern for linguists and anthropologists as well as everyone concerned with issues of cultural identity in an increasingly globalized culture. Linguists reckon that only 600 of the 6,000 or so languages in the world are 'safe' from the threat of extinction. Language loss is known throughout history, yet language death today differs in character, extent, and implications. The destruction of cultural diversity by means of processes that overwhelm local languages and cultures include natural catastrophe, social and economic genocide, destruction of habitat, displacement, economic factors, migration, language suppression through assimilation, the global electronic universe, and especially television, what Michael Kraus calls "cultural nerve gas" (6).

The main causes of language death are structural forces and power relations (Skutnabb Kangas, 29), when a dominant culture's language pervades everywhere, reinforced by daily economic and cultural pressures (Crystal, 78). That is to say, a minority people's language and cultural heritage begins to disappear and the loss of domains accelerates at an alarming rate such that its language, what "lies at the heart of what it means to be human"

(Crystal, 33-34), goes extinct. Language loss amounts to the "loss of inherited knowledge" (34) and is a tragic loss because, as Marianne Mithun notes, languages "are not interchangeable [...] they represent the distillation of the thoughts and communication of a people over their entire history" (quoted in Crystal, 38). A language constitutes both "an element of culture" as well as "the basis for all cultural activities" (Bloch and Trage [1942:5], quoted in Crystal, 39). Mamadou Kouyaté, a West African *griot* avers that performers embody oral traditions: "We are vessels of speech [...] the memory of mankind; by the spoken word we bring to life the deeds and exploits of kings for younger generations" (42). Community elders, leaders, and educators acknowledge that their language is "as an expression of their whole society and history [...] a means of conveying the past [...], their myths and legends [...] chief mechanism for rituals [...] and beliefs about the spirit world [...] to new generations [...] "expressing their network of social relationships [...] and commenting of their interaction with the landscape" (48-49). The demise of local languages and cultural systems is the loss of "priceless products of human mental ingenuity" (Ken Hale, cited in Crystal, 53). Except in the rare cases where a writing system is in use, when a language perishes it leaves no physical trace (Evans, *Dying Words,* viii); speech is evanescent and unless a form of recording is employed to capture its utterances, the texts survive only in oral traditions (Evans, 21). Cultural assimilation affects language in three ways: social or economic pressure to speak the dominant language; bilingualism that may rapidly devolve to monolingualism; and abandonment of the mother tongue everywhere but in the home (78). Such developments contribute to a diminished prestige for the indigenous language (83) and prestige is a *sine qua non* for language survival.

The August 11, 2013 edition of the Times of India reported that India lost in just 50 years 20 per cent of its languages, and among those UNESCO listed as endangered figure: Bodo, Dimasa, Hmar, Karbi, Mizo, Angami, Baitei, Deuri, Khasi, Kabui, Koch, Ao, Konyak, Meteit, and Mech. Dilip Kumar Klita, director of the Anundoram Borooah Institue of Language, Art and Culture is quoted as warning that "the northeast region "might lose its rich cultural heritage and diversity in the long run." Let me place the issue in the context of my own country. In July of 2012 Gladys Thompson, the last fully fluent speaker of Kiksht, a dialect of Clackamak spoken in the Pacific Northwest, died, and with her death Kiksht became extinct. Some months before her demise, Gladys Thompson explained her thinking on the plight of people who do not speak the mother tongue (Oregon Public Broadcasting, March 8, 2012):

> You're losing your culture once you lose your language. And you go completely into today's society and you know nothing about yourself. And the elders tell you that you're lost in this world. You don't know who you are or what you're doing once you lose the language and the traditional values."

Each language tells its own story in its grammar, lexicon, botanical and zoological, encyclopedia, and collection of songs and stories. In the social coordination of the community of speakers and in the mind of the individuals who know and use it language is doubly articulated. The entire mechanism of language, and its traditional verbal arts, requires human memory.

In a survey of endangered languages in mainland Southeast Asia published in 1991, James Matissof notes that India is a center of linguistic diversity, counting 1,683 'mother tonges' of which 850 are in daily use. Of these, 107 belong to the Tibeto-Burman family, making India that language family's heartland, with its center of gravity in Northeastern India (205). Matissof discusses how some minority languages are able to absorb enormous amounts of foreign lexical borrowings and grammatical features without losing their basic identity (202), while others confront the invidious effects of the threat posed by the imposition of an alien belief system that undermines the languages' semantic and conceptual systems. One way this sort of semantic imperialism impoverishes a language is by suppressing its religious/poetic styles of discourse, stripping out archaic features of vocabulary and grammar (202). The death of a language, Matissof observes, is "comparable to the extinction of a plant or an animal species," it is "an irreparable loss of "linguistic genes," [...] yet he recognizes a counterbalancing weight. An individual abandons a dying mother tongue in favor of a viable language that offers the irresistible potential for personal benefit, "allowing the individual to be 'mainstreamed' into a more powerful majority culture" (202).

Professor E. Annamalai's 1998 report on language survival in India indicates that tribal communities in general have maintained their language in limited domains, such as the home, for limited purposes, maintaining community identity and networking. As have other researchers, Professor Annamalai links the spread of literacy to the loss of minority languages and to the language's perceived economic value: "languages have a cultural value, but their culture does not have an economic value" (24). He cites the case of the Bodos in Assam and the Meithei in Manipuri as examples of the reversal of language shift and resistance to cultural and linguistic assimilation (25). Recognizing the power of the State to give economic value to ethnicity, he ennumerates the factors required to invigorate tribal languages: literacy, economic opportunity, awareness of rights, and language skills, all of which augment linguistic prestige. Though the work of the Indira Gandhi National Centre for Arts, the Anthropological Survey of India, and the Central Institute of Indian Languages in documenting minority languages is mentioned, Professor Annamalai locates the motive force for successful maintenance of minority languages in local community action, requiring political support in order to create: "awareness of the value of tribal culture and language, to counter the hegemonic pressure for self-deprecation [...] and to educate [minorities] about the realities [...] of the material progress [envisaged] through adaptation of the dominant culture and language" (29). In an article entitled "Identity Politics and Social Exclusion in India's Northeast," Nava Kishar Das observes: "Language has always been in the center stage of ethnic turmoil in the Northeast" (550) where tribal peoples have experienced the existential anxiety triggered by the threat of "near extinction of their original language and religion" (551) seeing themselves become "a minority in their own homeland" (552). Professor Das reviews the multiple factors at play in the region's fraught modern history—economic, demographic, political, sociological marginalization, deprivation, identity loss, as well as movements for self-determination and autonomy—stressing the need for "peace, development" and political consensus in order to safeguard "harmony in the region" (556), and concludes that the minorities' aspirations should be regarded as "a pre-requisite for distributive justice, which no nation-state can neglect" (556).

In the course of his survey the Tai languages spoken in Assam, Stephen Morey recognized that among communities that have lost a part of their language and culture, what remains is often sacred and its custodians refuse to disclose it to outsiders. He reports that among the Ahom, those with a vestigial knowledge of the language are priests, their texts are religious, and the language itself has acquired sacred status in modern society (24). He reports that from the perspective of speakers of these Tai languages, documentation is their foremost concern, the messages conveyed by the texts are considered as important as the means for conveying them (104). Morey translates a Tai Phake text, "Grandfather Teaches Children," thus: "Words are sweet as molasses. Food taken through the mouth nourishes the whole body. Young children should remember the words spoken by grandfather for thousands of years. O my dearest grandchildren, do not forget the old customs and traditions" (83). Grandfather's injunction, and the sentiment of the Tai speakers Morey mentions, describe the dilemma of the survival of the oral traditions transmitted by languages cornered against the wall of extinction and oblivion.

References

Abello, James, Broadwell, Peter, and Tangherlini, Timothy R. "Computational Folkloristics." *Communications of the ACM* 55.7 (July 2012): 60-70.

Annamalai. E. 1998. "Language survival in India: Challenges and Responses." In Kazuto Matsumura, ed., *Studies in Endangered Languages, Papers from the International Symposium on Endangered Languages, Tokyo, November 18-20, 1995*, 17-31. Tokyo: Hituzi Syobo.

Bauman, Richard. 2008. "The Philology of the Vernacular." *Journal of Folklore Research* 45.1:29-36.

Becker, A. L. "The Elusive Figures of Burmese Grammar: An Essay." In William Foley, ed. *The Role of Theory in Language Description*, 61-85. Berlin: Mouton de Gruyter.

Ben-Amos, Dan. "Introduction." *Research in African Literatures*, 14 (1983): 277-82.

Ben-Amos, Dan. "Do we Need Ideal Types (in Folklore)? An Address to Lauri Honko." NIF Papers No. 2. Turku: Nordic Institute of Folklore, 1992.

Boyer, Pascal. 1990. *Tradition as Truth and Communication: A Cognitive Description of Traditional Discourse*. New York: Cambridge University Press.

Brunner, Jerome. 1991. "The Narrative Construction of Reality." *Critical Inquiry* 18:1-21.

Crystal, David. 2000. *Language Death*. Cambridge: Cambridge University Press.

Das, Nava Kishor. 2009. "Identity Politics and Social Exclusion in India's Northeast. A Critique of Nation-Building and Redistributive Justice." *Anthropos* 104.2:549-58.

Diamond, Jared. 2001. "Deaths of Languages." *Natural History* 110.3:30-38.

Dundes, Alan. 1968. "Introduction." In Vladimir Propp, *Morphology of he Folktale*, 2d ed., xi-xvii. Austin: University of Texas Press.

Dundes, Alan, 1984. "Defining Identity through Folklore (Abstract)." *Journal of Folklore Research* 21:149-52.

Evans, Nicolas. 2010. *Dying Words: Endangered Languages and What They Have to Tell Us.* Wiley-Blackwell.

Fillmore, Charles. 1977. "Scenes-and-Frames-Semantics." In Antonio Zampolli, ed. *Linguistic Structures Processing*, 55-79. Amsterdam: North-Holland Publishing.

Finnegan, Ruth. 1991. "Tradition, But What Tradition and For Whom?" *Oral Tradition* 6.1:104-24.

Finnegan, Ruth. 2003. "Oral Tradition: Weasel Words or Transdisciplinary Door to Multiplexity." *Oral Tradition* 18.1: 84-86.

Fishman, Joshua. 1991. *Reversing Language Shift: Theoretical and Empirical Foundations of Assistance to Threatened Languages.* Philadelphia: Multilingual Matters.

Geertz, Clifford. 1973. *The Interpretation of Cultures.* New York: Basic Books.

Glassie, Henry. 1994. "On Identity." *Journal of American Folklore* 107:238-41.

Gumperz, John J. 1974. "Linguistic Anthropology in Society." *American Anthropologist New Series* 76.4: 785-98.

Hale, Ken, 1992a. "On Endangered Languages and the Safeguarding of Diversity." *Language* 68:1-3.

_____. 1992b. "Language endangerment and the Human Value of Linguistic Diversity." *Language* 68:36-42.

Handler, Richard, and Jocelyn Linnekin. 1984. "Tradition, Genuine or Spurious." *Journal of American Folklore* 97:273-90.

Harris, Roy. 1989-2001. "Does Writing Restructure Thought?" *Language & Communication* 2-3:99-106

Honko, Lauri. 1995. "Traditions in the Construction of Cultural Identity and Strategies of Ethnic Survival." *European Review* 3:131-46.

Jacobs, Melville. 1959 *The Content and Style of An Oral Literature: Clackamas Chinok Myths and Tales.* University of Chicago.

Jason, Heda, 2000. *Motif, Type and Genre. A Manual for Compilation of Indices & A Bibliography of Indices and Indexing.* Helsinki: Suomalainen Tideakatemia; Academia Scientarum Fennica.

Jensen, Mina Skafte. 2005. "Performance." in *A Companion to Ancient Epic*, 45-54. Ed. John Miles Foley. Cambridge, Mass: Blackwell Publishing.

Katz, Joshua T. 2005. "The Indo-European Context." *A Companion to Ancient Epic*, 20-30. Ed. John Miles Foley. Cambridge, Mass: Blackwell Publishing.

Kharmawphalang, Desmound. 2006. *Khasi Folktales and Songs*. New Delhi: Sahitya Akademi.

Krauss, Michael. 1992. "The World's Languages in Crisis." *Language* 68:6-10.

Lindhal, Carl. 1977. "Some Uses of Numbers." *Journal of Folklore Research* 34: 263-73.

Mahapatra, B.P. 1991. "An Appraisal of Indian Languages." In Robert H. Robins and Eugenius M. Uhlenbeck, eds. *Endangered Languages,* 177-88. Oxford/New York: Berg.

Marzolph, Ulrich. 2003. "'Folktale,' 'Tale Type'." In *South Asian Folklore, An Encylcopedia*. Ed. by Margaret A. Mills, Peter J. Claus, and Sarah Diamond. New York and London: Routledge. pp. 220-22.

Matisoff, James A. 1991. "Endangered Languages of Mainland Southeast Asia." In Robert H. Robins and Eugenius M. Uhlenbeck, eds. *Endangered Languages,* 189-228. Oxford/New York: Berg.

Morey, Stephen. 2002. "The Tai Languages of Assam: A Grammar and Texts." Ph.D. Dissertation, Monash University.

Noyes, Dorothy. 2009. "Tradition: Three Traditions." *Journal of Folklore Research* 46:233-68.

Noyes, Dorothy. 1995. "Group." *Journal of American Folklore* 108:449-78.

O Giollain, Diarmuid. 2003. "Tradition, Modernity and Cultural Diversity." *Folkloristica* 13:35-47.

Radin, Max. 1935. "Tradition." In E. R. A. Seligman, ed. *Encycloaedia of the Social Sciences*, vol. XV, 62-67. 16 vols. New York: MacMillan.

Reichl, Karl. 2007 Ed. and trans. *Edige. A Karakalpak Oral Epic as performed by Jumabay Bazarov*. Helsinki: Academia Scientiarum Fennica.

-----. 2016. "Oral Epics into the Twenty-First Century: The Case of the Kyrgyz Epic *Manas*." *JAF* 129:327-44.

Rubel, Paula and Abraham Rosman. 2003. "Introduction: Translation and Anthropology." In *Translating Cultures. Perspectives on Translation and Anthropology*, 1-22. Eds. Paula Rubel and Abraham Rosman. Oxford: Berg.

Shils, Edward. 1971. "Tradition." *Comparative Studies in Society and History* 13:122-59.

Skutnabb Kangas, Trove. 2012. *Linguistic Genocide in Education or Worldwide Diversity and Human Rights.* New York: Routledge.

Snelling-Hornby, Mary. *The Turns of Translation Studies.* Amsterdam, Philadelphia, PA: J. Benjamin, 2006.

Spicer, Edward. 1971. "Persistent Cultural Systems." *Science, New Series* 174 (no. 4011, Nov. 19, 1971):795-800.

The Quest for Meaning in Folklore and Belief Narrative Studies (with Special Reference to Assam)1

Ülo Valk

Throughout its history folklore research has gone through several transfigurations, although we can also note a few more or less persistent trends and tendencies. The discipline has constantly grown as new forms of expressions have been discovered and the spectrum of genres being studied has expanded. In addition, scholars have always been fascinated by the attempt to grasp the depths and by looking inwards for the origins of folklore, its genesis, history, and hidden meanings. Johann Gottfried von Herder (1744–1803), one of the pioneers of folklore studies, was mainly interested in songs as expressions of the soul of the people, but he also considered them resources of memory and thus comparable to archival sources. Jacob Grimm (1785–1863) and Wilhelm Grimm (1786–1869) became the founders of the theory of folk prose, offering the basic characteristics of folktales (*Märchen*) and legends (*Sagen*). Just like Herder they tried to understand folklore through a historical perspective and postulated a link between the pre-Christian heritage and

---

1   The article is a revised version of the plenary lecture delivered at the seminar Orality: The Quest for Meaning, held at Bodoland University (May 26–27, 2016).

later folk tales, poetic elements of which they explained as survivals of ancient myths. The discovery that folklore can store elements from the past was very important for the future of the field, leading to several developments. In the 19th century a whole mythological school emerged that tried to discover the hidden meanings of European folktales. Max Müller (1823–1900) discovered the importance of solar deities in Rigveda and became a great authority in philological studies, followed by scholars hoping to find ancient solar deities in folklore. The Danish folklorist Bengt Holbek (1933–1992), who thoroughly analysed the history of folktale studies, has shown that this approach led to a dead end in fantastic speculation that was of no use in understanding the meaning of folklore for the people. For example Franz Linnig interpreted the tale Little Red Riding Hood (ATU 333) as a remote reflection of proto-Indo-European mythology. According to Linnig, the little girl with red cap represents the dawn, corresponding to the goddess Ushas in Vedic mythology; her opponent is the wolf Fenris in Scandinavian mythology, whose Indian parallel is the evil dragon Vrtra, a creature who has also been called *vrika* ('wolf') in Indian myths. (Holbek 222–23) Such interpretations of the possible mythic origin of folktales and their hidden meanings appeared in many 19th century works but the school declined during the 20th century as scientifically more solid methodologies appeared.

The quest for meanings in folk narrative studies

Whereas the mythological school of Max Müller failed, the geographic-historical, Finnish school had more success. Instead of looking for some cryptic, hidden meanings within folklore it studied its spread in time and space. Systematic comparative philological research and the compilation of indexes of folktales established the ground for discipline to take a firm position in academic institutions. This brief historical introduction cannot be more than sketchy. Thus, it might be enough to say that the basic research questions of the Finnish school remained too narrow for socially oriented folklorists, many of whom left the libraries and archival collections for actual fieldwork.

During the second half of the 20th century innovative approaches emerged in the USA when a new generation of scholars, including Roger D. Abrahams, Dan Ben-Amos, Alan Dundes, Richard Bauman, Américo Paredes and others distanced themselves from philology and shifted towards synchronous studies of live traditions and folklore events in social settings: not folklore as a ready-made product, but the processes of its making was of interest. One of the landmarks of this approach was the collection of articles entitled *Towards New Perspectives in Folklore* (Paredes, Bauman 1972). Comparative and analytical work with archival manuscripts and old records lost much of its attraction and folklorists concentrated on fieldwork, with 'performance' becoming the key concept. Attention shifted from texts to the social life of folklore and its psychological relevance to performers and their audiences. Whereas in North America contextual research gained momentum and most folklorists took interest in live traditions, many European scholars maintained their more conservative research traditions, focussing on manuscripts and printed sources. However, it became clear that documenting folklore and studying its textual transmission was not sufficient to comprehend its social life and to see folklore as a tool and mode of thinking and as an expression of worldview.

In the 1970s, the quest for meaning emerged as a significant trend in folkloristics, represented by Alan Dundes, Lauri Honko, Bengt Holbek, Lutz Röhrich, and many other scholars, whose analytical and interpretive works tried to reach a better understanding of folklore genres, not only considering the explicit textual level, but also deeper symbolic and structural layers. It is not surprising that the Europeans took the leading role, as the problem of meanings becomes more acute in archival research. The temporal distance between the moment of the textualisation of folklore and its reception several generations later is an obstacle to understanding. The fact that the performer and scholar are socially distant, that the language has changed and the predominantly rural environment has been replaced with urban settings, is another complication. Hence, it became important to develop hermeneutical methods of scholarship. In 1984 the 8th congress of the International Society for Folk Narrative Research (ISFNR) was held in Bergen, Norway, and one of the main topics of discussion was 'folk narrative and the quest for meaning'. Some of the questions, asked at the congress were as follows: "Does the meaning of folklore lie in the text or the context? Is the meaning obvious or hidden? How can meaning be studied? Whose meanings should the folklorists be interested in? What is the position of different genres in speaking of meaning? Has meaning been overlooked in research?" (Lehtipuro 1) These questions are equally relevant today, more than thirty years later.

Let us discuss briefly some answers that were offered. Alan Dundes (1934–2005) noted that asking questions about the meaning of folklore should be a part and parcel of fieldwork: "One cannot always guess the meaning from context. For this reason, folklorists must actively seek to elicit meaning from the folk." (Dundes 51). Remarkably, the quoted article "Metafolklore and Oral Literary Criticism", in which Dundes stressed the need to study the context of folklore in order to understand it, was first published as early as 1966. In the same article he noted: "There is no one right interpretation of an item of folklore any more than there is but one right version of a game or song. (We must overcome our penchant for monolithic perspectives as exemplified in monotheism, monogamy, and the like.) There are multiple meanings and interpretations and they all ought to be collected." (Dundes 52). Understanding folklore as an endless art of oral and written variation without a standard template is today common, but in the 1970s and 1980s this contextual approach, which celebrated the overflowing abundance of folklore with a broad range of meanings, was new. It was necessary to articulate what meaning is and find ways to study something so subtle, which remains hidden behind the folkloric texture. Finnish scholar Lauri Honko (1932–2002) belonged to those who remained sceptical about retrospective research in archives. He noted that meaning is generated in the process of communication. He also emphasised that the context of situation and performance plays a crucial role in the formation of actual meaning, and characterised "stored, inactive texts, be they conserved in human memory or in folklore archives, as empty, devoid of meaning." (Honko 41)

Others, however, tried to find reliable methods to study the meanings in this stored folklore of the past. Danish scholar Bengt Holbek (1933–1992) examined different schools of interpretation, listing four basic trends: firstly, focusing on the historical development and original forms, secondly concentrating on the social and cultural conditions of the storytellers and their audiences, thirdly studies of mind (including Freudian and Jungian approaches), and finally deriving meaning from narrative and conceptual structures (1982: 20–21). He found it discouraging that these schools are incompatible and rather exclude than support each other in their common goal – the quest for meaning. Holbek compared archival recordings of folktales with faded photographs that convey a frozen, reduced expression of the original performance. He noted that we know next to nothing about the narrator and the audience, but we do have the texts and we possess some knowledge of the wider context. (1982: 27) According to Holbek, "the task of the interpreter concerned with traditional storytelling is to explore the white patches in order to formulate hypotheses about the *meaning* structuring a complex process of which only some parts are known" (ibid.). In his later monograph "The Interpretation of Fairy-Tales" (1987) Holbek tried to formulate the consistent method of interpretation of their marvellous elements, describing the genre as a common language that has been mastered by many storytellers. According to Holbek, the genre is tied together by certain syntagmatic and paradigmatic models that provide framework for the formation of symbolic expressions. Hence, he tried to formulate a scientific method of interpreting the symbolism of fairy-tales, bearing in mind the perspective of story-tellers and their primary audiences in traditional European rural society.

German scholar Lutz Röhrich (1922–2006) stressed that the "meaning of a text is not a fixed constant but is a variable, determined by the development of culture and ideas, fashions and trends, and dependent on rulers and ruling ideologies, not to forget the education and cultural awareness, the sex, age, religion and ethnic group of the consumer" (128). Röhrich also drew attention to the fact that meanings and expressive forms of folklore are in correlation. He made a distinction between metaphoric genres with hidden meanings (such as riddles, proverbs and jokes) and non-metaphoric genres (such as legends and fairy tales). However, he showed that the latter also contain messages, such as wish-fulfilment in fairy tales and overcoming anxieties and fears in legends. Röhrich wrote: "Creatures of lower mythology are usually embodiments of human fears, projections of anxiety and the repression of these. Water sprites and water-nymphs embody the enticement, but also the danger and fathomlessness of water. Werewolf legends point to the wolf-like traits in human beings. (---) Belief in witches is the vehicle for a great many different fears and the attempt to find a scapegoat for these fears. The motives often are envy, hate, greed and jealousy." (Röhrich 132) The psychological relevance of folk narratives in expressing conflicts certainly helps to explain why certain stories spread so widely. As fears about accidents, failures and misfortunes can hardly be overcome, there is a consistent need for stories that address them. However, whether these narrative responses contain supernatural elements and demonic adversaries or remain more realistic depends on religious context. It is also significant that, according to Röhrich, there is a correlation between folklore genres and semantics. Some genres tend to be charged with metaphors but others are more explicit and it might be useless to speculate about their hidden meanings.

As the semantics of folklore appears open-ended and enables various interpretations, the same is true of genres as expressive modalities. Genres are easily adaptable. Although they narrow down the limits of communication, they also enable improvisation, creativity and deviations from habitual discursive patterns. Genres can be identified in comparison and in relationship to each other as complex clusters of expressive forms that folklorists have described as systems, scholarly models that reveal the interconnections and interdependence of genres. Different models of genre systems have been sketched, such as William Bascom's (1984) set of prose narratives (myth – legend – folktale) or the taxonomy of Roger Abrahams that differentiates genres on the basis of interaction between performer and audience. He has distinguished conversational genres, play genres, fictive genres and static genres (61–69). Kaarina Koski (2008) has shown that spatial and temporal distance to the narrate events can help to map various dimensions of storyrealms. Wendy Doniger (2013) has drawn attention to the fact that written and oral texts can have both fixed and fluid forms – they can be frozen and reproduced in a rigid manner or rendered creatively through free variation. Whereas frozen forms are typical to charms and magical formulas, prose narratives are more open for artistic storytelling and creative developments.

Contemporary genre theory tends to avoid normative patterning and finalised models and explicates relationships between different expressive forms. On the one hand single genres have been identified and described by comparing and contrasting them with each other. This approach can be called analytical as it has developed genre systems towards further particularisations. On the other hand the multiplication of genres has been balanced by a synthetic approach that looks for common traits in genres and aims to overcome the fragmentation of the broad expressive spectrum. The category of belief narrative that we discuss next represents such synthetic thinking.

What are belief narratives and how can they be understood?

The notion of belief narrative brings together several genres that had been separated by former taxonomies, including myths, legends and religious legends, but also urban legends, rumours, oral histories and other narratives told as true stories that contribute to transmitting and reproducing knowledge about the supernatural and mundane dimensions of the world. Stories on most diverse topics, such as individual wellbeing, health, the polluted environment and climate change, political or religious convictions, conspiracies, corruption, ethnic or other stereotypes, as well as demonic encounters, witchcraft and divine help from above can be considered belief narratives. It seems useless to construct a comprehensive list or typology of belief narratives as it could never be completed. The idea is not to aim at a more detailed classificatory system but to study the role of narratives in constructing shared reality, of reproducing and representing reality in credible accounts. The truth can be something hidden, to be disclosed in storytelling, or it could be something that is well known. If the stories reveal nothing new, they reaffirm something that is worth repeating about reality as it is perceived. Often narratives verify some general truths by rendering factual cases – for example about somebody bribing a politician (which also proves overall corruption); about a fellow villager being involved in sorcery; one's friend having recovered after visiting a temple or through using some powerful medicine; about an ominous dream that predicted an accident or a great success. All these particular episodes also give evidence of some substantial aspects of reality.

Legend is one of the belief narrative genres that has been widely discussed and theorised in Western folkloristics. In her seminal monograph "Legend and Belief" Linda Dégh (1920–2014) critically examined the existing approaches to the genre and its various subcategories, and concluded that legend is an overarching term for a multitude of stories that nevertheless share a common core (23–97). She claimed: "The legend is a legend once it entertains debate about belief. Short or long, complete or rudimentary, local or global, supernatural, horrible, mysterious, or grotesque, about one's own or someone else's experience, the sounding of contrary opinions is what makes a legend a legend." (Dégh 97) Elliott Oring shifted the discussion on the genre from the notion of contested belief to matters of truth. He showed that legends make claims about the truth of an event that is perceived to be extraordinary, and that therefore these stories "require the deployment of a rhetoric to allay doubts and foil challenges" (Oring 107). Oring characterised legends as narrations that invoke the rhetoric of truth. He also noted that folklorists have "acknowledged that a narrative does not have to be false to qualify as legend"; nevertheless, as he remarks, "folklorists gravitate to narratives that they almost invariably believe to be false" (Oring 151). It is remarkable that both Dégh and Oring do not define the genre of legend on the basis of its content but through its communicative and rhetorical aspects. The category of belief relates legend to something that lies beyond its textual boundaries – to the supernatural world, to a true but extraordinary event that has triggered the story, to real people with their emotions, aspirations and life stories. In addition, the notion of "truth" in legend narration implies the relationship between the story and something bigger – objective reality, history, life experience or religious world view. The observances of Dégh and Oring offer solid ground for further theorising of belief narrative as a new category, which was coined after Dégh and Oring had published their respective works (Dégh 2001, Oring 2008). "Belief narrative" was brought to life during the 15th congress of the International Society for Folk Narrative Research (ISFNR) in Athens on June 25th, 2009 when a group of folklorists had gathered to establish the ISFNR's Belief Narrative Network in order to promote scholarship in legends and the related genres. During this meeting the originally proposed overarching term to define the research focus – "belief tales" – was replaced with "belief narratives". The suggestion of better formulation was made by Welsh folklorist Robin Gwyndaf to avoid the semantically somewhat obscure notion of "tale" and better match the ISFNR name, which refers to "narrative" (Sepp, Tomingas-Joandi). Later symposia of the Belief Narrative Network of the ISFNR followed: in St Petersburg (2010), Shillong (2011), Novi Sad (2012), Vilnius (2013), Zugdidi and Pécs (2014) and have helped to fill the term with contents and meaning. However, as a category belief narrative is still undertheorised and its uses in international folklore scholarship have been limited.

Next, let us analyse and discuss some belief narrative examples from contemporary India. During my field trips to Assam I have met several people who have shared with me their stories about encounters with spirits and demons and experiences with magical practitioners. The classical book by Benudhar Rajkhowa, *Assamese Demonology* (first printed in 1905), presents a survey of the world of spirits as it appeared more than a century ago. It also offers a rich background for the dominant beliefs and the related narratives that are circulated today. One of the clusters of stories that seem to be widely spread in Assam at the beginning of the 21st century discusses *bira*s as dangerous spirits who can be controlled by magicians and sent out on various missions, very often with harmful tasks, which is confirmed by multiple personal experience narratives. The following story was told in January 2014 by Sankar[2], a student from one of the universities in Guwahati:

S: We were living in a rented house in Guwahati itself. This was a house with four or five apartments and we were living in one of

---

2   The names of the two informants have been changed.

them. And one new family came to the apartment, which was on the ground floor. Once my mum was introduced to that lady of the new family. The lady said that we have been facing some problems with *bira*s. Some of my enemies have sent the *bira* to my house to destruct me, to destroy me and to do miserable things, which I cannot bear. My mummy did not believe that.

Time goes on, we often hear that whenever they used to take their dinner or their lunch sometimes some unusual things happen, like plates automatically move around or a plate falls on the ground from the dining table. One day we experienced that. That lady came to our floor, to our apartment and she was taking tea, talking to my mummy; I was beside in my room. That lady said that since I am at your home now that *bira* can cause some trouble, don't be afraid of that. My mummy said, 'No, I believe in God too much, so that thing [the *bira*] cannot do anything in my house'. What happened – the door was automatically locked from outside and it was strange. And we were calling from inside for the help – 'Somebody please open the door, somebody please open the door!' And coincidently what happened, the three apartments – this is our apartment in the middle, this is the apartment on the right side, this is the apartment in the left side – all of the three apartment doors were closed. Strange. People were inside but the doors were closed from outside. And the house owner came from downstairs. He thought that something wrong is happening. He came up and he opened the door. We were curious and asked who closed the door? The house owner said: "Who will close the door? There is no one to close the door. All the servants and all the people are inside the house only, who will close the door?" That was a mystery even for me and my mummy. This was the experience we have faced – one of my experiences.

Ü: So this was a kind of trick played by a *bira*?

S: Yeah, trick of a *bira*. That lady said that that *bira* may cause some problems because he follows me wherever I go and tries to disturb me by any means. We had done a lot of tantras and mantras but we were unable to send that *bira* [away] because the person who sent the *bira* knows much more powerful magic than our magician. That's a real fact.

Obviously, Sankar was talking about an event that he had witnessed and I had no reason to doubt in the veracity of the story. It is not so easy to find explicit employment of the rhetoric of truth in this narrative. The obvious question is: is there no rational explanation to the locking of the doors other than blaming the *bira*. One of the devices of storytellers' truth rhetoric is to discount alternative interpretations (Oring 129–130). Closing the doors might have been a prank of some of the neighbours, and this explanation is, indeed, eliminated by the story-teller. He indicates that only the owner of the house was around and obviously he had no reason to harass his tenants. Anyhow, the rhetoric of belief in the narration remains subtle. Sankar did not suggest himself that the door was locked by a *bira*, and as I listen to the recording I am somewhat surprised that this explicit interpretation was offered by me instead. Obviously, I was convinced by the logic of the narrative.

Even though we can find elements of the rhetoric of truth and its effects in the story, it nevertheless seems difficult to consider it as its most distinctive feature. Rather, we can say that it is narrative about a strange event, witnessed by the teller himself and told in a neutral manner without emphasising the supernatural. However, the story does reveal something significant about the belief world, such as the conviction of the mother that faith in God should eliminate troublesome *bira*s. The story also opens up a whole realm of belief narrative motifs about mischievous *bira*s and powerful magic. We also learn that some people in Assam are more affected by supernatural powers than the others, including the storyteller, for whom this demonic world seems somewhat distant and strange. A single story hardly convinces anybody of the existence of *bira*, although it probably confirms the pre-existing belief in these entities. In any case, by sharing somebody's experience the story works as a vehicle that carries general information about *bira*s.

Secondly, let us take an example from another rich array of contemporary belief narratives about accident-prone places and demonic encounters on the roads of Assam. These belief narrative motifs often actualise in somebody's personal experience, as is the case in the story, told on the same evening by Arun, another student from Guwahati:

> A: It was 19th of May, I forgot the year but it was 19th of May and it was my birthday. I used to live fifteen kilometres away from my home in a small town named Lakhimpur. That day together with my father and my parents and some of my friends I was celebrating my

birthday. At nine my father, my mother and my sister returned to my village home. It was 9.30 PM, there was a bridge nearby my house and at the end of the bridge there was a mango tree, which was around 45 to 50 years old. And as it was Tuesday, there was a market in our own place, there used to be a big market on Tuesdays. My father saw a lady coming across the way. She was looking like a Boro woman.

Ü: She crossed the road?

A: Yeah, my father was crossing the bridge and saw her. Suddenly she crossed the way and disappeared in the mango tree. And my father had an accident. As my father, my mother and sister were attached together, therefore the woman – the spirit – couldn't harm them. My father thinks that if they were separated from each other, she could harm them. And my father shared this story with my grandfather. My grandfather said that in Assamese we use to say *bhūt*, external soul or these types of thing – spirit.

Ü: So the accident happened immediately after?

A: Yeah, immediately after the woman crossed. My father wanted to save the woman, and that's why the accident happened. But she was not a woman, she was a spirit only and she disappeared in a mango tree.

Haunted places on the roads in North Eastern India – as discussed in folk narratives – have recently attracted the attention of several scholars. Margaret Lyngdoh has shown how the vanishing hitchhiker stories among the Khasis do not only express supernatural beliefs but also address conflicts inside families and the shifting balance of gender roles as women lose power in the matrilineal society (Lyngdoh 2012). Shibani Sarmah has discussed legends about a haunted tree and ghostly encounters in a village in Nalbari district and shown the continuity of traditional supernatural motifs in contemporary storytelling (Sarmah 2015). The belief narrative above represents some widely known story patterns and scary experiences that occur time and again. It does not manifest explicit rhetoric of truth or attempts to convince me that dangerous spirits live in big trees. Frankly, I did not doubt the veracity of the story and even if I had been sceptical, it would have been rude of me to suggest that my conversation partner was fantasising or simply lying.

Thirdly, let us read a third story on the same topic, which followed the previous one:

A: There is another story that I shared with you yesterday about my friend's brother's accident. My friend's brother was coming from Dhemaji to Lakhhimpur. It was around 11.30 PM. At that time one *mandir* ['temple'] was there nearby my house. This happened on the highway, and it was a sharp turning. He could not hold his handlebars; he got into an accident and died.

After one month his uncle was coming the same way. He was not having any drinks, he didn't use any intoxicants. He was talking with his friend and driving the car. When he reached the same spot, his car started to go the wrong way. He put on the brake and stopped the car. He said that automatically it had been going in the wrong way. He told his friend that some external power was pulling him to that spot. At that time we came and helped him and we said that you please stay for a while and afterwards you go.

In a conversation that followed, Arun told me that his family had constructed a little shrine beside the road in order to avoid traffic accidents. They had put some flags there so that people could easily find the right way. He also told me about the tradition of his Sonowal Katchari tribe to have small shrines in the jungle, called *Gozai-mandir*, dedicated to local deities (*Gozai*, in Assamese *Gohain*). These deities received sacrifices once a year and there were taboos regarding the shrines. Spitting or other defiling acts would entail punishment by the deities, who would cause serious accidents. The conversation reveals that the same beliefs were transferred to shrines on roadsides and tragic accidents could be the consequence of somebody's former sacrilegious behaviour. Again, in the story above it is not easy to discern that the rhetoric of truth has been employed consciously in order to convince me or argue against my possible disbelief about ghosts who cause accidents. However, the narrative does evoke the world of beliefs and activates memories of proper conduct and of how to deal with haunted places and remain safe. If we compare the three stories, we can see that they all discuss moments of crisis that somehow rupture the flow of everyday life. The story about the *bira* is mysterious and somewhat grotesque (as Linda Dégh characterised some legends), the story about encountering the ghost near the bridge is dramatic but has a happy ending, and the last story, consisting of two episodes (about the brother of Arun's friend and his uncle) includes a fatal traffic accident. All three narratives address single episodes, particular and unique events in peoples' lives.

Final remarks: on genres and meanings

There is no reason to doubt if the events described in the narrative above actually happened or not. Although the relationship between truth and fantasy is one of the fundamental genre theoretical issues, both in vernacular and scholarly discourses, applying a fictionalising perspective towards the stories above would seem to misdirect us from something obvious – the narrative mechanisms of transmitting notions of reality. I cannot see that the rhetoric of truth has a definitive or significant role in the above narratives although the stories share other generic traits. Arguing for belief would seem more likely if somebody from the audience expressed scepticism or disbelief. Whether or not people share the same basic knowledge about tangible and intangible reality, belief or disbelief does not seem to be the main trigger of storytelling. In the examples above it was my questions about the world of spirits and magic that elicited the stories – my lack of knowledge on the one hand and the storytellers' generous willingness to share it on the other hand. However, I don't think that this folkloristically staged storytelling would alter some of the basic functions of belief narratives – to affiliate single cases and life episodes to broader fields of meaning and tie them to the shared and tradition-bound world of knowledge. Stories make connections; the examples above offer interpretations of some extraordinary, dramatic and tragic events. Each story is a vernacular case study of something that has happened and a commentary that makes the event meaningful. Stories also evoke a myriad of associations with other narratives, memories, behaviour patterns, values and beliefs that remain invisible for outsiders.

The quest for meanings in the works of some leading folklorists that we discussed in the first half of this article guided us to studying narratives in context – if possible, working together with the people whose knowledge transcends the stories and encompasses the big jungle behind the single trees. The more we know about the social and cultural environment and the world of beliefs, the more meaningful the stories become. However, the goal of research cannot be to understand belief narratives in the same way as the people do (who have the experiences and who know the world from their perspectives). As analytically thinking folklorists we also have something to contribute – our critical perspectives and conceptual tools, which open the stories and the related experiences from angles that are hard to discern from inside the vernacular discourse.

International folkloristics has offered us a common terminology, a set of research methods, foci and basic problems. However, it has also burdened us with ideological baggage and with some theoretical constructs that might obscure our vision if we are unable to find alternatives. Cemented theoretical ground and pre-constructed concrete walls of classification without alternatives are not a good starting point for research, especially if the master builders have come from distant cultures and are inclined to look for cross-cultural similarities, not for differences. The tripartite scheme of folk narratives, consisting of myths, legends and folktales, might be one of such burdens compelling scholars to look for non-existent genres, to misunderstand those that exist and overlook those that are actually prevalent. The obsolete understanding of legends as historically oriented narratives (following the theory of the Grimm brothers) seems to have become an obstacle in legend studies in several countries that have suffered from the legacy of folkloristics as a colonial discipline (see Briggs, Naithani). The notion of belief narratives seems to be an alternative to some rigid traditional classification schemes. True, legend is far from a frozen category as it has been time and again reconceptualised and revived. However, sometimes the obsolete, reified definitions of legend prevail as the rejuvenated discourse about the genre in international scholarship does not reach ethnic and national research traditions. Belief narrative is a new concept without a heavy semantic burden and this makes it attractive. Applying it to different cultures and ethnic traditions might reveal something new – not only about legends but also about all the genres in their multiplicity that evoke the rhetoric of belief and make us perceive reality as we do.

Acknowledgement

This research has been supported by the Estonian Ministry of Education and Research (Institutional Research Project IUT2–43).

References

Abrahams, Roger D. *Everyday Life: A Poetics of Vernacular Practices.* Philadelphia: University of Pennsylvania Press, 2005.

Bascom, William. "The Forms of Folklore: Prose Narratives." *Sacred Narrative. Readings in the Theory of Myth.* Ed. by Alan Dundes. Berkeley, Los Angeles, London: University of California Press, 1984. 5–29.

Briggs, Charles L.; Naithani, Sadhana. "The Coloniality of Folklore: Towards a Multi-Genealogical Practice of Folkloristics." *Studies in History* 28 (2). SAGE Publications: Los Angeles, London, New Delhi, Singapore, 2012. 231–270.

Dégh, Linda. *Legend and Belief: Dialectics of a Folklore Genre.* Bloomington, Indianapolis: Indiana University Press, 2001.

Doniger, Wendy. "Impermanence and Eternity in Hindu Epic, Art, and Performance." *On Hinduism.* New Delhi: Aleph, 2013. 509–522.

Dundes, Alan. "Metafolklore and Oral Literary Criticism." *Analytic Essays in Folklore.* Mouton, The Hague, Paris, New York: Mouton Publishers, 1979 [1966]. 50–58.

Holbek, Bengt. "The Many Abodes of Fata Morgana or The Quest for Meaning in Fairy Tales". *Journal of Folklore Research* 22. 1 (1982): 19–28.

Holbek, Bengt. *Interpretation of Fairy Tales. Danish Folklore in a European Perspective.* Folklore Fellows' Communications No. 239. Helsinki: Suomalainen Tiedeakatemia, 1987.

Holbek, Bengt. "Tendencies in Modern Folk Narrative Research." *Nordic Institute of Folklore Papers* No. 4. Turku: Nordic Institute of Folklore, 1992.

Honko, Lauri. "Folkloristic studies of meaning. An introduction." *ARV: Scandinavian Yearbook of Folklore* Vol. 40. Uppsala, Stockholm: The Royal Gustavus Adolphus Academy, 1984. 35–56.

Koski, Kaarina. "Narrative Time-Spaces in Belief Legends." *Space and Time in Europe: East and West, Past and Present.* Ed. by Mirjam Mencej. Ljubljana: University of Ljubljana Press, 2008. 337–353.

Lehtipuro, Outi. "The 8th Congress for the International Society for Folk Narrative Research. Berge, June 12th–17th 1984." *NIF Newsletter* Vol 12: 2 (1984): 1–12.

Lyngdoh, Margaret 2012. "The Vanishing Hitchhiker in Shillong Khasi Belief Narratives and Violence Against Women." *Asian Ethnology* 7. 2 (2012): 207–224.

Oring, Elliott. "Legendry and the Rhetoric of Truth." *Just Folklore: Analysis, Interpretation, Critique.* Los Angeles, California: Cantilever Press, 2012 [2008]. 104–152.

Paredes, Américo; Bauman, Richard (eds). *Towards New Perspectives in Folklore.* Austin and London: The University of Texas Press, 1972.

Rajkhowa, Benudhar. *Assamese Popular Superstitions and Assamese Demonology.* Guwahati: Gauhati University Press, 1973.

Röhrich, Lutz. "The Quest for Meaning in folk-narrative research. What does meaning mean and what is the meaning of mean?" *ARV: Scandinavian Yearbook of Folklore* Vol. 40, 1984. Uppsala, Stockholm: The Royal Gustavus Adolphus Academy. 127–138.

Sarmah, Shibani. "The Haunted Tree of Kendukuchi: Finding Elements of Folk Belief, Specific Messages and Motif in Urban Legends." *Journal of Folkloristics.* Vol III. Ed. by Anil Boro. Department of Folklore Research, Gauhati University (2015): 80–86.

Sepp, Tiina; Tomingas-Joandi, Siiri. "15th Congress of the ISFNR in Athens, the Belief Tales Session." *ISFNR Newsletter* No 5, May 2010. 16–17. (http://isfnr.org/index2.html)

Orality: The Quest for Meaning

Kailash C. Baral

We humans are meaning making animals; perpetually in quest for meaning simply because we order our lives through or around the meanings that we derive of the world. The world is made meaningful or gets illuminated by the word. Language as a transparent medium holds the key to all meanings at least in certain cultural traditions—predominantly, Semitic. The world of words is divided into two primary domains of speech and writing with the problematic of meaning tagged to them, for without being meaningful nothing makes sense. Western theories of meaning starting with hermeneutics (following the Biblical exegeses) to post-structuralism deal primarily with the written text. Fore grounded in written language, a text when interpreted produces meanings, according to the Western tradition, depending on the context and the interpretive method that is in operation. Such interpretive acts also characterize the nature and properties of linguistic registers to suit a particular genre. Whether the oral is amenable to the interpretive modes developed in the context of written textual forms or not is an issue that needs to be examined. Furthermore, what is of significance is to understand the power of the spoken word with the problematic of meaning in the interplay of temporalities of time in the complex dynamics of the oral discourse with diverse cosmologies and epistemological horizons.

Let us start with a set of provisional questions:

1. Is there a difference between the ontological and epistemological assumptions of the oral and the written? This is an important question for the written cultures always emphasize on ontological/epistemological difference. For example, they contend that discourses like philosophy and grammar could not have emerged in the context of cultures without writing.

2. As an extension of the above, we may add whether the folk/oral traditions have their own meaning making modes;

3. Should then traditions of interpretation of the written texts be applicable to the interpretations of the folk?

4. Is intertextuality in oral forms different from the written ones; if so how do we critically deal with oral intertextuality which appears in the forms of citation, allusion (musical, tonal, thematic, idiomatic etc) as well as in rituals, performative and body arts?

5. What is the role of cultural memory in oral discourses in identity formation subject to temporalities of time and the utterances having "a greater dependence on nonverbal contextual clues through more use of fillers and repetitions than written texts" (Payne and Barbara 2010: 512)?

These are some of the provisional questions that I set out with in my presentation today. The first and the second questions could be taken up together as there are basic theoretical issues that need to be addressed. As we know, Derrida's critique of Logocentrism, in other words of the Western metaphysics of Presence, has exploded certain myths of origin/beginning thereby unsettling hitherto secured and stable world of meanings and their processes. For Derrida, Western conception of ontology is essentially centric and this is derived from onto-theology that underlines the presence of Logos, the Divine at the centre and theology that constitutes the humanistic conceptions of being. If the theologically derived textualized world provides a particular structure of knowledge, the oral world on the other hand produces a different structure where there is a creator not necessarily equivalent to the theologically conceived God; interestingly having a substructure of the world of spirits independent of the Creator and the most dominant powers who dominate the lives and existence of humans who are non-theologically produced within the folk domain. These spirits function within an elaborate system of rituals. The rituals don't include the notion of personal salvation or redemption but connect the past to the present as in case of ancestral spirit worship. Further on rituals signify social life and such events including births, deaths, festivals and other modes of community life. In the oral domain, the meanings are produced through rituals in which nature is emblematic in all aspects from which the cultural forms are generated contrary to the proposition that the relation between nature and culture are contra-directional. Within this epistemological horizon we need to put the domains of written/ oral, theological/non-theological and other differentiations. The question then could be asked if the written and oral domains are structured differently how far we can apply the traditions of interpretation developed around written texts to oral forms. If we accept that nothing exists outside the text implying that all forms are textual could we then say that there should not be any difference in the applicability of interpretive methods irrespective of the forms whether verbal or written. This is where we are confronted with the most crucial question when the two domains are structured differently should not then the oral forms be interpreted by their own modes? In doing so should they seek the support of some other methods/modes for production of meaning as such? For example, semiotics, a product of structuralism, may be productively applied to interpretations of the oral as it effectively unbares the layers of meaning around a sign. This assertion takes care of the third question wherein the fourth one confronts us with the argument whether the intertextuality of a written text is similar to oral forms which needs some elaboration. Working through the three dimensions of temporalities of time, memory works as a dynamic force that serves both as an archive of traditional knowledge and also keeps the folk alive and relevant. I shall be dealing with some of these issues in my presentation connecting each to my understanding of the complex structure of the oral. Let me start with the traditions of interpretation advanced by folklorists.

Levi-Staruss advanced the argument that the primitive man can produce meaning in terms of binaries such as black and white implying that his less evolved consciousness could not negotiate with multiplicity of combinations. The oral imagination that is demonstrative of activities that are ritualistic, performative and has produced a structure of thought having a creator and other forces within a particular world view cannot be reduced to a simple binary, according to Jack Goody and Ian Watt, that the oral and the written belong to two distinct "technologies of the intellect" (Goody and Watt 1968:

27). The oral imaginary is generative, according to John D. Niles (1999), for a society defines, celebrates and re-creates itself through oral narratives: oral narratives as verbal art possess the "cosmoplastic power, or world-making ability" (3) of a community. There exists a complex symbiotic relationship between oral literature and a society that produces it. For Walter Ong: "Oral cultures indeed produce powerful and beautiful verbal performances of high artistic and human worth, which are no longer even possible once writing has taken possession of the psyche" (2002 [1982]: 14). What obtains from these citations is that the oral world indeed is full of meanings constituting of "thick descriptions" to use an expression of Clifford Geertze (following Philosopher Gilbert Ryle) that he developed as an interpretive theory of culture (1973). All oral forms are culturally derived and socially produced over and over again connecting the present to the past.

Alan Dundes made his interventions in folklore study following both Levi-Strauss's binarism and Vladimir Propp's structuralist approach in his work *The Meaning in Folklore* (2007 edited by Simon J Bronner). Dundes' analytical approach covering a wide variety of folk genres "linked dualism (particularly the importance of "double meaning") in psychoanalysis to Vladimir Propp's syntagmatic approach relating to a sequential pattern of plot functions and to Claude Lévi-Strauss's paradigmatic approach relating to a thematic set of contrasting relations. The process is often set in opposition to one another in surveys of structuralist approaches that Dundes united "to reveal mental processes underlying the structural patterns of fantastical expressions" (Ibid: Intro-5). Although Dundes used binarism more as a method if not as a philosophy, for he was drawn to Freud making the relationship between the inside with the outside and the manifest with the latent to study productively patterns that are often circular not linear. By asserting that the unconscious is made conscious the way the latent reveals through the manifest, Dundes has provided an opportunity to go beyond the fixed notions of meaning. Walter Ong in a famous essay "Before Textuality: Orality and Interpretation" has elaborated upon the methods of interpretation starting with hermeneutics to reader-response theories providing a perspective on understanding of the written. What according to him is of significance in interpreting the oral is to make the differentiation between the one who creates and the one who interprets? He maintains: "An interpreter is in between his interlocutor and the noninterpreted phenomenon...Ultimately meaning is not assigned but negotiated, and out of a holistic situation in the human life world: the speaker or writer in a given situation, which is shared by speaker and hearer in oral communication, but in written communication not shared" (267). The meanings intended by the creator and the interpretations derived by the interpreter are two different positions, for Ong interpretation is an "in between" act, a kind of doubling of the idea. Ong and others don't point out clearly the methodological dilemma that an interpreter may face in the act of interpreting the oral if attempting to move beyond binaries. However, his idea of *inbetweenness* is instrumentally useful within a cultural approach. The cultural approach is important for it provides a context to an event and also helps understand the intertextual connections within the cultural matrix.

In view of the above discussion, let us take for example the origin myths in the context of oral societies in Northeast. We could see a pattern in the origin of a tribe either by descending from above what is emblematic of the ladder trope or emerging from the earth/stones as autochthonous. The arrivants get distributed across clans, clans then distributed across sub-clans as in case of the original seven huts of the Khasis indicating original seven clans and in case of Mizos, characterized socially as the Raltes are different from the Sailos and then places of origin are marked with narratives of either a definite place of origin or chosen by the tribe as said in migration myths as in case of Aos (Longterok) and Konyaks (Longphang, Alamkaphen means "gate of the sun") respectively. The multiplying of the narratives suggest the generic nature of the myth even as at one level identity based on single origin myth get dispersed across with variations of particular narratives identifying say different groups within the same formation. Further on the dispersal also suggests the totemic variations and rituals. In this brief discussion what I'm trying to suggest is to acknowledge the consolidation and displacements that take place simultaneously. In the context of plural narratives with some difference from the original meaning can be fixed at some level but cannot be hold on to when the narratives about a particular origin differs and multiplies. Each narrative is intertextually produced as in case of performing arts but again gets dispersed across contexts that also multiply. The point that I'm driving at is that the cultural field is semiotically rich and contextually diverse. Hence any meaning that has to be made pertinent has to be negotiated all the time in looking at the layers of thick descriptions of an oral product.

The study of oral cultures in the Northeast as we know has been shaped to a large extent by colonial ethnography. Colonial administrators turned anthropologists such as J H Hutton, J P Mills, John Shakespeare, T.H. Lewin, N.E.Parry[1] and a host of others continued to have their authority in occupying academic positions in the Universities of Cambridge and Oxford after their retirement from the colonial service. Although some of these writers were sensitive to local social-ritual practices but in most cases what purportedly pursued was a descriptive approach—things and people were reported and written about as they were seen— that lacked a nuanced understanding of deeper cultural meanings and values that a community had evolved over centuries wherein some of the tribal practices were central to the ethnic groups' worldview, cosmology and indigenous belief systems. Instead, the tribal practices were mostly classified on the basis of what was supposedly civilized and what was not in applying the western parameters to study a group of people already colonized, subjugated and were voiceless. Therefore the contemporary debate to have an alternative method outside the Western paradigm is relevant.

Working within the hermeneutics of suspicion, exemplifying and figuring out the notorious/innocent *wink*, Clifford Geertze starting with E B Taylor's notion of culture as the "most complex whole" then following the classification offered by Clyde Kluckohn to Gilbert Ryle's "thick description" maintains that culture is a web and its interpretation should not follow the method of "an experimental science in search of law (as most modern ethnographic studies do in the name of objectivity: added) but an interpretive one in search of meaning" (311). The thick description is laid upon semiotic resources that the cultural web incorporates. Meaning that is apparent and observable becomes meaningful only when that which is invisible and latent is known. The whole process following Ryle depends on "Thinking and Reflecting" in which a cultural way of thinking, feeling and believing occurs. S N Balagangadhara who emphasizes on the Indian reflective tradition expands on the cultural approach to meaning in following comparative science of religion arguing that the western approach to understanding non-western cultures has its inherent limitations. The formulation that culture, a configuration of learning revealed in performative knowledge is significant. Balgangadhara argues that there is not only a process of learning that takes place in the cultural domain but also learning to learn (meta –learning) with the social community. This pedagogical process as it continues in reorganizing itself through the temporalities of time shapes the cultural predicament. In the west, it is religion that lends to the structure of thought wherein it plays the dominant role even shaping the western theoretical structures the way knowing about the world happens. In *The Heathen in His Blindness*, Balgangadhara demonstrates how the layered cultural web in the context of India through the configuration of learning crystallizes the ritual culture that imparts practical knowledge leading to performative acts. Extending upon this central understanding, he further argues in *Reconceptualizing India Studies* that cultural learning needs to be understood through comparative science of culture. He discards some of the established anthropological theorizing that enables us to see the individuation of culture considering how a person uses the resources of his socialization. Another central argument of Balgangadhara is cultural difference. The questions that follow the proposition are: what kind of difference is cultural difference and what difference does it make? These questions help us to differentiate cultural difference from social difference and other forms of difference in anthropological approaches. For him, the western consideration of religion as a cultural universal is unacceptable whereas in India cultural difference is not based on religion but in ritual; further ritual is also diverse as each ritual has an objective different from other rituals and with same objective the form of ritual is different from one community to another, for example the ritual for spirits that cause sickness is different from ancestral worship. Ritual apart when culture is embodied in the performative context the body becomes significant; similarly the body in a different context holds a different meaning for example tattoos an inscription on the body. The intangible folk resources and also the tangible aspects of social practices are laid out between the spiritual and the material contexts of culture; hence cultural difference becomes pertinent. Keeping this line of argument and following Balgangadhara, epistemological discontinuity has to be noted between the Western/Christian and the so-called pagan/heathen cultures. The epistemological discontinuity implies different configurations of cultural learning outside the assumption where the West assumes non-western cultural forms as its own variants. This argument could be connected to my earlier position how the onto-theologically driven western thought brings a critical difference between the oral and the written cultural forms. Once we accept this fundamental difference the mode of interpretation will follow different horizons.

Following Balgangadhara, given the example of origin myth among the Khasi, Mizo and Naga tribes, the ontological difference have to be noted as cultural difference. Similarly in case of other forms of oral practices and traditions we may find the differences across tribes and across cultures. What are Indian cultural assumptions should emerge from these differences as they throw up some patterns of similarity even across differences. The same is true of performative arts as well as ritual gestures. Problematic as it may seem, difference holds the key to cultural knowledge and learning. It is through (re) learning that we deepen the meanings of oral practices.

Once we understand the differences in learning configurations, we begin to make sense of our own experiences visa-a-vie European descriptions of non-western cultural traditions. The challenge before us is therefore to recontextualize our stories, rituals and performative arts in an effort to shape an alternative theory to the study of oral cultures in Northeast India.

Note:

1. J H Hutton, J P Mills, John Shakespeare, T.H. Lewin and N.E.Parry were colonial bureaucrats who turned anthropologists in producing ethnographic writings about the Naga and Mizo tribes of Northeast. Their ethnographies have presented a lot of distortion of the actual meaning and import of oral cultural practices.

Works Cited:

Balgangadhra S N. 1993. *'The Heathen in His Blindness'...Asia, The West and the Dynamic of Religion*. Leiden: E.J. Brill

_____. 2012. *Reconceptualizing India Studies*. New Delhi: Oxford University Press.

Dundes, Alan.2007. *The Meaning in Folklore:The Analytical Essays by Alan Dundes*, ed. Simon J Bronner. Logan: Utah State University Press.

Geertze, Clifford. 1973. *The Interpretation of Cultures*. New York: Basic Books.

Jack Goody and Ian Watt, 1968. *Literacy in Traditional Societies*. London: Cambridge University Press.

Niles D John. 1999. *Home Narrans: The Poetics and Anthropology of Oral Literature*. Philadelhia: University of Pennsylvania Press.

Ong, J Walter. [1982] 2002. *Orality and Literacy: The Technolozing of the Word*. London and New York: Routledge.

_____. 1988. "Before Texuality: Orality and Interpretation". *Oral Tradition*, 3/3:259-269.

Payne, Michael and Barbera Rae Jessica. 2010. *A Dictionary of Cultural and Critical Theory*: Wiley-Blackwell,2013,2ⁿᵈedition Web: http://www.black wellreference.com/public/book?id=g9781405168908_9781405168908, visited on 16ᵗʰ Jyne 2016.

"Little Red Riding Hood in different itineraries: Female characters in Argentinean folk narrative"

Maria Inés Palleiro

Key words: Little Red Riding Hood-Argentina-Legend-Belief narrative
In this presentation, I analyze Argentinean oral versions collected in fieldwork, as well as theatrical and choreographic recreations of tale type ATU 333, Little Red Riding Hood. This analysis is focused on narrative representations of female body. I consider both the combination with local legends regarding the mysterious apparition of an elf called the *Pombero*, who makes a sexual attack on the young girl, already studied in Palleiro (2012). I contextualize this synchronic analysis with a diachronic overview of this tale type, from French versions supposedly from the Ancient Régime as discussed by Darnton from a historic perspective, to others analyzed by Mary Douglas from an anthropological feminist point of view. I consider in this way the intertextual intertwining of tale and legends in the theatrical version *Caperucita* by Javier Daulte (2009) and the Argentinean choreographic version *Voraz* (2006) by Charles Trunsky, dealing with the representations of female corporality by means of "narrating bodies" (Palleiro 2016) This analysis deals as well with the fictionalization process of believing in the folk narrative texts and performances. My main hypothesis is that

believing has a strong influence in the constructive process of folk narrative, erasing generic boundaries, such as story, legend and myth. These boundaries are erased as well by of performers and dancers, who deconstruct cultural stereotypes by recreating folk narrative matrices by means of embodiment procedures.

Little Red Riding Hood: fictional and legendary characters

Little Red Riding Hood is a fictional creature associated with the realm of fairy tales. Her "trials and tribulations" (Zipes 1993) are contextualised in different social and historical environments in which she interacts with "local" beasts and monsters which act as metaphors of social beliefs. One of these metaphoric representations of the beast is the wolf, as it happens in the version provided by Darnton and in those studied by Mary Douglas. The wolf can also be found in the "classical" written versions of the French Charles Perrault and the German Brothers Grimm. Cartoons as well as media recreations, including the Disney Studies Productions, in which one of the main characters is the "big bad wolf". The aforesaid Zipes (*op. cit.*) analyzes different versions and variants of this tale-type in different sociocultural contexts. Of this vast tradition, I focus my attention on Argentinean versions, in which, for instance, the wolf is replaced by the *Pombero*, an elf who makes sexual attacks not only to young girls but also to grown up women as the Grandmother, depicted as an old witch, associated also with the "Pachamama", an earthly indigenous female goddess. II deal as well with theatrical and choreographic Argentinean versions, in which Little Red Riding Hood is either a young woman who lives in Buenos Aires city and works in a supermarket, or a dancer interacting with the voracity of her partner.

The folk matrix is flexible enough to favour the polyphonic intertwining of different discourses. In this way, this narrative pattern enters both the realm of collected beliefs, and reflects as well the social role of old and young women in different cultural contexts

This analysis also deals as well with corporal performance, embodiment and belief narratives in Argentinean contexts. I consider belief, from a semiotic perspective, as statements which express an intersubjective consensus regarding the truth value of discourse (Greimas and Courtés,1982). I characterize narrative as a a cognitive principle of sequential organization of experience

(Bruner 2003). In this sense, embodiment is analyzed in its relationship with collective beliefs and cultural identities, as represented in different itineraries of a folk narrative matrix. I consider rhetoric as the art of persuading, dealing with argumentative discursive strategies. I focus as well my attention in somatic images as they are reflected in different narrative versions and recreations. In this way, the corpus includes both oral narratives, theatrical and coreographic recreations of the aforesaid tale type. I analyze both fictional versions of a folk narrative matrix which includes discursive representations of female corporality. In previous researchs, we analyzed how social beliefs are framed in different narrative genres, such as oral tales regarding this narrative matrix (Palleiro 2012). In this new presentation, I focus my attention in the narrative construction of fictional discourses dealing with embodiment and synechdotic representations of female body. The aim is to identify argumentative strategies dealing with legitimation of corporality associated with cultural patterns. I connect as well such rhetoric with fragmenting and disciplinating corporality as an expression of social control.

In short, the versions and recreations of this narrative matrix are considered as a point of departure to analyze rhetoric of somatic expressions connected with collective beliefs and female social roles. The aim is to identify in the corpus argumentative strategies dealing with a "rhetoric of female corporality" in Argentinean contexts.

Giving continuity to previous research (Palleiro and Krmpotic 2016), the aim is to inquire into the discursive construction of corporality in oral narratives collected in Argentinean contexts, in an intertexual comparison with European ones. I give priority the semiotics of corporality, addressing the body as signic network, which inform expressions of identity. I associate performativity with a praxis, i.e. with actions produced in a context from speech acts, verbal and iconic statements, musical and body language. I understand the performance, both as an act of producing an aesthetically message as spectacularized representation of social life. The aim is to identify in the narratives strategies of legitimizing social beliefs, dealing with a a rhetoric of embodiment and care, articulated in narrative form. The expected results tend to study the rhetoric construction of corporality and to articulate a theoretical reflection regarding the relationship between body, narrative and local social beliefs in folk matrices of a universal tale type such as Little Red Riding Hood.

Little Red Riding Hood:
tale types and the legendary discourse

The thematic description of the tale type ATU 333, "Little Red Riding Hood", mentions not only "the wolf" but also "other monster" who attacks "human beings": *"The wolf or other monster devours human beings until all of them are rescued alive from his belly"*.

The Argentinean *Pombero* is described in different Argentinean legendary discourse as a sort of elf whose appearance frightens both children and adolescents who dare to remain awoken late at night or in the early afternoon, instead of going to rest. It is also said that he tempts sexual attacks to girls and women[3]. So it happens in the Argentinean version I deal with, in which the protagonist is not Little Red Riding Hood but the Grandmother, who plays an active role whose climax is a sexual rapport with the *Pombero*. Such reference to this mythical being transforms the narrative message into a complex discourse, whose distinctive feature is the intertextual gap between orality and literacy, fiction and belief.

Little Red Riding Hood: folktale, legend and belief

The name of the protagonist of different narrative versions takes the audience to the realm of fiction, which is the distinctive feature of fairy tales, but the boundaries of this realm are extremely flexible, since they also linked with legends and social beliefs. Folktales are in fact living expressions which are reshaped to please different audiences. This happens with contemporary versions of Little Red Riding Hood, in which ATU 333 is mixed up with other narrative forms, such as legendary discourse. As Marzolph (2012) points out, folk narratives serve as verbal expression of social identity, which may be as well highly codified items, such as folktales and fairy tales, or even fairly simply, such as legends and anecdotes. The Argentinean oral version I deal with provides a blend of these narrative forms, in which a fairy tale character such as Little Red Riding Hood interacts with a mythical creature. Oral and literary registers are mixed up in this version in a polyphonic message, in which this fictional creature crosses the boundaries of belief discourse.

---

[3] Some of these versions can be found in Vidal de Battini (1984)

The term "legend" (Latin *legenda:* "things to be read") shows itself this intertwining between oral and written culture. The legend is a short episodic, historicized narrative performed in a conversational mode, reflecting a symbolic representation of folk belief and collective experiences. Such narrative message serves as a reaffirmation of commonly held values of the group to whose tradition it belongs (Tangherlini 1990). When Brothers Grimm defined legend as a folktale historically grounded, they affirmed this connection between fairy tale and legend which can be seen in the Argentinean version of Little Red Riding Hood and the *Pombero.*

Dégh (2001) stresses that "all legends are based on beliefs to the extent that the term "belief legend" is a pleonasm. In different narrative itineraries, ATU 333 is mixed up with local legends, such as the one of the guaranythical *Pombero,* or with other social beliefs regarding lycanthropic transformations. In a choreographic language, also Carlos Trunsky recreates this matrix, dealing with social beliefs about voracity and cannibalism of human relationship in contemporary urban societies. Such connection with the social context has wisely been pointed out by Darnton, and also analysed by Mary Douglas from a contextual gender perspective. All these narrative itineraries show the close linkage between this folk narrative matrix and social beliefs both in rural and urban contemporary contexts. In fact, stories are embedded in the society they circulate in, and they are part of daily life experience (Blécourt 2012).

Dégh (2001) considers the legend a characteristic form of folklore in contemporary civilization, able to survive technological innovations. By mixing up ATU 333 with legendary discourse, Little Red Riding Hood is recreated also in other channels of discourse, in which moving corporality plays an important role. Legendary discourse deals in fact with supernatural encounters such as the one between Little Red Riding Hood and the *Pombero,* or with other monsters such as werewolves or other lycanthropic manifestations of social beliefs close not only to the peasant culture but also to the urban and industrial world. The theatrical performance directed by Javier Daulte deals in fact with an urban protagonist, who lives in a urban flat with her mother and her grandmother, and interacts as well with a "human wolf" who is also a parapsychologist. All these narrative forms in different channels of discourse reveal the way how folk narrative patterns change constantly while responding to the exigencies of surrounding societies and cultures (Marzolph 2012).

Oral and literary versions

The folk narrative pattern ATU 333 reached a written form with Charles Perrault's "Le Petit Chaperon Rouge". This was the earliest known printed version, published in 1697, in the collection *Tales and Stories of the Past with Morals. Tales of Mother Goose*. According to this title, Perrault's primary concern was teaching children moral lessons, so he simplifies the story into one about "vanity, power, and seduction" (Zipes *op. cit.*). The "attractive, well-bred young lady" of this "story" is a village girl who gives the big bad wolf the necessary information to find her grandmother's house successfully. As soon as he arrives, the wolf eats the old woman, avoiding being noticed by woodcutters working in the nearby forest. Then he lays a trap for the Red Riding Hood, who puts on the Grandmother's clothes, and asks Little Red Riding Hood to climb into the bed. Then he eats her, and so the story finishes. In Perrault's version, there is no happy ending. Instead, he includes a moral ("From this story one learns that children, especially young ladies, pretty, courteous and well-bred, do very wrong to listen to strangers. And … the Wolf is thereby provided with his dinner…. Alas! Who does not know that these gentle wolves are of all such creatures the most dangerous!") In this way, the narrative serves the function of an *exemplum,* that is to say, an ancillary tale, illustrating a moral lesson (Welter 1927).

One century later, in 1812, Brothers Grimm published "*Rotkäppchen*". Dundes (1989) considers that "Rotkäppchen" is probably a reworking of the French version of the tale, rather than an authentic German folktale. The Grimms' version reinstalled a happy ending, wherein a woodsman saves Red Riding Hood from the belly of the wolf. The intervention of the hunter, who is a symbol of order in contrast with the chaotic nature of the wolf, saves the protagonist. Through an additional anecdote, the Grimms add another moral lesson. While Red Riding Hood journeys again to her grandmother's house, she encounters another wolf. This time, she goes directly to her grandmother and warns her, so they plot together to fend off the wolf. In her first encounter with the wolf, Red Riding Hood leaves the path against her mother's warning, and as a result, both she and her grandmother are nearly eaten alive. When she obeys her mother and stays on the path, going directly to her grandmother's house, they are able to prevent a catastrophe.

Both Perrault and the Grimms had specific goals in mind when reworking ATU 333. Each one of them had the same general goal of influencing the behaviour of children, but where Perrault's version gives a lesson about the dangers of seduction and rape for pretty little girls and disciplinating young female bodies, the Grimms' version gives a lesson about the dangers of disobedience. Both in "Le Petit Chaperon Rouge" and "Rotkäppchen" the wolf is not the focus. In contemporary versions dealing with legendary discourse, instead, the wolf or the elf play an important role, dealing with cultural symbols of social beliefs in different societies.

For many years, these two versions have been considered as canonical material. Anyway, ATU 333 "Little Red Riding Hood" is a folktale, which has been reworked again and again both by folk narrators and literary authors, and it has been as well largely interpreted by literary critics (Zipes *op. cit.*, Dundes *op. cit.*). A short Latin verse recorded in the early eleventh century whose main character wears a red tunic and becomes captured by a wolf. As Dundes (*op. cit.*) states, "it is never appropriate to analyze a folktale on the basis of a single text". Different narrative itineraries as the ones I deal with in this presentation prove the folkloric origin of this narrative matrix.

Little Red Riding Hood and the Ancient Régime: the version provided by Robert Darnton

In *The Great Cat Massacre and Other Episodes in French Cultural History*, Robert Darnton (1999) provides a version of Little Red Riding Hood supposedly contextualised in the French Ancient Régime. Darnton's research deals with oral tradition and literary culture. From this standpoint, he analyses cultural motives and practices during Europe's transition between literate and illiterate eras. His main hypothesis is that actions are perceived in different ways by different cultures at different times. In this way, Darnton focuses his attention in social identities, and he considers that fairy tales, when viewed in a historical context, should offer a new way of understanding humanity and history.

In the chapter regarding "The Meaning of Mother Goose", Darnton explains why historical context is important for understanding the true meaning behind a fairy tale. He accomplishes this by demonstrating the relevance of French historical context of the Ancient Régime, neglected in the analyses of "Little Red Riding Hood" provided by psychoanalysts Fromm and Bettelheim, dealing only with sexual maturation. Darnton uses the Freudian description of "Little Red Riding Hood" to prevent readers of the oversimplification of the psychological interpretation of such tales. He points out how the typical versions of "Little Red Riding Hood" neglect some variants provided by French oral traditional versions. In this way, he affirms that Fromm and Bettelheim only take from these tales what they want to find[4]. Although each tale contains universal meanings about the human condition, these universal meanings don't offer any new information about the minds of people in different contexts. Darnton provides the following version, to discuss his thesis regarding the relevance of historic context in folktales:

Once a little girl was told by her mother to bring some bread an milk to her grandmother. As the girl was walking through the forest, a wolf came up to her and asked where she was going.

-"To Grandmother's house"- she replied.

-"Which path are you taking, the path of the pins or the path of the needles?"

-"The path of the needles".

So the wolf took the path of the pins and arrived first at the house. He killed Grandmother, poured her blood into a bottle, and sliced her flesh onto a platter. Then he got into her nightclothes and waited in bed.

"Knock, knock!"

-"Come in, my dear!"

-"Hello, Grandmother!"

-"I' ve brought you some bread and milk!"

-"Have something yourself, my dear! There is meat and wine in the pantry"

So the little girl ate what was offered; and as she did, a little cat said: -Slut! To eat the flesh and drink the blood of your Grandmother!

Then the wolf said: - "Undress and get into bed with me!"

-"Where shall I put my apron?"

-"Throw it on the fire! You won't need it anymore!"

For each garment – bodice, skirt, petticoat, and stockings - the girl asked the same question; and each time the wolf answered: -Throw it on the fire! You won't need it anymore!

---

[4] Darnton affirms that psychoanalytical interpretations reconstruct the tale in their own way: "Fromm and a host of other psychoanalytical exegetes did not worry about the transformations of the text–indeed, they did not know about them–because they got the tale they wanted. It begins with pubertal sex (the red hood, which does not exist in French oral tradition) and ends with the triumph of the ego (the rescued girl, who is usually eaten in the French tales) over the id (the wolf, who is never killed in the traditional versions). All's well that ends well." (Darnton *op. cit.,* p.282)

When the girl got in bed, she said: - Oh, Grandmother, how hairy you are!

- "It's to keep me warmer, my dear!
- "Oh, Grandmother, what big shoulders you have!
- "It's for carry firewood, my dear!
- "Oh, Grandmother, what long nails you have!
- "It's for scratching myself better, my dear!
- "Oh, Grandmother! What big teeth you have!
- "It's for eating you better, my dear!

And he ate her.

In his commentary of this version, Darnton affirms that fairy tales reflect the ideas of values of the time in which they were written or narrated, and their meanings can be accurately discovered when read from a historical perspective. He considers as well that the changes in society and culture over time are evident in fairy tales. From this standpoint, he points out the relevance of the social context of the Ancient Régime, where "fathers allow their daughter to get married with wolves", and in which young girls wandered around paths and forests where the wolf use to be seen in the desert fields because there was not an efficient police.

The path of pins and the path of needles

The sequence regarding the path of the pins and the path of the needles provided by Darnton, which does not appear in this Argentinean versions but in others, has been also interpreted by the anthropologist Mary Douglas in her article "Red Riding Hood: An Interpretation from Anthropology". In an analysis based on other versions of ATU 333, Douglas affirms that, in most of oral versions, the girl has to choose between a path of pins and a path of needles, and provides an interpretation regarding her approaching womanhood. Douglas thus explains that pins were easy but temporary solutions representing girlhood and needles, as used for more skilled permanent craft, have sexual connotations representing womanhood. The author examines different versions collected by Ivonne Verdier between French peasants in the XIXth Century, in which Little Red Riding Hood escapes from the big bad wolf by asking him to go to the bathroom, where there is a window. The girl escapes of Grandmother's house going out from this window, with the help of some peasant women who are working as launderers. Douglas provides a contextual interpretation of this sequence from a gender perspective. She points out the relevance of the sequence of the "magic flight" (ATU 313), which is an addition to the folk narrative matrix. She underlines the solidarity of these working women, who are able to rescue a young girl in danger, and to protect her in the context of a masculine world. All these "details", considered by Mukarovsky (1977) as basic semantic units in folk art, provide different meanings to this narrative pattern. All these interpretations deal with social believings regarding the historic context. While Darnton focuses his attention in danger and ferocity of the social context of the Ancient Régime, Douglas (1995) is mainly interested in the social position of peasant women. According to Douglas, pins and needles deal with female roles in peasant French society. She affirms that young French peasant girls in their teens used to pass the winter period in the dressmaker's house, where they learned how to use well the needles and other domestic skills, and they learnt as well to be careful in sexual matters. Once reached sexual maturation, they turned back home where there were able to face permanent sexual unions such as a weddings, symbolized by the needles. Such contextual aspects regarding cultural roles in French society introduce transformations in the way of interpreting these folk narrative versions. In the Argentinean version I deal with, pins and needles are not mentioned since the sexual and intellectual maturation of the young girl is not associated with domestic skills but with her ability of approaching ugly beasts such as the *Pombero*. The Argentinean version is focused in the danger of going all alone to wander around in the forest, where such ugly creatures may appear in lonely paths.

The alternative itinerary of the magic flight: from Little Red Riding Hood to Snow White in Argentinean contexts

The motif of crossing the forest to reach an old woman's house can be found in other Argentinean versions, in a curious intertwining between oral voices and audiovisual communication. One clear example is the one of this version by Sonia de la Fuente, who was 9 years old when I collected it in 1988 in La Rioja, Argentina, classified as "story", heard from his mother and sister. The protagonist is not Little Red Riding Hood but Snow White, and as the narrator itself pointed out, she associated this folkloric character with the one of the protagonist of the videofilm "Snow White" whose copyright belongs to Disney Entertainment Co. However, the version presents an alternative itinerary, dealing with ATU 313 *"The magic flight" whose thematic description*

is: The hero and his helper escape from the ogre's house. The fugitives throw
magic objects behind them, which become mountains, wood or sea; or they change
themselves into various animals or objects.

The version narrated by Sonia de la Fuente is the following:

Snow White was lighting the fire. And a cat arrived by chance, peing on the fire, and in this way Snow White remained without fire. Since she ran out of matchsticks, she dedided decided to ask for matchsticks to the only human being who lived in the forest, an old witch. So she went out of the house with her old shoes, and she walked a lot. She arrived to the house of the witch, and she knocked at the door. So the old maid opened, and she asked her what she was looking for. And Snow White asked her if she could lend her some matchsticks, some embers, some coals to make fire. And the made gave her the embers. And she also gave her a pair of scissors, some needles and a thimble.

So Snow White went away. And when the witch arrived home, she told the maid that thre was a smell of human flesh in the air. But the maid told her that she hadn't seen anyone. But the witch began wandering about, until she saw Snow White walking fastly through the forest. So she began pursuing Snow White across the forest, mounted on a pig. And when she was about to catch her, Snow White threw her needle, and the needle became a a big "pencal" forest, and the witch could not pass. So the witch went on trying to catch Snow White, mounted on her pig. And when she was about to catch her for the second time, Snow White threw the thimble, which became a high mountain. And the witch couldn't climb the mountain, so she had to take another longer way. And when finally she was about to catch Snow White for the third time, Snow White threw the scissors, which became a big river. And the witch couldn't pass. So she took another longer way, always mounted on her pig. At last, she arrived to the house where Snow White lived with the seven dwarfs, protected by a lot of dogs.

And the dogs began pursuing the witch, and the witch had to run away, and she never returned. So Snow White lived happily ever after with the seven dwarfs.

This alternative itinerary of "Snow White", focused on "The magic flight", presents some similarities to those of "Little Red Riding Hood" above discussed. Such similarities deal not only thematic topics but also the compositional and rhetorical articulation. Thus the action is centred in the "flight" of Snow White, who escapes from the witch with the help of magical items like a needle, a thimble and scissors. These objects have the power to transform in obstacles which are respectively a pencal forest, a high mountain and a river which hinder the pursuit of her antagonist and facilitate the arrival of Snow White to the" house the Dwarfs with the matchsticks that allow her to light the fire. As in the Old Regime Riding Hood, the flight is associated with items dealing with the domestic sphere of feminine arts. Thimble, needle and scissors are related to the domain of the seam, and the fire burning, with food and the warmth of home. The output of the protagonist is aimed at the preservation of this area, threatened by the cat, which acts as a representative of the same Antagonist class to which the witch belongs. As the needles marked the way of permanent joints in Darnton's version of Little Red Riding Hood, the proper use of the elements of stitching allows the young to succeed in their flight and to scare the witch, performing efficiently in her homecoming. In Darnton's version, the cat also plays a narrative role, but he acts as a messenger who heralds the tragic end, revealing the cannibalistic dimension of the action of eating and drinking flesh and blood of her grandmother performed by the young protagonist. This dimension is suppressed in the version of the young Argentinean narrator, who adds instead other items, regarding the topography and the rural vegetation of Argentinean Northwestern context, such as the "Pencal" and the "mountains. The axis of the compositional and rhetorical structure is, as in Little Red Riding Hood, the antithesis between the girl and, in this case, the witch instead of the wolf. Both the witch and the wolf can be considered, along with the cat, as metaphorical condensation of external dangers that threaten the domestic universe, built around symbols of feminine skills such as needle, scissors and thimble. The wolf adds as well sexual connotations to such threatening, erased in the version by the young girl, in which the dwarfs can be also interpreted as a symbol of catration. From a gender perspective, the way Snow White in the forest and success to overcome obstacles with the help of a magical helper has to do, like in Red Riding Hood, with the transition to his female maturation. The same witch is related to the female universe, which can be hostile and envious towards younger women.

The happy end of the arrival of Snow White, unharmed, to the house of the dwarves, is associated with the return to everyday household life. This itinerary of "Snow White" reflects, in short, the role of women in the social context in which the story was registered has to do with its effectiveness to perform domestic chores. The deletion of the marriage to the Prince of other versions can also be associated with the structure of La Rioja cuasimatriarcal rural areas. At the time in which I collected this version, most of the women of the rural areas were heads of households, with the consequent weakening of marriage as an institution. It was not frequent even the coexistence in stable unions, because men, as the dwarves of folk matrix, spent long periods away from home in search of different jobs. The contextualization of the narrative matrix reflects in this way the social organization of the group.

This alternative itinerary of "Snow White", close to the one of "Little Red Riding Hood" regarding pins and needles presents, in short, a sequential development centered on the magic flight, around which the narrator builds a metaphorical net linked with feminine roles. This net has as its correlate a metonymic association of some properties of certain items, such as the sharpness of the needle, the protrusion of the thimble and the potential of cutting of the scissors, with elements of other semantic spheres endowed with similar qualities, such as thorny plants, high mountains and a river that cuts the aridity of the way. Contextualisation processes deal both with the direct reference to local vegetation and with the oblique reference to the social role of women. The similarities between these versions regarding Snow White and Little Red Riding Hood deal with the dangers of the forest and its strategies to avert them. Such topics, with its rhetorical structure characterized by the use of metaphors and symbols, interpretable as manifestations of the unconscious, which appear in oral discourse of the most diverse times and places, can be also found in children's voices as an updated echo of different cultures. In all of them, however, as Isabel Cardigos (1999) even if fairy tales are inextricable bound to patriarchal worldviews systems, there are also indexical signs of complex contrasts that lead to a paradox. Even if the feminine social role is the one of a patriarchal society, the possibility of going fastly across the forest and the capacity of returning home safe gives the protagonist a sense of freedom and mastery of space, along with self-reliance. Even if wolfs or ugly witches represent a danger, there is a sense of wisdom that saves the protagonist in contemporary itineraries of the folk narrative matrix, such as the one of Snow White by Sonia de la Fuente and the other regarding the Pombero I will deal with in the next section.

"Little Red Riding Hood and the elf": the Argentinean oral version

I registered this oral narrative in Buenos Aires city in 2002, from Norma Benvenuto, doctor in Medicine, who presented her version as a reported speech, heard from an illiterate patient born in the Argentinean province of Formosa, aged 65. In Benvenuto's narrative, there is an intertextual gap (Briggs and Bauman 1992) between the version told by the illiterate narrator and the recreation. The polyphonic tension between these two voices is the distinctive feature of this text, which mixes up oral and written registers. The title itself, "Little Red Riding Hood and the elf", shows from the very beginning the intertwining between fictional and belief discourse, since, as Benvenuto pointed out, the illiterate narrator believed in the "real" existence of the elf, described as a "mysterious creature who attacks young girls and women in the woods".

The *Pombero*: a legendary and mythical creature

The Pombero is a small mythical creature of Guaranythical culture, located in Northeastern Argentina and Paraguay. As Benvenuto referred, the illiterate narrator from Formosa described him as "a short being, with hairy hands and feet", who wears a large hat hiddinghis ugly face. She also added that he dwelt in rural areas, in the Northeastern Argentinean forest, and he also liked to enter abandoned houses.

In a large research I carried on in the Argentinean province of La Rioja, from 1985 until 2000, I registered different oral versions regarding such elf with an ugly face hidden by a big hat, hairy hands and long fingers. In La Rioja, this elf is called the *Mikilo*. Although he is called with different names, this strange elf has more or less the same characteristics in different Argentinean regions, such as La Rioja and Formosa. Some narrators added that he had iron arms and hands, and others specified that he had iron fingers in his right hand, and wooden ones in the left one. Others told that he used to appear at noon, when young children were supposed to rest after lunch. It is said that he used to hide behind the trees or the plants, and that he appeared in the early afternoon or late in the evening, to take away the children who dared to be out of their houses. It is worth mentioning that both in La Rioja and in Formosa, people use to rest in the early afternoon after lunch, since the weather is very hot. During this time, the streets and paths are desert, since most part of the people stay at home. Such resting time, called *siesta,* is one of the moments of the day in which this ugly creature would commit sexual attacks not only to young girls but also to grown up women. According to Blache (1982), who studied narratives of guaranytical cultures, the significance of the *Pombero* and other mythical creatures deals with the aim of regulating social conducts that might cause danger to young children, young girls or even grown up women, such as returning late at night, visiting abandoned houses or wandering around in hours in which people use to rest such as the *siesta* period, in the early afternoon. From this standpoint, such narratives can be considered as warning messages to regulate social conducts, preventing people from encounters with this ugly creature. There is also a collective belief regarding this mysterious elf, attributed both to the *Pombero* and to the *Mikilo*. It is said that he uses to have sex with old witches.

The text provided by Dr. Norma Benvenuto was registered in occasion of an informal conversation before a medical check-up. The patient told the doctor about different kind of illness connected with witchcraft, and about the narratives told to the children to warn them about dangerous creatures such as the *Pombero*. Dr Benvenuto encouraged her patient to tell her one of these narratives, regarding Little Red Riding Hood. Some months later, she retold it as a reported speech:

…Therefore, my patient told me that she was from the province of Formosa, and that she did knew a lot about that elf, the *Pombero*. But I said: - And do you know any story regarding the *Pombero*? Then, she answer: -Yes, of course I know it! –And well, please, do tell me!

So she said: -Well…There was… a young girl who had…a red cloak…a red hooded cape…And then, one day, her mother asked her to go to visit her grandmother. And the young girl went to visit her grandmother. And when she was walking through the woods, wandering around, she met the elf, the *Pombero*. And the *Pombero* asked her:

-Where are you going to?

- Oh, I' m going to visit Granny. So, he said: -Can I come along with you?

So they went together, the girl and the elf, the *Pombero*. They went along walking through the forest.

And when they arrived to the grandmother's house, Little Red Riding Hood said [to her grandmother]: – Let me introduce you the elf, the *Pombero*! Here he is!

And the *Pombero* began to speak to the grandmother. He said to her: -Oh, what big eyes you have!

And Granny answered: It's to see you better!

And then, the elf said: - And what big nose you have!

- It's to smell you better!

- Oh, what big ears you have!
- It's to hear you better!
- Oh, what big arms you have!
- It's to embrace you better!

So the grandmother embraced the elf, the *Pombero*, and he hid inside the grandmother's dress…and so he disappeared

And this tale reminded me a poem I learnt by heart when I was a young student, whose author was Juan Carlos Dávalos. This poem said "Young guy, here it comes the eddy/. Please hold your hat and tie up "Saint Pilate" with the handkerchief /The elf of the eddy is coming/ He is coming very angry / And hides under the women's skirts [Dr Benvenuto then refers other anecdotes told by this patient, regarding illness and traditional healing]

The opening clause of this version includes a description of thee protagonist as "a young girl who had…a red cloak…a red hooded cape…" Such description is focused in the young girl's clothes, whose red colour can easily be associated with "Little Red Riding Hood" of ATU No. 333. The narrative structure is based on the antithetical tension between this tale type and the local legend regarding the *Pombero*. The opening clause provides as well a spatial orientation, which locates the action "in the woods". This is the setting of the sequence of "the meeting" with the *Pombero,* a local elf of the forests, whom the protagonist meets in her way to the grandmother's house. This local elf, which replaces "the big bad wolf" of other versions, can be considered as a metaphoric expression of all dangers from the outside world that a girl must face when she goes out alone for the first time, in her transition from childhood to sexual and intellectual maturation.

The rhetoric construction

With a simple rhetoric structure and a spontaneous style, the narrator presents a sort of theatrical dramatization of the narrative action, based on a formulaic repetition of questions and answers. She avoids the antithetical dynamics of other versions between the big bad monster and the innocent young girl, since the main character is here the grandmother, depicted as a witch. The bifurcation of different paths is not mentioned in this version. Instead, the narrator refers that the girl and the *Pombero.* arrive at the same time, walking all together, to Grandmother's house. The encounter between the Grandmother and the Pombero is the point of the following sequence, which takes place inside the house ("And when they arrived to the grandmother's house, Little Red Riding Hood said [to her grandmother]: – Let me introduce you the elf!"). The rhetoric construction of this sequence is very similar in different versions. Such similarity deals with the formulaic structure of dialogue, based on a polyphonic counterpoint between the voice of the young girl, the one of the grandmother and the one of the elf. Although there is a strong parallelism between the different allusions of the elf and the replies of the grandmother in different versions, there is as well a relevant difference. In this text, the Grandmother herself replies not to the girl but to the elf, and in this way she makes room for the sexual contact, by embracing him. In the same way as in other versions, the dialogue consists of a formulaic repetition of indirect questions and answers, based on a metonymic fragmentation of different parts of the body (eyes, nose, ears). In this rhetoric construction, the big size of each part of the body is emphasized by a means of a hyperbole ("… what big…you have"). This allusion to the corporal functions is connected with the social uses of the body in specific contexts. The exclamations are modal signs of the affective commotion of the Grandmother, who is the real protagonist of this sequence. Such active role of the Grandmother makes room to the action of the *Pombero,* who has a sexual approach to the Grandmother. This sexual encounter of an old woman with an elf can be considered as also a mythical allusion which gives a new meaning to the narrative message, dealing with local legends and collective beliefs. In fact, the grandmother is depicted as a sort of witch similar to the ones who use to have sex with this ugly mythical creature.

Oral and literary discourse: the intertextual gap

This Argentinean version mixes up not only story and legend, but also orality and literacy, in an intertextual blend. Benvenuto presents in fact a curious intertwining between the oral version heard from an illiterate narrator and literary recreations of legendary discourse. In this way, the final clause includes an intertextual connection between "the elf" of this oral version and an allusion to "the elf of the eddy" of a poem by the Argentinean writer Jaime Dàvalos. ("The elf of the eddy is coming… very angry / And he is looking for a woman to hide under her skirt …") Such intertextual connection can be extended to the German film *The tin drum (Die Blechtrommel)* by Volker

Schlöndorff (1979), based on the novel by Günter Grass. In the opening scene of this film, there is a similar allusion of the mythical conception of the hero[5]. In this film, the female farmer Anja Bronski is harvesting in the fields when a desperate soldier, escaping from the Kaiser's police, asks her to hide him behind her skirt. The soldier catches the occasion, and he has a sexual encounter with the woman, as a result of which the protagonist, Oskar, is born. Such modality of sexual rapport is connected with mythical beings such as "the Pombero" and "the elf of the eddy". Such intertextual gap (Briggs and Bauman 1992) between oral, literary and filmic discourse reveals the complex texture of this version,..

The comparative approach:
variants and alternative itineraries

The variants of ATU 333 deal with the intertwining with belief legends regarding the *Pombero*, who replaces the wolf of other oral and written versions. In those versions, such as Darnton's one, there is a dialogue between Little Red Riding Hood and the big bad wolf, in which the young girl asks different questions to the wolf. In this Argentinean narrative the elf replaces the girl in the role of asking questions, and the grandmother replaces the wolf in answering them. In this oral version, the *Pombero* does not attack the girl, as happens in local legends. Instead, he accepts a sexual encounter with the grandmother, who herself invites and almost compels him to have sex with her. In this way, the protagonist is not the young girl but the Grandmother, who is presented as a local witch whose distinctive feature is her interest to have sex with this ugly monster. Such sexual encounter replaces the happy end of other oral versions, such as one Argentinean version collected by Diana Pedrini from a young Peruvian narrator aged nine[6]. The version provided by the Peruvian young narrador, collected by Professor Diana Pedrini, analysed in Palleiro (2005), is the following:

Once upon a time there was Little Red Riding Hood, and her mother asks her: - Little Red Riding Hood, go and take these *kekes* and these cookies to Granny… Oh! And be carefull, because in the forest, you can meet the big bad wolf! And so she goes through the forest. While she is wandering around in the forest, picking up flowers and playing with the animals, the wolf sees her,

---

[5]   The iconic illustration of this opening scene can be seen in Moeller and Lellis (2002), p. 166.

and he hides behind a tree. Then he dresses as if he were a man, in human's clothes. Then, fastly, he takes the longer path [sic] and he arrives first to the Grandmother's house. He breaks the door, and he enters the house. And it says...that he puts Granny into a closet, into a big wardrobe. An then, he dresses with Granny's clothes, and he goes to Granny's bed. In that moment, Little Red Riding Hood knocks at the door, and he says: -Please, come in!. Little Red Riding Hood enters Granny's room, she sees the wolf in Grann's clothes, and she says: - "Oh, Grandmother, what big eyes you have! - "It's for seeing you better, my dear! - "Oh, Grandmother, what big nose you have! - "It's for smelling you better, my dear! - "Oh, Grandmother! What big hands you have! - "It's for hugging you better, my dear! - "Oh, Grandmother! What big mouth you have!- "It's for eating you better, my dear! So, when Little Red Riding Hood hears these words, she gets away from the house quicky, and she returns to the forest. There, she finds a hunter, and she asks him for help. She says: - Help me, help me, please! The big bad wolf put Granny in the wardrobe, and now he wants to eat me!. So the hunter says: - Show me where he is!. So Little Red Riding Hood takes the hunter to Granny's house, and he goes, and he kills the big bad wolf, by shooting at him. And then, they rescue the grandmother, who was still in the wardrobe. And then, they all have a big party, and they live happily ever after. (Pedrini in Palleiro 2005)

This oral version, referred by a young male narrator, includes the topic of the long and the short paths, but not the disjunction between pins and needles, connected with feminine roles. The text mentions as well contextual details such as the "kekes", a local food. The antagonist is the "classic" wolf, instead of local monsters or animals of the vernacular fauna. It replaces as well the tragic end of Perrault and Darnton's versions, in which Red Riding Hood is eaten by the wolf, by a happy end in which a woodcutter rescues both the young girl and the Grandmother, and kills the big bad wolf.

In ATU 333, Little Red Riding Hood refers not only the story of a little girl wandering around the forest and bringing food to a sick grandmother but a young girl's trip towards adulthood, culminating with her loss of virginity (Bettelheim 2006). In fact, when Red Riding Hood encounters the wolf, as referred both in the oral version by Pedrini and in Darnton's written one, she is ready to reach sexual maturity (Litch 2006). In the Argentinean oral version, instead, the sexual encounter takes place not between the girl and the wolf, but between the grandmother and the elf, and this encounter is associated with local beliefs dealing with supernatural creatures. The grandmother, identified with a witch, seduces the elf by embracing him, in a sort of invitation to a sexual rapport. In this way, Little Red Riding Hood's trip deals mainly with encountering supernatural creatures in the woods. The encounter of the young girl with the *Pombero,* a sort of little monster with sexual maturity, acknowledges the fronteer between children and adult world. The young girl joins the *Pombero* and they go together to Grandmother's house, where she acts as a witness of a sexual encounter between grown up beings. In this way, she reaches sexual maturity not by going through terrible experiences such as being attacked by a wolf but by seeing her grandmother, a sort of expert old witch, interacting with the elf.

"Caperucita Coya": stereotypes, contextual variants and didactic uses of folk narrative

In her MA Thesis in Folklore and Traditional Cultures intitled: "From the Humahuaca creek to the tramel of the kultrum: didactic uses of folkloric expressions in schools of José C. Paz, Argentina", developed under my guidance, Deborah Franco dealt with a didactic "local" stereotyped recreation of Little Red Hiding Hood illustrated by Argentinean writer and painter Walter Carzon, recently published in Argentina. Such recreation locates Little Red Riding Hood in Humahuaca creek, going to visit Granny with a basket full of algarroba (algarrobo fruit) and "tamales" (boiled corn put in a sort of package with the leaves of corn plant). On her way to Granny's house, she meets a "thin wolf" (sort of fox) who becomes a dangerous animal because he doesn't have enough food to eat. A shepheard helps Red Riding Hood to arrive safely to Granny's house, where the wolf arrived firstly, looking for some food. He fires the fox away and eats "tamales" together with Red Riding Hood and Granny. This stereotyped female character is depicted as a "Coya", that is to say, as an indigenous Red Riding Hood from Northwestern Argentina. Deborah Franco MA used this recreation to encourage her young students to recreate the tale in another ways, according to their own traditions. She pointed uot that this Coya Red Riding Hood picks up flowers, worships the Pachamama (a local indigenous earthly divinity) and she is also a friend of "llama" shepheard (the "llama" is an animal who lives in Northwestern Argentinean mountains). The focus of Deborah's recreation is not exactly the stereotyped one, but other in which she underlines Coya Red Riding Hood's capacities to distinguish good "animals" from dangerous ones, especially those who become dangerous being hungry. In this way, she focuses the attention in the skills of the protagonist to survive in a cultural context such as the Humahuaca creek where she learns to keep away from the dangerous ones, such as the "thin" wolf who is hungry. There is an intertextual gap (Briggs 2001) between the stereotyped written recreation of the folktale "Caperucita Coya" for Argentinean children and the version told to the children of José C. Paz, which is as well a difficult context where learning surviving skills is one of the most important lessons that can be taught to the students. Other of the recreations Deborah dealt with has been the "Patagonian Red Riding Hood" who goes to the Pehuen forest playing the kultrum, and there she meets an elf, who escapes away when he hears the sound of the Kultrum, a sort of cosmic sacred drum, played in honour of God Nguenechén. In her comparative approach, Deborah pointed out that Coya Red Riding Hood learns to live close to nature, and to be aware of dangerous animals, while Patagonian Red Riding Hood saves herself by avoiding dangerous elfs and worshiping cosmic local divinities such as 'Nguenechén. After having worked with the Patagonian version, Deborah also organized a workshop with Mr. Inalef, member of the Mapuche indigenous community. In this workshop Mr Inalef planned different activities to teach the children both some words in Mapuche indigenous language and how to play the Kultrum as Red Riding Hood. He also showed the students the different Mapuche trees and plants of the Patagonian forest, such as the Pehuen, and the taught also some aspects about Mapuche rites and religious beliefs. In this way, the stereotyped recreations of Little Red Riding Hood served the function of encouraging the students to know different indigenous cultures. In this sense, Deborah encouraged the young students to tell their own versions of Little Red Riding Hood and to draw and paint different sequences of the folktale, mixing up sequences of different narrative itineraries. The aim of this activity has been to encourage the students to accept cultural diversity as a relevant aspect of Argentinean plural identity, being the point of departure the approach to folk stories.

Little Red Riding Hood: a ferocious performance" ("Caperucita: un espectáculo feroz"): a theatrical version by Javier Daulte

This theatrical performance directed by Javier Daulte took place in 2009, in the "Multiteatro" Theatre of Buenos Aires city, starred by Valeria Bertuccelli,

Alejandra Flechner, Verónica Llinás and Héctor Díaz. I deam "performance" as a spectacular representation of social life (Schechner 2000) which, in this case, deals with a recreation of this folk narrative matrix in Argentinean urban context. As Marzolph (*op. cit.*) points out, living performance of folk texts goes together with dramatic enactment and a visual representation. In fact, the pretextual matrix of Little Red Riding Hood has been transformed by Daulte in a living performance dealing with human rapports in a contemporary family, composed by three generations of women. As Daulte himself pointed out in an interview held by Natalia Blanc (2009), this new "Little Red Riding Hood lives in Buenos Aires and works in a supermarket…She is twenty years old and she is the daughter of a single mother".

This version is focused in human and family rapports, theatrically represented in a dialogic performance with scenes of seduction, music and dance. In the aforesaid interview, Daulte emphasized the relevance of the historic contextualization of this version in Buenos Aires city, as a resource to recreate this folk matrix as a real contemporary conflict dealing with family rapports. He faced also the creative process of this version, faced as a research work:

> In Little Red Riding Hood, there is a monster, and moreover, there is a curious point: why does the mother send her daughter to the Grandmother's house, instead of going herself to visit her own mother?. It seemed to me a nice point to begin a research work.

As Daulte himself stressed, the focus of his research is the connection between the monster, motherhood and Little Red Riding Hood. He also pointed out that one of his main ideas when creating his theatrical version has been "to create this character of the young woman who goes to visit her grandmother to the hospital…" One of the clues of this version is the problem of illness, connected with social uses of the body. Such social uses of corporality have been also underlined by Darnton and Mary Douglas.

In Daulte's *performance*, the meaning deals with the different vital cycles of three generation of women who move themselves in scene, in a sort of ballet dance. Such dance plays an important role, connected with the progression of the sequential action, which ends in a tragicomic way. In this way, in the final sequence, the human "wolf" kills her mother. But, in Daulte's words, this end is not the most relevant aspect of this performance, based on the exhibition of the female body, as watched by a man, who acts both as a spectator and protagonist of a theatrical performance.

The way of recreating this narrative matrix from a perspective dealing with human rapports in the context of a family it is also connected with social beliefs regarding the "werewolf" in contemporary urban societies. Such wolf, who is ready to attack and even to murder either the mother or the grandmother, could be hidden behind any handsome man. Legendary discourse dealing with the *lobizón* (the werewolf) is here recreated in the daily context of contemporary Argentinean society, within a family in which three women live in a narrow space, in an urban context. The variant is that the wolf murders not the grandmother but the mother who oppresses the protagonist.

The same female roles considered by Darnton and Mary Douglas, reappear both in Argentinean oral and theatrical versions. Daulte's performance adds the rhetoric of illness, expressed in the metaphoric space of the hospital. The hospital replaces in this version Grandmother's house, since this is the place where the protagonist visits the Grandmother. The contextualization in an urban environment gives a new sense to the narrative matrix, recreated in a multisemiotic version, in which the living presence of the actors and the public plays an important role in the communicative situation.

"Voraz" (Voracious) by Carlos Trunsky: the inner wolf in choreographic discourse

"Voraz" (Voracious) is a choreographic performance directed by Carlos Trunsky. This choreography, performed by four dancers (two men and two women), has been presented in 2006, in the *Teatro del Sur* of Buenos Aires city. Like Daulte's theatrical version, this one also deals with human rapports, recreated in choreographic language.

The aim of Trunsky, as he affirmed in a personal interview held in Buenos Aires in November 2006, was to explore social behaviours regarding power and fear, as well as the ambiguity of sexual and cultural rapports between men and women. The moving body of the dancers displays poetic signs in the significant space of the scenery, with a narrative order dealing with the sequential articulation of choreographic movements. The artistic movements of the moving body display the evolutions and involutions of the rapport between two couples of dancers (Inés Armas-Emmanuel Ludueña and Mariela Alarcón-Leonardo Haedo) until the climax of the total separation of one of them from the others which n provokes the deconstruction and reconstruction of the rapport between the other three ones. The different choreographic scenes are structured both in quartets, couples and solo dancing. The homosexual, bisexual and heterosexual rapports are explored by means of the moving body as a material support of the choreographic narrative. The body acquires a metaphoric dimension, in which the changes of human rapports tend to be similar to the lycanthropic transformations of the folk narrative matrix of Little Red Riding Hood (ATU 333), mixed up with legendary discourse. Trunsky includes in his choreography a dancistic recreation of folkloric games such as the rhythmic entertainment of shaking hands, with the rhytm of the children's song "*Le coq est mort*". Such games serve the function of cohesion resources which separate the different evolutions and involutions between the couples of dancers. The narrative plot is based on such evolutions and involutions performed in the scenic spaces, in different sequences whose climax is the destruction of one of the characters, who is at the same time the avenger and the victim of the other's voracity. Such voracity, which comes to light within scenic movements of the dancers, is connected with the folk narrative matrix of Little Red Riding Hood. In this way, the idea which Trunsky tends to express is that the wolf is hidden in each one of us, no matter the sexual orientation, along with the willingness of challenging the beast which characterizes Little Red Hiding Hood.

The mise en scene is absolutely simple, tending to underline the significance of the body, which sustains the narrative tension, along with music and illumination. In this way, the bright illumination by Eli Sirlin tends to establish a chromatic contrast with the dark clothes of the dancers and with the few dark objects displayed in the scenery. The body of the dancers acts as a metaphoric sign of sexual, cultural and social identity acted out in choreographic movements. The folkloric composition, whose distinctive feature is fragmentarism (Mukarovsky 1977), tends to construct a complex message by mixing up music, dance and monosyllabic articulated language. All these aspects converge in a polyphonic discourse composed by a combination of both rigid and flexible movements, which create a disruptive effect, in a visual metaphor of the ambiguity of human rapports. This performance is based on the wolf's voracity, which is the axis of the choreographic recreation of the narrative matrix. The dancing movements represent the transformation of a human being into a beast. Such transformation generates as well significant changes in the social group, represented by the other three dancers. The small group acts in this way as a metaphor of any society, in which the human rapports are always complex and ambiguous. The semiotic richness of the dance reaches in this performance its highest expression. The dance is the main language, enriched by visual, tactile and sonorous signs which combine illumination, clothes, music, gests and monosyllabic verbal language, mixed up in a complex semiotic net. Such poetic combination of different discourses recreates the narrative matrix in a brilliant choreography which attracts the attention of the audience during the whole performance.

Final considerations

The different narrative itineraries of "Little Red Riding Hood" (ATU 333) show the intertwining of narrative genres such as folktale and legend, which shows the the dynamics between orality, literature and living performances. From the versions supposedly dated in the French Ancient Régime to the literary recreations by Perrault and the brothers Grimm, all recreations are connected with social beliefs regarding werewolves and other monsters which interact with human beings in different cultural environments. As well as these narrative itineraries, also Argentinean oral, theatrical and choreographic versions show contextual transformations of the narrative matrix. Such transformations deal with differential identity of local cultures, in a dynamic tension with the global *spectrum* of recreations. The universal message of a young girl in her way from childhood to womanhood is recreated in different ways, dealing with local beliefs in transformations of human beings into beasts, such as the *Pombero,* the *lobizón* or any other lycanthropic *metamorphosis.* These ways of recreating ATU 333 include as well, theatrical and choreographic performances which show the "somatic dimension" of oral narrative, in a complex message. Such complex message mixes up sound, dance and visual resources, enriched by technological resources.

All these alternative itineraries of "Little Red Riding Hood" reveal the flexible boundaries between folk narrative genres, connected with social beliefs of different cultural contexts. Such social beliefs do influence in the constructive process of folk narratives, erasing generic boundaries between story and legend. These flexible boundaries make room to the most different recreations, such as the Argentinean one, in which the mythical *Pombero* interacts both with Little Red Riding Hood and with the grandmother, or others in which Red Riding Hood is no more a girl but a young woman who works in the urban context of a supermarket. One of the main aspects of the different discursive itineraries is the rhetoric construction of female corporality, based on a dynamic intertwining between synechdotic logic of fragmentation and metaphorical condensations of symbols dealing with sexual awakening. Such rhetoric construction reflects the image of the woman and her different vital cycles in different cultural contexts, from the Argentinean one in which the young girl learns about sexual development by watching the rapport between her grandmother and the mythical *Pombero,* up to the European version in which both the young girl and her grandmother are victims of the wolf's voracity. Both in theatrical and choreographic recreation, there is an embodiment process in the narrative matrix, in which the actors and the dancers give new senses to the narrative matrix, by deplacing or deconstructing the narrative plot. Daulte transforms the pretextual matrix of Little Red Riding Hood in a living performance dealing with human rapports in a contemporary family, composed by three generations of women. The theatrical plot is based on the exhibition of the female body, as watched by a man, who acts as a "wolf". This point leads to another problem, dealing with who is the real wolf. The answer that Trunsky tends to express in the choreographic language is that the wolf is hidden in each one of us, no matter the sexual orientation, along with the willingness of challenging the beast which characterizes Little Red Riding Hood. Besides, the transformations of the narrative matrix make room to didactic transformations, such as Coya or Patagonian Red Riding Hood, which serve the function of symbols of differential identities, used as tools to teach cultural diversities to young children.

In short, the different itineraries of this matrix express a rhetoric of corporality, both as a metaphor of sexual awakening and as a synechdotic fragmentation of parts, dealing with the cultural significance of the female body in different cultures. The counterpart of such rhetoric is the question about who is the real beast and which is the real home, hidden in the dark forest of the outside world.

Bibliography

Blache, M. (1982) *Estructura del miedo. Narrativas folklóricas guaraníticas.* Buenos Aires: Plus Ultra.

Blanc, N. (2009) "El teatro no debe anhelar la perfección. Entrevista a Javier Daulte", *ADN Cultura,*

Blécourt, W. de (2012). "The Problem of Belief Narratives: A Very Short Introduction", *Newsletter of the International Society for Folk Narrative Research,* No. 6: 36-37.

Briggs, Ch. and R. Bauman. (1992). "Genre, intertextuality and social power", *Journal of Linguistical Antropology,* II: 131-172.

Carter, A. (1993) *The Bloody Chamber and other stories.* New York: Penguin.

Darnton, R. (1999). *The Great Cat Massacre and Other Episodes in French Cultural History.* New York: Basic Books.

Dégh, L. (2001) *Legend and Belief: Dialectics of a Folklore Genre.* Bloomington and Indianapolis: Indiana University Press.

Douglas, M. (1995) "Red Riding Hood: An Interpretation from Anthropology. *Folklore* No. 106: 1-7.

Douglas, M. (1998). *Estilos de pensar. Ensayos críticos sobre el buen gusto.* Barcelona: Gedisa.

Dundes, A. (1989). *Little Red Riding Hood: A Casebook.* Madison: University of Wisconsin Press.

Fromm, E. (1972) *El lenguaje olvidado.* Buenos Aires: Hachette.

Grass, G. (1975) *The tin drum.* New York: Houghton, Mifflin and Harcourt Publishing.

Greimas, A. y J. Courtès (1982). *Semiótica. Diccionario razonado de la teoría del lenguaje.* Madrid: Gredos. Bettelheim, B. (1975). *The Uses of Enchantment: The Meaning and Importance of Fairy-Tales.* New York: Random house.

Grimm, J. and W. (1909-14) *Household tales,* Vol. XVII, Part 2. New York: Collier & Son.

La Nación Digital. Publicado el 1/11/2009. Consultado el 2/11/2009.

Licht, R. (2006) "Undertones in "Little Red Riding Hood": The Relationship Between Childhood Innocence and Adult Knowledge." Washington, George Washington University Web. http://www.gwu.edu/~uwp/fyw/euonymous/2005-2006/06-lichtfinal.pdf (Consulted March 1, 2012)

Marzolph, U. (2012) "Presidential Address at the Opening of the ISFNR Interim Conference", *Newsletter of the International Society for Folk Narrative Research,* No. 6: 4-11.

Moeller, H. and G. Lellis (2002) *Volker Schlöndorff's Cinema: Adaptation, poltics and the "movie- appropriate".* Carbondale: Southern Illinois University Press.

Mukarovsky, J. (1977) "Detail as the Basic Semantic Unit in Folk Art.", *The Word and Verbal Art: Selected Essays* ed by J. Burbank and P. Steiner. New Haven: Yale University Press, pp. 180-204

Palleiro, M. (2005) *Narrativa: identidades y memorias.* Buenos Aires: Dunken.

Palleiro, M. (2011) *Jornada "Archivos de Narrativa Tradicional Argentina".* Buenos Aires: María Inés Palleiro editora.

Perrault, Ch. (2006). *The tales of Mother Goose.* Teddington: The Echo Library ed.

Schechner, R. (2000). *Performance. Teoría y prácticas interculturales.* Buenos Aires: Ediciones Libros del Rojas.

Tangherlini, T. (1990). "'It Happened Not Too Far From Here...': A Survey of Legend Theory and Characterization" *Western Folklore* 49: 371-390.

Üther, H.(2004). *The types of International Folktales: a classification and bibliography, based on the system of Antti Aarne and Stith Thompson.* Helsinki: Academia Scientiarum Fennica.

Vidal de Battini, B. (1980-1984). *Cuentos y leyendas populares de la Argentina.* 9 vols. Buenos Aires: Ediciones Culturales Argentinas.

Welter, J. Ch. (1927) *L'enxemplum dans la littérature religieuse et didactique du Moyen Age.* Paris: Tolouse.

Zipes, J. (1993 [1983]). *The Trials and Tribulations of Little Red Riding Hood.* New York: Routledge.

Films and Videotexts

Jordan, Neil and Angela Carter (1991). *The company of wolves* Los Angeles: ITL Entertainment eds..

Schlöndorff, Volker (1979) *The tin drum.* Frankfurt: Bioskop Film.

Hardwicke, Catherine (2011) *Red Riding Hood.* Los Angeles: Warner Brothers.

Living performances

Daulte, Javier (2009) *Caperucita: un espectáculo feroz.* Buenos Aires: Multiteatro

Trunsky, Carlos (2006-2007) *Voraz.* Buenos Aires: Teatro del Sur

Folklore as a Mode of World Transformation: A New Paradigm of Folklore Studies in Thailand

Onusa Suwanpratest

Abstract:

This article aims to investigate the development of folklore studies in Thailand since it was established as a scientific field of study in 1967. The data were collected from related documents, research studies and interviews.

It is found that the first 30 years of folklore studies in Thailand is considered the oral-tradition data collection period. Local folklore was appreciated and recognized as a National heritage. In the decade that followed, scholars attempted to employ western theories such as Cultural Diffusion Theory, Psychoanalysis, and Structural Functional Theory to analyze folklore data. However, it can be observed that all the folklore researchers at the time studied only the Thai and Tai cultures due to the fact that during the time the study of folklore was affiliated with the department of Thai. Consequently, researchers could not conduct studies in areas that were considered "unrelated" to the context of the Thai and Tai cultures.

A significant progress of folklore studies in Thailand took place in 2005 when Department of Folklore was established at Naresuan University. Since then, the subjects of the studies have broadened and are no longer limited to the Thai and Tai cultures. The paradigm of the field has also transformed from Essentialism to Universalism. The studies now focus on Perennial Philosophy to enable researchers to understand universal and world philosophy. At Naresuan University, the study of folklore is a quest for meaning and value in life. The ultimate goal of the study is to become "transparent to transcendence."

Keywords: Folklore, Folklore Studies, Thailand, New Paradigm

Introduction

Oral tradition data are considered to be of great significance as the information derived in this manner, though written down in later periods, reflects the ancestors' great wisdom which has been imparted from generation to generation (Ong 7). The recognition of the importance of such oral tradition has led to academic studies of folktales, folksongs, folk beliefs, etc. comprising traditional ways of living of different groups of people. The emerging field of study is known as Folklore.

Folklore studies were originated in the West around the 19th century when the concepts of romanticism and nationalism were influential in the western nations. Jumping on the bandwagon, many scholars then embraced the interest in an investigation of folk culture. The term "Folklore" was coined by William Thomas in 1846 (Dundes 4).

In Thailand, the interest in Folklore could be said to have existed since the olden days. The academic study of Folklore based on a system recognized internationally, however, began around 50 years ago and has seen a steady progress. On the other hand, no study could be found that documented the historical development of Folklore studies in Thailand. The existingrecords tackling this subject matter related merely the beginning phase of the studies of Folklore in Thailand. This article, therefore, attempts to explore the development of Folklore studies in Thailand from the past up to the present time in order to provide a complete picture on this subject and to highlight the new paradigm that has emerged during the development. The results are expected to have certain contributive value to Folklore studies both in Thailand and in other countries.

Objective

The objective of this article is to study the development of Folklore studies in Thailand from 1967, when Folklore was first studied as a scientific field of study, to 2016 (the present day).

Methodology

1. Data Collection
1.1 Study the history and status of Folklore studies in Thailand from related documents and research works.

1.2 Conduct an interview with Professor Dr.Kingkeo Attagara, the first Thai person with a doctorate in Folklore from Indiana University, U.S.A., and the pioneer who inaugurated the western system of Folklore studies in Thailand.

2. Data Analysis
2.1 Analyze the data from the documentary study and the interview by means of Content Analysis in order to sum up the historical development of Folklore studies in Thailand.

2.2 Present the results by means of Descriptive Analysis.

Results

1. Background of Folklore Studies in Thailand
The information derived from the data collection suggests that Folkloristics first became known among the academia in Thailand in 1967 as a result of the pioneering effort of Professor Dr.Kingkeo Attagara, the first Thai nationality with a doctorate in Folklore from Indiana University, U.S.A.

This by no means suggests that the interest in Folklore in Thailand had been non-existent prior to the year 1967. Documentary evidence points out that King Chulalongkorn (King Rama V) of the Chakri Dynasty composed a literary work titled *Praratchapithee Sipsong Duean (The Twelve-Months Royal Ceremonies)* in 1888, which provides detailed information on a collection of royal ceremonies. In addition, during the reign of King Vajiravudh (King Rama VI) (1910-1925), nationalism was promoted by the monarchy (Fry, Nieminen and Smith 9), and consequently the promotion of art and culture, both royal and local, was championed in earnest. Traditional lullabies and local myths were collected and printed to be preserved as manuscripts (Wetchasat 3). The interest in these cultural aspects, nevertheless, merely led to the collection of the information considered as a cultural heritage. The science of Folklore remained yet to be introduced.

Around the year 1957, higher education institutes began to integrate cultural instruction into their curricula although the term "Folklore" was not yet applied to such instruction. Professor Khun Ying Kularb Mallikamas, a notable scholar, translated excerpts from Stith Thompson's *The Folktale* and published them in 1964 in tandem with samples from Thai literary works and beliefs in *Khati Chaoban (Lore of Rural People)*. The data in the book, however, were illustrated but not analyzed (Attagara 211).

In 1967, Professor Dr.Kingkeo Attagara completed a doctorate in Folklore, came back to Thailand and introduced the study of Folklore based on systematic and universal Folkloristic theories and methodology, and thus began the systematic and universal study of Folklore in Thailand (Wetchasat 4). Professor Dr.Kingkeo Attagara's doctoral thesis titled *The Folk Religion of Ban Nai, a Hamlet in Central Thailand*, a field study of a village in Na Pa Sub-district, Muang District, Chonburi province, is hailed as Thailand's first research study in Folklore (Patrachai 45).

Kingkeo Attagara, the pioneer of Folkloristics in Thailand, coined the Thai terms "Khatichon" and "Khatichon Withaya" to be used in place of the English term "Folklore". "Khatichon" is used to mean information in the form of the product of culture, and "Khatichon Withaya" is used to refer to a discipline. (Nimmanahaeminda 23-24)

2. Folklore Studies in Thailand from 1967-1996

Folklore studies in Thailand during the first 30 years evolved around collecting and categorizing oral-tradition data from different local areas. Localism, subsequently, became increasingly ingrained in the people's awareness. After completing a doctorate in Folklore, Kingkeo Attagara came back to Thailand and offered Folklore as a course in the Master's program of Department of Thai both at The College of Education, Prasarnmit Campus (now Srinakharinwirot University), and at Chulalongkorn University. As a result, a number of Folklore research studies were produced, with subject areas related to all regions of Thailand. Examples of the studies are *Wannakam Khao Khong Phak Neu (Khao Literature of the North)* (Saneha Bunyarak,

1976), *Laksana Wannakam Isan (Characteristics of the Literature of the North-East)* (Jaruwan Thammawat, 1978), *Wikhro Samnuanwoharn Lae Sanyalak Nai Plengklomdek Phak Tai (An Analysis of the Expressions and Symbols in the Lullabies of the South)* (Winai Chanprim, 1988), and *Kan Suksa Wikhro Nithan Pheunban Phak Klang (An Analysis of the folktales of Central Thailand)* (Chanthana Yennan, 1996).

Nevertheless, it was found that most of the research studies in this era featured the collection of data for a literary analysis. This is to say that the studies were conducted to understand the characteristics of the literary works. If the data comprised folktales, the studies tended to include an analysis of the plots, characters, themes and settings. If the data derived from folk songs or proverbs, the studies often involved a linguistic analysis of the expressions, comparative statements or cultural values found in the songs or the proverbs (Patrachai 56). Examples of such studies are *Wannakam Chak Tambon Srikirimas Changwat Sukhothai (The Literary Works of Srikirimas Sub-district, Sukhothai Province)* (Prachak Saisaeng, 1973), *Wikhro Wannakam Pheunban Tambon Thamai Amphur Prankratai Changwat Kamphaengphet (An Analysis of the Folktales of Thamai Sub-district, Kamphaengphet Province)* (Sunthree Duangthip, 1982), and *Kan Suksa Khunkha Wannakhadee Isan Reung Siao Sawad (A Study of the Value of the Isan Literature Siao Sawad)* (Nonglak Khuntawee, 1986), etc. Furthermore, there were also studies comparing the same type of Folklore exhibited in different groups of people such as *Kan Suksa Prieptiep Reung Phra Rot-Meree Chabap Tang Tang (A Comparison of Different Versions of Phra Rot-Meree)* (Nantaporn Puangkaew, 1984), and *Kan Suksa Prieptiep Wannakhadee Reung Nang Phom Hom Chabap Lanna Kap Isan (A Comparative Study of the Lanna and Isan Versions of Nang Phom Hom)* (Siwaporn Wattanarat, 1989).

Even though the Folkloristic theories and methodology were being adopted into the research works, studies of this nature were still a rarity. Some examples of the studies are *Nithan Phrasuthon-Nangmanorah Kan Suksa Nai Rabiepwithee Phummiprawat (The Tale of Phrasuthon-Nangmanorah: A Study Based on a Historic-Geographic Approach)* (Sukanya Sujachaya, 1978), *Rammakian: Kan Suksa Nai Ngae Kan Phrae Krajai Khong Nithan (Ramayana: A Study on the Diffusion of a Tale)* (Siraporn Thitathan, 1979), and *Kan Suksa Cheung Wikhro Baepreung Lae Anuphak Nai Panyasachadok (An Analytical Study of Tale Types and Motifs in Pannasa Jataka)* (Uenthip Peerasathian, 1996).

When the Thai Studies program was offered in various universities in and around the year 1986, Folklore research became more varied, extending from verbal folklore research to non-verbal folklore research such as studies on folk music, folk handicraft and mixed-folklore such as folk performing arts, folk games, etc. (Patrachai 47)

3. Folklore Studies in Thailand from 1997-2005

During this period, Folklore studies in Thailand became more diversified. Thai Folklorists adapted western theories in their research studies in an effort to comprehend the meanings of the data. The theories popularly adopted included Cultural Diffusion Theory, Psychoanalysis, and Structural Functional Theory. Examples of research studies in this period are *Baeprueang Nithan Sang Thong: Kwam Phraelai Lae Kan Taek Rueang (The Sang Thong Tale Type: Its Popularity and Reproduction)* (Watcharaporn Distapan, 2002) and *Kwam Khatyaeng Lae Kan Praneepranorm Nai Tamnan Parumpara Thai (Conflict and Compromise in Thai Myths)* (Poramin Jaruworn, 2006), etc. In addition, it could be seen that the studies were shifting from focusing only on textual research to investigating the media employed to convey performing arts, including studies on contemporary Folklore in the digital age, net lore, popular culture, and dynamics of Folklore.

Yet, it could be observed that almost all of the studies involved the Folklore data from Thai people or Tai ethnic group since the Folklore course was offered by Department of Thai as part of their study programs. Even with the extension of the curricular contents into Thai Studies, the research topics remained constrained by the scope of the curriculum as well as the department with which the researchers were affiliated.

4. A New Paradigm of Folklore Studies in Thailand (2005-present)

The year 2005 marked an important milestone in the field of Folklore Studies in Thailand when Division of Folklore was inaugurated at Naresuan University in Phitsanulok province to offer a doctoral program in Folklore, independent of Department of Thai. This inauguration greatly expanded the scope of Folklore studies in Thailand. In the past, a study of Folklore was considered to be within the area of Thai language and literature, and the thesis studies were more or less restricted by this notion. As a result, the folklore research in the earlier period was invariably related to Thailand or the Tai ethnic group. The establishment of Division of Folklore helped liberate the concept of Folklore studies in Thailand from the monopoly of the Thai and Tai contents.

Up to the present time, Naresuan University has remained the first and the only higher education institute in Thailand that offers degree programs, both Master's and Doctoral, in Folklore. Other institutes that offer graduate instruction on Folklore confer a degree in Thai, not in Folklore. (Suwanpratest 26)

Kingkeo Attagara, Thailand's pioneering figure in Folklore, played a vital role in the advancement of Folkloristics during this phase in becoming a full-time lecturer at Naresuan University since the conception of Division of Folklore and designing Folklore curricula based on a modern concept which focuses on a quest for the divine excellences and powers. In other words, Folklore has since, and thus, been regarded as the power behind both cultural and spiritual drives.

Culturally speaking, this concept of Folklore embraces both the Great Tradition and the Little Tradition, which are connected to provide an insight into the equality of different cultures and contents in terms of human philosophy. The diversity of expressions by different groups of people is regarded merely as different masks and shades.

Spiritually speaking, this mode of Folklore studies is influenced by concepts concocted by Joseph Campbell and Aldous Huxley; hence, the study of mythology based on Perennial Philosophy. Mythology is regarded as a significant type of Folklore that contributes to man's spiritual uplifting, a metaphor for an understanding of life in and beyond this world.

The structure of the world and the universe is not by any means limited to the material world. The mental structure consists of countless components and details. The material world of the universe constitutes the macro cosmos, whereas the human world of each individual constitutes the micro cosmos. Each human organ has already been conditioned to function as well as to communicate and interpret messages. Certain behaviors have been conditioned to generate conflicts and problems while other behaviors lead predictably to harmonious operations and the coherence of the entire system of the universe. Mythology relates such incidents. Ancient instances indicate right from wrong – 'right' refers to harmony and coherence whereas 'wrong' refers to obstruction, problem and damage. Mythology connects the human spirit to the condition of life, providing clues to problems and acting as an alarm signal system. (Attagara 9-10)

According to Kingkeo Attagara, "the birth of Folkloristics at Naresuan Universityrevitalized my Self. It was as if I myself had been reborn. I had turned away from Folklore for 25 years to fulfill other missions. The Folklore I had been engaged in concerned the collection of folk data and the dissemination of theories essential for fundamental understanding of the course, and when my time was up, it was left at just that. Now that I have revived that engagement, I feel uplifted because I have already done what my great teachers have imparted to me; that is to perceive Folklore and Folkloristics as cultural and spiritual dynamics." (Attagara, 2016, interview)

Under this conceptual framework, a number of research studies have been produce, for example, *Cheewit Lae Khunupakan Khong Joseph Campbell Tor Kan Suksa Theppakoranam (The Life and Contributions of Joseph Campbell to the Study of Mythology)* (Baranee Boonsong, 2009), *Somdet Phra Naresuan Maharat: Phalang Khapkluen Buenglang Prachachat (King Naresuan the Great: The Dynamic Power Behind the Nation)* (Onusa Suwanpratest, 2009), *Archetype Awatan: Prakottakan Thang Theppakoranam Nai Satsana Hidu Lae Phraphutthasatsana (Avatar Archetype: A Mythological Phenomenon in Hinduism and Buddhism)* (Catthaleeya Aungthonggumnerd, 2014), *Moommong Thang Khatichon Withaya Kap Prakottakan Kwam Sattha Tor Ponruea-ek Phrachaoborommawongther Krommaluang Chumphon Khet-udomsak (Folkloristic Overview and the Phenomena of Beliefs in His Royal Highness Admiral Prince Abhakara of Chumphon)* (Pakpoom Sookcharoen, 2015), and *Thong: Kwammai Lae Khunkha Nai Watthanatham Thai (Gold: Its Meaning and Value in Thai Tradition)* (Suwannee Thongrot, 2015).

Conclusion

When the overall historical development of Folklore studies in Thailand is taken into account, Professor Dr.Kingkeo Attagara shines as a torchbearer in the field. It could, therefore, be said that the development of Folkloristics in Thailand is the trophy of a lifelong quest of Kingkeo Attagara, who set up a standard of Folklore studies in Thailand after receiving a doctoral degree in Folklore from Indiana University, U.S.A., thus generating academic interests in Folkloristics among Thai scholars. Moreover, Professor Dr.Kingkeo Attagarahas created a "new paradigm" for the study of Folklore, which has transformed the Essentialist approach, in which the conservation of the oral-tradition culture and the quest for the identity of an ethnic group constitute a major occupation, into Universalism which focuses on mythological studies based on Perennial Philosophy. The goal of a study of this nature, then, is to understand the system and mechanism of the world and the universe including the human philosophy, with Folklore acting as the answer to the quest for meaning and value in life, and with the ultimate goal to become "transparent to transcendence".

This development of the study of Folklore provides an insight into the nature of Folklore data – that despite the diversified character of the data, they can be conceptualized into one universal theory, which signifies the universality of the essence of life.

What Folklore is expected to do is to "connect" the cultural data – masked in different forms and shades – in order to interpret and understand the meaning and value of life so that the harmony and compassion generated as a result of that realization will help prevent social discords. Folklore theories, therefore, must help create understanding, peace and spiritual elevation towards the noblest of existence.

References

Attagara, Kingkeo. *Khatichon Withaya (Folklore)*. Bangkok: Department of Teacher Education, 1976.

---. *Pleroma*. Phitsanulok: Surasrigraphic, 2015.

Dundes, Alan. (Editor). *The Study of Folklore*. U.S.A.: Englewood Cliffs, N.J. Prentice-Hall, Inc, 1965.

Fry, Gerald W., Nieminen, Gayla S. and Smith, Harold E. *Historical Dictionary of Thailand*. Third Edition. UK: Scarecrow Press, Inc, 1942.

Nimmanahaeminda, Prakong. "Professor Phraya Anuman Rajadhon: Contributions to the Study of Folklore and Folk Life." *The Journal of the Royal Institute of Thailand*. Vol.I, 2009, pp.21-36.

Ong, Walter J. *Orality and Literacy*. 2nd Edition. U.S.A.: Routledge, 2002.

Patrachai, Sukanya. "Sathanapap Lae Phathanakan Withayanipon Thang Khatichon Withaya (Status and Development of Folklore Thesis)." *Khatichon Kap Khon Thai-Tai (Folklore and Thai-Tai People)*. Nathalang, Siraporn and Patrachai, Sukanya. (Editors). Bangkok: Chulalongkorn University, 1999, pp.44-57.

Suwanpratest, Onusa. "Kwang Kwa Lok Nuea Chakkrawan Khopkhai Un Phaisan Khong Wicha Khatichonwithaya" (Wider than the Earth, Above the Universe: The Unlimited Scope of Folklore). *Withayajarn*. Vol.111/3, January 2012, pp.25-28.

Wetchasat, Kanyarat. "Wongkan Khatichonwithaya: Phubukberk lae Phonngan (Folklore Academic Circle: A Pioneer and Contributions)." *Khatichon Kap Khon Thai-Tai (Folklore and Thai-Tai People)*. Nathalang, Siraporn and Patrachai, Sukanya. (Editors). Bangkok: Chulalongkorn University, 1999, pp.1-22.

Interview

Kingkeo Attagara. 8th April, 2016.

Orality and the Quest for Truth in the Thai Forest Tradition

Dr. Dipti Visuddhangkoon

Abstract:

This paper discusses dhamma propagation as based on orality and a non-text oriented form of teaching method that had once been employed by many well-known forest tradition monks of Northeast Thailand. The Northeast, popularly known as Isan, has been particularly fortunate in having begotten many great meditation masters whose lineage has flourished until the present time. Rigorous consistency in meditation practice, strict adherence to the monastic disciplinary codes (*vinaya*), and a highly regimented life-style based upon austerity in living conditions have made the forest tradition monks accomplished meditation masters. The profound teachings of highly venerated monks like Ajahn Sao, Ajahn Mun, Ajahn Thet, Ajahn Chah and many other monastics from the tradition form a corpus of ethico-spiritual guidelines for the cultivation of reflexive thinking that has inspired Buddhist and non-Buddhist alike, from prison inmates in the West to monastics and lay devotees in Southeast Asia. But most interestingly enough, none of these monks had ever tried their hands at writing down any of their teachings. This paper analyzes the richness of this form of oral teachings and the philosophical dimension of self-reflexivity that is reflected in the teachings. What is decipherable in the oral dhamma expositions of almost all the forest tradition monks is the mindful deconstruction of dichotomous thought-processes. In the teachings of Ajahn Chah, for instance, it is not just language, but the human Ego in all its *kammic* dimensions – linguistic, ethico-spiritual, and socio-cultural orientations – get dismantled time and again, as do all dualistic mental states arising from attachment to 'me' and 'mine', 'Self' and the 'Other'. By consciously defying reification of all mental formations, conditioned states, dichotomous predilections and conventional signs – be it the written word in its varied embodied textuality, or a concept in its mere conceptuality – the simple, direct, and profound teachings bring to the fore the effectual significance of cultivation of self-reflexivity in daily life in order to break through and go beyond the dualities in all conventional realities.

Keywords: The Thai Forest Tradition, orality, quest for truth, self-reflexivity

Introduction

Northeast Thailand (Isan) has been the home of many great meditation masters whose lineage is being well preserved, both in theory and practice, until the present day. The sagacity in the practice of meditative mindfulness that accompanied the strict adherence to *vinaya* or monastic disciplinary codes have had transformed many monks of the forest tradition from their ordinary status of unknown renunciants dwelling in forested monasteries to accomplished meditation masters, whose profound teachings are today widely disseminated across the globe. All the monks in the entire lineage starting from Ajahn Mun, Ajahn Sao, Ajahn Thet, Ajahn Doon, Ajahn Kamdi, Ajahn Chah, Ajahn Liem down to Ajahn Sumedho and many other living masters underwent rigorous self-training through the practice of insight meditation and close scrutiny of the mind with contemplative and rationalistic understanding of the Buddha's teachings on the Four Noble Truths (*ariyasacca*) and the three characteristics of existence (*tilakkhana*).[7] The praxis of mental training that has been developed and nurtured under the aegis of the above mentioned and many other forest tradition monks, both dead and those still living, has come to epitomize the

---

[7]   In Thailand, the laity addresses a senior monk with such honorifics as *luangpoo* (venerable grandfather), *luangpho* (venerable father), or *ajahn* (variously spelt as *ajarn*, *ajan*, *achaan* and meaning respected teacher).

true Buddhist way of monasticism which is marked by such characteristics as non-clinging, egolessness, mindfulness, equanimity, compassion, simplicity, material frugality and contentment. Their collected teachings form a corpus of reflective guidelines for the cultivation of mental well-being that is not only conducive to individual moral growth but also for communal spiritual health and mental well-being along the path set forth by the Buddha more than two millennia ago. But most interestingly enough none of these monks had ever written down anything in their own hand. Rather, they opted for orality and the quest for truth by focusing on practice and communicated their experiential knowledge through dhamma talks, delivered mostly in the Isan dialect and occasionally in central Thai which were either recorded on tapes or jotted down by their disciples.

In the recent past, Buddhism as a social institution has undergone tremendous changes as Thai society began to adapt itself to the process of modernization under the swaying influence of both capitalism and consumerism. As Buddhists, most Thais today confine themselves to ritualistic worshipping and acts of merit-making more than any reflective practice of dhamma in daily life. Across the country great emphasis has been laid down upon the structural expansion of Buddhadhamma, starting from the construction of huge Buddha images, preaching halls, elaborately decorated temples and convenient monastic dwellings. The message of selfless renunciation, which forms the core essence of Right Thought (*sammā sankappa*), an essential factor leading to wisdom as incorporated in the Noble Eightfold Path (*ariya-atthangika-magga*), is at times completely lost from the scene. It is against this backdrop one needs to take a look at the way of life and practice of the *dhutanga*[8] tradition of Northeast Thailand that has begotten such great meditation masters as mentioned above. These monks who underwent rigorous self-training through the practice of insight meditation (*vipassana*) and close scrutiny of the mind with reflexive and rationalistic understanding of the Buddha's teachings of the Four Noble Truths (*ariyasacca*)[9]

---

[8]   The tradition of forest monks who voluntarily choose to follow a more austere way of life dates back to the Buddha. Besides Thailand, this tradition still exists in Laos, Myanmar and Sri Lanka.

[9]   The Four Noble Truths are – 1) Suffering (*dukkha*), 2) The arising or origin of suffering (*samudaya*), 3) The cessation of suffering (*nirodha*), and 4) The way or path leading to the cessation of suffering (*magga*).

and the three characteristics of existence (*tilakkhana*)[10] have come to epitomize the authentic Buddhist way of living and mental development. The praxis of mental well-being that has been developed and nurtured under the aegis of the forest tradition monks have set up the solid foundation for holistic well-being of the individual and the community in relation to the social and natural environment. The universality in the praxis can be applied at any time and situation by any interested person irrespective of religious and cultural background. Buddhist and non-Buddhist alike can gain from the teachings because the underlying messages embodied in them are free from sectarianism. The universal garb of the teachings can be understood from the praxis of mental well-being developed by these monks, the different levels at which their practice benefitted the mind, and their contemplative thinking which is deconstructive in nature. But all the benefits that we are talking about had the origin in a form of practice that was based on an approach that was non-textual, non-canonical and strictly practice-oriented and the knowledge arising from which was conveyed and shared by the masters through extempore dhamma talks.

Why did the forest tradition monks opt for orality?

While the modern Thai centralized type of education system was not readily available to them in their remote villages in the late 19th- and early 20th-century, the forest tradition monks still had access to ecclesiastical literacy when they ordained as novices and monks in the village temples. As for instance, most of them had learnt the Thaam and Thai Noi scripts, two major languages in which manuscripts used to be written in NE Thailand for centuries. Moreover, they also learnt fundamentals of Pali, the Theravada canonical language, and in their Lao-speaking local context they were also exposed to central Thai, the *lingua franca* used for general communication across the country. Yet, what strikes us most is the fact that most of the forest tradition monks deliberately opted for orality as the mode of practice for dhamma exchange, discussion, and dissemination and refrained from committing themselves to writing and compiling any text. While many of them preferred to propagate in a non-script/non-text/non-Canon based style, relying exclusively on the Isan dialect in its spoken form, it is as if they themselves and their powerful verbal teachings

---

[10]   The threefold characteristics of existence are – impermanence (*anicca*), suffering (*dukkha*) and non-substantiality (*anattā*).

formed a great living and self-generative text. The self-imposed orality and the quest for truth by focusing on practice became the hallmark of their teaching technique that has yielded very positive results. Not only did their timeless teachings attracted the native Thais but also drew a large number of non-Thais, especially western disciples from time to time. Ajahn Chah, the founder of the first international monastery in Thailand for western disciples, communicated his experiential knowledge on mindfulness cultivation and *dhutanga* practice through numerous dhamma talks, delivered mostly in the Isan dialect and occasionally in central Thai. The dhamma talks were either recorded on tape cassettes or jotted down from memory by the ardent disciples. It should be noted that the recording of dhamma talks became more common only when Westerners came to live in the monastery as fully ordained monks and began to engage in question and answer sessions with the master. Later the disciples transcribed the dhamma talks from tape cassettes and put them down in written form. Today, most of the teachings are available for free on different websites and are being translated into many different languages such as French, German, Hebrew, Chinese etc. Perhaps the most influential master when it comes to teaching to non-Thais, Ajahn Chah has been continually honoured (even decades after his demise) by his disciples through translation and proliferation of his teachings far and wide. Currently, his dhamma talks are available in more than fifteen different languages and most of his disciples; especially those who are still in robes are actively engaged in the teaching and propagation of Theravada Buddhism.

Initially, all the forest tradition monks (including Ajahn Chah) have always preferred to lead a wandering life, practicing meditation in outdoor settings – in tiger and cobra-infested forests, mountain caves and forsaken cremation grounds – before settling down and establishing monasteries, especially to make themselves available to the lay community that sought their abiding teachings. The ascetic way of life and rigorous outdoor meditation practice made them austere renunciants enabling them to detach from all physical comforts and surviving on mere minimal requirements. From the voluntary cultivation of severing ties with material possessions and all physical comforts, they developed the mental prowess to face every difficulty, be it physical or mental, in a detached, yet courageous manner. And most importantly, the rigorous outdoor meditation practice had provided the fertile ground for the realization and reflective internalization of the three characteristics of existence – impermanence (*anicca*), suffering (*dukkha*) and non-substantiality (*anatta*) and the Law of Dependent Origination (*paticcasamuppāda*)[11] that clearly depicts the cycle of birth and rebirth starting from ignorance (*avijjā*). When monasteries grew around them, these monks implemented strict discipline to continue their way of practice themselves and to inspire their disciples to cultivate morality, mindfulness and wisdom through the practice of insight meditation in the same manner. Out of their dedicated effort a praxis of mental well-being took shape. In the numerous dhamma talks of the renunciant monks of the forest tradition, it is clearly reflected that the trained mind of a meditator transcends its own ego and at a higher contemplative level proceeds to deconstruct all dualistic notions starting from the very concepts of me and mine, I and the other. As Ajahn Chah succinctly expresses, "Give up clinging to love and hate, just rest with things as they are. Do not try to become anything. Do not make yourself into anything. Do not be a meditator. Do not become enlightened. When you sit, let it be. When you walk, let it be. Grasp at nothing. Resist nothing."[12]

Deconstruction and binary oppositions

If one goes by the conventional understanding of what philosophy is, or could be, then certainly the forest tradition monks' teachings do not directly fall within the category of philosophical exposition in the strictest sense of the term. Yet, at a close introspection it appears that most of them incessantly worked within the matrix of a mode of practice that can be categorized as deconstruction-in-praxis since it laid emphasis on certain wholesome practical aspects like strict adherence to monastic codes, mindfulness cultivation and living out the principle of 'letting go' in daily life. The teachings are bereft of any emphasis on external means and ritualistic excess. The tools employed to impart the deep knowledge of Buddhism were simple and down-to-earth,

---

[11] The twelve elements of dependent origination are: ignorance (*avijjā*) → mental formation (*saṅkhāra*) → consciousness (*viññāna*) → mind-and-body (*nāma-rūpa*) → six sense-bases (*salāyatana*) → contact (*phassa*) → sensation (*vedanā*) → craving (*tanhā*) → clinging (*upādāna*) → becoming (*bhava*) → birth (*jāti*) → decay-and-death (*jarā-marana*).

[12] All the quotes of Ajahn Chah's dhamma talks are taken from the book *A Still Forest Pool* edited by Jack Korn- field and Paul Breiter. Hereafter reference will be made to the specific dhamma talk from the book with the corresponding page number. Quoted above is "The Simple Path", p.5.

for example, Ajahn Chah used a human skeleton, a fetus in a glass jar, and ordinary images from nature which he held up to profound metaphoric level.

To understand the Buddhist non-reification of binaries we may now as well try to reflect upon Derridean deconstruction that sees the influence of the traditional binary oppositions such as true–false, original–derivative, unified–diverse as infecting all areas of life and thought, including the evolution of western philosophy from the time of Plato to Heidegger. The well-known French philosopher and founder of deconstruction, Jacques Derrida (1930-2004) upholds the idea that the task of the thinker is to twist free of these oppositions, and of the forms of intellectual and cultural life which they structure. Derrida draws our attention to the important issue that the individual terms of the 'binaries' do not really have the same 'status'. There exists an imbalance in the structure of the pairing in which one of the terms inevitably dominates the other (e.g. presence/absence, light/dark, man/woman etc.) So the first necessary action is to reverse the binary as a sign of justification. By doing so one is actually raising philosophical objections as well as uncovering socially oppressive operations of one of the terms of the binary. But mere reversal is not enough. Derrida points out that reversing the binary is but the *first step* that deconstruction has to undertake. The *second*, and even more radical step is to make the binary redundant by "thinking it through". The second step will help prepare the ground for analyzing the conditions of possibility for that binary so as to get it displaced. If there is no displacement but mere reversal then there exist the perils of repeating the original imbalance – earlier structure with a negative notation. It merely puts a mark of negation onto something that was valued earlier. Such a naïve kind of reversal is to the previous order of domination what negative theology is to theology as Aniket Jaware puts it humorously "the worshippers of the Devil make the Devil into their God…and thus end up with a God after all."[13] What needs to be done is to *neutralize* the binary, not merely negate or reverse it. To this extent, deconstruction as a method of philosophizing and 'reading' of any text is extremely bold and radical since it helps to generate momentum and critical questioning of dualistic hierarchies.

While the Derridean call for dismantling of dualistic hierarchies might be radical as a new exegetical tool possessing a self-righteous analytical

---

[13]   Jaware, Aniket. (2001). *Simplifications*. New Delhi: Orient Longman Lt, p. 435.

edge,[14] from the Buddhist perspective of 'letting go', however, it appears to be a metaphysical *cul-de-sac*, since it cannot detach and dislodge itself from the act of parasitical engagement with the play and teasing apart of binary oppositions.[15] On the other hand, a careful and attentive reading of the forest tradition monks' play of paradoxes in their dhamma talks, reveals the fact that there is always an objective distancing from the process of giving rise to an 'Ego' that rejoices in the unraveling of the paradoxes, quite unlike in Derrida and the gamut of texts generated under his powerful influence by academically-oriented philosophers and literary critics, who do not hesitate to be pretentiously opaque at times camouflaging personal socio-cultural biases under the rubric of critical radicality.[16] In one of his dhamma talks Ajahn Chah says, "You must go beyond all words, all symbols, all plans for your practice.

---

[14] As the well known deconstructionist critic, Gayatri Spivak once said in an interview "Deconstruction seems to offer a way out of the closure of knowledge. By inaugurating the open-ended infiniteness of textuality by thus 'placing in the abyss' (mettre en abime) as the French expression would literally have it – it shows us the hue of the abyss as freedom. The fall into the abyss of deconstruction inspires us with as much pleasure as fear. We are intoxicated with the prospect of never hitting bottom."

[15] It's as if the deconstructionist-fetus continues to live cozily forever in the dark womb of mother-post-structuralism, drawing nutrients from the umbilical cord of the binary-pair and swimming endlessly in the amniotic sac of abstruse jargon-loaded linguistic games and gimmicks, while forever postponing that final hour of emergence from the womb, severing the cord, and leading a life of its own – apart from the binary pair.

[16] As for instance, the anti-Semitism of Paul de Man and more distinctly Gayatri Spivak's narcissistic, navel gazing attitudinal disposition towards highlighting her own Bengali culture while purposefully side-stepping the imperialistic trend within that culture. In this context it is worth throwing some light on the fact that Spivak never deconstructs the Bengali gentleman's imposition of his language and culture upon the non-Bengali states of Northeast India. Moreover, while she seeks to draw attention in her talks to exploitation of the Bengali-dialect speaking Rohinyas in Myanmar, she never utters a single word about the brutality inflicted for decades by Bangladesh upon non-Bengali speaking minorities and indigenous people, the Jummas of Chittagong Hill Tracts. Persecuted, attacked and forced off their ancestral land, the situation of the ethnic Buddhists is extremely bleak in their own homeland. So the question is what does a critic like Spivak have been deconstructing at all? Appropriating the Gramscian concept of subaltern to develop the postcolonial discourse she overlooks imperialist trends within her own linguistic community that has had devastated the indigenous ethnic cultural identity of many northeastern states like Tripura, Assam, Meghalaya, and parts of Arunachal Pradesh.

Then you can see for yourself the truth arising right there. If you don't turn inward, you will never know reality."[17] This turning inward does not imply aggrandizement of the individual ego, but rather its objectivization through the realization of its workings within the natural paradigmatic truth of existence – *anicca*, *dukkha* and *anattā*. He has reiterated the message of empting the mind in most of his dhamma talks – "When you practice, observe yourself. Then gradually knowledge and vision will arise of themselves. If you sit in meditation and want it to be this way or that, you had better stop right there. Do not bring ideals or expectations to your practice. Take your studies, your opinions, and store them away."[18]

The forest tradition vis-à-vis Derridean deconstruction

The forest tradition monks as followers of the Buddha themselves worked very much within the framework of a form of deconstruction that we may as well name as empirical deconstruction. These monks who emphasized on the *thudanga* practice geared their deconstructive endeavours to none other than the dawning of an inner peaceful state upon the transcendence of their ego, conventional truths, mental-formations and attachment to such mental states. They developed and adhered to a life's philosophy that was based on a rigorous deconstructive mode of practice that gave rise to a practical discourse of annihilation of the ego and the resultant understanding of any state of 'being' (both mental and physical) as it-is-in-itself. This mode of practice can thus be categorized as empirical deconstruction or deconstruction-in-praxis. Such a way of practice does not valorize the 'written' text, but renders the practice a moment-to-moment phenomenal and empirical garb without at the same time erecting a 'mega-narrative' of the self-at-practice; hence the deliberate choice for orality. Through the numerous talks what get manifested is that critically reflective Buddhist deconstruction creates the fertile ground for a form of self-introspective practice/scrutiny that goes hand in hand with moral practice and non-attachment to the self and the practice practiced.

The deconstructive similes and metaphors that Ajahn Chah uses are thought provoking. In all his dhamma talks there are some extremely pithy statements/sentences that are located at strategic points. One such example

---

[17]   "Go Beyond Words: See for Yourself" p.10.
[18]   Ibid.

is: "Regardless of time and place, the whole practice of Dhamma comes to *completion* at the place where there is *nothing*. It's the place of surrender, of emptiness, of laying down the burden. This is the finish. It's not like the person who says, "Why is the flag fluttering in the wind? I say it's because of the wind." Another person says because of the flag. The other retorts that it's because of the wind. There's no end to this! All these things are merely *conventions*, we establish them ourselves. If you know these things with wisdom then you'll know impermanence, suffering and not-self. This is the outlook which leads to enlightenment."

What distinguishes Ajahn Chah's deconstruction from Derrida's deconstruction as centered upon word game is an unwillingness to indulge in prolix and convoluted wordplay. For Ajahn Chah, lexical and conceptual deconstructions are merely a means of breaking through conceptuality and attachment leading to a transformed state of consciousness. The essential difference between Derridean philosophy and Ajahn Chah's philosophy is that the deconstructive tool through which Ajahn Chah seeks to dispose of all self/ego arising positions helps lead to enlightenment beyond language and conceptuality. Ajahn Chah's deconstructive endeavours are geared to none other than the dawning of an inner peaceful state upon the transcendence of language, conventional truths, conceptual thinking, mental-formations and attachment to such mental states. It has arisen from practical lessons learnt from the practice of renunciation and insight meditation, quite unlike Derrida whose way of philosophizing is based on theoretical exposition of the philosophical and socio-cultural road map of the European civilization and the Jewish experience as the "other".

Derrida in his text *The Gift of Death* states that: "I cannot respond to the call, the request, the obligation, or even the love of another, without sacrificing the other other, the other others."[19] That is why for Derrida it seems that the Buddhist desire to have attachment to nobody and equal compassion for everybody is an unattainable ideal. He does, in fact suggests that a universal community that excludes no one is a contradiction in terms. According to him, this is because: "I am responsible to anyone (that is to say, to any other) only by failing in my responsibility to all the others, to the ethical or political generality. And I can never justify this sacrifice; I must always hold my peace

---

[19] Derrida, Jacques. (1992). *The Gift of Death.* Trans. David Wills, Chicago: University of Chicago Press, 1995.

about it…What binds me to this one, remains finally unjustifiable."[20] Derrida hence implies that responsibility to any particular individual is only possible by being irresponsible to the "other others", that is, to the other people and possibilities that haunt any and every existence. Such deconstructive way of arguing appears glib when placed against the Buddhist emphasis on taking into account *'cetana'* or intention that guides any willed action.

It is understandable that Derrida's standard arguments or counter-arguments have arisen in the context of a Judo-Christian outlook that functions within the matrix of a discourse that takes the self (whether divine or human) as a centre, quite contrary to the Buddhist concept of non-substantiality/non-self or *anattā*. The radicality of Derrida's deconstructive practice appears to be limited when it is placed vis-à-vis the concept of Buddhist non-substantiality. The above quotes from Derrida also reflect the western mode of philosophizing that is based upon the edifice of structured argumentation guided by mere logical progression. But looked at from the Buddhist perspective, the *Derridean aporia* of equating non-attachment to non-compassion (for Derrida, Buddhist desire to have attachment to nobody and equal compassion for everybody is an unattainable ideal) appears to be rather naïve and simplistic since it implies that compassion is rooted in attachment or compassion cannot arise without attachment. On the contrary, the teachings of the forest tradition monks clearly reflect that compassion to be compassion at all should be rooted in non-attachment. In other words, true compassion which is universal in garb and non-restricted to any particular individual (as it is all-inclusive in nature) cannot actually arise with attachment.

The dismantling of binaries in the dhamma expositions of Ajahn Chah

Given the antiquity and ubiquity of binary thought processes dominating every human discourse, it is interesting to see how in almost all of Ajahn Chah's extempore dhamma talks, binary thoughts get ceaselessly dismantled time and again. Ajahn Chah's form of teaching does not involve grandiose theory, but a form of dhamma exposition that is simple, direct and yet profound at the same time. While the entire Derridean deconstructionist mode of critical practice engages in the practice of *neutralizing* the binary, Ajahn Chah stretches on

---

20　Ibid.

undoing the whole thing and going beyond it by mindfully defying reification of all mental formations, conditioned states and conventional linguistic signs be it the written word or the verbal utterance. Thus, in his dhamma talks the dismantling of binary oppositions occurs at various levels – linguistic/discursive, ontological and meditative.

Linguistic deconstruction

Ajahn Chah adheres to a non-logocentric approach through his defying of linguistic reification of all conditioned states and terms that denote such states. In his dhamma talk *Go beyond Words: See for yourself* he emphasizes on going beyond all words and symbols, even to the extent of giving up all overriding wishes and plans for practice. While any plan in the conventional sense involves external issues like fixed retreat time, day, and routine, the plan of No-plan is one that involves an inward moving attitudinal disposition that nullifies all external plans, once and for all. The true meditation retreat is a reflexive act of seeing the self for oneself. This turning inward is a metamentation process that brings to self-recognition the aggrandizement of the individual ego, and leads to its objectivization through the realization of the ego's subtle workings vis-à-vis the natural paradigmatic truth of existence – impermanence, suffering and non-self.

Ajahn Chah urges his monastic and lay disciples to go beyond words and not to cling to concepts. The mind should be focused upon seeing through and mindfully recognizing the process of changeability both within and without oneself. In the above dhamma talk, he reiterates, "If you are interested in Dhamma, just give up, just let go. Merely thinking about practice is like pouncing on the shadow and missing the substance. You need not study much. If you follow the basics and practice accordingly, you will see Dhamma for yourself. There must be more than merely hearing the words. Speak just with yourself, observe your own mind. If you cut off this verbal, thinking mind, you will have a true standard for judging. Otherwise, your understanding will not penetrate deeply. Practice in this way and the rest will follow."[21] Through the challenge to cut off the verbal/thinking mind the issue of 'metaphysics-of-presence' of the Ego in rendered at once redundant.

---

[21] "Go Beyond Words: See for Yourself" p.11.

In his dhamma talk *Ending Doubt,* Ajahn Chah echoes what the Buddha once said to the Kalamas. "Outward, scriptural study is not important. Of course, the dhamma books are correct, but they are not right. They cannot give you right understanding. To see the word *hatred* in print is not the same as experiencing *anger,* just as hearing a person's name is different from meeting him. Only experiencing for yourself can give you true faith."[22] Non-logocentrism gets provocative expressions in yet another of his powerful sayings in the dhamma talk *Study and Experiencing* – "When our innate wisdom, the one who knows, experiences the truth of the heart/mind, it will be clear that the mind is not our self. Not belonging to us, not I, not mine, all of it must be dropped. As to our learning the names of all the elements of mind and consciousness, the Buddha did not want us to become *attached* to the words. He just wanted us to see all this as impermanent, unsatisfactory, and empty of self. He taught only to let go."[23]

Ontological deconstruction

The hierarchical order of binary structures tacitly promotes a first-term sequence (male/right/good) at the expense of a second-term sequence (female/left/evil) and has generally resulted in privileging of unity (albeit, superficially), identity, and temporal and spatial presence over diversity, difference, and deferment in space and time. Going against and beyond the general paradigm of polarized and dichotomous thinking, Ajahn Chah's teachings focus on the truth that all things exists only in relation to each other not with any permanent or absolute intrinsic attribute. At times meanings of conventional terms are desacralized and shown as constructed by the exigencies of a shared system of relational signification only without any transcendental importance as a point of reference and validation. In order to cultivate right understanding which is beyond the workings of polarized thought processes, he emphasizes the need to recognize the contradictions and binary oppositions involved in traditional discourses and our ordinary perspectives. In his dhamma talk *The discriminating mind* he explains this graphically –"Right understanding ultimately means nondiscrimination – seeing all people as the same, neither good nor bad, neither clever nor foolish; not thinking that honey is sweet and

---

22   "Ending Doubt" pp.8-9.
23   "Study and Experiencing" p.14.

good and some other food is bitter. Although you may eat several kinds of food, when you absorb and excrete them, they all become the same. Is it one or many? Is a glass big? In relation to a little cup, yes; when placed next to a pitcher, no. Our desire and ignorance, our discrimination *color* everything. This is the world we create. There are always differences. Get to know those differences, yet learn to see the sameness too. Learn to see the underlying sameness of all things, how they are all truly equal, truly empty. Then you can know how to deal with the apparent differences wisely. But do not get attached even to this sameness."[24]

Referentiality, in the Buddhist context is always empty, or non-self. Reference is not denied, however; it is perpetually put under erasure – problematized, bracketed, and relativized. If Derrida questions meanings or texts on the basis of differences, Ajahn Chah comes at these things from the other end – there inherent sameness – the sameness of emptiness or non-substantiality that permeates everything. While Derrida's way of philosophizing hinges upon the teasing apart of differences, Ajahn Chah puts under erasure these differences too through drawing attention to the permeating emptiness and proceeding to drop even the emptiness of emptiness, thus making the entire premise of deconstructive practice redundant. The mindful recognition of this redundancy renders Ajahn Chah's deconstructive mode a *lived* experience, both at the conceptual as well as spirituo-experiential level.

Through ontological deconstruction Ajahn Chah aims to focus on the practice of identifying the source and mode of one's delusion. Delusion occurs through our failure to recognize and accept the true nature of our ontological reality which is marked by conditioned states that are constantly changing and hence are marked by impermanence and non-substantiality. Ajahn Chah further attempts at problematizing the binary system prevalent in the ethical categories as well, because none of these categories has its own essence to distinguish itself from its opposite; both good and evil exist through conditioned causality and are thus empty of essence. With emphatic focus on non-reification of provisional distinctions and categories, Ajahn Chah made oppositions vanish or be transcended upon on recognition of it. His strident dismantling of all notions of absolute distinction is well reflected in the dhamma talk *Underground Water* – "The Dharma is not out there, to be gained by a long voyage viewed through a telescope. It is right here, nearest to

---

[24]   "The Discriminating Mind" p.34.

us, our true essence, our true self, no self. When we see this essence, there are no problems, no troubles. Good, bad, pleasure, pain, light, dark, self, other, are empty phenomena. If we come to know this essence, we die to our old sense of self and become truly free."[25]

The important thing in Buddhism is that the 'coming-to-rest' of using names to take perceptions (*saññā*) as 'self-existing' objects actually deconstructs the 'objective' everyday world. In the dhamma talk *The Timeless Buddha*, Ajahn goes to the extent of deconstructing the Buddha as a historical figure vis-à-vis the clarity of the unmoving mind. He explains, "We take refuge in Buddha, Dhamma, and Sangha. This is the heritage of every Buddha that appears in the world. What is this Buddha? When we see with the eye of wisdom, we know that the Buddha is timeless, unborn, unrelated to anybody, any history, any image. Buddha is the ground of all being, the realization of the truth of the unmoving mind. So the Buddha was not enlightened in India. In fact he was never enlightened, was never born, and never died. This timeless Buddha is our true home, our abiding place. When we take refuge in the Buddha, Dhamma and Sangha, all things in the world are free for us. They become our teacher, proclaiming the one true nature of life."[26]

Deconstruction of meditation

Buddhist deconstruction as put into practice by Ajahn Chah is not simply a strategic reversal of categories; it mindfully seeks to *undo* a given order of priorities and the very system of conceptual framework and discursive practice that makes that order possible. The identity of separate entities is subverted as entities are demonstrated to be inextricably involved the one in the other. Traditional interpretation places *samatha* and *vipassanā* meditation as distinct phases, levels, stages or methods in formal meditation training, but in Ajahn Chah's interpretation the dichotomy collapses altogether giving way to interdependence and inextricable linking. When asked about the practice of meditation, Ajahn Chah replied in the dhamma talk *Study and Experiencing*, "Meditation is like a single log of wood. Insight and investigation are one end of the log; calm and concentration are the other end. If you lift up the whole log, both sides come up at once. Which is concentration and which is insight?

---

25   "Underground Water" p.175.
26   "The Timeless Buddha" p.179.

Just this mind. You cannot really separate concentration, inner tranquility, and insight. They are just as a mango that is first green and sour, then yellow and sweet, but not two different fruits. One grows into the other; without the first, we would never have the second. Such terms are only *conventions* for teaching. We should not be attached to the language."[27] Thus Ajahn Chah's form of deconstruction is more of an 'undoing' than 'destruction', of polarized categorization and manifests itself in the careful teasing out of forces and layers of signification within a given text/context.

His kind of contemplative and rational understanding of meditation helps to deconstruct the actual act of meditation practice thereby removing from it any mark of fetishization. He dispels the aura around meditation retreat by reducing it to a mundane activity of watchful and attentive awareness of one's various moods and feelings which give rise to suffering. Mindful watching of the mind is most essential to attain lasting inner peace. He alerts his disciples by saying – "Peace is within oneself, to be found in the same place as agitation and suffering. It is not found in a forest or on a hilltop, nor is it given by a teacher. Where you experience suffering, you can also find freedom from suffering. To try to run away from suffering is actually to run toward it."[28] His timeless teachings thus emphasize not just formal meditation practice for the sake of it, but on real meditation that has to do with attitude and awareness in any activity, not just with seeking silence in a forest cottage.

He emphatically points out that when the mind does not grasp or take a vested interest, does not get caught up, things become clear. Right understanding arises from the attempt at looking very objectively at a particular situation or event and understanding it as it-is-in-itself and not colouring it with our subjective views that arise from personal likes and dislikes. He clarifies this vividly in one of the dhamma talks – "When you take a good look at it, the world of ours is just that much; it exists just as it is. Ruled by birth, aging, sickness, death, it is only that much. Great or little is only that much. The wheel of life and death is only that much. Then why are we still attached, caught up, not removed? Playing around with the objects of life gives us some enjoyment; yet this enjoyment is also just that much."[29]

---

27   "Study and Experiencing" p.15.

28   "Right Understanding" p.30.

29   "Just That Much" p.41.

His dhamma talks endlessly indicate the necessity for a thoroughly self-conscious reading, one that subjects its own assumptions to close scrutiny. More practice and more reflection, the greater the practice the deeper is the 'letting go'. He reiterates this more focused awareness while simultaneously dispelling the aura of human being as a 'superior' being by citing the example of a harness animal, the buffalo – "We must train our mind like a buffalo: the buffalo is our thinking, the owner is the meditator, raising and training the buffalo is the practice. With a trained mind we can see the truth, we can know the cause of our self and its end, the end of all sorrow."[30] Ajahn Chah uses the deconstructive mode of self-reflexive understanding of changeability and selflessness not only in regards to non-reification of entities in relational existence as *samatha* and *vipassana*, but also about such absolute truths as arahantship. At a gathering in one of his overseas trips when someone from the audience asked him whether he was an *arahant*, he compared himself to a tree laden with fruits and the tree's indifference to all the birds (and their chirping) that come to feed and rest in its shade.[31]

Conclusion

The Thai forest tradition monks were *dhutanga* monks whose main focus was mindfulness practice and not reading or writing of the dhamma. They deliberately refrained from higher ecclesiastical education and displayed no inclination to join Sangha administration. The Buddha had no plan to become a priest but a practitioner of the right path, so do the forest tradition monks. But every word they have uttered, every example they have cited have become a text in itself because it has deep meaning embedded in it, the meaning that derived from putting the dhamma into real practice. When practice becomes the stronghold, orality becomes the deliberate choice. This choice manifested in the case of Ajahn Chah too and was never an impediment in spreading the dhamma far and wide. In fact he became one of the most successful meditation

---

[30] "Starving Defilements", p.32.

[31] By answering in a spontaneously non-reified metaphoric language he fulfilled three important points – adhering to the Buddha's wise advice on non-declaration of arhantship by any monastic, the cultivation of the spirit of indifference to such states of spiritual accomplishment, and finally, pointing out tacitly the irrelevance of the question – 'Are you an Arahant?' (for the session was conducted to reflect upon one's own self i.e. cultivation of mindfulness and self-reflexivity and not on probing another person's mind, especially the master's spiritual advancement).

masters of the twentieth century teaching the dhamma not only to the Thais but also to Western disciples from different countries and diverse linguistic, socio-cultural and religious background. Through his non-written text, non-Canon centric mode of practice he directed his teachings to both his ordained disciples and lay followers in confronting and working directly with their own problems of greed, judgment, hatred and ignorance. His direct and simple teachings always turn his followers back to their own minds, the source and the root of all trouble. His teachings emphasized that understanding the *tilakkhana* and putting this understanding into practice leads to understanding everything in life and nature as-it-is-in-itself. This understanding is not inaction and passive acceptance as some people might hastily conclude. Enlightenment does not mean deaf and blind. On the other hand, enlightened understanding leads to empirical deconstruction of the 'self' and the 'self-in-action'. Time and again Ajahn Chah emphasized on seeing through the process of thought construction so as to recognize from one's own experiential reality the fact that when the mind is stirred from the normal state of tranquility, it leads away from right practice to one of the extremes of indulgence or aversion, thereby creating more illusion, more thought construction. A true understanding of the nature of the mind helps people to free it from the clasp or bondage of conventional realities and so the mind is not enslaved by codes, customs, traditions, conventions, linguistics choices, personal predilections, etc. Once this state can be achieved, all binary oppositions get automatically collapsed leading to no more creation of dichotomy/polarity and slavish clinging to its hierarchical chasm.

The dhamma of the forest tradition is down-to-earth, yet difficult to understand and realize, especially when the mind is ceaselessly caught up in the quagmire of defilements and lack of mindfulness. It requires moment-to-moment 'self-scrutiny' and mindful practice of 'letting go'. In this form of existentialistic deconstruction that involves conscientious and mindful teasing apart of all binary oppositions and getting released from their bindings, there is no room for *aporia* or conflictual and conceptual hiatus. Although Ajahn Chah was not a philosopher in the conventional sense of the term, nevertheless, his numerous dhamma talks reveal the truth that he incessantly worked within the matrix of a mode of practice that can be categorized as deconstruction-in-praxis. Such a mode of practice does not valorize any 'text', not even the Buddha, but renders the training a moment-to-moment phenomenal and empirical garb through the rigorous practice of both insight meditation and austerity in tandem. The deconstructionist approach of Ajahn Chah helps to dispose of all Self/Ego arising positions and leads to a clear and reflexive understanding of the teachings of Buddhism.

References

Ajahn Chah. *Living Dhamma*. Ubol Rajathani: The Sangha, Bung Wai Forest Monastery, 1992.

Ajahn Sumedho. *Cittaviveka – Teachings from the Silent Mind*. Hertfordshire: Amaravati Publications, 1984.

Derrida, Jacques. *Of Grammatology*, trans. Gayatri Chakravorty Spivak. Delhi: Motilal Banarsidass Publishers Pvt. Ltd., 1976.

_____. *The Gift of Death*, trans. David Wills. Chicago: University of Chicago Press, 1995.

Kornfield, Jack and Breiter, Paul, ed. *A Still Forest Pool – The Insight Meditation of Achaan Chah*. Illinois: The Theosophical Publishing House, 1985.

Jaware, Aniket. *Simplifications*. New Delhi: Orient Longman Lt., 2001.

Magliola, Robert. *Derrida on the Mend*. West Lafayette: Purdue University Press, 1984.

Mahanta, Dipti. Deconstruction deconstructed: A study of Ajahn Chah in the light of Derridean philosophy. Research monograph, Bangkok: Buddhist Research Institute 2012.

Mahasi Sayadaw. *The Great Discourse on Not Self (Anattālakkhana Sutta)*. Bangkok: Buddhadhamma Foundation, 1996.

Park, Jin Y. ed. *Buddhisms and Deconstructions (New Frameworks for Continental Philosophy)*. Rowman & Littlefield Publishers, 2006.

_____ *Buddhism and Postmodernity: Zen, Huayan, and the Possibility of Postmodern Ethics*. Lexington Books, 2010.

Payutto, P.A.*Buddhadhamma*, trans. Grant A. Olson. Albany: State University of New York Press, 1995.

Rahula, Walpola. *What the Buddha Taught*. Bangkok: Haw Trai Foundation, 1990.

Seeing the Way – An Anthology of Teachings by English-speaking Disciples of Ajahn Chah. Hertfordshire: Amaravati Publications, 1989.

Steve Odin. "Derrida and the Decentered Universe of Chan/Zen Buddhism", *Journal of Chinese Philosophy*, Vol.17, Issue 1, March 1990.

Wang, Youru ed. *Deconstruction and the Ethical in Asian Thought*. New York: Routledge, 2007.

Oral History in North East India

Salam Irene

Oral history which can be characterized as a body of knowledge, comprising folklore, myths, legends, ballads, traditional practices, chants, taboos, omens, is undoubtedly a part of the Intangible Heritage of North East India. In North East India, historians' gives special importance to Oral History, because in the region there exists societies for whom there is little or no recorded history for various phases of their development. Many North East Indian communities were pre-literate for centuries. Even the history of Manipur before the Christian Era, cannot be traced with any degree of certainty, except bits of information collected from folklore and other references made in passing, in the chronicles of adjoining kingdoms. The problems of study of the regional history of North East India, whether it relates to origin, migration settlement, primeval religion, customary law, traditional practices, chieftainship, etc. are due to paucity of sources of information, especially in the ancient period, the multiplicity of ethnic, linguistic and culture groups at different levels of civilization and culture, which is both a problem and challenge to any student of history, and the inter-regional variation in the North East regions, which is at the same time a cultural, political and ethnic zone.

For the Khasis of Meghalaya, the Mizos of Mizoram, the Nagas of Nagaland, the tribals of Manipur, historical writing is a comparatively recent development. The comprehensive history of the whole region has not been completely written.[1] But a contemporary Indian historian Romila Thapar wrote: 'Historical consciousness need not necessarily take the form of historical writings. Each version of the past which has been deliberately transmitted has significance for the present. The record may be one which historical consciousness is embedded, myth and genealogy, or alternatively it may refers to the more externalized forms: chronicles of families, institutions and regions, and biographies of persons in authority.[2] We depend upon local traditions, and though as historical evidence, they individually leave much to be desired, it is difficult to disregard them on any point, where they are unanimous or nearly unanimous.[3] A good example would be the migration of five Naga tribes in Nagaland viz Angami, Chakhesang, Rengma, Sema and Lotha who traced their origin to the village of Khezakhenoma from folktales and legends. The oral tradition of the Shupfomei forefathers claims that Shupfomei came from different directions and finally reached Makhel. From Makhel (in Manipur) Makhrufu, they dispersed by different routes. Such legends of dispersion of their ancestors are told and retold for the benefit of posterity.[4] Many of the village elders often spoke of a certain 'hole' but they could never mention any specific place, location and time. It is told that from this hole people were just crawling out like moles.[5] This is similar to the mythical origin of Chhinlung, Sinlung, Khul, etc. as narrated by Chin, Kuki and Mizos. A folksong proves their Khul origin –

> *Famous Sinlung (Chhinlung, Khul)*
> *Is my motherland*
> *And home of my ancestors*
> *If it could be called back like chawngzil*
> *The home of my ancestors.*

> *Kan seina Sinlung ram hmingthang*
> *Ka nu ram ka pa ram ngai*
> *Chawngzil ang kokir thei changsien*
> *Ka nu ram ka pa ngai.*[6]

From Oral Tradition it is evident that the Marings lived and dwelled in Leinung (cave) called 'Nungmuisho' in about 10,000 B.C. to 1800 B.C. According to Maring mythylogy, after the Leinung was opened by a male shrim (Mithun – an animal that resembles a buffalo or ox), the Marings migrated to the upper region of the earth.[7] Most tribes have made attempts to trace their origin. The Vaiphei believe that their progenitor Zahawng found the door of the Khul (cave) closed by a great serpent, so he cut it into three pieces with his sword. It is because of this, that when his descendants (Suantaks) killed an enemy or tiger, they shout or chant 'Hanla' (songs of the brave).

Kathange, Kathange, Khulsin, Dongkot Kahonge i.e. I am famous, I am famous, I open the gate of the cave.[8]

Most of the Naga tribes believe that they came from a 'Khur' or 'Khol' (hole) in the earth. This tradition of cave origin is further corroborated by the folksongs of the different Naga tribes. 'Ah, the days of old, when we first emerged from the khol, the broad teak leaves were our make belief gongs which we playfully tolled, the whole day long, and the grasshopper would be our cattle, you know, as we prodded and poked them a long time ago.' In Anal dialect it reads: *Kholo-nahang sanpe Hnakhal o langdal pathusin nu-o, Hedum patel sinnu – o, Khelwung – o – limsor, pathusin nu – o, Hedum patel sinnu – o, Hari – o, Hari – o.*[9]

The Mizo have an interesting tradition of origin now generally referred to as Chhinlung tradition that brings their progenitors from the bowels of the earth. This belief is apparent from the Hmar folksong – *My famous home Sinlung, My Motherland, My Fatherland, and I pine for, I would if it could be called back as Chawngzil, My Motherland, My Fatherland; Ka Siengna Sinlung ram hmingthang, Ka Nu ram, Ka Pa ram ngai, Chawngzil kokir thei changsien, Ka Nu ram, Ka Pa ram ngai.*[10]

From all the above it is apparent that many tribes lived in a subterranean world. The challenge is to reconstruct the material culture of all these tribes during their period of settlement beneath the earth's surface. This will become possible through Oral History. Oral History is a means to collect otherwise unwritten recollections of prominent individuals to fill in the gaps in our knowledge, necessary for future historians, for research, and as a tool for orally based biography. There are many societies in this region, where there is a total lack of recorded history. If the historical evolution of these societies have to be reconstructed and analysed, then recourse to the traditions of oral history becomes almost mandatory. As Paul Thompson wrote: the term 'oral history' is new.....but it does not mean that it has no past. It was the first kind of history. The discovery of Oral History by historians is not only a discovery but a recovery. It gives a future no longer tied to the cultural significance of paper documents. Oral history tradition therefore holds out hope for understanding the historical evolution of those societies, where beginnings might have to be made with interpretation of legends, myths and folklore.[11] For instance King Bhaggya Chandra's scribes had the task of writing or reconstructing the proto-history of Manipur, presumably from oral sources and memory, and perhaps also from scattered written records.[12]

The geopolitical significance of North East India cannot be overemphasized. Oral tradition deals with origin, migration, settlement, history, rites, rituals, social customs and the evolution of polity, society and culture.

A good example is the song of Feast of Merit. The Rongmeis (Kabuis) believe that a man goes to heaven when he dies, if he is able to host feasts of merit during his lifetime. Maku Lu is a Song of the Feast of Merit.[13] (There are a number of such songs).

Before conversion to Christianity, hill tribes did not possess written records of the past. But knowledgeable villagers (elders) could discuss the structure and process of change in tribal societies. The tribal who was very concerned with the status of chieftainship in different tribes, the mode of selection, particularly whether it was based on hereditary or elective principle, or on popular oligarchic selection, subject to public confirmation, was found to have practical implication in interpreting the land holding system. The Tarao have a distinct form of land system, different from the Kuki-Chin; the Tarao have a socialistic pattern of land holding, whereas in the case of the Kuki-Chin, the chief is the absolute ounce of the whole village.[14] The Mizo Chieftainship originated and developed on its own-among the family having more men, the strongest of them was invited to be a leader of the clan.[15]

There is a co-relation between deep-rooted forms of cultural activities and productive activities. Tribals invoked the grace of the ancestors in their traditional form. Ancestor worship is an important feature of Khasi society. Of all deceased ancestors, the Khasis revere 'Ka lawbei' the most (grandmother) Kawbei is the primeval or ancient ancestors of the clan. She is the tribal mother of the Khasis.[16]

The tribal account of their past, preserved through oral tradition is believed to be authentic. The Nagas have their history in folk-lore, hymns and songs and migration accounts, the Kuki tribes keep their authentic genealogy for generations, centuries even, as thoroughly as possible. The social identity of an ethnic group includes their common past of history, cultural heritage, linguistic affinity, their shared experiences, struggle and suffering, with a strong sense of belonging to each other. And while the art of writing developed at a very early stage of the Meitei civilization, the record keeping or chronicle keeping was started only in the 15th century.[17]

There are many areas where there may not be any numismatic or epigraphic sources. For such societies, the tapping and interpretation of oral history becomes a very real need.[18] Some legends give an insight into the world view of a people. The legend 'Ai Kuangpui Sial – pre-Christian sacrifice for success in hunting, along with others derived from oral tradition, are used to project that the Mizo are descendants of one of the lost tribes of Israel. The priest chants: 'those above, and those below, go away, flee, we the children of Manmasi are coming.' The value system of the tribes and sub-tribes of the North East are essentially reflected, as in a mirror, in the Hynniewtrep's value system. At the first Divine Dorbar in Heaven, the momentous decision was taken to send the Hynniewtrep to control the world for a definite purpose – to rule, to govern, to administer, according to the maxim: 'Ka Nia, Kaba Tam' i.e. reason, discussion and consensus.[19]

Oral history is not only a tool or a method, it is also a theory of history, which maintains that the common people and the dispossessed have a history.[20] Oral historian activists use oral sources to right an imbalance in historical records, which have favoured the literate and the formally educated, over those whose culture has not left written records. Oral history can also document the literacy culture of a period. At a time when many historians believe that the narrative offers the most promising structure for solving interconnected problems of specialization and interpretation, the study of memory may provide the most promising entrance to the possibilities of narrative and oral history may provide one of the most promising entries into memory.[21] Oral traditions are historical sources couched in a form suitable for oral transmission, and that their preservation depends on the powers of memory of successive generations of human beings.[22]

Broadly, one can list three main classes of oral tradition: recognized literary forms, generalized historical knowledge and personal recollections. First there is oral literature – various types of both prose and poetry which correspond to literature in literate societies. Praise poetry can lead to insight into the values and ideals of society, or one group at least. Religious poetry can be conservative. Lyrics and songs for weddings, dance, work, love and so forth can throw light on values and personal pre-occupations of a particular society at a particular time. For example, the Song of Rice – Mazaah Lu. The song is sung on the occasions connected with the harvest such as Napmu, Pukphaa, and the day of the first harvest – it sings of the Goddess of Rice.[23] Topical and political poems can be an excellent source. The historical poetry of the epics provides the best and most relevant source for the historian. Myths and narrations about creation, deities and so on, can be useful for throwing lights on local attitudes. A narrative (legend) about arrival in an area need not necessarily be interpreted as the migration of the whole people (refer to Shakespear's Old and New Kukis in Manipur). Travels, conquests and arrivals are common themes in stories, but one must be cautious about accepting them literally.

General historical knowledge may consist of beliefs about recent events or may include references to the remote past. Informal historical knowledge includes not only general notions of what happened in the past, but also a few elements that take a somewhat formalized shape to include places, praise, names and genealogies. For example, ballads of the Marings provides the dialectical and also balladical name of their seven clans.

Dialectical Name	Balladical Name
Dangsawa	Darleiya
Khulpuwa	Thoubunga
Kansawa	Parshunga
Makunga	Yorshunga
Lamthaka	Selleiya
Tontanga	Roupiya
Khlewa	Darshanga [24]

Personal collections are much nearer the primary facts than similar accounts which have been handed down through generations.[25]

To dismiss the oral tradition narrative because it cannot be used in the reconstruction of objective history is to ignore the community perception of its past, and to disregard the complex interaction between psychology, narrative function and historicity in oral historical research. When oral history is passed on to another person, usually of the succeeding generation in that family or lineage, it becomes oral tradition.[26] For instance, through 'oral tradition' it is clear that the corpse of a 'Nungkih' (divorced woman among the Kukis) is not taken for burial outside through the front door, but is instead taken through a hole made in the wall.[27] (The practice is now extinct).

A great deal of the history of North East India commenced with the British historians who colonized the area. The primary characteristic of 'colonised' history is that it is the view of outsiders and not people themselves. Oral history from which oral tradition emerges, offers an alternative way of conceptualizing history, and a means by which to recover that past. It captures the human spirit of the people.[28]

In North East India, there is a growing consciousness of ethnicity and nationalism. When a group's unique customs, tradition and history falter, a drive for preservation and celebration often surfaces. In non literate societies, oral tradition has an institutionally recognized place and purpose in the culture. The function of oral testimony may range from myths aimed at providing an explanation of the creation of the world, and of society as it exists, to those providing a pedigree for tribal rulers, or to a justification of the political structure. The oral testimony can be legalistic, didactic and explanatory, and its structure and mode of presentation may vary accordingly. Whatever its function, its social purpose is officially valued in these cultures.[29]

Wherever oral traditions are extant, they remain an indispensable source for reconstruction. Oral history has matured into a branch of historiography which seeks to understand all forms of subjective experience. In order to conserve and protect oral tradition, various measures may be taken. Oral tradition tapes and transcripts, films and documentaries, must find their way into a library or archive, narrators of oral tradition could be invited to an annual gathering, to link the present with the past. New technologies, such as computerized research aids and personal computers have made professional oral history collections more capital intensive. Museums can incorporate oral material into exhibits. Through radio, television and film, producers can raise popular historical consciousness, to broadcast to the woman or man in the street, to develop historical mindedness. Electronics and mass media are leading outlets for publicizing oral history findings. Documentaries on specific themes – indigenous festivals, ways of worship, modes of craft and handloom production, silk weaving, use of medicinal plants, etc are all ways of preserving our Intangible Heritage. This can sensitise various players to the cultural and other values of Intangible Heritage to recognize the sustainable use of it for the economic and social benefit of local and national communities.[30]

And finally Oral Tradition reminds us of the magic magnitude of our inherited past. It rescues that which is the everyday thing, the transcendental, the historical fact expressed by word of mouth. There are many untold and destroyed histories that must be told and reconstructed. There is a resurgence of interest in the everyday event, the ordinary. Its significance serves in the reconstruction of historical processes and in the illustration of life styles from different times and circumstances. Oral Tradition humanized history, making it alive, social and dynamic. Oral Tradition places us in direct contact with individual and social sectors that have been ignored for a long time. The idea of rescuing, safeguarding and conserving oral testimony, becomes a task of strengthening a historical memory.[31] Oral Tradition honours the past but is always open to the present.

Notes:

1. Gangmumei Kamei – On History and Historiography of Manipur, pp. 70-71, Akansha Publishing House, Delhi, 2006.
2. Manorama Sharma – History and History Writing in North East India, p. 15, Regency Publications, 2006.
3. Irfan Habib – The Agrarian System of Mughal India, p. 159, Oxford University Press, 2000.
4. William Nepuni – Socio-Cultural History of Shuofomei Naga Tribe, p. 35, Mittal Publication, Delhi, 2010. According to the 1994 Revenue Census, Makhel is a small village of 127 houses with a population of 863 on Highway 32 in Senapati, north district of Manipur. Cit. CF, Sani Ashiho Mao – The Shepoumaramth in the Naga National Movements, p. 16.
5. Ibid, p. 37.
6. Ginneihching – The History and Culture of the Simte Tribe in Manipur, p.23, Unpublished Ph.D Thesis 2012, Manipur University.
7. Molung Dominic Maring – History and Culture of the Marings, pp. 8, 10, Unpublished Ph.D Thesis 2014, Manipur University.
8. S Kamminlun Vaiphei – The Genealogy and Ancient Appeasement Practices of the Vaiphei Tribe, pp. 116-117, in Salam Irene Editor, An Anthology of Historical Essays, Ruby Publications, Delhi, 2006.
9. Ningreishim Kashung Shimray – Origin of the Tangkhul Naga through their Oral Tradition/Folksongs, p. 70, in Salam Irene Editor, Op.cit.
10. Lallianzuali Chhangte – Mizo Origin Myths, p. 6, Cit Rochunga 1963:21 in Mizo Narratives – Editors Malsawmdawngliana and Rohmingmawii – Scientific Book Centre, Guwahati, 2013.
11. Manorama Sharma, Op.cit, p. 22
12. Saroj Nalini Arambam Parrrat – The Cheitharol Kumpapa, Court Chronicles of the Kings of Manipur, p. 4, Routledge, 2005.

13. Ragongning Gangmei – Folksongs of the Rongmeis (Kabui), p. 17, R.G Centre for Arts and Culture, Imphal, 1994.

14. Jacob Luiram – Tarao Land Holding System, p. 34 in Salam Irene Editors, Op.cit.

15. Lalchhuanawma – The Origin and Development of Chieftainship in Mizoram, p. 45 in Malsawmdawngliana and Rohmingmawii Editors, Op.cit.

16. Nambam Babita – Traditional and Customary Socio-Religious Practices and Modernisation of Khasi Women, pp. 87-88, Unpublished Ph.D Thesis, Manipur University, 2002.

17. Gangmumei Kamei, Op.cit, pp. 55,56,111.

18. Manorama Sharma, Op.cit, p. 92.

19. Salam Irene – Socio-Cultural Life of the Tribal before the Advent of Christianity, p. 2, Cit. Sylvanus Sngi Lyngdoh – The Tribal Value System and the Impact of Christianity on it.

20. Gary Okihiro – Oral History and the Writing of Ethnic History, p. 12, Cit. in Editors David K Dunaway and Willa Buam – From Oral History – An Interdisciplinary Anthology, Alta Miira Press, 1996.

21. David Thelin – Memory and American History – Journal of American History, 4th March, 1989.

22. Jan Vansina – Oral Tradition and Historical Methodology in Eds. – David K Dunaway and Willa Buam, Op.cit.

23. Ragongning Gangmei – Op.cit, p. 7.

24. Molung Dominic Maring – Op.cit, p. 47.

25. Ruth Finnegan – A Note on Oral Tradition and Historical Evidence, pp. 127-131 in Eds. David K Dunaway and Willa Buam, Op.cit.

26. Gary Okihiro – Op.cit, p. 204.

27. Salam Irene – Women of Manipur – An Alternative Perspective, p. 19, Cit. Arfina Haokip – Position of Women in the Kuki Society of Manipur – A Historical Study – Unpublished Ph.D Thesis, Manipur University, 2012.

28. Gary Okihiro, Op.cit, p. 211

29. Tanara Hareven – The Search For Generational Memory, pp. 245-246, Cit. in Eds David K Dunaway and Willa Buam, Op.cit.

30. Salam Irene – The Intangible Heritage of North East India, p. 523 in Intach-Heritage and Development, Delhi, 2008.

31. Eugenia Meyer – Generational History in Mexico and the Carribean, pp. 345-349, Cit. in Eds. David K Dunaway and Willa Buam, Op.cit.

Women Narratives

Rashmi Narzary

India's north-east comes alive in the voice and narratives of its women. By nature and instinct, women tend to delve into and observe the microcosm of the situation she is surrounded by, more intensely than do men. She is more sensitive to what goes on about her and because she feels and receives in a more in-depth manner, she also has the ability to reproduce and narrate her surroundings in an equally well expressed and profound manner. Quoting eminent writer Mitra Phukan, 'gender colours perspective'. The same social, economic, political or cultural situation is bound to be seen by men and women, each from a different perspective. In the context of women narratives of the ethnic societies of India's northeast, narrations made by women are seen to be rooted each in its unique, social backdrop. It is hoped that study of such a narrative will throw new light on the quest for meaning of ethnic societies of the northeast. However, women narratives may also be made by men, in which case it is narratives made by men about/for women. Again, women narratives may also be about/for/by the third gender as well. Third gender narratives and cross dressing form a significant part of Indian mythology and folklore.

FRAMEWORK

Narrations have always been an imperative part of our social fabric, but back in the days of yore these narrations were more an oral tradition, theoretically termed as *Orality*. The written narrative came in only later, when we felt the need to document the traditions and tales our old folks told us. By the time these narrations started to be documented, sadly, much of the oral narrative passed away with the passing away of the older generation. So we see that narratives and orality cannot be studied in isolation of each other. Orality is included in narratives. Refer to the following flow chart.

The figure below shows the categories and sub-categories of Women's Narratives

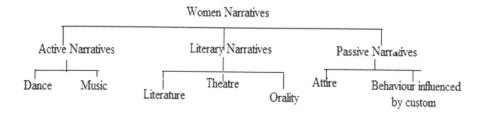

From the above figure it is seen that Women Narratives fall into three broad categories

1. **Active Narratives are the narrations which need to be actively performed and are in the 'doing' mode. But when inert, these do not narrate.** These cannot be performed and saved for later reference. Examples, Narratives in the form of dance and music. Here, each reference will require a live performance. Yes, dance and music can be digitally recorded and replayed. Such replays nevertheless see the narrations in action, in the 'doing' mode. When a dance posture is not in live performance but is a photograph or in a pause, then it becomes a passive narrative.

   a) **Dance Narratives** have integrally spoken about our traditions and identity. Every tribe has its own harvest dance, war dance, religious dance and dance to celebrate births, new year, and other rituals. On close observation, it is seen that the entire dance form narrates in totality a particular story. In the bodo context, the *kherai*, the *thungri sibnai*, etc are all narratives in the form of dance. For instance, if we observe the movements, rhythm and poise of the kherai dance, we can feel the bodo religious pulse as expressed through the active dance form. Again, when the young girls dance the bagarumba during bwisagu, the pulse shifts from the religious to the fun-loving, sometimes lightly flirtatious, festive mode. Even those who do not understand or relate to the bodo language can understand that there is a difference between these dance forms by just observing the body language, facial expression and tone of the accompanying song. They can also gauge that one is spiritual and the other is entertaining. This exactly is the power of narratives. However, while not in performance, these expressions, body language and tone remain dormant. This is why such forms of narratives are called active narrative.

Within this narrative, it may be mentioned that since the days of yore, cross dressing had been evident in bodo plays, often called the **jatragaan**, and also during bwisagu when groups of young men went from house to house, dancing in the courtyards and blessing the homesteads they went to. The women in these groups were actually young men who donned the dokhna (bodo women's traditional attire) and appeared as women!

b) **Music Narratives** too are a similar feature, which, when not in performance, cease to be active narratives.

2. **Literary Narratives are those narratives which use reading or composing in any form or context.** These are different from natural narratives in the sense that these add to, omit from, rearrange or sensationalize the basic elements of storytelling. These hold on to literature and sometimes, as in the case of Orality, to the undocumented verbal rendering of tales and traditions.

a) **Literature** forms the major part of Literary Narrative. This includes all forms of narratives that use the written word. This is one realm which has seen key developments in recent times and consequently, tribal societies are more pronouncedly observed and portrayed on the global platform from various perspectives, each perspective being an eye-opener into women's role in these societies.

b) **Theatre** is that form of Literary Narrative which is an active rendition of the otherwise passive written form of narrative. It brings the abstracts in a written narrative to life through performance. What is abstractly referred to as, for instance, sorrow, anger or poverty in the passive written form is brought to life by theatre, simply by performing the abstract human conditions. However, it is a literary narrative because some kind of literary preplanning and composing goes into the creation of a theatrical performance.

c) **Orality**, as mentioned earlier, is the undocumented, verbal rendition of tales, experiences, traditions and folk cultures. Orality plays a significant role in tribal societies because the written word made its inroads into these societies much, much later and is comparatively of a recent origin as compared to the written word in other societies. And so the entire responsibility of keeping alive and carrying forward our cultures and traditions, our identity and existence, was borne solely by Oral Narratives, technically termed as Orality. Orality in itself is a vast field of study.

3. **Passive Narratives are those narratives that speak or express about a tribe, its history, traditions, lifestyles and heritage by just its passive, inert existence, by being what it always is.** Unlike Active Narrative, it need not be re-enacted or performed to be brought to life to narrate a tale.

a) **Attire** is an example of Passive Narrative. The designs, colour, technique of wrapping a particular costume around the body, all have stories to tell, stories about each tribe and within each tribe, each gender. And yet, the costume need not perform any live activity to narrate the culture of the tribe or community it belongs to.

b) **Behaviour influenced by custom** is one of the most significant yet silent pointers a society can have. These pointers include, a women's right to vote at the village level, age of marriage, how much she is allowed to be educated and so on.

However, this study being a part of a social science, there can be no rigid demarcation between its various categories and sub-categories, unlike in a pure, physical science. Hence, though for convenience we categorize narratives into active, literary and passive, in practice there is all chance of the categories merging and /or overlapping and being embraced into one another.

Therefore, this paper welcomes discussions and suggestions on the categorization of women narratives with the objective of bringing in more themes into its purview

1. to study these themes on a comparative basis with gender issues of other societies
2. to facilitate social change with a view to adapt to gender equalities which become necessary with changing times
3. and to assist policy makers with inputs and feedback to bill and frame such policies as would give women her due rights, acknowledgements and social standing keeping in view her social, political and overall environment.

OPINION

For the purpose of this seminar on Orality, I intend to look at women narratives from the creative writer's perspective and not from that of the academician's. As such, any academic interpretation to the views presented herein are wholly welcome.

Well then, let us be honest and put forward the fact that women in tribal societies of northeast India have, in general, little say in decision making. This is true right from the micro unit of the family to the macro unit of the greater tribal society at large. Though some amount of claim to equality among the genders exists, in reality this claim is a challenged one. How much ever we shy away from admitting, male dominion or male priority has definitely affected a woman's relationship with her father, her brother, her husband and even her son. Time and traditions have conditioned her into submission and acceptance of whatever is doled out to her, in contrast to what she rightfully ought to have received. And yet, a woman DOES NOT seek freedom from her relationship with her father, her brother, her husband and her son. What she instead seeks is freedom WITHIN these relationships.

So when her voice is suppressed and it creates turmoil within her being, she gives vent to her feelings and her needs in the form of narratives of all forms and context. This is exactly where the urgent need to pay serious attention to women narratives arises. Because oftentimes, she voices her grievances and demands her rights through these narratives. What a women is barred from expressing in reality, she may express that in the form of a tale, a song, a costume, body language or even in the form of the written word, through fiction and storytelling. Again, she may just as well like to proclaim the beauty of her land, the peace therein, the richness of her heritage or the trauma of riots and insurgency and life in relief camps. She may make a first person narrative or she may speak through a protagonist in her tale. She may speak for herself or for the greater interest of the women of her tribe or community. However, the protagonists, the song, the dance etc are all only media through which the narrator actually voices her own feelings.

Then again, apart from presenting her needs through such narratives, she may also bring to the narrative the kind of climax she hopes to find in real life. Hence arises the urgent need to observe and study woman narratives with great indepth. Because somewhere in those narratives will lie the clue to what women in general desire in her social standing, and how much of that desire is logical and feasible. A clear understanding of this matter will aid in the framing of many a social change policy. Because the narratives may just be one woman's subtle way of placing a key claim on behalf of the majority of her gender within their community.

As an author, I strongly feel that women narratives (of the literary form) composed in the local languages ought to be translated into more and more languages, especially languages that cater to a global audience. This would assist in carrying the voice of the tribal women out onto a global platform. This would also convey the message to the world that apart from unrest and turmoil in the region, there exists side by side beauty and positive growth.

CONCLUSION

In conclusion, as an author, I only have this to say that there can be no right way or wrong way to look into women narrative or to study such a narrative. There can only be varied ways and varied angles to look at women narrative. Every such way and angle will give a different significance to women and women narrative and a new quest for meaning!

In this context, allow me to present a brief excerpt from the bestselling book "His Share of Sky", published by Leadstart Publishers (India HQ at Mumbai). The excerpt, from the above mentioned book, is from the short story titled *GHOST.* The excerpt focuses on the belief among the Bodos about the existence of a certain *banshee.*

The next evening too while dusk settled into night, the boys settled around grandfather for more of his stories. And as he told the stories, he would today prick two to three small fish at a time onto an old spoke from Okhonda's bicycle which he used as a skewer to barbeque fish on evenings like this.

'So then,' grandfather started his tale, 'this was just there, in yonder Habrubil.'

And he gestured towards Habrubil with his left hand while with his right hand he kindled the fire with a twig.

'This bald, naked, dwarf, he appeared out of nowhere and after showing himself to only some, disappeared as suddenly again. He was like the banshee who wailed and forewarned people about death in the family by appearing only to them.'

The boys listened intently.

'Might he appear even here, grandfather?' Barsau asked.

Mergau and Derha instinctively glanced across the dark courtyard and looked at the other's heads to see if the heads were bald or had hair on them.

*'Who knows, child, he may. But for Bathou's** sake don't speak thus, my boy, don't. If he does then I am the oldest around here now and I shall have to be the first to get aboard that hearse. And I don't want to…not now…' and the old man became pensive.*

'Oh grandfather, come on now!' Derha said reassuringly. They actually and very dearly loved the old man.

'So what happened at Habrubil, grandfather?' Mergau asked.

'Ah yes! That…' and the old man resumed as he leisurely poked his skewer into three-four small fish through their mouths and brought it out through their tails.

'…*that dwarf—the bawnaswr— people said had appeared in villages around ours and whenever and wherever he did, death inevitably struck. Some even say that if two persons walked together and bawnaswr appeared, only the one in whose threshold death stood would see him.*

'*Did he wail too?*' *Derha asked.*

'*No. That he didn't,*' *grandfather replied. A twig in the fire crackled sending little splinters up into the night sky.*

'*So what happened at Habrubil, grandfather?*' *Barsau asked, his pulse almost stopping lest it made too much noise and didn't let them hear if bawnaswr walked into their midst.*

'*Hmm…it was late afternoon…no, later than that because the sun was almost setting. But there was enough light yet to enable you to see upto quite some distance beyond your nose. And adwi Jibe, you know him, don't you?*'

'*Oh! Adwi Jibe? He saw bawnaswr with his own eyes?*'

'*He did. He was standing just outside his gate by the street when he saw bawnaswr suddenly appearing and walking past his gate. Jibe thought it was a little boy who must have wandered away from home. Jibe had just about parted his lips to ask the boy where he was going all alone when bawnaswr vanished! As abruptly as he had appeared!*'

Barsau shuffled and quietly moved closer to grandfather. Derha kept turning to look behind him as if someone with a height upto his neck as he sat might any moment appear right behind him and breathe down his nape. Grandfather rotated his skewer to bring the uncooked sides of the fish to the fire.

'*Jibe was taken aback and stood dumbstruck for a while. And immediately following bawnaswr came up a rickshaw, its puller humming to himself. Jibe asked him if he saw a little boy walking along the road without any clothes or any companion…*'

'*Did he…?*' *Barsau interrupted, unable to hold the suspense.*

'*Did he see?*' *Derha in turn interrupted Barsau.*

Grandfather looked calmly into the faces of his grandsons. Then at the fish. He had this amazingly patience-testing way of pausing just when the boys would like to race into the climax.

'*Did the rickshaw puller see bawnaswr, grandfather?*' *lastly quipped Mergau.*

Grandfather smiled, 'No, he didn't. That evening bawnaswr appeared only to Jibe. He appeared like the banshee…'

'But adwi Jibe is alive and in good health, grandfather,' Barsau asked, almost hoping that the bawnaswr's foreboding had been defied. 'He is, son, but bawnaswr's premonition never goes a waste. Do you forget that Jibe's sister got widowed soon after? And that his father too passed away not too many days later?'

Legal Instruments to Combat Witch-hunting

Shyamal Prasad Saikia

Keywords: Witch-hunting, witch-craft, laws, legislations, India

INTRODUCTION:

The witch-occult, comprising different elements like witch-craft, witch-trials and witch-hunts have been in existence ever since the dawn of mankind, both in the primitive and advanced cultures round the globe (*Sharma, 2015*). All the three aspects of the phenomena viz. witch-craft, witch-trials and witch-hunts show both spatial and temporal variability. In India, these phenomena have dominated in at least twenty-two tribal dominated states of India. It has been compared with infectious diseases as it is slowly spreading to newer and newer areas (*Vaishnavi, 2015*). Going by the data obtained from the National Crime Records Bureau (NCRB), during the period from 2000 – 2012, around 2100 cases of witch-hunting have been registered across India, of which 363 incidents were from Jharkhand alone. Despite the existence of an anti-witchcraft law in the State, incidents of witch-hunting continues to plague the State (*Sarkar, 2015*). Since the Chhattisgarh Witchcraft Atrocities (Prevention) Act, 2005 came into place, the State has witnessed 1268 incidents of witch-hunting till 2015, including 210 women, who were beaten to death (*Drolia, 2015*). The Odisha Prevention of Witch-hunting Bill, 2013 was passed by the State Assembly in December 2013 which became an Act in February 2014. However, there is no perceptible change in the crime graph scenario regarding witch-hunting (*Dixit, 2015*).

OBJECTIVE AND METHODOLOGY:

The above facts bring a very pertinent question to our minds – do the different laws of the land serve to provide exclusive keys for elimination of this prevailing social injustice? In this piece of research, the researcher focuses on the legal aspects of witch-hunting in the international as well as national and state level perspectives. The primary objective of the present work is to examine the different clauses that are outlined in the various anti-superstition legislations, including anti-witch-hunt legislations that have been drafted by the respective governments from time to time and to present a comparative as well as a critical analysis. Information presented in this work has been derived from various primary as well as secondary sources. The primary sources for the study include RTI information obtained from the Police Department as well as case studies. A number of websites carry information on the different witch-hunting events that take place in different localities. Investigative journalism by journalists attached with some of the leading international and national dailies and magazines provide insights into different cases along with their matured observations and judgments. All the different legislations, status reports and consultation reports that are easily accessible in the World Wide Web have been examined. All the available information have been synthesized with the personal experience and opinion of the author during the course of studies made on the witch-hunting victims belonging to the Rabha community of Assam.

INTERNATIONAL LEGISLATIONS:

A number of various international level legislations exist, as of date, which have got both direct and indirect bearing upon their potentiality to deal with the witch-hunting phenomenon. Some of these are detailed below –

The Universal Declaration of Human Rights (UDHR), 1948: In the words of Ban Ki-Moon, United Nations Secretary General, *"The Universal Declaration of Human Rights remains as relevant today as it was on the day in 1948…It provides* *a foundation for a just and decent future for all, and has given people everywhere a powerful tool in the fight against oppression, impunity and affronts to human dignity...*" The witch-hunting phenomenon violates as many as five articles, amongst thirty articles that are enlisted in the UDHR, 1948, as detailed below –

Article 3: *Everyone has the right to life, liberty and security of person*

Article 5: *No one shall be subjected to torture or to cruel, inhuman or degrading treatment or punishment*

Article 12: *No one shall be subjected to arbitrary interference with his privacy, family, home or correspondence, nor to attacks upon his honour and reputation ....*

Article 13: *Everyone has the right to freedom of movement and residence within the borders of each State*

Article 19: *Everyone has the right to freedom of opinion and expression*

The International Covenant on Civil and Political Rights (ICCPR), 1966. It was adopted by the General Assembly of the United Nations on 19 December 1966 and came into force from 23 March 1976. The witch-hunting phenomenon violates as many as six articles out of the fifty three articles that are enlisted in ICCPR, 1966 as detailed below –

Article 6 (1): *Every human being has the inherent right to life...No one shall be arbitrarily deprived of his life.*

Article 7: *No one shall be subjected to torture or to cruel, inhuman or degrading treatment or punishment.*

Article 9 (1): *No one shall be deprived of his liberty....*

Article 12 (1): *Everyone...has the right to liberty of movement and freedom to choose his residence.*

Article 17: *No one shall be subjected to arbitrary or unlawful interference with his privacy, family, home or correspondence....*

Article 19 (1): *Everyone shall have the right to hold opinions without interference.*

The International Covenant of Economic, Social and Cultural Rights (ICESCR), 1966. It was adopted by the United Nations General Assembly on 16 December 1966 and came into force from 3 January 1976. India acceded to the ICESCR on 10 April, 1979. It encompasses thirty-one Articles of which six articles may be linked with the witch-hunt victims -

---

Article 1(1): *All peoples…freely pursue their economic, social and cultural development*
Article 1(2): *All peoples…freely dispose of their natural wealth and resources…*
Article 6: *….recognize the right to work…*
Article 9: *…recognizes the right of everyone to social security, including social insurance*
Article 10(1): *…widest possible protection and assistance should be accorded to the family…*
Article 11: *…the right of everyone to an adequate standard of living…*
Article 12 (1): *…the right of everyone to the enjoyment of the highest attainable standard of physical and mental health*
Article 12 (2c): *The prevention treatment and control of epidemic, endemic, occupational and other diseases*
Article 12 (2d): *The creation of conditions which would assure to all medical service…*

The Declaration on the Protection of All Persons from Being Subjected to Torture and Other Cruel, Inhuman or Degrading Treatment or Punishment, 1975. The United Nations General Assembly having regard to the Article 5 of The Universal Declaration of Human Rights (UDHR), 1948 and the Article 7 of The International Covenant on Civil and Political Rights (ICCPR), 1966, adopted this Declaration on 9 December, 1975. This Declaration comprised 12 Articles, which provides for legal protection for any civilian who is subjected to torture or to cruel, inhuman or degrading treatment or punishment.

The Convention on the Elimination of all forms of Discrimination Against Women (CEDAW), 1979. The CEDAW was adopted by the United Nations General Assembly on 18 December 1979, vide resolution 34/180. Bearing in mind the great contribution of women to the welfare of the family and to the development of society, the State Parties agreed on thirty different articles that were enlisted in this Convention amongst which as much as five articles may be linked to the witch-hunt victims -

> *Article 2 (e):* *To take all appropriate measures to eliminate discrimination against women…*
>
> *Article 2 (f):* *To take all appropriate measures … to modify or abolish existing laws … which constitute discrimination against women*
>
> *Article 3:* *… guaranteeing them the exercise and enjoyment of human rights and fundamental freedoms …*
>
> *Article 13:* *…to eliminate discrimination against women in other areas of economic and social life…*
>
> *Article 14 (f):* *To participate in all community activities*
>
> *Article 15 (4):* *… accord to men and women the same rights … to the movement of persons and the freedom to choose their residence…*

The Convention Against Torture and other Cruel, Inhuman or Degrading Treatment or Punishment (CAT), 1984. The CAT was adopted by the United Nations General Assembly on 10 December 1984, vide resolution 39/46. The State Parties to this convention agreed upon thirty-three Articles, of which as many as seven articles may be linked with the witch-hunt victims.

> *Article 1:* *… the term 'torture' means any act by which severe pain or suffering, whether physical or mental, is intentionally inflicted on a person…*
>
> *Article 2 (1):* *… take effective legislative, administrative, judicial or other measures to prevent acts of torture…*
>
> *Article 4 (1):* *… shall ensure that all acts of torture are offences under its criminal law…*
>
> *Article 6 (1):* *…any State Party in whose territory a person alleged to have committed any offence … shall take him into custody or take other legal measures …*
>
> *Article 13:* *… shall ensure that any individual who alleges he has been subjected to torture in any territory under its jurisdiction has the right to complain to…ensure that the complainant and witnesses are protected against all ill-treatment or intimidation…*
>
> *Article 14 (1):* *… shall ensure in its legal system…the means for as full rehabilitation as possible …*
>
> *Article 16 (1):* *… shall undertake to prevent in any territory under its jurisdiction other acts of cruel, inhuman or degrading treatment or punishment…*

Over and above, there are different domestic laws existing in some countries, which are directly and indirectly related to witch-craft and other superstitious beliefs. Some examples include Witchcraft Suppression Act, 1957 and the Witchcraft Suppression Amendment Act, 1970 (South Africa), the amended Witchcraft Suppression Act, 2006 (Zimbabwe), The Witchcraft Act, 1911 (Malawi), The Fraudulent Mediums Act, 1951 (United Kingdom) [repealed in 2008], Consumer Protection from Unfair Trading Regulations, 2008 (United Kingdom), etc. Other countries like Kenya, Uganda, Tanzania, Cameroon, Indonesia, etc also do have certain pertinent laws (*CSSEIP, NLSIU Report, 2013*).

NATIONAL LEGISLATIONS:

Presently, there is no national law in India to battle witch-hunting. However, different Constitutional provisions and other domestic laws seek to provide indirect relief to all affected persons in the witch-hunting incidents. Some of the pertinent provisions in the Indian Constitution are listed below –

Article 14 (Equality before law): It guarantees equality before law and states that, "*The State shall not deny to any person equality before the law or the equal protection of the laws within the territory of India*"

Article 15 (Prohibition of discrimination on grounds of religion, race, caste, sex or place of birth):

Clause 3: "*Nothing in this Article shall prevent the State from making any special provision for women and children*"

Clause 4: "*Nothing in this Article or in Clause (2) of Article 29 shall prevent the State from making any special provision for the advancement of any socially and educationally backward classes of citizens...*"

Article 21 (Protection of life and personal liberty): It seeks to uphold human dignity by guaranteeing protection of life and personal liberties, "*No person shall be deprived of his life or personal liberty except according to the procedure established by law*".

Article 29 (Protection of interests of minorities): It states that, "*Any section of the citizens ...having a distinct language, script or culture of its own shall have the right to conserve the same*".

> ***Article 51*** (Promotion of international peace and security): It states that, *"The State shall endeavour to …foster respect for international law and treaty obligations in the dealings of organized peoples with one another".*
>
> ***Article 51A*** (Fundamental Duties) Clause (h): It states that, *"It shall be the duty of every citizen of India to…develop the scientific temper, humanism and the spirit of inquiry and reform".* In addition, the Supreme Court jurisprudence states, *"whatever has received the common consent of civilized nations must have received the assent of our country, and that too which we have assented along with other nations in general may properly be called international law, and as such will be acknowledged and applied by our municipal tribunals when legitimate occasion arise for those tribunals to decide questions to which doctrines of international law may be relevant".*

Going by the provisions of the Indian Constitution as well as the Supreme Court jurisprudence, India needs to comply with the different international legal obligations. Signing of international treaties under the ***Vienna Convention on the Law of Treaties, 1969***, also makes India to refrain from those acts which would defeat the object and purpose of the treaty. Article 18 (a) provides that, *"A state is obliged to refrain from acts which would defeat the object and purpose of a treaty when it has signed the treaty…".*

The account given below examines some of the national level legislations that exist in India for providing relief to the witch-hunt victims of the country, and which are in consonance with different international legislations.

The Indian Penal Code (IPC), 1860. The IPC contains 511 different Sections, included within 23 chapters. Several sections of the IPC have been commonly invoked against the perpetrators of the witch-hunting cases in different States of India, which do not have specific laws to deal with this problem. Cases are registered under different sections of the Indian Penal Code (IPC), viz. *Sec 302* (punishment for murder), *Sec 320* (grievous hurt), *Sec 323* (punishment for voluntarily causing hurt), *Sec 351* (assault), *Sec 354* (assault or criminal force to woman with intent to outrage her modesty), *Sec 364a* (kidnapping for ransom), *Sec 376* (punishment for rape), *Sec 503* (criminal intimidation), etc. (*Vaishnavi, 2015; Masoodi, 2016*). In addition, several other sections have been observed to have been invoked against the perpetrators in different witch-hunting cases that took place in Assam, as revealed from information obtained from the State Police Criminal Investigation Department, viz. *Sec 34* (acts done by several persons in furtherance of common intention), *120B* (punishment of criminal conspiracy), *Sec 148* (rioting, armed with deadly weapon), *Sec 149* (every member of unlawful assembly guilty of offence committed in prosecution of common object), *Sec 201* (causing disappearance of evidence of offence, or giving false information to screen offender), *Sec 325* (punishment for voluntarily causing grievous hurt), *Sec 326* (voluntarily causing grievous hurt by dangerous weapons or means), *Sec 342* (punishment for wrongful confinement), *Sec 365* (kidnapping or abducting with intent secretly and wrongfully to confine person), *Sec 379* (punishment for theft), *Sec 427* (mischief causing damage to the amount of fifty rupees), *Sec 447* (punishment for criminal trespass), *Sec 448* (punishment for house-trespass), *Sec 506* (punishment for criminal intimidation), etc.

The Drugs and Magic Remedies (Objectionable Advertisements) Act, 1954. This is an Act to control the advertisement of drugs in certain cases, to prohibit the advertisement for certain purposes of remedies alleged to possess magic qualities. As defined in the Act, '*magic remedy*' includes "*a talisman, mantra, kavacha and any other charm of any kind which is alleged to possess miraculous powers for or in the diagnosis, sure, mitigation, treatment or prevention of any disease in human beings…*". It has been opined that if this act is properly enforced in Andhra Pradesh, many babas, swamijis and other fake priests and hermits can be put behind bars (*Navayan, 2011*).

The Code of Criminal Procedure (CrPC), 1973. At one point of time, there was no uniform law of criminal procedure for the whole of India. For the guidance of the courts, there were separate Acts which were applicable in erstwhile provinces and the presidency towns. The Acts which were applicable in the presidency towns were first consolidated by the Criminal Procedure Supreme Court Act (16 of 1852). The Code has been amended from time to time by various Acts of the Central and State Legislatures. The Code of Criminal Procedure Bill having been passed by both the Houses of Parliament. It had received the assent of the President on 25th January, 1974. It came into force from 1 April, 1974 as *The Code of Criminal Procedure, 1973* (2 of 1974). This legislation contains 484 Sections, classified into 37 chapters.

The Scheduled Castes and Scheduled Tribes (Prevention of Atrocities) Act, 1989. This Act was formulated, "*to prevent the commission of offences of atrocities against the members of the Scheduled Castes and the Scheduled Tribes…*". The punishment under this Act provides for imprisonment ranging from six months up to life imprisonment. It has been suggested that the perpetrators of different witch-hunting cases in Andhra Pradesh, can be booked under this act, since majority of the victims belong to SC and ST communities (*Navayan, 2011*).

The Protection of Human Rights Act, 1993; The Protection of Human Rights (Amendment) Act, 2006. The purpose of these Acts are, *"to provide for the constitution of a National Human Rights Commission, State Human Rights Commission in States and Human Rights Courts for better protection of human rights and for matters connected therewith or incidental thereto"*. The different functions of these Commissions are to inquire, *suo motu* or on a petition presented to it by a victim into complaint of violation of human rights as well as several others.

The Prevention of Witch-Hunting Bill, 2016. This Bill was introduced in the Lok Sabha as Bill No. 66 of 2016 by Raghav Lakhanpal, M.P. on 11 February, 2016. This Bill is, *"meant to provide for more effective measures to prevent and protect women from 'witch-hunt' practices to eliminate their torture, oppression, humiliation and killing by providing punishment for such offences, relief and rehabilitation of women victims…"*. The punishment norms as provided in the Bill is segmented into eleven categories, that includes imprisonment in the range of three months up to life imprisonment, and/or a fine amount ranging from one thousand rupees to fifty thousand rupees. Several provisions of the Indian Penal Code, 1860 have also been sought to be invoked in certain cases.

STATE LEGISLATIONS:

International law is not merely binding on the national government; rather, states too must ensure, through legislative and executive acts and court decisions that they are in compliance with international treaties and covenants (*Cornell International Human Rights Clinic*).

The Prevention of Witch (Daain) Practices Act, 1999 [Bihar]. The State of Bihar, although being a backward state in many respects, was the first state in India to frame laws for curbing the menace of witch-hunting. This Act provides for, *"effective measures to prevent the witch practices and identification of a woman as a witch…"*. The Act prescribes a jail term in the range of three months to one year and fine in the range of one thousand to two thousand rupees.

The Prevention of Witch-Hunting Practices Act, 2001 [Jharkhand]. Jharkhand was the second state in India to pass another act, two years after

Bihar. This Act was meant, *"to provide for effective measures to prevent the witch practices and the identification of a woman as a witch and their oppression…"*. The Act prescribes a jail term in the range of three months to one year and fine in the range of one thousand to two thousand rupees.

The Chattisgarh Tonahi Pratadna Nivaran Act, 2005 [Chhattisgarh]. The State of Chhattisgarh was the third in the line to frame legislations against witch-hunting. Every offence committed under this Act is triable by the Judicial Magistrate First Class. Every offence punishable under this Act is cognizable and non-bailable. The Act provides for a jail term of one to five years as punishment, along with fine. There is no mention of the fine amount; however, when fixing the amount of fine, the court shall take into consideration the physical and mental damage caused to victim, including any cost of treatment.

The Odisha Prevention of Witch-Hunting Bill, 2013 [Odisha]. This Bill was passed by the Odisha State Assembly on 5th December 2013 and has become enforceable in the state of Odisha from February 2014 in the form of an Act. Thus Odisha became the fourth state in India to have special legislation against the practice of witch-hunting. This Act provides for, *"effective measures to tackle the menace of witch hunting and to prevent the practices of witch craft in the State of Odisha"*. The Act prescribes a jail term in the range of one to seven years and fine in the range of one thousand to ten thousand rupees. It has also been provided that when a Court imposes sentence of fine, it may order the whole or part of the fine recovered to be awarded as compensation to the victims.

The Maharashtra Prevention and Eradication of Human Sacrifice and other Inhuman, Evil and Aghori Practices and Black Magic Act, 2013 [Maharashtra]. The State of Maharashtra is the first in India to pass a comprehensive legislation for protecting people from being exploited in the name of superstition. This Act was passed on 13th December 2013 (*Gadgil, 2013*). After passing, the bill witnessed criticisms from different organizations like Shiv Sena, Bharatiya Janata Party, Hindu Jagran Samiti etc on the alleged grounds of being anti-Hindu (*Das and Banerjee, 2015*). This Act aims, *"to bring social awakening and awareness in the society and to create a healthy and safe social environment, with a view to protect the common people in the society, against the evil and sinister practices thriving on ignorance, and to combat and eradicate human sacrifice and other inhuman, evil, sinister and aghori practices…"*. Nothing in the Act applies in respect to certain religious practices like *Kirtan*,

Bhajan, Haripath, Pradakshina, Parikrama, Upasana, Upvas, Vastushashtra, etc and all religious rites at places such as home, temple, dargah, gurudwara, pagoda, church or other religious places which do not cause physical injury or financial loss. The Act encompasses the commission of twelve different superstitious acts, under the category of inhuman, evil and aghori practices. The Act prescribes a jail term of not less than three months which may extend up to seven years and fine in the range of five thousand to fifty thousand rupees.

The Rajasthan Prevention of Witch-Hunting Bill, 2015 [Rajasthan]. The State of Rajasthan became the fifth Indian state to adopt a witch-hunting Bill. It was introduced in the State Assembly on 31 March 2015 and thereafter passed on 9th April 2015. This Bill is mean, *"to provide effective measures to tackle the menace of witch-hunting, and to prevent the practice of witch craft in the State of Rajasthan…"*. The Act prescribes a jail term of not less than one year and which may extend up to life imprisonment and fine in the range of ten thousand to one lakh rupees. The net proceeds of the fine shall be utilized in the rehabilitation and resettlement of the victims. It also seeks to impose collective fine on residents of different areas, where witch-hunting occurs.

The Assam Witch-Hunting (Prohibition, Prevention and Protection) Bill, 2015 [Assam]. The State of Assam became the sixth Indian state to adopt a witch-hunting bill. It was passed by the State Legislative Assembly on 13th August 2015. This Act provides for, *"effective measures to prevent and protect persons from witch hunt practices and to eliminate their torture, oppression, humiliation and killing by a section of the society…"*. The Act provides for a imprisonment term ranging from three years up to life imprisonment and the fine amount being in the range five thousand to five lakh rupees. It also proposes to set up special courts for the trial of witch-hunting offences. The significance of the Bill is that Sec. 438 of CrPC will not apply and no person can seek anticipatory bail in connection with any case. All fines realized from the accused would be paid to the victim as compensation. There is also provision for free counseling, medical and legal aid.

Apart from all the legislations as detailed above a few other legislations are also in the pipeline in different States in India. Some of these could not materialize due to various administrative setbacks and other reasons. Some of these are mentioned below -

The Rajasthan Women (Prevention & Protection from Atrocities) Bill, 2011 [Rajasthan]. The Rajasthan government had also taken the initiative to draft this bill in 2011. When the Criminal Law Amendment Act, 2013 came into force, many of the sections of this Bill was taken care of for which the Ministry of Home Affairs directed the Govt. of Rajasthan to pass the witch-hunting bill as a separate bill. Simultaneously, the Rajasthan High Court requested the Govt. of Rajasthan to draft a law for preventing witch-hunts (*Srivastava et. al., 2015*).

The Karnataka Prevention of Superstitious Practices Bill, 2013 [Karnataka]. Following the lead of Maharashtra, Karnataka also drafted this bill in 2013, through The Centre for the Study of Social Exclusion and Inclusive Policy (CSSEIP) at the National Law School of India University (NLSIU), Bangalore. This bill has been criticized and opposed by the Hindu groups (*Das and Banerjee, 2015*).

The Karnataka Prevention and Eradication of Evil and Inhuman Practices Bill, 2014 [Karnataka]. It was prepared by the Karnataka State Law University.

The Karnataka Evil, Inhuman and Superstitious Practices Prevention and Eradication Bill, 2014 [Karnataka]. The Law Commission of Karnataka vide its thirty-fourth report dated 6 December 2014, had approved for passage of this Bill. While preparing the report, the Law Commission had also taken into account The Karnataka Prevention of Superstitious Practices Bill, 2013 and The Karnataka Prevention and Eradication of Evil and Inhuman Practices Bill, 2014.

SUMMARY AND CONCLUSION:

In spite of the numerous legislations that have been enacted from time to time, witch-hunting has never subsided in our country, and the occurrence perspectives have changed over time. Social sanction given to the practice is a factor which has contributed to the rising incidents. However, in many cases, it has been observed that witch-hunting cases also do occur on different pretexts. A section of people have adopted a modus operandi to disgrace and ostracize the victims through conspiracy for the purposes of fulfillment of various self interests like grabbing of various movable and other immovable properties, settling scores, family rivalry or even as a measure to punish for turning down sexual advances of someone influential in the village. Widows who are reluctant to relinquish claim over their husband's properties may be threatened and charged with being a witch (*Akula, 2015*). If a woman happens to be too assertive, and questions social norms, then also she is at risk of being branded as a witch (*Rakesh, 2010*). The link between ownership of land and persecution of women in witch-hunting cases is well established (*Das Gupta, 1993*). There are also several instances when members of the family themselves conspire to brand a woman as a witch and subject her to torture. One such is an instance from the Ranchi district in Jharkhand, in which the husband of the victim conspired to get his wife raped by hired goons on the accusation of her being a witch as she had apparently tried to dissuade her husband from selling a plot of land (*Rajalakshmi, 2000*). In another instance from Rajasthan, the husband of a woman conspired to declare his wife to be a witch, in order to marry another woman (*Shalz, 2013*). Witch-hunting has also been linked with politics. In Madhya Pradesh, a Dalit woman contested against a backward-caste woman in the Panchayat elections. Thereafter, the land-owning castes conspired to brand the Dalit woman as a *tonahi* (witch). Yet in another instance, a tea garden worker who actively campaigned for Left Front candidates in the Panchayat elections was declared a witch after a conspiracy hatched by the members of the Indigenous People's Front of Tripura, and later murdered (*Rajalakshmi, 2000*). Witch-hunting has therefore emerged as a popular extra-judicial and extra-legal method to gain masculine dominance over women. Creating awareness amongst the gullible sections of the people for doing away with the superstitious practices shall yield results only when the people act or react on the basis of superstition, ignorance and illiteracy. But if the community members takes recourse to witch-labeling and witch-hunting on the pretext of certain hidden vendetta, then the question of creation of awareness will not be relevant and valid, and only strictest lawful action can only prove out to be effective. The Government ought to send a strong message to the communities endorsing and practicing witch-hunting that it would not be tolerated and should instill a sense of fear and terror amongst those who indulge in these acts of crime against women. However, change in law will hardly prove satisfactory, unless there is a corresponding structural change in the administrative wing of the justice disposal system (*Rawat, 2014*).

It has transpired from case studies that the headmen of the villages just remain mute spectators to the entire sequence of events of many incidents. This important class of people of the rural society must be brought within the ambit of the legal provisions. Certain administrative mechanisms can be devised wherein the village headman or village defence parties can come to the police station for periodical meetings. This system will provide a regular update on the happenings within the remote hamlets, which are susceptible to witch-huntings. The provisions enlisted in *The Rajasthan Women (Prevention & Protection from Atrocities) Bill, 2011 (Chapter V, Sec. 17-2)* and in *The Prevention of Witch-Hunting Bill, 2016 (Chapter IV, Sec. 20-2)* are relevant in this point. The powers vested in the State Government to impose collective fines on the community [*The Rajasthan Women (Prevention & Protection from Atrocities) Bill, 2011, Chapter VI, Sec. 19; The Rajasthan Prevention of Witch-Hunting Bill, 2015, Sec. 8*] constitute another significant mechanism that might act as an effective tool to combat witch-hunting. Such a step will act as a deterrent for all the community members who would think twice before going for holding trials in 'kangaroo courts' and indulging in mob violence.

The provisions incorporated in *ICESCR, 1966 (Article 9)* is a very pertinent point which the Indian lawmakers had not included in the legislations so far enacted within the Indian Territory. The provision of social insurance schemes, if can be made available amongst the identified classes of people in the different States, might go a long way in alleviating the misery of the witch-hunt victims.

REFERENCES

Akula, Dinesh. *"How witch-hunting grips Chhattisgarh tribal villages."* Governance Now, 8 Aug. Web. 03 Feb. 2016.

CSSEIP, NLSIU Report. N.p. 12 Jan. 2016. <http://oppanna.com/wp-content/uploads/2013/11/superstitionbill2013.pdf>

Cornell International Human Rights Clinic. "International Law Memorandum: Jharkhand's Obligation to Prevent Witch-Hunting." N.p. 14 Jan. 2016. http://www.lawschool.cornell.edu/Clinical-Programs/international-human rights/upload/-1-Witch-Hunt-Brief-2.pdf

Das, Rolla and Banerjee, Suparna. *"Are we even ready to talk about superstition."* India Together, *23 Jun. 2015. Web. 30 Aug. 2015.*

Declaration on the Protection of All Persons from Being Subjected to Torture and Other Cruel, Inhuman or Degrading Treatment or Punishment, 1975. 11 Jan. 2016. <http://insanhaklarimerkezi.bilgi.edu.tr/media/uploads/2015/08/01/IskenceyeKarsiBildirge.pdf>

Dixit, Rakesh. "Witch-hunting on the rise in Maoist-hit Odisha as tribal districts cling to superstition." *Daily Mail*, 16 Mar. 2015. Web. 03 Feb. 2016.

Drolia, Rashmi. "Chhattisgarh witnesses 1268 incidents of witch hunting, a doctor offers to rehabilitate survivors in 332 pending cases." *Times of India, TNN*, 30 Sept. 2015. Web. 26 Jan. 2016.

Gadgil, Makarand. "Maharashtra Assembly passes anti-black magic Bill." *Live Mint*, 13 Dec. 2013. Web. 03 March, 2016.

Khan, Saif Rasul. "Witch Hunting in Assam: Critique of the Assam Witch Hunting Bill, 2015." International Journal of Research and Analysis 3.2 (2015): 281-287. Web. 18 Dec. 2015.

Massodi, Ashwaq. "Witch hunting – Victims of superstition." *Live Mint*, 28 Feb. 2016. Web. 18 Mar. 2016.

Navayan, Karthik. "Killings in the name of witchcraft." *Round Table India*, 19 Dec. 2011. Web. 12 Jan. 2016.

Rajalakshmi, T.K. "In the name of the witch." *Frontline*, 17.23, 11-24 Nov. 2000. Web. 04 Mar. 2016.

Rakesh, Renu. "Rajasthan's Shame: Witch Way DO These Women Go?" *Boloji*, 26 Sept. 2010. Web. 18 Mar. 2016.

Rawat, Anjali. "Witch Hunting in India: Much Darker Than Black Magic." *The Indian Police Journal* LXI.4 (2014): 186-197. Web. 9 Mar. 2016.

Sarkar, Suparno. "Witch Hunt: Villagers Kill 5 Women in Jharkhand; Victim's Daughter Narrates Horror." *IB Times*, 8 Aug. 2015. Web. 21 Nov. 2015.

Shalz V. "Victims of Witch Hunting." *Dreams Beyond Basics*, 1 Jul. 2013. Web. 18 Mar. 2016.

Sharma, Gaurav. "Witchcraft: Demystifying the decapitation, rape and banishment of women." *Newsgram*, 22 Jul. 2015. Web. 11 Dec.

Srivastava, Kavita et. al. "Rajasthan Prevention of Witch-Hunting Bill 2015: A critique by women organizations." *The Hindu*, 2 Apr. 2015. Web. 19 Sept. 2015.

The Chattisgarh Tonahi Pratadna Nivaran Act, 2005. 11 Jan. 2016. <http://cgpolicekorea.in/korea_Police/Laws/tonhi%20pratadna%202005CG17.pdf>

The Code of Criminal Procedure, 1973. 11 Jan. 2016. <http://www.icf.indianrailways.gov.in/uploads/files/CrPC.pdf>

The Convention Against Torture and other Cruel, Inhuman or Degrading Treatment or Punishment, 1984. 11 Jan. 2016. <http://www.ohchr.org/Documents/ProfessionalInterest/cat.pdf>

The Convention on the Elimination of all forms of Discrimination Against Women, 1979. 11 Jan. 2016. <http://www.ohchr.org/Documents/Professional Interest/cedaw.pdf>

The Drugs and Magic Remedies (Objectionable Advertisements) Act, 1954. 11 Jan. 2016.<http://www.rfhha.org/images/pdf/Hospital_Laws/Drugs_magic_remedies_(%20advertisement)_act.pdf>

The Indian Penal Code, 1860. 18 Jan. 2016. <http://ncw.nic.in/acts/ THEINDIANPENALCODE1860.pdf>

The International Covenant on Civil and Political Rights, 1966. 21 Jan. 2016. <https://treaties.un.org/doc/Publication/UNTS/Volume%20999/volume-999-I-14668-English.pdf>

The International Covenant of Economic, Social and Cultural Rights. 25 Jan. 2016. <http://www.ohchr.org/Documents/ProfessionalInterest/cescr.pdf>

The Karnataka Evil, Inhuman and Superstitious Practices Prevention and Eradication Bill, 2014. 25 Jan. 2016. <http://www.karnataka.gov.in/ lawcommission/Reports/Report%20No.34%20(English%20Version). pdf>

The Karnataka Prevention of Superstitious Practices Bill, 2013. 12 Jan. 2016. <https://www.nls.ac.in/results/superstitionbill2013.pdf>

The Rajasthan Prevention of Witch-Hunting Bill, 2015. 8 Jan. 2016. <http:// rajassembly.nic.in/BillsPdf/Bill20-2015.pdf>

The Maharashtra Prevention and Eradication of Human Sacrifice and other Inhuman, Evil and Aghori Practices and Black Magic Act, 2013. 8 Jan. 2016. http://bombayhighcourt.nic.in/libweb/acts/Stateact/2013acts/2013.30.pdf

The Odisha Prevention of Witch-Hunting Bill, 2013. 10 Jan. 2016. <http:// odisha.gov.in/govtpress/pdf/2013/1669.pdf>

The Prevention of Witch (Daain) Practices Act, 1999. 10 Jan. 2016. <http:// razahmed2003.blog.com/2011/03/09/witch-hunting-in-jharkhand-a-curse-on-the-society/>

The Prevention of Witch-Hunting Bill, 2006. 11 Mar. 2016. http://164.100.47.4/ BillsTexts/LSBillTexts/AsIntroduced/4572LS.pdf.

The Prevention of Witch-Hunting Practices Act, 2001. 2 Mar. 2016. <http:// razahmed2003.blog.com/2011/03/09/witch-hunting-in-jharkhand-a-curse-on-the-society/>

The Protection of Human Rights Act, 1993 and The Protection of Human Rights (Amendment) Act, 2006. 2 Feb. 2016. <http://nhrc.nic.in/documents/ Publications/TheProtectionofHumanRightsAct1993_Eng.pdf>

The Rajasthan Women (Prevention & Protection from Atrocities) Bill, 2011. 2 Mar. 2016. <http://wcd.rajasthan.gov.in/docs/raj-womwen-bill-2011.PDF>

The Scheduled Castes and Scheduled Tribes (Prevention of Atrocities) Act, 1989. 2 Mar. 2016.Web.

The Universal Declaration of Human Rights, 1948. 2 Mar. 2016. <http:// www.un.org/en/udhrbook/pdf/udhr_booklet_en_web.pdf>

Tracing Lost Tunes of Manipur

Ksh. Premchandra Singh

Throw me in the fire, I bloom like a flower. Sprinkle water on me, I wither and die. Who am I?
- Manipuri riddle.

Abstract:

Agriculture is not only the science of farming but also a storehouse of knowledge and culture. In Manipur it is a shared responsibility as well as source of her rich oral traditions. Many of Manipuri (Meitei) hymns, rites, rituals, customs, beliefs, proverbs, jokes, etc. come from the practice of agriculture. However, changing times and tastes have brought about, if not decimated entirely, changes in the rites and rituals associated with agricultural practices. The so called old/ancient/primitive practices have receded after the introduction of modern farming tools and techniques. As a result, human values associated with agri-culture have diminished significantly. The agri-culture of Manipur is a dying culture. Existing *puyas* (old Manipuri texts/ tracts left in manuscript forms - *Pudin, Soubon Yairen Chanu, Loutaron, Phouwoibi Waron,* etc.) remain reliable sources for the tools and implements the farmers used in those days (ancient) and the associated oral traditions. Some of these hymns and songs are still with the *Maibas* and *Maibis* (high priests and priestesses) and other 'living heritage' in the oral form. Agricultural rituals are displayed prominently in Lai Haraoba. Phouoibi (Goddess of bounty and also Rice Spirit) is worshipped throughout the valley of Manipur and songs and hymns were composed and written in her praise. Like other societies, the domestication and cultivation of rice also marked a change in Manipuri society. In this paper, the researcher makes an attempt to explore the oral traditions associated with agricultural practices which once reverberated the green fields of Manipur.

Keywords: culture, agri-culture, rites and rituals, hymns, oral songs

We believe that our gods and goddesses still reside in our valleys, dales, rivers, hills, meadows, etc. They gave us seasons and crops. They taught us the art and craft of weaving. They played *sagol kangjei* (polo) and passed the game down to us. They gave us our dance, our movements. Our respect and devotion for our gods and goddesses enabled us to devise our belief systems and, subsequently, our religious practices emanated from those belief systems. These beliefs and practices united us into one single spiritual community. The process of cultural self identification of this community started when efforts were made to locate ourselves within the symbolic order of the universe. In establishing our relationship with the 'ones' we revere and worship. Our songs, dance, rites and rituals, games and sports, etc. are powerful metaphors for our yearnings for peace, death and disease free villages, and villages with surplus crops (Meitei concept of existential equilibrium). And *Lai Haraoba* is a live performance passed down from one generation to another earnestly seeking the much required existential equilibrium for the community. It is also a repository of Meitei social history, folklore, food history, games and sports, agriculture, etc. What one finds in *Lai Haraoba* is what Walter Ong calls 'orality'. Because, Manipuris stored important aspects of their rituals, traditions, orature, music, dance, economy, polity, etc. in oral form in *Lai Haraoba*. It is their way of practicing traditions before the advent of 'literacy'. Before tradition becomes discourse.

Manipuri singing styles (tunes) are divided into nine broad areas. They are:

1. Leimarel sheisak
2. Panthoibi sheisak
3. Nongthangleima sheisak

4. Ayangleima sheisak
5. Hepli pabot
6. Hepli thangyei
7. Shikaplon/Huikaplon
8. Kalen cheijing
9. Lam-een sheisak[32]

One may get to hear these tunes in *Lai Haraoba* and other rituals. What one witnesses in *Lai Haraoba* is the ritualisation of oral materials (fostered by a ritualized setting). Hence, the language used in these oral songs can be regarded as ritual language which is different from the language of the common people. These tunes/singing styles were also used outside the ritualized settings of *Lai Haraoba*, palace ceremonies, *sagei lai*[33] worships, etc. These singing styles were mostly used in eulogising nature's beauty, hardships of life, glory of kings, great love stories, simple household tales, legends, etc. while performing agricultural activities, and other everyday activities.

Like other great Southeast Asian kingdoms, Manipur also got developed as an agrarian kingdom based on intensive wet-rice cultivation. Though wet cultivation had been in practice in Manipur for long (in other methods), transplantation method was introduced to Manipur by Muslim migrants in the early 1600s during the reign of King Khagemba (1597-1652 CE). Manipuris indulged in both *pamlou* (shifting cultivation) and wet cultivation. There are three methods of plantation. The first method is known as *pumhun* and is probably the oldest technique in both shifting and wet cultivation. The process of *pumhun* is held in the lunar month of *Kalen* (May) in which the dry seeds are sown after ploughing the field. The second method of *pamphen hunba* differs from the first method. In *pamphen hunba* the rice is soaked in water for two three days and dried for germination. The germinated seeds are sown after pulling harrow over the wet field. The third is the transplantation method or *lou lingba*. And in this method, a particular area is reserved for sowing the seeds. Such a process is known as *louhon hunba* and it has two techniques, i.e. *kang-louhon* or *pumhun louhon* in which the dry seeds are sown in the soil. *Chaiji louhon* or *pamphen louhon* differed from the previous methods. In these methods germinated seeds are sown in the wet area. Then the grown up plants are uprooted and transplanted. During the working hours, talented singers sing various songs.

The following songs, associated with agricultural practices, reverberated the green fields of Manipur in bygone days.

Louta eshei

Louta eshei (the tilling song) was sung when village folks worked in the fields for the first time in a harvest year. The song eulogises the community work which was an important aspect of agriculture in Manipur:

> Poirei khunja hup
> Tayum naija tin
> Yotlei nongthang kup
> Thouri lisang toi
> Tengpak lallu sa
> Haru nongga fou,
> Porom mata sham,
> Kaithet maru tup,
> Yupa khuman tan,
> Yangdou mamei sham,
> Wahi koktai tup
> Louri shungdai yan
> Piren machi khom
> Khalei ngam thungle.[34]

> Assembled are the village folks
> Attendants are also gathered
> Lightning spades strike
> Conquering the length of the earth
> Crushing the land into crumbles
> Grass covered earth is dried
> And, the grass are hewed
> Useless plants are destroyed
> Digging what is dug up again
> Repeating the strikes of the spades
> The heads of *wahis*[32] are chopped off

---

[32] *Wahi* – an insect

The edges of the *louri*[33] are cleaned
And, the grass are collected and dumped
The earth thus is covered.

[my translation]

This song of five syllables (in Manipuri) in one line talks about the collective efforts of the peasants in preparing the earth for plantation in the month of *kalen* (June/July). The tools used in agriculture were not mechanized. So, a good number of labourers, both males and females, were needed to carry out the tasks and this gave an opportunity to share the ups and downs of rural life at the work place. Apart from the hymns dedicated to the forces of the earth and the supreme beings, Manipuris added recreational songs which later became our folk songs.

Louyan eshei

Louyan eshei (*Lou*-paddy field+*yan*-to dig/till, *eshei*-song) which is sung at the very beginning of the agricultural process has these lines. The singing style/tune of this song is *shikaplon awangba*.

Epa louni yalluhe	He yanse.
Epu louni yallu he	He yanse.
Leipak mara tapnaba louni yallu he	Hey yanse
Ningthou punsinaba louni yallu he	Hey yanse
Khunjao leichao louni yallu he	Hey yanse
Mahei marong chumnaba louni yallu he	Hey yanse
Punshi nungsang lounida yallu he	Hey yanse
Shougri mayangba lounida yallu he	Hey yanse
Lomba fadigom lounida yallu he	Hey yanse
Fourel foujao lounida yallu he	Hey yanse
Singkha singthum louni yallu he	Hey yanse[35]
My father's field it is	Hey yanse [Let's till/dig].
My forefathers' field it is	Hey yanse
Till the field for a peaceful kingdom	Hey yanse

[33] *Louri* – elevated strips of earth that separate fields

Till the field for the king's long life	Hey yanse
Till the field for a prosperous kingdom	Hey yanse
Till the field for bountiful crops	Hey yanse
Till the field for long lives	Hey yanse
Till it for it is the field for *sougri* and *mayangba*	Hey yanse
Till it for it is the field for *lomba* and *fadigom*	Hey yanse
Till it for it is the field for *fourel* and *foujao*	Hey yanse
Till it for it is the field for *singkha* and *singthum*[34]	Hey yanse

[my translation]

This *eshei*/song establishes the fact that Manipuris consider land as inherited from their forefathers. The second line (Hey yanse) is repeated after every sentence and this line is the chorus. One person sings the first and others join in to complete the song. This song came down to us probably from the pre-agrarian period in which land was owned by individuals but agricultural activities were carried out together. The sense of community service and of helping one another could be seen in this song. Agricultural rites were one of the important socio-religious and economic observances of early Manipuris. According to the traditional belief, the neglect of paddy or rice provoked the anger of Phouoibi (Goddess of paddy). The rites and rituals of the goddess were performed to ward off possible misfortunes that could come to the peasants. The song also reiterates the notion of existential equilibrium in which simple peasants ask the deities for peace and prosperity and for the wellbeing of the king.

Phousu Eshei (*phou*-rice+*su*-to grind/pound *Eshei*-song = pestle and mortar song)

Introduction of rice mills in Manipur rooted out the traditional practice of husking rice using *suk*[35] and *sumbal*[36]. Before the introduction of machanised rice mills in Manipur, every family had *suk* and *sumbal* and all the rice husking and other grinding works were done using these simple tools. Young girls as well as married ones worked on this rice husking process at their free time especially in moonlit nights. They also indulged in reciprocal/community work

---

[34]   Words in italics are names of Manipuri herbs, vegetables, rice, and eatable roots

[35]   A long wooden rod encased with iron on one end used in pounding rice (wooden pestle)

[36]   A hollowed out piece of wood for rice husking and other grinding purposes (Wooden mortar)

culture which they call *khutlang* (khut-hand, *langnaba*- to reciprocate/return). Such a workplace often turned into meeting grounds and merrymaking when young unmarried men take part in this rice husking work. When two young male and female pound the *suk* in the *sumbal* there emanated a rhythm and they sang songs expressing their desires. They also entertain themselves with riddles laced with their inner feelings. Stories of wit and humour are sung or narrated to make progress to the work. The song given below is an example from a repertoire of *phousu esheis* associated with the husking process.

> *Hayum yanaba koudrang ko*
> *Sing challak-u hairaga*
> *Phou purakpa yannaba*
> *Nangna chakpu hairaga*
> *Fougak chajik namthiba*
> *Chakpu sana pijage.*
>
> *Nangna yenshang hairaga*
> *Lafu yendem thumnamdabi*
> *Yenshangbu sana pijage.*
>
> *Nangna ngabu hairaga*
> *Khongbandagi ngachakna*
> *Ngabu sana pijage.*
>
> *Nangna thumbu hairaga*
> *Faklang leibak oinamba*
> *Thumbu sana pijage.*[36]

Hayum yanaba koudrang ko
Told you to collect firewood
But brought paddy instead

So, when you demand cooked rice
Will offer in its place
Stinky *fougak*[37] leftover

---

[37]   fougak

When you want cooked vegetable
Will treat you
Salt less *lafu-yendem*[38] stew

When you want fish
Tadpole from a *khongban*[39]
Will be offered instead

When you say salt
Tasty earth from the earthen wall
Will be given as a substitute.

[my translation]

This song is humorous and witty. It talks about someone who is told to do something but ends up doing another. So the speaker here warns the person that one reaps what one sows.

Mishigi sumbal maipakpi
Shei-yi sukti tunanbi
Leihou sintak pathetla
Monugi yangkok mangda tham
Shei-yi sukti tunanbi
Khurak leika yetna pai
Hayumgi koloi toyna shon
Shei-yi sukti tunanbi
Korou thakta thangkatle
Monugi pukshit huithapna
Malem leida thadare
Nuragi khwangdi polhainei
Hayum koloi shonduna
Panthougi shumang mathoupung
Chengja maingou tanshido.

---

38 A boiled based stew of plantain tree and *yendem*
39 A *nalla*

Broad-faced mortar made from *mishi*[40]
Clean and shining pestle made from *sayi*[41]
Leihou sintak pathetla[42]
Placing a woman's *yangkok*[43] in front
Clean and shining pestle made from *sayi*
Holding it by both the hands
Chanting the glory of Hayum[44] repeatedly
Clean and shining pestle made from *sayi*
Raising it towards the sky above
A woman's belly is shrunk
Lowers it towards the mortar
A woman's hips move to and fro
Chanting the glory of Hayum
Turning the father's courtyard into a workplace
Let's pound to produce the whitest rice.

[my translation]

Shinnai Eshei

Song and dance conform to a Manipuri's daily activities. Various hymns, songs, and ballads describing events, daily/routine activities, plants, animals, and natural phenomena are composed and sung. These songs (*sheitharol*) filled with the knowledge of the people and their natural habitats are passed down from one generation to another. Some have survived the taste of time. Some of these *seitharols* did enter the court and became parts of king's revelries and peace and prosperity festivities. Some of them are passed down as hymns sung at the appeasement rituals of deities. These *seitharols* are; *khutlang eshei, leiron, shinnai eshei, khutlang eshei awai akhum,* etc. These songs are rather for the stage and seminar halls now.

---

[40] A kind of tree especially for making mortar
[41] A kind of tree for making handles for axe, spade, etc.
[42] A reference to *yangkok*
[43] *yangkok*: a round bamboo product used in isolating rice from the chaff with intricate hand movements
[44] Supreme Being

Thangol thoudabana lou ngamnei
Thanglen pamdabana
Tolloi mana pungnei
Thangol thoudabana lou ngamnadou sharuk
Thanglen pamdabana
Tolloi mana pungnadou sharuk
Pallem pheira tajinthak
Khomlang mayoknaringei
Khomlang hanna aman khamlei kumlamlabadi
Thangol thoudabana lou ngamnaba
Thanglen pamdabana tolloi mana pungnababu
Khanglamloidabani.

Nonglao eshei

Agriculture in Manipur depended much on rainwater as there was no irrigation system in olden days. When there is no rain or scarcity of rain, *maibas* and *maibis* of the land perform rain rites or rain making rites to invoke rain at *nongju khong* at Langjing Hills. *Nonglao eshei* (rain making song) is sung at such a ceremony. From the *Puya* called *Chinglon Laihui* we get the following *nonglao eshei*:

Nong-o chutharo
Langjing maton thumhatlo
Pashoi nurabi taotharo
Unam pakhang khunjaro
Kouba kounu nong-o
Loiji loiya nong-o
Ereng engtham nong-o
Thangjing koyren nong-o
Wangbren thanachaoba nong-o
Shambun maharaba nong-o
Chingkhei nongpok nong-o
Haokap chingsang nong-o
Khunpham ngangjeng nong-o
Leiri nongli houro.
Leikhong nongkhong nemmo

Korou khongdum khonglak-o
Malem leiburumbi lumkhatlak-o
Laijaethabi nang thabirak-o
Laija ekhiba nang khithabirak-o.[37]

Pour down O rain
Submerge the tip of Langching
Wash down the maidens of Patsoi
Collect the young lads of Unam
Rain of the Koubru hills
Rain of the foothills and hillocks
Rain of the river Iril
Rain of the Thangching hills
Rain of Wangbren thanachaoba
Rain of Shambun maharaba
Rain of the East
Rain of the Haokap Hill ranges
Rain of the Khunpham ngangjeng
Sprout rainclouds in heaven and earth
Lower the firmaments of the sky
Bring the roaring thunders
Make the sky heavier than ever
Come down O Laijaethabi
Pour down O rain.

[my translation]

Many of our *puyas* (old Manipuri texts/tracts left in manuscript forms) are the sources for the tools and implements the Manipuris used in ancient times and the associated hymns, rites and rituals emanating from their use in everyday life. *Pudin, Soubon Yairen Chanu, Loutaron, Phouoibi Waron,* etc. reveal much about the rites and rituals practiced by Manipuris in the pre and post Vaishnavism period. What was widely practiced is with the *Maibas, Maibis* (high priests and priestesses), and other 'living heritage' in oral forms. Various hymns and folk/ritual songs sprang from the recesses men and women took due to rain and sun while working. Many of these songs were not written down but composed on the spot, a mimetic rendition of plants and seasons, of hardships of life and yearning for the Supreme Being. Familial as well as social events/incidents were added later on in these songs.

Many songs, including the ones discussed above, once enthralled the green fields of Manipur. They were part of our oral memorization. Our tradition in practice has become a tradition of discourse in no time. I don't know how much has lost in this transition and translation. It is said that 'the word in its natural, oral habitat is a part of a real, existential present'.[38] That 'oral habitat' of the bygone days seems to have lost its poetic powers. No one sings in the green fields of Manipur any longer. No one composes new songs any more. Nowadays, you get to hear noises from the diesel engines only.

Notes and References

This classification is done by R. K. Nabindra in his book Kanglei Haraoba. But in the book Shri Shri Goura Govinda Thouram Pareng written by Gulapi Singh, Manipuri tunes are classified as, 1. Naheirol, 2. Shikaplon, 3. Huikaplon, 4. Jat-Lameen, 5. Hiri Pabot, 6. Hiri Thangyei, etc. This book is quoted by Shri Soukrakpam Chanbi Singh in his unpublished seminar paper "Bangadesh Esheigi Raag Raagini" presented at Jawaharlal Nehru Manipur Dance Academy, Imphal organised by Manipur State Kala Academy, Imphal, from 11-12 January, 1974.

Lineage deities
N. Khelchandra Singh. Ariba Manipuri Sahityagi Etihash (Imphal: by the author himself, 2011) p. 8. Print.
N. Khelchandra Singh. p. 8.
Phousu eshei
From Chinglon Laihui
Walter J. Ong. Orality and Literacy (London: Routledge, 2002), p. 99. Print.

The Tribal Heritage:
Quest for 'Meaning' in Bodo Folk Dances

Deepak Basumatary

" *When an old woman hears the dance she knows her old age deserts her*" writes Chinua Achebe in *Things Fall Apart* (1958). Eloquently and succinctly summed up in this beautiful line is the significance and power of dance in tribal societies which transcends barriers of age, gender, social hierarchies and class barriers. Tribal people are primordial *homo sapiens*, unique and different from the rest, ancient and new at the same. Their culture carries accumulated wisdom of generations together which are found in the Oral traditions, their lives display vigour and energy in sync with nature, and there is a vibrancy of colours in their attire/ dresses. Going further, Ashish Mohan Khokar in his book *Folk Dance Tribal Ritual and Martial Forms* (2003) lauds the import of folk dance amongst the tribes in the following lines;

> "*They believe that their dance is a kind of prayer to Nature and its puissant gods, a prayer that invokes and propitiates, as well as gives thanks.*" [1] (8)

Dance, then becomes a form of reverence, a communication with the gods themselves meaning that it's not simply a matter of pastime or festivity but a statement.

Homo sapiens are meaning generating animals, they express in a number of ways that are difficult to discern, deduce, and comprehend for meanings or ideas. Signs and symbols, movements and actions, gestures and words all these form a complex system of communication and expression for mankind. They at all times 'mean' and 'express' their thoughts and feelings through these media under different circumstances and situations which varies from one culture to the other. Every activity of an individual, person or community connotes a certain meaning in one form or the other. While some meanings are explicit in the structure of the verbal language, some are subtle and nuanced expressions of a deeper thought which contains wealth of knowledge, philosophy and imaginations of the community. For the tribes, the primordial *homo sapiens* Oral traditions form a veritable encyclopaedia of their cultural heritage. There is a rich texture of meanings in the Oral traditions of the tribes which come alive in performances. Dance which is a vital cog in the tribal life cycle is a performance of the tribal ethos. Folk dances accompanied by traditional music and songs are loaded with idioms of expression and articles of imagination that give verve to 'meaning' generation.

Post-colonial studies in recent times have spurred interest in the study of non-Western cultures and multiculturalism. This has significantly provided impetus towards the renewed study of 'Orality' or unwritten verbal sources around the world. In this context it is noteworthy to recall Miles Foley's words who have claimed in the book *Teaching Oral Traditions* (1998) that the 'rediscovery' of Oral traditions is an important "achievement of the twentieth century" in unearthing wealth of knowledge. In the pan-Indian context this statement becomes a core doctrine in folkloristics as the very idea of India harps on the diversity of its culture. It is necessary to understand these multitudes of cultures from cross-cultural and holistic perspectives taking into account the importance and significance of Oral narratives as an important source of meaning gathering. The modern nation state of India has evolved through a gradual process of cultural contests, and new texts have emerged out of these numerous cross-cultural contests. A number of indigenous tribes have endeavoured to preserve their distinct identities in the face of constant pressures of globalization, dominance of mainstream cultures and the rise of popular cultures. The India of today is a result of the negotiation of the Western ethos with that of the natives in the colonial times which needs to be re/read from a non-Western perspective that is unbiased and holistic. For this purpose it is important to re-orient the fundamental way one reads and interprets history, traditions and cultures of the people by placing into the forefront the 'folk' and their 'lore' from Oral traditions in performance contexts. N. Scott Momaday, an American Indian writer in an essay 'The Man Made of Words' (1979) offers the most comprehensive and simple definition of Oral tradition. In his words;

> *"The oral tradition is that process by which the myths, legends, tales and lore of a people are formulated, communicated and preserved in language by word of mouth, as opposed to writing. Or it is a collection of such things."*[2] (167)

While this definition is comprehensive enough focussing on the medium and matrices of language it rather restricts itself to the spoken word or utterances of verbal language. Going beyond this restrictive and reductive meaning of language if one considers language as a system of signs, an organized and scientific way of communicating ideas or feelings by use of conventionalized signs, sounds, gestures, or marks having understood meanings then 'Orality' connotes a far wider compass. In this case one can include many other forms of folk performances other than the verbal language like — dances, songs, music, attire/ dresses, etc. which speak or communicate ideas, thoughts, feelings through gestures, sounds, colours, motifs, etc.

Thus far, it has been a norm in the construction and reading of non-Western history and culture by the West and the academia to interpret non-Western cultures from Western ethnocentric prism which is considered uncouth and unworthy of intellectual debate, attention, and discourse. North-east region of India is inhabited by a large number of tribes of different hues and tongues; blessed with abundant natural resources, flora and fauna the cultures of these tribes reflect the beauty of nature. For instance, these tribes have numerous dance forms that reflect their close affinity with nature. These dance forms have been passed on from one generation to the next by means of an Oral tradition strongly revealing the extant traditional beliefs of the 'folk' which constitutes the traits of their culture.

Tribal people love to dance, it is their passion. Whether in peace or war, work or leisure there are various dance forms for each and every occasion in tribal communities. The rhythmic movement of the body is symbolic of the movement of nature — from one landscape to the other, from one season to the next and the harmonic adaptation of the human body with it in tranquillity. For the tribes, dance is a form of expression which releases pent-up feelings and uplifts them from the ordinary and humdrum mundane life to delight and joy. It renews them with a new spirit of imagination.

The large repertoire of folk dances which are found in the tribal communities of the north-east region of India is a narrative of their history, tradition and cultures. This has not been given adequate attention it deserves in the 'normal' Western discourses as it belongs to the 'Other' non-Western histories and cultures so far. One reason is that the West prioritize the 'written' over Orality as more reliable and authentic source of the past. However, for non-literate indigenous tribal cultures writing, being a relatively recent invention is largely an alien form of recording of experiences, traditions, history, proverbs, tales, and beliefs. For them Oral traditions is the primary means or vehicle through which cultural memory is recorded and passed on from one generation to the next. There is scanty number of 'written' literature as such in tribal cultures to begin with. It is the Oral traditions which constitute a large chunk of cultural memory. This offers a better understanding of their imaginations and the rich general lore of the tribal folk, who have lived for generations together with the other animate and inanimate objects in nature. Scribing or writing has now become a dominant mode of recording ideas, thoughts, knowledge, imagination and feelings. However, it does not and cannot replace Oral traditions altogether because writing is secondary to speech. "Writing is nothing but the representation of speech;" writes **J. J. Rousseau,** "it is bizarre that one gives more care to the determining of the image than to the object."[3] (*Fragment inédit d'un essai sur les langues.*) Written accounts serve to add another dimension to Orality, which later become staid and frozen in time as against the dynamism of Oral traditions. Against this backdrop, a folkloristic perspective of folk tales, folk life, folk traditions, folk beliefs, and folk performances offer a vast gamut of dynamic living narratives with a long and rich texture.

It is in recent times that a paradigm shift has taken place in folkloristic researches wherein the 'folk' and their 'Oral traditions' have become the 'centre' of investigation which takes 'Orality' as its primary source material as it is found in living contexts. There has come about a perceptible change in the approach towards the critical method of studying the 'folk' and their 'lore' which places Orality as a kind of canon. Orality is a narrative of living history in particular contexts as it offers a genuine source material which directly comes from the 'folk'. It is therefore, authentic and reliable as compared to the 'frozen in time' written sources in libraries. It offers a genuine understanding of the people through the living contexts of the 'folk'. It is the Oral traditions that give a nuanced perspective of the people, their lore or wisdom gathered through generations and provides a glimpse of their philosophy, their character and behaviour. In the book *Folkloristics and Indian Folklore* (1991) eminent American folklorists Peter J. Claus and Frank J. Korom have emphasized the significance of living contexts of folklore as it is the contexts that make the 'meaning' of the 'texts' comprehensible in the course of time, place and history.

The 'rediscovery' of the Oral traditions as put forth by Foley is particularly apt in the case of north-east India which is home to a large number of indigenous ethnic tribal people. North-east region of India remains a largely unknown, exotic and enigmatic part of the country even to this day largely because, to a very large extent, the culture, traditions, beliefs, and history of this region have scarcely been 'rediscovered' from the perspective of Oral traditions. It has mostly relied on a few numbers of writings that exist in the form of colonial accounts and anthropological/ ethnographic works by the missionaries and historians which offer only partial, one-sided and distorted views on the region and its people. Rather than 'rediscovering' the culture, traditions, and history of the diverse tribal populace of the region by its oral traditions and narratives, it looks at it from the lens of Western ethnocentrism and comparison with other developed cultures of mainland India. At best it offers only an exotic panorama and a passing reference to these multitudes of tribal cultures of north-east India which have only served to mystify it further.

Thus, the Oral traditions and the verbal art of the Bodo tribe represent living folk performance contexts which have a long history steeped in folk beliefs, folk tales, and folk traditions. Folk performances of the Bodos like dance have not received adequate intellectual attention and debate so as to discern the encoded meanings that it carries. Folk dance is a performativity of cultural mores and it provides a visual dimension to Oral traditions/ narratives of the folk. Folk performances of the Bodos are not a spectacle but a larger narrative of the extant cultural practices extant that has been inherited from the preceding generations. A folk performance in the form of folk dances brings it alive and makes it relevant to the contemporary generation. All the tribal cultures have rich and varied dance forms which tell stories of their traditions, and history constituting a kind of oral discursive narrative. Performances give wings to the imaginations of the folk, it becomes Oral narrative. Folk dances, invariably accompanied by traditional music and songs, are structured movements of the body performed according to the traditional culture; it is an expression of the community through rhythmic movements that symbolize a deeply held belief and imagination of the mind.

If one were to define culture as dynamic, non-static and ever-evolving art that is not structured, fixed and reified system for posterity, then folk dances, which are performed in certain living contexts, provide ample opportunity for interpretation of the Oral traditions and the verbal as well as visual art. It is a source of oral narratives wherein many of the unwritten codes and conventions come alive in the performances. Consequently, 'meanings' of Oral tradition are better understood through these performances which situates 'texts' in its 'living contexts' across time and space.

Ashma Shamail in her essay 'Orality and the Re-enactment of Memory: History, Ritual, and African-Caribbean Resistance in the Chosen Place, the Timeless People' says —

> *"Dance, music, customs, and festivals describe not only events of cultural importance inscribed in memory and passed through generations, but serve to express or record the hardships, sufferings, defeats and victories among populations".*[4]

In other words 'dance, music, customs, and festivals' constitute the matrices of the 'cultural memory' of the tribal people which is basic in the 'rediscovery' of the Oral traditions. The tribal communities in the north-east region of India have abundant folk dance forms which are varied and vibrant. The Bodo tribe too have a number of dance forms out of which **Bwisagu, Bagurumba, Naa Gurnai, Baardwi Sikla** and **Dahal-Thungri Mwsanai** are the most popular folk dances that reflect their extant Oral traditions. Performed during specific occasions, time and place (contexts) during the course of the year it encapsulates wealth of meanings, expressed and articulated through the different traits, motifs, symbols, signs, movements, sounds, and speech as the folk dance performances become living Oral narrative. The vitality, vivacity and verve in the Oral traditions of the Bodos come alive in these performances which are characteristically expressed through collective performances. These folk dances of the Bodos provide a rich texture of Oral narratives which significantly gives 'living' contextual meaning and can be read from a gender perspective.

The folk dances of the Bodos are a part of rituals and festivals; a performance of the masses who are not professionals but rustic people's spontaneous performances. Primarily an agricultural community, 'nature' for the Bodos is the root and the basis of existence. It is the gift of life it offers and the tremendous possibility of leading a joyous life in the lap of nature that fascinates the collective imagination of the Bodo community as a whole. The folk dances of the Bodos therefore have a close affinity with nature, which form an important component of their culture and Oral traditions. Their lives and activities accentuate the rhythm and flow of nature throughout its seasonal cycle and it is these aspects in nature that the folk dances imitate the animate as well as inanimate objects. The songs appreciating the beauty, grace and grandeur of nature wherein the rivers, birds, butterflies, plants, flowers, etc. become a part and parcel of the oral narrative constitute a kind of 'animism', a belief and practise which is germane to the traditional Bodo faith *Bathou* that attributes conscious life to the phenomena of nature. The folk dance of the Bodos, its rhythmic movements imitates nature and attributes conscious life to it. The animate and inanimate objects of nature, the rivers, birds, butterflies, plants, flowers or the flora and fauna — are subsumed in the thoughts and imaginations of the folk and become an integral aspect of their cultural life.

Nature during spring adorns glorious beauty and poise as the trees put on new and tender leaves that bring about a lustrous and sensuous ambience to the surrounding environment. This brings about a delirious excitement in the young and old, men and women alike. Like nature the people too adorns new outlook, zest and spirit in life with a renewed energy forgetting for a while all the troubles and worries of the harsh realities of life. The young and old, men and women sing and dance together in groups expressing their joy and gratitude to nature. The passion for nature lifts the spirit of the ordinary Bodo people from the mundane life into ecstasy which is expressed through dance. The Bodos love to dance because they are filled with ecstasy with the forming of a close filial bond between Man and Nature. Dance is a characteristic feature of the tribal people because they live close to nature. For them dance is not a simple structured or rhythmic movement of the body but a special gesture, a symbolic association with mother nature and an expression of gratitude through performance. In the words of Omkar Sharma, an academician and linguist — "gestures reflect the social and cultural preoccupation, habits, and

beliefs of the concerned community performing the art." This observation
holds true for the Bodo folk dance performances as each and every gesture in
the folk dances reflects the abiding social and cultural preoccupation, habits,
and beliefs of the community.

The folk dances of the Bodo tribe who live in sync with nature are best
manifested in the annual spring festival popularly called *Bwisagu* in Bodo.
This festival *Bwisagu* brings alive the spirit of the people in all its glory in a
'carnival' like atmosphere during the festivities. *Bwisagu* songs and dances of
the Bodos are an appreciation of the beauties and bounties of nature in all its
glorious manifestation. The songs accompanied by dances are an expression
of the fact that the Bodos as a whole community feel indebted to nature and
the opportunities that it offers to lead a happy and contented life. As nature
appears in fullness with gay abandon, one timeless *Bwisagu* song —

> *"Bwisag Danni baar baarnaijwng/ Dao kou ou ni gabnai dengkhw jwng/
> Jaolia gwsw aa gwswni khwtakou/ Fwrmaigoumwn fwrmaigoumwn
> aagwi/ Gami nuhurnai gupurwi baleng leng nainw mwjang*
>
> *Bwisag okhapwr purnima horao/ Gwsw khangbai nwngkou sona
> khalou-bilou/ Nwng dongmwn bla, lwgwmwnbla/ Gwswni khwta kou
> bungprugoumwn aagwi/ Gaami nuhurnai gufurwi baleng-leng nainw
> mwjang*
>
> *Bwisag Danni baar baarnaijwng/ Harsa mungjwng moose, Boro
> munjwng moose/ Daha tabai aagwi gwswni khwta kou/ Gwswni khwta
> kou fwrmainw mwnnai ao"*

(collected from Oral source: Loknath Goyary, an academic and folk
artist)

[An English translation would to some extent mean/imply the following:]

> With the gentle breeze of the spring,
> With the mesmerising song of the cuckoo,
> My heart goes insane in love for you,
> I wish to express, I wish to convey
> My love, Oh dear beloved

To the one from the next village
The graceful, svelte, and beautiful lady

In spring's moonlit night,
I feel and miss you, agonizingly
If you were somewhere nearby,
I could have met you
To pour out my love, my beloved
The one from the next village
The graceful, svelte, and beautiful lady

With the gentle breeze of the spring,
With the mesmerising song of the cuckoo
Graceful, svelte, and beautiful
A charming Bodo lady, lovely and beautiful
Beyond words, beyond description
Woe betide my heart
For I cannot express my love

sums up the prevailing mood of the rustic folk revelling in the lap of nature in a carnival spirit and gay abandon just like nature itself. Through this *Bwisagu* performance (song & dance) the Bodo men folk take the liberty to express their feelings of love to the ladies where no offence is meant or taken. In a joyous and humorous mood the women folk too react to these proposals of love and marriage that comes their way. Here, the song cleverly orchestrates the emotional side of man with the rhythm and tune of nature which shows that there is a symphony of the human mind with the sights and sounds of nature. The carefree spirit of nature during spring brings out the emotional side of man and he is able to shake off all his inhibitions to express his feelings for the lady love he discreetly pines for. Nature fills the core of their lives; it is the fountainhead of the spirit in man, and fills *Homo sapiens* with attributes of emotions, feelings, thoughts and imaginations. The Oral tradition manifested in this *Bwisagu* songs reveal that even feelings of love, emotions, sense of beauty and appreciation are envisioned and facilitated by nature. The *Bwisagu* festival exemplifies the inter-connection and the close affinity of the life and well-being of the Bodos with Nature — their lives, traditions and culture revolve round it.

'Texts' of this sort which reveal the centrality of nature in a human life living in close affinity with nature are produced through Oral narratives in the everyday vocabulary of the masses — active as well passive. The *Bwisagu* festival provides a live cultural 'context' for demystifying Oral traditions that exists in performances like songs, dances, rituals, or games containing layers of oral meanings which get a concrete shape during performances. In this context A.K. Ramanujan has stated that —

> *"Written and hallowed texts are not the only kinds of texts in a culture like India's. Oral traditions of every kind produce texts. "Cultural performances" of every kind, whether they are plays, rituals, or games, contain texts, written and oral. In a sense, every cultural performance is a text in itself."*[5] (Collected Essays 16, 18)

Perhaps the best and well known folk dance of the Bodo tribe is *Bagurumba*. Performed by women with their colourful *dokhna, jwmgra* (fasra) and *aronai* to the tune of *kham, siphung, serja* and *jota*, the traditional musical instruments played by men, the *Bagurumba* song goes this way —

> *"baa baa bagurumba/ hai lwgwfwr/ baa baa bagurumba/ jaat nonga bwbla/ khul nongabwbla/ thabwrwm homnanwi/ bamnanwi lagou mwnka/ hai lwgwfwr lagoumwnka*
>
> *sen sena sen daosen/ jwngni lagwaalai dajen/ gwsw hwsar hwsar mwsade/ hai lwgwfwr mwsade*
>
> *baa baa bagurumba/ hai lwgwfwr/ baa baa bagurumba/ jaat nonga bwbla/ khul nongabwbla/ thabwrwm homnanwi/ bamnanwi lagou mwnka/ hai lwgwfwr lagoumwnka*
>
> *dwi jiri jiri samo kingkiri/ sonani jinjiri/ hai jinjiri*
>
> *baa baa bagurumba/ hai lwgwfwr/ baa baa bagurumba/ jaat nonga bwbla/ khul nongabwbla/ thabwrwm homnanwi/ bamnanwi lagou mwnka/ hai lwgwfwr lagoumwnka"*

(*Bagurumba is a well documented dance form of the Bodos, the most popular and well-known. Collected from Oral source: Mr Barlangfa Narzary, an acclaimed Bodo folk artist)

(An English translation of the same would to some extent imply as follows)

if it weren't for the ethnicity,
if it weren't for the cultural traditions
my friends, i would have snatched
quite a handful and cuddled in my arms

in love, peace, or war
let my village be always victorious
dance with all your heart
dance with all your soul
dance my friends, dance

if it weren't for the ethnicity,
if it weren't for the cultural traditions
my friends, i would have snatched
quite a handful and cuddled in my arms

In the crystal clear rivers
The snail makes an impression
a golden chain, my friend
dance my friends, dance

if it weren't for the ethnicity,
if it weren't for the cultural traditions
my friends, i would have snatched
quite a handful and cuddled in my arms

It was performed by young damsels in leisure in the past generally after the season of sowing and harvesting when there was lesser workload after a hectic period of work in the fields. The dance embodies colourful motifs of nature. It imitates the rhythmic movement of the butterflies, waves of the wind, the smooth ebb and flow of the rivers, the sounds and music of birds and animals, etc.

In a very short and crisp lyric the *bagurumba* song gives expression to the mindset, outlook and the cultural ethos of the Bodos and their love of nature from which they draw their sustenance in everyday life. In essence, the Bodo women folk articulate their deepest feelings of love and anxiety saying that if it were not for the cultural ethos by which they swear their allegiance to, the love for their beautiful village/ place she would have followed her heart in matters of love otherwise. However, their love for their culture and nature surpasses all other personal longings of desire and love.

Another important folk dance of the Bodos, *naa gurnai mwsanai* is a dance symbolizing the tradition of fishing by the Bodo women in the lakes, springs and rivulets that dot the landscape of the foothills of the great Himalayas which the Bodos vastly inhabit. It displays the skill of women folk and the bond that it fosters among the fellow women of the villages as they tell stories amongst themselves when they go out for fishing. This folk dance celebrates the bounties of nature, the means of sustenance and livelihood it offers, the skill of Bodo women in fishing and the traditional cuisines of the Bodos, one amongst them being *nafaam* (fermented fish).

In the song a young damsel exhorts her friends to catch hold of a *Jekai*[6] and *Kobai*[7] and go out for fishing in the streams and rivulets of the village showcasing the tribal heritage.

> "*Fwi hai lwgwfwr jekai laa/ Fwi hai lwgwfwr khobai laa*
>
> *Bilw budangao/ Juguru jugurub naa gurni/ Bala habruao dangwrwm dangwrwm samu konni /Haikhang gafa khobai fa/ Obla wngkri ao hwsonggafa/ Obla wngkri ao hwsonggafa/ Jaaya jaalaigwn wngkam gwrlwijwng/ Khaja kou roto roto hai jwnglai khaja kou roto roto*
>
> *Fwi hai lwgwfwr jekai laa/ Fwi hai lwgwfwr khobai laa*
>
> *Haikhanggafa khobaifa/ Orr jwng fwrannawi dwnfwifgafaHiakhangafa khobaifa/ Nafaam denanwi dwntumgafa/ Khumbra bwraijwng songnanwi jaalaigwn/ Bwswr puraijase/ Hai jwnglai bwswr puraijase/ Bwrw bwrw lwgw bwrw bwrw/ Bese burja mwnkw nwngha lwgw/ Bese burja mwnkw nwngha lwgw/ Naa bwtia thurirakeb/ Naatur junai ganda gageb/ Mwna mwnlaibai khobai gwdwnase/ Hai anglai khobai gwdwnase*

Fwi hai lwgwfwr jekai laa/ Fwi hai lwgwfwr khobai laa

Sunna habbai belasibai/ Tudw lwgw noao thangfindini/ Naa sainangou mwigong khanangou/Wngkham wngki songtarnanou

Fwi hai lwgwfwr jekai laa/ Fwi hai lwgwfwr khobai laa"

(collected from an Oral Source: Mr Barlangfa Narzary, an acclaimed Bodo folk artist)

(An English translation of the same would to some extent imply as follows)

Come my friends pick up the *jekai*
Come my friends pick up the *khobai*

Let's go for fishing in the lake
As much as we can
From the moorland and the clear waters
Till we fill up to the brim of the *khobai*
With fishes and snails
And prepare the curry to our delight
And have it with the new rice

Come my friends pick up the *jekai*
Come my friends pick up the *khobai*

Let's go for fishing in the lake
As much as we can
From the moorland and the clear waters
Till we fill up to the brim of the *Khobai*
And dry it, ferment it
And stock it for the whole year
Cook it with the white gourd to savour

Well my friends show me, show me
How much have you caught today
Have you filled it to the brim of the *khobai*

With fishes and prawns
Come my friends pick up the *jekai*
Come my friends pick up the *khobai*

Now the sun is setting, the night is approaching
Let's go back to our homes
Need to pick vegetables from the orchards
And prepare the food for the night

Come my friends pick up the *jekai*
Come my friends pick up the *khobai*

The significance of the dance form is not so much about fishing per se but the fact that the tradition of fishing gives women the scope to share/ ventilate/ express their thoughts, feelings, hopes and aspirations among themselves. For many a poor Bodo household, *naa gurnai* has given a scope for livelihood, for some a hobby and favourite pastime but, the ultimate appeal of this aspect of Bodo tradition is that it gives a platform to women for voicing their grievances.

Another two very significant folk dances of the Bodos are *Baardwi Sikla Mwsanai* and *Dahal-Thungri Mwsanai*. These two folk dances do not have a song and both are performed (only by women) to the beat and tune of *kham, siphung, serja* and *jota* usually played by men. *Baardwi Sikla Mwsanai* (literally meaning the dance of storm-wind lass) follows the web and flow of the storm-wind during the onset of monsoon. During the performance the dancers tap their feet imitating the fall of raindrops and the movements depicts the caressing of the body by the *baardwi* (storm-wind). It is said that this dance symbolises the sensuous side of nature conspiring with a women's physique for fertility and agricultural productivity of the soil. Sexuality and desire of a women's body is aesthetically syncretised with the natural cycle of seasons to express a deeper and concrete aspect of life. The *baardwi* (storm-wind) symbolizing the sexuality, the desire and the raindrops suggesting the menstrual cycle of women's body which are both critical to the sustenance of life on earth.

Dahal-Thungri Mwsanai is originally said to have evolved or developed from the practice of paying obeisance to *Bathou*[8] by the women for protection in battle-field for their men and after the eventual victory in the battle. Performed only by women with a *dahal* (shield) and *thungri* (sword) to the beat of *kham* (drum), *sipung* (flute) and *serja* (stringed musical instrument of the Bodo tribe which looks like a violin) the women show the martial/ warrior side of the primarily agricultural community. In a sense, through the dance, women show their gratitude and respect to their men for putting their lives at stake for the well-being of their women.

However, the significance of the Bodo folk dances goes beyond this usual narrative, and is suitably placed in the gender relations. There is a common thread that runs through these five popular folk dances and this is the predominance of women in the performances. With an exception to the *Bwisagu* dance where men and women dance in equal number and measure all the other folk dances are performed by women with 'marginal' roles by men who are confined to play the traditional musical instruments. The predominance of women in the performances is because nature is considered as an embodiment of the female body which is crucial for the sustenance of life on earth, and by extension of this logic, the very survival of culture itself. Therefore, the female body becomes a medium of expression and means of sustenance of a culture. Folk dance by the Bodo women is a performativity of gender norms in the traditionally patriarchal social set-up of the Bodo society. The woman's body is used as a canvass and frame for expressing/ articulating the cultural heritage and ethos, and to situate them in the patriarchal social hierarchy. The ability to perform these folk dances with poise and grace is seen as an accomplishment of ideal womanhood. More or less, every woman is expected to conform to this norm in the traditional Bodo society which is in a sense an imposition from without on the women a certain trait/ norm of subjectivity based on a patriarchal cultural norms. Through the dance performances the patriarchal society is basically assigning 'gender roles' to women.

In the *Bwisagu* performances there is usually a kind of light hearted bantering among men and women. These light-hearted bantering gives women a little space to express their mind without hurting the sentiments of the other sex, which in normal circumstances are not acceptable in a polite society. In a traditional social set-up of the Bodos, under 'normal' circumstances women are supposed to remain silent and demure in front of their male counterparts 'performing' the role of an 'ideal' woman. It is on this occasion of *Bwisagu* festival that women are allowed a window to be themselves and not perform gender roles assigned to them for a brief period of time.

The *Bagurumba* dance ironically conveys that the women themselves inspite of their assigned gender roles imposed on them by the patriarchal society they are more than willing to abide by this rules by their own sweet accord as it is this custom that holds together their cultural identity, although their hearts now and then desire for the forbidden aspects in life. The *Bagurumba* dance celebrates the voluntary sacrifices that women make in order to keep the culture and traditions of the community alive.

Baardwi Sikla dance, as mentioned earlier, is a dance which celebrates feminity (womanhood) and fertility in an aesthetically rhythmic movement of the body that is syncretised with the natural seasonal cycle to suggest that it is the woman's body and the earth that brings life on this earth, and the pain that it undergoes for this reason are suggested by the *baardwi* (storm-wind) in the process.

Dahal-Thungri Mwsanai is normally read as a dance of obeisance to *Bathou* in times of war. At the cost of banality, however, it may be repeated here that a patriarchal Bodo society expect their women to be submissive and demure but, when the need arises their women are prepared to take up the cudgel (sword & shield) to protect their land and dignity like a man.

These five major folk dance forms of the Bodo tribe are significant because it goes beyond the usual definition of folk dance to reveal the fine prints of gender relations. The tribal societies although patriarchal give space/ room to their women through art/ performances to let themselves be what they are — a woman. It is a performativity by women as themselves, what they essentially are, and a performance that expresses their womanhood.

Notes:

1. From *Folk Dance Tribal Ritual and Martial Forms* by Ashish Mohan Khokar, 2003, p-8.
2. Momaday, N. Scott in the essay 'The Man Made of Words' in The Remembered Earth: An Anthology of Contemporary Native American Literature. Edited by Geary Hobson 1979 University of New Mexico Press, Albuquerque, p-167.

3. Quoted from the book *Of Grammatology* (by Jacques Derrida, (translated by Gayatri Chakravarti Spivak from *De la Grammatologie*), Chapter Two, p-27.

4. Quoted from the essay 'Orality and the Re-enactment of Memory: History, Ritual, and African-Caribbean Resistance *in the Chosen Place, the Timeless People*' by Ashma Shamail in International Journal of Humanities and Management Sciences (IJHMS) Volume 3, Issue 6 (2015) ISSN 2320–4044 (Online) www.isaet.org/images/extraimages/EA0116021%20updated.pdf

5. From *The Collected Essays of A. K. Ramanujan*. Edited by Vinay Dharwadker, New Delhi: Oxford University Press, 1999, p 16,18.

6. Traditional fishing equipment made of bamboo.

7. Traditional equipment to hold fish while fishing.

8. Traditional deity of the Bodos, represented by Sijou plant (euphorbia splendis).

Works Cited:

1. Achebe, Chinua; *Things Fall Apart*, Heinemann Publishers (Pty) Limited, Johannesburg, South Africa, 2000, Reprint.

2. Bauman, Richard & Briggs, Charles L; 'Poetics and Performance as Critical Perspectives on Language and Social Life', Annual Review of Anthropology, Vol. 19 (199), pp. 59-88. Web.

3. Claus, Peter J. & Korom, Frank J; *Folkloristics and Indian Folklore*, Regional Resources Centre for Folk Performing Arts, Mahatma Gandhi College, Udupi, India, 1991, Print.

4. Derrida, Jacques, trans. Gayatri Chakravarti Spivak; *Of Grammatology*, John Hopkins University Press, 1976 (corrected paperback edition). Chapter Two, p-27. Print.

5. Dharwadker, Vinay (ed.); *The Collected Essays of A. K. Ramanujan*, Oxford University Press, New Delhi, 1999, Print.

6. Foley, John Miles (ed); *Teaching Oral Traditions*, The Modern Language Association, New York, 1998, print.

7. Kharmawphlang, Desmond L. & Sen, Soumen; *Orality and Beyond: A North-East Indian Perspective*, Sahitya Akademi, New Delhi, 2007, Print.

8. Khokar, Ashish Mohan; *Folk Dance Tribal Ritual and Martial Forms*, Rupa &Co., New Delhi, 2003, Print.

9. Momaday, N. Scott 'The Man Made of Words'; Hobson, Geary (ed.) *The Remembered Earth: An Anthology of Contemporary Native American Literature*, University of New Mexico Press, Albuquerque, 1979, Print.

10. Shamail, Ashma; 'Orality and the Re-enactment of Memory: History, Ritual, and African-Caribbean Resistance *in the Chosen Place, the Timeless People*', International Journal of Humanities and Management Sciences (IJHMS) Volume 3, Issue 6 (2015) ISSN 2320–4044 (Online)

Legends in Bodo Historiography

Jeetumoni Basumatary

Abstract:

Legends, an important sub-genre of folktales, are considered to be accounts of events of a recent past, which are believed to be true by its tellers and listeners. In his essay "The Way Legends Grow", E.M.R. Ditmas classified between two types of traditions of which one is, "a kind of folk memory which is kept alive by those who have an interest in the recollection of some local event such as a great victory or a disastrous defeat, or of some outstanding personality". A look at the various works published between 1993 (formation of Bodoland Autonomous Council) and 2003 (formation of Bodoland Territorial Council) reveals a conscious attempt at the revival/ retelling of significant Bodo legends. Important works of this period are Chanakya Brahma's *Gwdwni Solo Batha* (1999), Dr. Anil Boro's *Folk Literature of the Boros: An Introduction* (2001), Kameswar Brahma's *An Introduction to the Myths and Legends of the Bodos* (2004), and a series of legends in the novel form by writers like Madhu Ram Boro, Bidyasagar Narzary, etc. While Dr. Boro attempted a theoretical analysis of Bodo folklore, Kameswar Brahma followed suit and worked on Bodo myths and legends. Writers like Madhu Ram Boro and Narzary produced historical novels from the legends of folk heroes to ensure that they are not lost to the community. The decade 1993-2003 and the years that followed, was a crucial point in the history of the Bodo-Kacharis. It was a period of (re)construction of history and recovery of traditions.

My paper would look at the social, political and historical function of the publication of legends such as the narratives of Jwhwlao Dwimalu, Jaolia Dewan, Raja Iragdao, Swmdwn (Sombhudon Kachari), Bigwsri Sikhla and Gambari Sikhla and attempt to determine their roles in the construction of a historical narrative of the much claimed glorious past of the Bodos.

The word 'history' comes from the ancient Greek word 'historia' which means knowledge arrived at through investigation and inquiry. An important element in this inquiry and arrival at knowledge is the practice of recording what has been or has happened in the past. However, history cannot be simply defined as the written record of what happened in the past, because a lot goes into its craft as well as in the choices of sources made during the recording process. History, despite its claims to objectivity is most often subjective and is reliant on the views, perceptions and choices of historical sources made by the historian. Historiography attempts to look at the craft used, the choices made, the validity of the sources used, and the motive of the author in composing the history. It attempts to look not only at the validity of the sources used and facts included, but also at the facts excluded. Therefore, historiography, a study of the process involved in the writing of history, has come to be an important discipline of study.

I am interested in the facts that are excluded from the writing of history, which may survive as oral history and the roles they play in a community or society. Primitive communities are often considered to lack history due to the absence of a written record. This is true of most ethnic and tribal communities. This absence in the written word does not mean that these communities are without a past. Traditions and oral narratives do exist among these people and they are disseminated not through the print media, but orally from one generation to another. In the language of folklorists, these orally transmitted narratives of the past may be called legends, an important sub-genre of folktales.

Legends are considered to be accounts of events of a recent past, which are believed to be true by its tellers and listeners. In his essay "The Way Legends Grow", E.M.R. Ditmas classified between two types of traditions of which one is the legend, "a kind of folk memory which is kept alive by those who have an interest in the recollection of some local event such as a great victory or a disastrous defeat, or of some outstanding personality". William Bascom in his *Contributions to Folkloristics* has defined legends as "prose narratives which, like myths, are regarded as true by the narrator and his audience, but they are set in a period considered less remote, when the world was much as it is today. Legends are more often secular than sacred, and their principal characters are human. They tell of migrations, wars and victories, deeds of past heroes, chiefs, and kings, and succession in ruling dynasties. In this, they are often the counterpart in verbal tradition of written history..." (98).

I cannot say for sure if oral traditions can be considered as valid sources for recording and writing down as history. But, what I can say with confidence is that, oral traditions or legends do play important role in the historiography of communities that live outside the periphery of standard history. Larry Moses in "Legends by the Numbers" identifies legends as those oral histories that have evolved into 'standardized literary form' (74). Communities that have only their oral histories in order to comprehend their past tend to provide much importance to legends which can be told, retold, and improvised as per the social and political demands of the times.

Legends are highly elastic in nature. In the process of making or narrating a folk narrative, there is always a process of ecotypification going on. The term 'ecotypification' was used by the Swedish folklorist Carl Wilhelm von Sydow to refer to the variations folklore undergoes from region to region and culture to culture. Timothy R. Tangherini understands this term as a reference to the "...process where the narrative is variated to fit the needs of the culture and its tradition" ("'It Happened Not Too Far from Here...': A Survey of Legend Theory and Characterization", 378). To this, I want to add time (historical moment), and say that legends constantly undergo a process of adaptation in keeping with the need and importance of the historical moment in which it is narrated. So, the various versions of the same legend might be a result of the demands of various moments in history when it becomes necessary to add, remove or highlight one or another motif in the narrative. My paper would therefore look at the publication history of Bodo legends such as the narratives of Jwhwlao Dwimalu, Jaolia Dewan, Raja Iragdao, Raja Nilambar, Gambari Sikhla and Birgwsri Sikhla and attempt to determine their roles in the construction of a historical narrative of the much claimed glorious past of the Bodos.

Legends, significantly among groups of people, whose stories have often remained outside standard history, constitute a vital component of their ethos.

As a result, while scholars of standard history consider them irrelevant, there is a tendency among the people themselves to give a primary importance to legends and other oral accounts. The traditional belief among the Bodos is that they were the first inhabitants of the Brahmaputra valley and had prosperously ruled the region till the onset of the Ahoms in the 13th century. This belief is validated by referring to the many names of places and rivers such as Dilao, Digaru, Dikhou, Diphlu, etc., all of which begin with the prefix 'di', the Bodo word for water, and therefore apparently hint at a Bodo-Kachari influence. That the Bodo-Kacharis have existed in the eastern part of the Indian subcontinent since ancient times is also validated by referring to the various mentions of the Kiratas in the *Mahabharata*. Despite having a glorious past, and despite the fact that Bodo-Kachari rulers continued to rule parts of Assam till the early 19th century, the Bodo-Kacharis do not have a written history of their own. This is a lament most common in the discourse of Bodo identity politics. These traditional beliefs, no matter how far their validity can be stressed, was the foundation on which the assertion of Bodo identity leaned on and have become a source for the (re)construction of Bodo history.

The earliest works on the Bodo-Kacharis and their social practices did mention a few folktales prevalent among the people. J.D. Anderson's *A Collection of Kachari Folk-Tales and Rhymes* (1895) and Rev. Sidney Endle's *The Kacharis*(1911) are two pioneering works on the Bodo-Kacharis. Interestingly both these works have no mention of the various myths and legends prevalent among the Bodos. This has led to my hypothesis that the telling/retelling of myths and legends are closely tied to the historical moment when it is done and hence to the community's need for an expression of its social or political identity.

From 1960s onwards, there seem to have risen an interest in the study of Bodo culture and traditions. Sukumar Basumatary's *Abou Aboini* Solo (1960), and *Boro-Kachari Solo* (1972) edited by P. Goswami and M. M. Brahma, *Boro-Kacharir Samaj Aru Sanskriti* (1966), *Boro Kacharir Jana Sahitya* (1966), and *Boro Kacharir Gitmat* (1966) by Bhaben Narji, and *Folk Songs of the Bodos* (1960) edited by Mohini Mohan Brahma are some of the books of Bodo folklore. Bodo folklore also made occasional appearances in books like *Folktales of Assam* (1969) by Mira Prakasi, *Ballads and Tales of Assam: A Study of the Folklore of Assam* (1970), *Songs and Tales of North-Eastern India* (1976), and *Tales of Assam* (1980) by Praphulladutta Goswami. It is also around this time that Kamal Kumar Brahma composed the historical play *Raja Iragdao*

(1978) and Dr.Mongolsingh Hazowary composed *Swmdwn* in 1979. Other works that were published around this time and must find mention here are *Sonani Maibang* and *Raja Nilambar*(1993) by Dwarendranath Basumatary, *Sandw Baodia* (1988) by Surath Narzary, *Gambari Sikhla*(1992) by Aniram Basumatary, *Jwhwlao Dwimalu*(1991) and *Jaolia Dewan*(1991) by Dr. Mongolsingh Hazoway.

The emergence of the various oral narratives into the above mentioned texts is significant, because it coincides with various important socio-political moments and events in the history of the Bodo people. The foundation of the Bodo Sahitya Sabha and the movement for and leading to the introduction of Bodo as the medium of instruction in the Government schools of Bodo-dominated areas, the formation of the All Bodo Students Union and then the Plains Tribal Council of Assam in the 1950s and 60s are important milestones in the Bodo's assertion of socio-political identity. In a time which demanded great awareness and consciousness on the part of the people about their Bodo culture and identity, the publication of Bodo folklore in its various forms must have had an important role to play. For, a community's folklore not only reflects the characteristics, customs, traditions and the belief system of a community, but also "give us an understanding of the identity and self perception of (the) people, how they position themselves both with regard to their natural environment and how they respond to the encroachment of outsiders into their geographical and social space" (Heredia 15-24). The re/appearance of Bodo folklore into text served the important function of not only reminding the Bodo people about their rich cultural heritage, but also articulating to the world beyond, the Bodo's perception of the self.

Historical plays like *Raja Iragdao* (1978), *Swmdwn* (1979), *Sonani Maibang* (1992), *Raja Nilambar*(1993), *Gambari Sikhla*(1992), *Jwhwlao Dwimalu*(1991) and *Jaolia Dewan*(1991) are based on legends that provide important lessons of heroism and patriotism that instilled in the Bodo man's heart, love and pride for his culture and race. These legends tell us about the heroic exploits of local heroes and chiefs, and are believed to be true by the folks among whom these stories are told. They are informative in nature and as such, functions as "verbal traditions of written history". The stories surrounding the great 19th century Bodo heroes of Western Assam such as Jaolia Dewan, Sikhna Jwhwlao, Birgashri Sikhla and Gambari Sikhla, gives us an idea of the state of the western part of the province as well as about the people inhabiting this region in the 19th century. But, what is more interesting is the appropriation (if I may say so), of legendary figures such as Jwhwlao Dwimalu, Raja Iragdao (Gobinda Chandra), and Swmdwn (Sombhudhon Kachari) of the Dimasas of the North Cachar Hills. The fact that these Dimasa heroes and legendary figures are spoken in one breath along with other Bodo heroes of western Assam serves the narrative of a great Bodo-Kachari race that includes the Bodo-Kacharis, the Dimasas of North Cachar Hills, the Kok-Boroks of Tripura and Sonowal Kacharis among others. It is significant that plays based on Raja Iragdao, Swmdwn and Jwhwlao Dwimalu appeared among the Bodo-Kacharis when it became pertinent for them to hark back to a historical (and royal) past in order to validate their cultural and political assertions.

I would also like to mention here, the various works published between 1993 (formation of Bodoland Autonomous Council) and 2003 (formation of Bodoland Territorial Council) and thereafter, reveals a conscious attempt at the revival/retelling of significant Bodo legends. Important works of this period are Chanakya Brahma's *Gwdwni Solo Batha* (1999), Dr. Anil Boro's *Folk Literature of the Boros: An Introduction* (2001), Kameswar Brahma's *An Introduction to the Myths and Legends of the Bodos* (2004), and a series of legends in the novel form by writers like Madhu Ram Boro, Bidyasagar Narzary, etc. While Dr. Boro attempted a theoretical analysis of Bodo folklore, Kameswar Brahma followed suit and worked on Bodo myths and legends. Writers like Madhu Ram Boro and Narzary produced historical novels from the legends already prevalent in the community. Kamal Kumar Brahma's *Raja Iragdao* which was first published in 1978, saw three more editions in 1994, 1999 and 2004. Dwarendranath Basumatary's *Sonani Maibang* and *Raja Nilambar* were brought out in their second editions in 2008. Aniram Basumatary's *Gambari Sikhla*, which was written in the Assamese script in 1992, was republished in 2007 in the Devanagri script (used by the Bodo language). Dr. Mongolsingh Hazowary's *Jaolia Dewan* and *Swmdwn* too returned to the readers' world in 2011. Not only new works were published, but also the older texts of the 1970s and early 90s were revisited.

The decade 1993-2003 and the years that followed, was a crucial point in the history of the Bodo-Kacharis. It was a period of (re)construction of history and recovery of traditions, and this time, the audience aimed at, was the larger world outside that of the Bodos or the Assamese. The aim was to portray the Bodo-Kachari community as one that has a rich cultural heritage and glorious political history and thereby, legitimise its demand for a separate state. The need of the hour was the portrayal of the community as a civilized people with a history, and with its roots buried deep in the soil of the Brahmaputra valley. This need was fulfilled by selectively appropriating, highlighting, shaping and reshaping traditional materials (oral narratives).

We all know folktales provide a huge degree of amusement to the listeners as well as the narrators. But that is not all the function of folklore. Folklore, Bascom says, "cannot be dismissed simply as a form of amusement." Though amusement is one of the important functions of folklore, beneath it there is a much 'deeper meaning' (55). This is truer of legends which represent the unwritten oral history of a community. Legends not only function as oral history among the Bodo-Kacharis, by providing to the people an idea of their past, but is often used by them to assert their identity. The remembrance of its past glory enables the community to be inspired and make an effort to regain it. Whenever the need arose, scholars, activists and politicians invoked the past and attempted to reassert their claim to the region. This is where I want to reiterate the point made by E.M.R. Ditmas that legends are "a kind of folk memory which is kept alive by those who have an interest in the recollection of some local event such as a great victory or a disastrous defeat, or of some outstanding personality". Folklore, despite its seeming distance from the political is not completely free from politics. Therefore, in her essay "The Political Face of Folklore – A Call for Debate", Joann Conrad draws her readers' attention to the problems that lie in "...an uncritical approach (to folklore) and (tries) to appeal to folklorists in general to acknowledge the politicized and politically motivated nature of folklore and folklorists' roles in it" (409).

Bibliography

Amos, Ben. "Towards a Definition of Folklore in Context." *The Journal of American Folklore*, 84.331 (1971):3-15. JSTOR. 6 Jun. 2009 <http://www.jstor.org/stable/539729>.

Bascom, William R. *Contributions to Folkloristics*. Meerut: Archana Publications, 1981.

Boro, Dr. Anil. *Folk Literature of the Boros: An Introduction*. Guwahati: Adhunik Prakashan, 2001.

Choudhury, Sujit. *The Bodos: Emergence and Assertion of an Ethnic Minority*. Shimla: Indian Institute of Advanced Study, 2007.

Cochrane, Timothy. "The Concept of Ecotypes in American Folklore." *Journal of Folklore Research*, 24.1 (1987): 33-55. JSTOR. 24 Feb. 2016.Web.

Conrad, Joann. "The Political Face of Folklore – A Call for Debate." *The Journal of American Folklore,* 111.442 (1998): 409-413. JSTOR. 06 May. 2016 Web.

Ditmas, E.M.R. "The Way Legends Grow." *Folklore*, 85.4 (1974): 244-253. JSTOR. 17 Mar. 2009. Web.

Goswami, Praphulladatta. "Demalu" and "Mainong Buri the House Goddess", *Tales of Assam*. Guwahati: Assam Publication Board, 1980.

Heredia, Rudolf C. "Tribal History: Living Word or Dead Letter?" *Economic and Political Weekly*, 35.18 (2000): 1522-1525. JSTOR. 18 May 2009 <http://www.jstor.org/stable/4409227>.

Klapp, Orrin E. "The Folk Hero." *The Journal of American Folklore*, 62.243 (1949): 17-25. JSTOR. 28 May 2009 <http://www.jstor.org/stable/536852>.

Moses, Larry. "Legends by the Numbers: The Symbolism of Numbers in the 'Secret History of the Mongols." *Asian Folklore Studies*, 55.1 (1996): 73-97. JSTOR. 17 Mar. 2009. Web.

Pegu, Jadav. *Reclaiming Identity:A Discourse on Bodo History*. Kokrajhar: Jwngsar, 2004.

Tangherlini, Timothy R. "'It Happened Not Too Far From Here…': A Survey of Legend Theory and Characterization." *Western Folklore*, 49.9 (Oct. 1990): 371-390. JSTOR. 24 Feb. 2016.Web.

---. "Legends and Legend Scholarship". *Interpreting Legend (RLE Folklore):Danish Storytellers and Their Repertoires*. Routledge, 2015.

The Oral-Literary transition:Bharath: An Epic of the Dungri Bhil

Jyoti Brahma and BhaskarJyotiGogoi

Orality

The signature line of Kabir: *Kahe Kabir suno* is remarkably well remembered and quoted amongst millions of Hindi speakers. By these lines Kabir calls attention to his own orality, and he repeatedly tells us that the ultimate experience of reality is in the sound, one that is profoundly different from those we ordinarily hear, yet still sound – the *anahadnād* (often translated as "unstruck sound", but more closely rendered as "boundless sound"). His style of poetry is uniquely associated with the *vocative* consisting of frequent direct addresses, questions and challenges to the listener reader-which emphasizes the oral character of his communication.

The direct development of Kabir traditions has been alive and transforming since he composed orally nearly six centuries ago. Most scholars of Kabir think it likely that he never wrote. This did not mean that they reject any kind of his written works lately but believe that the words of Kabir lived mainly through the voices of people who carried forward his legacy by singing and through recitation. They in turn made meaning out them and also changed them. Thus, in order to know Kabir, the series of conveyance (like packed in closely with a large crowd over roads, rails and trails through heat, cold and rain etc.) needs to be kept in mind while tacking the traditions of Kabir or for that matter any other living oral traditions of India. The experience of a place and it's worlds of meaning, discovering the relationships of texts, foods, social organizations, music, weather has to be absorbed and felt to get an inkling or understanding of any oral traditions. In oral tradition, there is no such thing as text without context. The contexts in the study of these oral traditions are the meaning makers and the interpreters of the text which is actually also the context.

From ancient times, great story-tellers and their stories were honoured and has been a rich source of wisdom for many cultures of the world. Evenin India, we have many storytelling traditions like the Pandvani, Harikatha, the Villu-Pattu, Burra Katha, Powada, the Baul and the Rathva communities among many others. One of the significant features of Indian culture is the presence of these rich, diverse and complex oral story-telling traditions. Orality is a significant presence and is universal as they have their dominant or subtle characteristics in many of the present as well as past cultures. It can be simply meant as a tradition, which has no textual antecedent. But, on the other hand if it's textual antecedent of a variant is found, it is assumed or often considered as the source of all later textual efforts of that variant.

Oral narratives of India have been not only a source of entertainment and recreation but also have been a part of the larger philosophical thought encompassing several major religious traditions. These oral narratives have been very significant in the dissemination of religious faith and practices. Oral literature can give us analogies to wide-ranging problems concerning folk-life and their history and relation to myths and rituals. The problematic arises especially for the oral/folk communities of India that is scattered in various parts of India. Of the major epics that have shaped the Indian sensibility, the Mahabharata is an oral epic. So were the puranas, in their initial stage. So, the possibility of regarding *Bharath* an epic of the DhungriBhils as transitional texts represents the culmination of a long tradition of oral poetry transmitted and sung by *sutas,* or bards.

Oral/ Literary Transition

No discussion of the oral/literary today can be complete without some consideration of the role of folk and classical. According, to A.K.

Coomaraswamy's folkloreinIndiais not similartothat of the classicaltraditions in Europe.In other words, Coomaraswamyasserts that in Europe folk and classical traditions are separate, whereas in India they share a common base. (14 Ramanujan). This is also perhaps the reason for the occasionally contradictory interpretation of the oral/literal transition.

The process of poetic composition as well as the conventions of literary reception was profoundly influenced throughout the history of India by the orality of literature. The principle mode of literary transmission was oral; but not all compositions were entirely oral. The meaning of orality itself was inadequately severed from its foundation. Certain kinds of Indian poetry have subsisted in oral tradition for centuries. But, these oral narratives have also a counterpoint and the division is between what is socially acceptable and what is not. This distinction gets expressed in the division of "folk" and the "classical", *Margi* and *Desi* or *Vaidic and Laukik*. The term *Desi* designates local or popular and *Margi* as highway styles represents the all-India paradigm. But, the irony of the contrast is that it is often used by the scholars but rarely by the folk themselves as an indigenous Indian expression of a folk /classical contrast. This position of division or the task of separating the folk from the classical is problematic in discussing the very seminal folk genre. The "folk" is ever evolving, open to rapid change with its flexible nature while the "classical" is conceptualized as structured and inflexible. Though it is certainly difficult not to compare it, the point remains thatthe folk and the classical in India share a common base and can be firmly located within it.

In India, we had simultaneous development of two streams of literature: the classical and the folk. The first stream constitute of the Vedas followed by the *Upanishads*, the latter followed by the epics and the epics followed by the *Mahapuranas*, the *Upapuranas* and the *Sthalapuranas.* The second stream constitute of *Brihatkatha* of Gunadhya later reincarnated as the *Kathasaritasagar* of Somdeva, the *Panchatantra* of Vishnusharma and the series of *Jataka-tales.* We should realize and fairly be sure that such parallels do also establish borrowings. The case of the "folk" becoming "classical" happens through a process of appropriation. All the so-called classical forms were once mixed, hybrid, confluential and folk. Once absorbed into the upper caste/class discourse, their disorderly worldview came to be leveled out and subjected to a canon.

In between these two streams of literature (*Vaidik* and *Laukik*), there developed an exclusive oral tradition, which clearly gave birth to a different genre. There were also pragmatic tales of both personal creativity and the necessity to solve the problem of everyday practical life. These tales were narrated by the wandering hermits and the mendicants to households. For example, *Tales told by Mystics* by Manoj Das is a retelling of a collection of tales that mostly prevailed as oral traditions and were used by the lost tribe of wandering mendicants to educate and enlighten the folks. These stories become diluted into a modern version codified by the transcreators of the regional version of our epics, the *Mahabharata* in particular like *Male Madeswara* of Kannada. So is also the case of *Bhilo nu Bharath*, the folk epic tradition, which resonates with the influence of *Mahabharata*. The over-powering oral tradition has flourished ever since it could not simply stop remaining oral. In the discussion on the "folk", the point needs to be highlighted that the folk is embedded in the oral as well as the written tradition. There is a co-relation in discussing the oral and written because it is expanded and exerts its influence back and forth. Walter J. Ong's *Orality and Literacy* gives a clear distinction between oral and the written; oral is often contrasted with the written. Whether narratives are oral or written on a palm leaf or on paper they are produced and circulated within human networks. Even when they are written narrative, pre-modern traditions still carry the legacy of oral delivery or aurally receiving processes. Literary and non-literary texts were presumably recorded as scripts in India in the fifth century B.C. In another sense poets recorded their texts in the palm leaves through the known scripts. Scholars have kept them alive by reproducing them. With the printing technology in India written records gradually replaced the oral tradition. But, nevertheless it could never be replaced completely. With the development of printing technology, the folk and classical traditions are transmitted and transformed. So, in reality the contrast is not on oral/written but oral/written/printed.

Bharath: An Epic of the Dungri Bhil

Epics are a living phenomenon in India. Epic performers carried and still carry out the epic tradition narrating and singing epics. Epic is a cultural narrative that embodies and highlights the cultural norms, and values enveloping heroism. The epic needs to be seen as a mega-story that contains a multitude of narratives of India, which shaped our culture. However, it is necessary to see a contrast between the different types of epic, which have passed from generation to generation by word or mouth. These types of "oral" or "primary" epics (such as Homer's *Illiad* and *Odyssey*) are known as folk epic. And, the epics that were composed with a pen like Virgil's *Aeneid* and Milton's *Paradise Lost* are known as "literary/secondary" epics. The folk epic better known as oral epic is referred by Felix J. Oinas's definition that "Folk epic (or oral) epic songs are the narrative poems in formulaic and ornamental style dealing with the adventures of extraordinary people." (Oinas 98)

The text *Bharath: An Epic of the Dungri Bhil* compiled and edited by Dr. Bhagwandas Patel translated by Nila Shah is the compilation of a living oral narrative tradition of the Dungri Bhil tribes living in the Khedbrahma and Danta districts near the northern border of Rajasthan and Gujarat. The orally transmitted *Bharath* are composed partly in prose and partly in verse. It is apparently hymns, lyrical in form and devotional in content that interiorize the narrative structuration. Dr. Bhagwandas Patel offers a minutely detailed socio-cultural interpretation of the narratives. These narratives are not meant for entertainment only but are also an integral part of the Bhil's cultural and social rituals. The narrative is called *bhajanvarta* and the chapters are called *pankhadi,* meaning petals. The Bhils perceive the narrative as a lotus flower that opens gradually and blooms with the recitation of each petal. Different *pankhadis* or episodes are sung while performing social or religious rites and rituals. The plot and structure are on the whole very simple. *Bharath* is an illuminating text, mainly on its account of its clarity and exposition of the idea of the Bhili world. The transmutations reveal to us the world of the tribal Bheels throughthe story and characters of the *Mahabharata*but also far beyond and sometimes completely different from the *Mahabharata.*

The main story of the Bhili *Bharat* is the same as the main story of the *Mahabharata.* But there are episodes, which are distinctly different. For example, the *Gita* is not included in the Bhili *Bharat.* Even the Satyavan and Savitri episode and the NalaDamyanti episode do not come in the Bhili *Bharath.* Interestingly the stories integrated into the folk epic, continued to function as independent tales after becoming part of the epic. The style and the local colour of the *Bharath*evoke the tribal ethos, though the emotional economy of *Bharath*is no less complex than the Sanskrit epic. The stylistic feature of *Bharath*is like Vyasa's direct narration. There is a sense of directness in the *Bharath* where the language is unembellished and is something similar like Vyasa's characteristic style. For example:

Once upon a time, a frog embarked on the pilgrimage to the river Ganga. He came across a big city on his way. While he was strolling around in the marketplace, a herd of cows happened to come that way. The frog tried to leap clear of the way but he could not do so. He was trampled by the cow. He died and his soul could enter into the womb of a Bania's wife which gave birth to a baby boy after nine months and nine days. The boy grew up into a bright young man eager for job. So, he seeks a job from the greatest man Indra from Indrapuri. 'Why have you come here', Indira inquired. 'Whichcommunity do you belong to?' 'Sir, I have come in search of work,' replied the youth. Indra employed the boy. One day there occurred an incident when the Bania's son was cleaning his teeth with a *datan*. He saw the sweeper woman busy doing her work. He then decided to adopt her as his sister and in return as a token gifted her clothes of gold. One day when the sweeper woman wore this, Indra saw it and asked her about the golden sari. She replied the bania servant has given her. Then when the trader boy confesses, he was dismissed from his job. But he demanded his due salary to Indra. He was given bags filled with money. (pp. 3-5 Patel)

It is no coincidence that *Bharath*, which means "war" in Dhungri Bhil languagederived from (Maha)bharata. Dr. Bhagwandas Patel, the scholar documented and made available *Bharath* to Gujarati literary world. The *Gujarati Bhilo nu Bharat/ Bharath* is loaded with a charm of rusticity balancing with its elemental epic quality and simplicity of the typical tribal life. *Bharath*must have undergone a "transitional period" in which oral and written cultures overlapped. In the case of the *Bharath*, the endeavor of the writers or "writing storytellers" to transform the oral stories into written texts would have to be considered as a kind of transition.

Therefore, we could assume that the endlessness of the epic material was not accidental. Dr. Bhagwandas Patel, in presenting these criteria for Bhili folk epic poetry in between 1984 to 1987 states that all the episodes of the epic *Bhilo nu Bharath* or Bharath were recorded on four hundred audio cassettes.

The oral/literary transition of the *Bharath* deals in a very subtle state and it draws and studies the poetry and culture of the still popular epic traditions through the lens of oral-performative traditions without the prompt apprehension of the written collections. Although it sometimes focuses on texts- their transmission by singers, and the dynamics of textual forms in oral performance, and the connections between texts in oral forms, written forms and other media cannot be ignored. Thus, the main contribution to this text is this transgression of the limits of usage about epic poetry from oral/literal transition.

Moreover, *Bharath* from its general nature of being anepic is replete with various kinds of knowledge as part of the folk wisdom. It plays a paramount significance in the Dungri Bhili context. In fact all the redactions of the *Bharath*agree remarkably in their form and content and with transformations and assimilationsbecome a single work. However, to deal with the genres of folk poetry and oral poetry, especially of the indigenous people like the Bhil tribes near the northern border between Rajasthan and Gujarat, it will be a self-defeating exercise if we cannot be a context sensitive. It is interesting to note that the recitation of the epic by the Bhil community is made in the public sphere, where everyone participates in the performance. During the celebration called *Bij*, a *mandala* via- a drawing of a particular pattern is made on a piece of cloth with white grains that depicts scene from the epic. Figures of the moon, sun, the Pandavas, Lord Hanuman, Vasuki (serpent God), cow, and horse among others are made. The constructed aspect of the folk epic scene creates a deep spiritual impact which is superimposed by the Bhils mentality. However in practice, they cannot ignore the crowd and the excited people during the performance *huro*, where this rite is performed only after the murder of one's kin is avenged. It cannot deny the most loved liquor under whose spell establishes the Bhils to let out a typical shriek called *kikiyari*. It relates to the fact of reality experience, which creates the atmosphere of valor in an appealing way. During that time episodes of bravery are sung. 'Karan, the Pandav', 'Dhofa and 'Vasang', 'Iko, the Danav Prince', 'Distribution of Land', 'Cloak of fire', 'Mighty Bow and Arrow', 'The skin of Rhino' are narrated on this occasion. Although the core of the epic remains unchanged, the idiom may alter according to the situation with time and occasions so that their cultural and social needs are fulfilled. It suggests a considerable degree of analytical thinking and acts as a part of the ritualistic nature of the Bhils. It is well known that some of the longer narratives are seldom sung or performed at a stretch from the beginning to the end. The apparent conflation of the *Bharath* is extraordinary in its extent and profundity. The episode of Dhofa and Vasang (Vasuki) the serpant king has been glorified in the Bhil *Bharath* whereas the character of Vasang (Vasuki) has been marginalized in the standard text. Even the story of the rape of Draupadi by the serpent king Vasuki is a new addition by the Dhungri Bhils. It quotes:

Vasang lifted the queen to her bed.
He lifted the queen to her bed.

He laid Dhofa on a high couch.
The queen tried to free herself in vain.
She tried to free herself in vain.
She struggled to get free. (pp. 78 Patel)

The text *Bharath* holds that "Gods and Goddesses behave as human beings" and share similar emotions like hatred, love, jealousy and other passions. Later in the same incident it is showsDraupadi as a woman who has quite willingly subjected to sexual ravishing. However this addition also could be matter from the oral/literary transition.

In outlining these points *Bharath*as a culturally embedded text does not have its own limitations. It is in some manner 'transformed' by the certain complex cultural phenomena while translating. An oral narrative, when transferred into a written text becomes static. For this reason, it is potentially misleading to ignore the fact that any oral narration owes its existence to many factors including active responses of the audience, mental state of the narrator at the time of narration, musical instrument etc. The latter affirms that who cannot access to the oral narratives has to take the help of the written source.

Even the convention of women being submissive or passive in relation to men is absent. It also treats the exceptional beauty of Draupadi with the beautiful description of golden hair and milky white complexion. Accordingly many of the socio-religious events have Dhofa (Draupadi) as the dispenser, ruling over all. In the folk epic Jethodar (Yudhisthir) acknowledges the power of a rapidly transforming woman Draupadi as Devi and performing aarti of Dhofa and worshipping her. Bhim, spying in from the arched window disliked what he saw and in furry wanted to kill his Bhabi (sister in law) or bhaiyya (brother) or himself.

He said remorsefully 'O mother, you and our bhabi are witches (dayyan).

This shows the great use a writer can make of a fable in a very interesting way. And its interest lies in the study to foreground the ideologies or the worldviews these narratives promote. There are two arguable implications (a) that the various tribes in Kheddanta can be clubbed together; and (b) that they will share a common world view.

Conclusion

To conclude it may be noted that the transgressive position of Indian folklore helps us to understand that the forms and features of the folk may be unique, but on some deeper levels its conceptual structure may have classical analogues. Thus, the transition of the epic from it's oral to it's literary forms is not a simple transformation whereby the folk epic was transmitted orally among a certain generation and got written down as it progressed down through subsequent generations. The transition is much more complex as is exhibited through the case example of the Bheel Mahabharata. The folk rendition of the Mahabharata prevalent among the Bheel community shows certain borrowings as well as conflicting standpoints to the Sanskrit/Classical version of it. Thus, the transition is not a simple borrowing or a radical retelling of the earlier version but is more of a process of mutual interactions. In the process of it being written down too it might have undergone tremendous changes in terms of it's stylistics and treatment of thematic concern to the classical version. Moreover, the folk also exhibits how the text in the case of the folk is more of a performance than being a "text" in it's written mode. In this process of transformation and transition it also becomes part of the culture and borrows from the locale setting, modes of thinking, values and traditions of the people concerned to become an integral part of the communal way of life of the community.

BIBLIOGRAPHY

- Dick, Ernest S. "The Folk and Their Culture" in Alan Dundes *Folklore: Critical Concepts in Literary and Cultural Studies.* Voume I. Routledge, New York. 2005. Print.
- Handoo, Jawaharlal. Honko, Lauri (Ed.) *The Epic: Oral and Written.* CIIL, Mysore. 1998. Print.
- Hess, Linda. *Bodies of Song.* Oxford University Press, New York. 2015. Print.
- Patel, Bhagwandas (Ed.) Nila Shah (Trans.) *Bharath: An Epic of the Dungri Bhils.* CIIL, Vadodara. 2012. Print.
- Ong, Walter J. *Orality and Literacy.* Routledge, New York. 2002. Print.

- Ram, Uma. Ram, K.S. *Tribal Songs, Ballads and Oral Epics of Bastar.* B.R. Rhythms, Delhi.2012. Print.
- Rao, Velcheru Narayan. "Epics and Ideologies: Six Telegu Folk Epics" in Blackburn, Stuart H., A. K. Ramanujan (Ed.) *Another Harmony: New Essays on the Folklore of India.* Oxford University Press, Delhi. 1986. Print.
- Sharma, Nabin Chandra. *Essays on Folklore of North-Eastern India.* Bani Prokash.Guwahati.1988.

A Study of a Bodo Urban Legend 'Sakondra'

Arnan Basumatary

Abstract:

Oral traditions of story-telling are in decline world-wide and that they have virtually disappeared from industrialized societies. Sakondra or child kidnapper, is a mythical figure among the Bodo community. The exploits of Sakondra, kidnapping children, which was once extant among the Bodos is now fast diminishing. Stories of Sakondra were orally transmitted to convey not morality, but sociability. It has been observed that, with modernization, Sakondra has updated and transformed, according to the time and setting of the environment. These are told, usually in informal settings, such as parties, as "really really true" stories of events that were reported in the media or actually happened to a "friend of a friend". One of the most interesting aspects of these "true" stories is that, although they often deal with modern situations and involve the latest technology, they are based on motifs that can be traced back to other cultures and even back to ancient myths and legends. Representative stories from neighbouring areas, reveal similar stories prevalent among many communities. In this study, an earnest attempt will be made to discuss, the common characteristics and motifs existing between the stories, not only of nations widely removed from each other by time and distance, but also neighbouring areas. Also, transformation of Sakondra with changing times.

Keywords- Urban legend, Bodos, Stories, Motifs, Belief.

Introduction

Oral traditions of story-telling are in decline world-wide, and that they have virtually disappeared from industrialised societies is what most people seem to believe, particularly those who see the trend as one of the evils of modern life, and who blame this deplorable situation on the advent of various electronic media. The assumption, then, is that people just don't sit down and tell each other stories any more. Folklorists, however, think otherwise. They have recognised and identified certain type of stories in oral circulation throughout the world which they have named as "urban legends". These are told, usually in informal settings, such as parties, as "really really true" stories of events that were reported in the media or actually happened to a "friend of a friend".

One of the most interesting aspects of these "true" stories is that, although they often deal with modern situations and involve the latest technology, they are based on motifs that can be traced back to other cultures and even back to ancient myths and legends. The fact that these stories, recounted as actual events, are in fact part of an oral culture of "urban legends" which has been popularised by folklorist Jan Harold Brunvand in The Vanishing Hitchhiker (1981). The Choking Doberman (1984) and The Mexican Pet (1986). The urban legends reveal many striking resemblance from age to age and from land to land, which lead us to realise that we are dealing everywhere with essentially the same human activity, and that the interest in a story is practically universal. Similarity in stories exists not only of nations widely removed from each other by time and distance, but also between those which are situated closely.

Oral tradition expresses self-identity and upholds social organizations, religious practices, ethical values and customary laws. While being a wealthy repository of mythical, legendary and historical past, it provides examples for the sustenance of contemporary social order. It articulates protest and dissent and simultaneously voices concerns of reform and redress. Orality is a complex phenomenon which configures its own ways and means of expression and transmission. It is that great highway of information where an exciting information of ideas, forms and styles takes place at different levels, creating processes and dialogues with inter-linkages between form and content, genre and theme, visual and aural, local and regional, traditional and contemporary.

Bodos, who are numerically and sociologically one of the most important tribes of North-Eastern India, particularly Assam have a host of folktales, legends, myths, songs, proverbs and riddles which have not been fully explored, preserved and brought to light. They live and breathe in their folk beliefs, institutions, practices, folklore and art. The oral lore of the Bodos date back to the primitive age about which our written history is completely in the dark. But it is inherent in the lives of the folk, although the growing multitude of the educated and enlightened section amongst them have tended to neglect and get rid of them. It is still the key to understand the folk around us. Bodos. J.D Anderson observed, "The river names of the whole Brahmaputra valley are Bodo names, and it is demonstrable that the Bodos were the aborigines of the valley." The Bodos are mainly agricultural people. They dwell near rivers. Their religion reveals the way of life and relationship with nature.

Objectives of the Study

a) To analyse the Sakondra tales extant among the Bodos.
b) To bring into focus how these tales have common characteristics and motifs.
c) To collect information on the urban legend and rumour of Sakondra as these tales are fast diminishing due to the impact of modernization.
d) The study focuses on the strong link which exists between rumours and urban legends. The relationship between rumours and urban legends cannot be denied. These two work in tandem and are dependent on each other for its sustenance.

Methodology

Datas for this study have been collected by conducting survey and interviews with informants from Kokrajhar town, Patgaon, Simbargaon and Samthaibari. Also, field survey was tried in Bhutan, but immigration officials did not issue necessary permit to interview the common people. Royal Government of Bhutan made announcement, 'warning' the general public not to talk about 'khegpa'. Most of the datas on Bhutan were gained from reliable internet sources. Photographs of various bridges and dams were taken during the field-work. Most of the materials for the study were collected through secondary analysis from books and internet sources. Participant observation was used to some extent in collecting the oral narratives.

What exactly is an Urban Legend? The term itself, is hard to define, as well as being quite a misnomer. Brunvand himself would rather call them "modern legends", since they are not restricted to cities (Brunvand,1984, ix). However in view of the antiquity of some of the basic themes, even that term will come to seem inappropriate. "Really Really True Stories" is cumbersome, yet, provided that we remember to include the all important ironic quotation marks, it captures the essential concept, and also helps to identify the genre immediately to anyone who has ever heard one of these legends. "Urban Legends", however is what folklorists are calling them, and, thanks to the popularity of Brunvand's books and television appearances, that is probably how they will be known for a long time.

The most effective way to recognize them is to be given a few examples. Most people will recognize at least one; then, all that remains is to demonstrate that, though they will undoubtedly have heard it told as a true account of something that happened to a friend of a friend of the teller, in fact the same story or a close variant of it has been collected by folklorists over several decades and in every part of the world. The clincher here is the statistical unlikelihood of the same specific details having happened to dozens of different people in different decades on different continents.

Characteristics of Urban Legend

1. They are "true"

Of all the characteristics of urban legends, the most striking is the teller's insistence that they are "true". This is a central and essential element. In fact, the teller's over-insistence on this element is often the main clue to an experienced listener that he is hearing an urban legend.

2. They are primarily oral

Urban legends are oral by nature, even though they can eventually appear in print; if nowhere else, at least in books about urban legends. More commonly they are found in newspapers and on television, in letters to advice columns and in "human interest" segments. Sakondra type of stories is found in the oral form. The oral origin of Sakondra is by no means a proven fact, but rather is assumed to be true on the basis of pretty convincing circumstantial evidence. This includes their short, incidental quality, and the fact that very few of them can be traced directly to written sources. In addition, the decidedly "gossipy" flavour noted in many of the stories indicates they were probably in oral circulation before being recorded.

3. They are short

Urban legends are short because they have to be remembered by the hearer in order to be passed on, and the same is true originally for *sakondra*, perhaps for the same reason. This is one of the characteristics to distinguish them from other oral traditions of storytelling, such as the epic poem or narrative. In those traditions, of course, astounding feats of memorisation were commonplace, but they were the preserve of professionals. Each urban legend relates essentially only one incident, and there is virtually no character development or complication of plot. This imitates the casual conversational style we use in daily life to report actual incidents. The three main characteristics of sakondra, all of which naturally apply to urban legends, and the first two of which emphasise their brevity:

1. They are generally short, taking no more than five or six written pages.
2. They are centred around some event, and the emphasis is on this event rather than the hero. Titles are thus often of the "How so-and-so encountered such-and-such and did such-and-such" variety.
3. The event depicted is almost always extraordinary in nature, but it is not something which would have been considered implausible by a contemporary audience.

4. They tend to be linked together

Another interesting parallel is that both genres seem to involve the linking of stories. As urban legends contain many similar motifs, an element in one story often provokes an association with another story and a chain of them ensues.

5. They tend to be unusually detailed

Detail is the spice of any narrative endeavour, fiction or otherwise. Without it a story is bland; it lacks flavour. A further characteristic of the minutiae is that they tend to be concrete. The kind of detail reported is that of dress and setting, including place names. It is quite quickly noticed that there is no psychological subtlety in these stories; the characters are broad stereotypes and the emotions and reactions ascribed to them are just what the audience would naturally impute to them, given the circumstances faced in the stories.

6. They cannot be traced to reliable witnesses

This is the most frustrating of the characteristics; the hardest one for most people to accept. The protestations of truth are so vehement, the witnesses seemingly so easy to trace, that many listeners simply cannot accept that there is usually not a shred of truth to the accounts. In his books, Brunvand gives several pathetic instances of conscientious journalists and curious laymen who spend months, not to mention money, trying to track down the source of a legend, always in vain. They are lured on by the tantalising technique used in telling the stories of implying that verification is just one or two informants away.

Representative Stories

The characteristics shared by certain Bodo tales and urban legends indicate that they are similar genres, but the connection becomes much closer when we find the same detailed motifs appearing in both traditions. It might not be too presumptuous in this light, to claim that urban legends are merely the current evolutionary form of *cubun colo* and similar traditions, or that certain *cubun colo* really are urban legends which have found their way into literature. This is by no means a rare phenomenon, in fact it is quite common. Brunvand mentions urban legends appearing in the works of Chaucer, Nathaniel Hawthorne and Thoreau (Brunvand 1984, 91, 108).

Sakondra: The Child kidnapper

Sakondra is a mythical figure among the Bodo community. He is known by different names in different areas such as *Khegpa* in neighbouring Bhutan.

In Peru, he is known as Pistachos or eyespuller. The *"Pistacho"* legend is scattered throughout an extensive portion of Peru. Besides from being called Pistacho, this character has different names such as *Nakaq, Degollador* and more recently *Sacaojos* (Eyespuller) according to the different regions in which it has been recorded.

Some charecteristics of the Sakondra are listed below:

1. A person who kidnaps children to remove kidney and eyes is a Sakondra. Kidnaps children for sacrifice in the construction of bridges and dams.

2. Physically, he is very tall and well built. He seem to possess great strength making it difficult to catch him. The character is similar to the *'Thlen'* practice among the Khasis of Meghalaya. A Khasi friend narrates, "He is tall and muscular and possess immense strength". Such people are engaged in the kidnapping of children among the Khasis.

3. Sakondra are usually stamped on the lower back of the body. This mark is not noticeable to the common people. Locals believe only police can identify and locate the mark. When a suspected Sakondra is caught by the village folk, the Sakondra is handed over to the police station. However, on finding the mark, police release him secretely. The motive behind releasing the Sakondra by the police administration is not known so far. Sakondra, thus, remains a mysterious figure among the Bodos.

4. A sakondra is believed to possess some form of magic. May be this is one reason, why he remains so elusive and hard to be caught.

5. There are reports of some getting caught but again no record of sakondra can be found in any of the police station. It is impossible to get access to written record of a Sakondra.

6. He is believed to stroll around at daytime carrying a large sack.

7. Mostly seen in black attire.

Laohati Incident

Laohati is located thirty kilometres away from kokrajhar, well known for a mini hydroelectric generating dam and a popular picnic spot. Locals believe, twenty-one human heads were sacrificed for the successful construction of the mini dam. People residing in the vicinity of the dam claimed to have heard sudden shrieks and crying of children at midnight. Here, the time of sacrificing highlights the importance of midnight as the auspicious time for the ritual.

The rumour goes that the person engaged in sacrificing humans is a mysterious person. He is seldom taken out from the hiding place. No one knows about his whereabouts and exact location. Labourers engaged at the construction site are clueless about the location of sakondra. The sakondra is hired especially for activities related to the sacrifice at the makeshift camp of the construction site.

Sakondra stories are believed and spread even today, albeit in a reformed character. Locals further claim, money is kept aside from the sanctioned amount of the construction project. These separate money is the fee to be paid to the sakondra upon successful kidnapping and delivery of the body at the construction site. The F.O.A.F, further claimed that it is impossible to catch a sakondra as he possesses some form of black magic power. The claim of black magic on the part of the narrator may be an assertion of belief to the audience.

A labourer engaged in four laning of national highway 31, claimed a goat was sacrificed on successful construction of a major bridge. On further query on human sacrifice, he said, "practice of human sacrifice occurred earlier but not in the present time."

Bhatarmari Incident

Tulunjoy is the storyteller and a resident of Bhatarmari. He is working as a surveyor in the NTPC plant located at Salakati, 17 km east of Kokrajhar town. He was present at the place of incident after the sakondra left the victim.

The incident occurred in the month between November to December, year 2011, when the weather starts turning little cold after the sweltering summer heat. Also, it is the time when a large number of cricket begin to come out from their holes and fly towards bright lights during night time.

The victim is Tulunjoy's next-door-neighbour. The incident occurred opposite Tulunjoy's house. The victim is a male aged about forty years. He is held as simpleton by the people of Bhatarmari. The victim had absolutely nothing to do. To pass time, he set out from his house in search of crickets near the street light. The cricket chutney called *khusengra bathwn* is one of the favourite delicacies of the Bodos. Since it was slightly cold outside, he wrapped himself with an '*Endi*' shawl. The incident took place between 7:30 – 8:00 p.m.

He was rendered unconscious by the sakondra and the body was dragged to a dark place full of wild vegetation. The plants were crushed by the dragging of the victims body. The sakondra was alone and he attempted to hit the eye of the victim but hit the bone by mistake which resulted in a deep cut above the eye of the victim. The younger brother of the colony chairman came riding a motorcycle at the spot. The flash from the motorcycle headlight towards the Sakondra alerted him. Sensing danger for fear of getting caught, the sakondra abandoned the victim and ran towards Gaurang river. Incidentally, the chairman of the village came across the sakondra, but could do little stop the Sakondra. The chairman later informed the colony people that the sakondra was way taller and physically stronger than him. A lady in the vicinity saw the scuffle but did not dare to rescue the victim since there was no male member of the family at that moment. After the sakondra left the scene of incident, neighbours from the area went to check and found to their horror, the simpleton lying unconscious in a pool of blood. On seeing the nature of the attack, locals concluded, Sakondra's motif was to remove the eye of the victim and sell it off.

Tulunjoy goes on to claim Sakondras are specially hired by doctors from the state of Haryana, Punjab, Delhi and other north-western Indian states to carry out the organ stealing job. This information also validates the claim of the physical description of Sakondra indicating people from outside the local region. Again, the Bhutanese claim the Khegpa to be dark, tall sporting beard, indicative of mainland Indian origin, which we will come across in Bhutanese versions later. He repeatedly asserts his belief oN the existence of Sakondra till date.

School story

During our schooldays we were gripped by the fear psychosis of Sakondra. Parents will warn their children not to venture outside in the fear of Sakondra lurking outside. Sakondras were in the lookout of unsuspecting children. To avoid kidnapping, going out was always in a group. Parents busy dropping and picking up their children out of fear. A incident occurred, when a boy from 4th standard was kidnapped after school hours. The unidentified kidnappers pushed the boy inside a gunny bag and drove away from the school. On reaching river Gaurang, which is only five kilometres away, the boy managed to free himself from the kidnappers. He jumped on the river but survived sans major injury. On his return home and upon query of the incident it was strongly believed that it was the handiwork of the sakondra. The boy left the school and joined another school.

About a decade ago, stories of child kidnapping was rampant in Kokrajhar. Mega construction work was the reason behind clandestine kidnapping of children. This fact is validated by the post liberalisation starting in the 1990s and the subsequent changes in the development scenario in the form of mega construction projects mushrooming. The children were rumoured to be taken to Bhutan. The pillars of Chukka dam and the Lodrai bridge in Bhutan is rumoured to be built by sacrificing children. Same is the case in the Meshka-Leshka project in the Jaintia Hills of Meghalaya. The case of Bhutan is different as majority of the Bhutanese people follow Buddhism, which prohibits killing of any living being. Question arises, "how can such activity take place"? Construction of hydroelectricity dams in Bhutan is mostly undertaken by Indian companies. Indian engineers and labourers, who follow Hindu religion believe in sacrificial rites. It is believed that every natural object such as tree, river, mountain, rain and others have guardian spirits, therefore, it becomes necessary to sacrifice, a gesture to appease the spirits of nature. It is believed that the sacrifice will ensure protection from natural hazards and the structure will remain strong and serve its purpose. Chilling as it sounds, rumour has it that many old bridges and dams in Bhutan have sacrificed human heads installed in the pillars. When the Indian engineers face repeated failures, they start believing in sacrificial power to accomplish the project. In Bhutan, the word *Khegpa* became synonymous with the *Sakondra* in instilling fear among the common people.

Black men stories during July 2012 riot

Suddenly the rumour of black men lurking in towns and villages at night became a common phenomenon. The mysterious black man is believed to move around at night in villages. There were reports of the black men getting caught and killed by the mob. The way he moves, the setting, attacking style indicates that the black men share similar character of Sakondra. On inquiry, the locals claimed the mysterious black men are the illegal Bangladeshis. The homeless illegal Bangladeshis during the riot were believed to be the 'black men'.

Some also claimed that the black men were the Indian soldiers working as spies in the villages to gain information on the whereabouts of the insurgents as there were reports of the insurgents attacking the illegal migrants. Black men rumour reveal how Sakondra type of stories emerge depending on the context of the situation and the physical setting.

Khegpa: Head hunter or myth

The whole neighbourhood was afraid of the rumour that the human head-hunter had arrived in their community. Locally, this mysterious person is called "Khegpa". Parents scare away children in the name of Khegpa in order to keep them indoors. Existence of khegpa could be a myth, rumour or even reality. No one knows for sure. Taw Penjo is well known in eastern Bhutan. He is popular for fraud and deceit. Despite several evidences, he is still a free man. He is known to be immune to legal prosecution because he is speculated to be a person who works for the common purpose. Legend has it that a human head should be installed inside important structures to ward away misfortunes. Ancient bridges in Bhutan are believed to have human head installed inside the foundation. This is a kind of offering to deities to protect bridges from disasters. To fulfil this quest, a khegpa plays an important role to bring human head secretly. For this reason, people fear them.

The local community alleged Taw Penjo to be a Khegpa. He never accepted their allegations; instead, he defended his status and tried to prosecute those people who alleged against him. Taw Penjo kept on gambling and drinking day and night without any source of income. This made people to suspect him. Even his wife agreed that something was wrong with him. She suspected some foul play when he brought home lot of money.

It was a full moon lit night. She was sleeping and she was about to doze off but she heard some strange and unusual cry of a baby. She thought that she was dreaming. She opened her eyes and listened carefully. She heard her baby crying. She confirmed that she wasn't dreaming and the cry was a real one. She was worried when she could not find her two months old baby who was lying beside her. She shivered and her voice stammered.

"Taw, wai Taw...where are you? Our baby is gone," She cried.

"Keep quite! She would be fine. Search carefully and keep quiet," He commanded.

She couldn't do anything. Her conscience froze and her mind was empty. In desperation, she ran outside her house. With moonlight, it was partially visible. She searched around her house for her baby. She finally went behind her house, which had a small window facing a thick forest. There she saw four tall man with turbaned head, all of them wearing thick beards. She gazed carefully and saw her husband Taw passing the baby to those strangers.

"Please help. Someone help me. My husband is a real Khegpa and he is selling my baby to those Indians," She shrieked in desperation. Nobody knew what happened to the baby but few months later, she died.

It was suspected that Taw Penjo had been assigned to bring a human head for the Kurichu dam construction in 1997, which he delayed and he attempted to give his own baby. This story is not based on the evidence or narration. It is part of the rumour Kelzang Dawa heard as a child.

Kurtoe farmers hunt Khegpa:

The villagers are on the lookout for two men in masks, wearing pants and t-shirts who have been knocking on their doors and going around their houses carrying torches every night this week.

All villagers have been sleeping in groups because of the rattling door latches and the torches at night, which have brought much fear and anxiety among us, Kurtoe gup Wangchuk Norbu said. There are about 190 households in the gewog.

He said that, while many were adamant that these men are Khegpas, some believe that they were thieves, taking advantage of the widespread headhunter rumour in many parts of the country.

We are being very careful because while we stay together in groups, these men might vandalise chortens and lakhangs, as the gup said.

The headhunter rumour first started in the mid 1980s. Khegpas are believed to be people in search of childrens heads to be buried under foundations of big constructions, especially hydropower projects.

While many, especially those in urban centres, say that these rumours could have started from elders years ago to frighten children from committing mischief, others say that it started following reports of numerous missing people. The construction of many hydroelectric projects in the country has heightened the khegpa rumour and fear, according to local leaders in the dzongkhags. Chhokhor gup in Bumthang said that all parents are busy dropping and picking their children from school and not letting them outside, with rumours rife about khegpas. A Thimpu resident also got a phone call this week from his parents in Trashigang asking him to warn his younger siblings.

A farmer in Kheri village, Pemagatsel, narrowly missed hitting his neighbour with a stone recently when he saw a man moving in the dark and when he did not respond to his repeated calls, thought he was a khegpa, according to media reports.

While a 27-year old man in Tsirang remains detained for allegedly telling people, especially children, that a headhunter was in the locality to abduct children, a monk in Tsholing village, Lhuentse, was also arrested and interrogated recently because villagers suspected him to be khegpa. The police let him go because we confirmed that he was new to the village and mentally unsound, said Lhuentse dzongda, Tshering Kezang.

The dzongda said that he got numerous reports from other parts of Lhuentse, I have asked them not to panic but be vigilant and report any suspicious incidents and characters to various authorities, he said adding that movement in Lhuentse town has also decreased, especially in the evenings. A new Bhutanese film was being shown in the town area but the producers were disappointed because nobody came to watch the movie.

Conclusion

By listing characteristics and giving examples, I hope to have identified what is meant by the term "urban legend", and to have shown conclusively that some of the stories in the oral narratives and colo batha collections belong to this new sub-categorisation of folklore. What I have not done and I am very much aware of it, is to define "urban legend", but then, folklorists themselves have yet to do this. The reason they have not is that the conscious awareness of this genre has only recently surfaced, incredible as that may seem. When Brunvand published his very important and comprehensive survey, The Study of American Folklore, in 1968, he vaguely referred to "urban tales", but these did not even merit a separate chapter. The situation is of course very different now, thanks to the same Professor Brunvand.

The genre, however, is still not defined; perhaps it can be delimited by showing how it differs from related genres. Urban legends, for example, differ from traditional legends in the fact that they take place recently, relative to the date of the telling. This is one factor in the continual updating that occurs in their transmission. They do not share, generally, fixed functions or elements such as those abstracted by Propp in his work on folk and fairy tales and when they do, they usually have only one or two elements, which puts them well outside the tradition of elaborate and lengthy developments.

Certain kinds of urban legends are very close to jokes and as has been said, the same story can show up either as a joke or an urban legend, depending perhaps on the level of sophistication or gullibility of the audience. It may be that when an urban legend is too preposterous to be believed by a certain group, it is told to them as a joke. Again, many urban legends resemble ghost stories, but have to be excluded by the fact that are readily believed by people who do not believe in ghosts. In any case, the two categories, jokes and ghost stories, must be considered mutually exclusive, except under the most contrived circumstances and therefore neither one can serve in the definition of urban legends.

Definitions will certainly emerge as the field is studied in more depth and as urban legends are exposed in the wide range of social circumstances where they occur – little has been made so far, for example, of their connection to certain kinds of quasi-superstitions. They are frighteningly insidious; even after long exposure to the genre, one can easily be caught innocently passing one on. At least their identification should be useful in categorising certain types of folklore and literary genres. It can be done with the group of secular urban legend tales of the Bodos that has upto now gone under the "other" category, or under no identity at all.

Whether told as literally true or not, whether fully believed or not, urban legends of the Bodos is transmitted in order to convey to the listener of what the world is like. The urban legends have "no special purpose". While it is true that all the stories in *zunatni colo* (animal tales) end with a moral, in the case of the secular tales this usually amounts to no more than something like: "These things happen". Nevertheless, the stories of urban legends clearly exist in order to admonish, to warn or to instruct, even though there appears to be no specific canon on which their didacticism is based.

The purpose of these stories is to promote not morality, but rather sociability. The messages are conservative and orthodox: "Be careful"; "Beware of new fashions'" like bee-hive hairdos, which can harbour spiders; "Beware of new technologies" like microwave ovens, which can behave unpredictably. "Do not be too quick to trust strangers"; "Do not let strangers prepare your food"; "Do not act precipitously"; "Things have a way of working out".

The narrator of urban legend and the reporter of media try to assert their claim in the truth of the story. They justify by saying: "If it's not true, it ought to be". With regard to the questions of the truth of the stories, of people's belief in them as well as of the motivation to repeat them on subsequent reflection, we are sometimes given pause by some implausible detail but this is usually forgotten, all the more quickly when we are impatient to pass on the good story in our turn. It is only after repeated exposures to urban legends that the hearer's nagging doubts turn into "urban legend alert" warning bells.

REFERENCES:

Boro, Anil Kumar. 2010. *A History of Bodo Literature.* Sahitya Akademi.

Brunvand, Jan Harold. 1996. *American Folklore: An Encyclopedia.* New York: Garland Publishing Incorporated.

Devi, P. *Social and Religious Institutions of Bodos.* Guwahati: Geophil Publishing House.

Dorson, Richard M. 1972. *Folklore and Folklife.* Chicago: The University of Chicago Press.

Kumar, B. B. 1993. *Folklore and Folklore Motifs.* New Delhi: Omsons Publications.

Sen, Soumen and Kharmawphlang D.L. 2007. *Orality and Beyond.* Sahitya Akademi.

Thompson, Stith. 1977. *The Folktale.* California: University of California Press.

The Modern Day Witch-hunt in the Kokrajhar District

Tamsin Aftab

Introduction: a sociological analysis

The art of performing charms, spells and rituals to seek or control events or govern certain natural or supernatural forces is generally termed as witchcraft. There have been various incidents happening in the state of Assam where people have been accused of witchcraft and they are hunted down for the same. No satisfactory explanations have ever evolved for the hunting of men and women in the region and the rate of witchcraft killing is alarmingly high among tribal communities and other minor communities in the state. According to local beliefs, a witch or diani, in Assamese, is a man or woman who has magical powers that bring misfortune upon the community. It is shocking to know that even in the present age witchcraft is a real belief system and one that is very much rooted in the popular mentality of people. This belief in Witches is manifest throughout the world but in our state it is more confined to the Kokrajhar district where the number of incidents outnumbers the rest. In British social anthropology, discussions about witchcraft have tended to take their departure from Evans-Pritchard's classic study of *Witchcraft, oracles and magicamong the Azande* (Evans-Pritchard 1976). Evans Pritchard used the Azandepeople's own distinction between what he translated as witchcraft and sorcery in his exposition of zande beliefs. Analytically, his main purpose was to show how for the Azande ideas of witchcraft functioned as a means of explaining misfortunes that were difficult to explain in other ways, these ideas were then, he argues harnessed to a way of settling suspicions between people. In this way witchcraft was used as a tool.

The belief in witches is one that can be said to be cultural and is found in various degrees among all cultures. Prosecution for alleged witchcraft can be traced back to early ages, where history has witnessed a series of events related to witch craft and witch hunting - the decline of Roman Empire; it caused the Protestant reformation, European wars of Religion, English Civil war, and the rise of African Independence movements. All these events in history were accompanied by a large number of witch prosecutions. Dating back to the Witch trials in Salem (colonial Massachusetts), one can see that many innocent victims lost their lives and more than two hundreds were accused during the Salem Witchcraft hysteria. There have been stronger factors behind the Witch hunts- the strict puritan lifestyle, a strong belief in the devil and witchcraft and the divisions within Salem Village. These factors led to such tragic and horrific incidents taking place in the history during 1690's. Coming back to the present scenario, Assam is not lacking behind in such incidents. There have been 77 deaths till last year in the state. The various charges that appear during witch-hunts involve accusations of crimes committed against the community or the society. It is the whole of collective existence that is at stake. When a charge is brought of being a witch what is happening is that a ritual contrast is being drawn between images of the corporate order and things, which would oppose it. This can be seen as a construction of the Durkheimian idea of the sacred-profane dichotomy in modern terms. Here the sociology of deviance and the sociology of religion are merged, for the idea of deviant and normal is but another form of the idea of sacred and profane. They both have the same function: a symbolic opposition to collective representations is drawn, and as such representations of the corporate community are redefined. (Durkheim, 1912).

Victor Turner added to the functionalist paradigm his notion of the social drama in which conflicts exposed the weakness of lineage organization and caused fission in social groups (Turner 1966[1957]). In Turners view, witchcraft accusations were seen as the surface indicators of underlying conflicts over land

and power. Turner's work on conflict and ritual became widely known and influenced the field of ritual studies in general. He saw witchcraft accusations as "social catalysts" that could precipitate unforeseen results.

Now what has magic to do with such incidents? Malinowski has given the answer to this brilliantly. It is always utilitarian (magic), whereas religion lacks utility. He did not view magic as a characteristic of particular kinds of societies, but thought that it could be found when human beings were confronted with a lack of knowledge or ability to control something important to their lives. Malinowski also observed that magic had social and moral functions that led to better cooperation among group members. In addition, it gave people access to what he referred to as "miracles," events that were unexpected or unlikely, thus giving them hope. In this way Malinowski explained magic in a positive way.

Soma Chaudhuristates that Witch Craft accusations are not exotic and primitive rituals of a backward *adivasi* community during time of stress but rather a powerful protest organized by a marginalized community against its oppressors. Here she brings the classical Marxian explanation behind the conflict between the two classes: The worker (in this case the tea plantation worker), and the owners (here the planters and the management). The workers are nothing but just a commodity in the eyes of the owners.

The area of study is Kokrajhar District, which is in Bodoland Territorial District, Assam, one of the North East States and territories of India. The study focuses on data collected from two villages namely East Tengaigaon (pub tengaigaon) under Serfanguri Police Station and also the village named Thaigirguri under the Kachugaon Police Station.

Sample of Study: Respondents are selected through stratified random sampling method and snowball sampling method. The study is based on 15 in-depth interviews.

Tools to be used: In order to get the most out of the respondents a semi-structured interview schedule was prepared. As Creswell stated the question will be broad and general so that the participants can construct the meaning of a situation, a meaning typically forced in discussions or interactions with other persons (Creswell).

In almost all of the interviews, the researcher was accompanied by a translator who would intervene only if a word or phrase required translation.

Techniques of data collection: Techniques of observation and interview schedule were used for the collection of data.

Law and witch hunting

Article 21 of the constitution of India, which guarantees the right to life, includes protection of life and property of all members of the society. The guarantees, as provided by the constitution of India with regard to life and property, cannot be taken away without due procedure established by law. Witch hunting is a gender-based violence, which undermines the very nucleus of this Article 21. Article 51A(h) of the constitution of India spells out the need to develop a scientific temper, humanism and the sprit of inquiry and reform as fundamental duty of every Indian citizen. But factors such as social inequality and lack of rational thinking along with illiteracy and extreme poverty manifests in the form of such inhuman practices based on superstitions.

As per 7th schedule of the constitution of India, police and public orders are state subjects and as such the state governments are primarily responsible for prevention, detection, registration and investigation of crime as well as for prosecution of the accused/criminal. Therefore it is also the responsibility of the state government to protect the life and property of the citizen and to take appropriate measure for providing necessary funds for providing adequate compensation to the victims, their legal representatives or dependents, as the case may be.

Section 357-A Cr.P.C. itself provides that the state government, in coordination with the central government has to prepare the said scheme for providing fund for the purpose of payment of compensation to the victims, their legal airs and dependents. This implies that the central government also has the responsibility all together for implementation of the provisions prescribed under section 357-A Cr. P.C. Thus, it is clear that the rehabilitation of the victim or their dependents and legal representative, as the case maybe is also a part of criminal justice delivery systems.

If one looks at the national laws, most of the witch-hunts cases are dealt by section 323 of the IPC, which prescribes one-year imprisonment and an Rs 1000/- fine to anyone who causes harm voluntarily. In other words, the punishment for brutalizing a woman by calling her a witch could be the same as that for slapping women. Other sections like 302(murder) of the IPC are invoking in witch-hunts cases that leads to a women's death.

After much speculations and discussions the witch-hunt bill 2015, has been passed recently. It makes Witch hunting a cognizable, non-bailable, and non-compoundable offence, and rules out anticipatory bail. Any death due to the practice, it says, should be prosecuted under Section 302 of the IPC that provides for punishment for murder. In other cases, it proposes fines and imprisonment. Apart from stricter punishment for terming someone a witch and for physical, sexual or mental torture leading to suicide and displacement, the Prevention of and Protection from Witch Hunting Bill, 2015, Assam, aims to check illegal practices by quacks. It also proposes action against negligence in investigation, formation of special courts for trial of witch-hunting cases and free legal aid to victims, among other provisions. If such a bill is passed at least there is a hope that acts like Witch hunting can be eradicated from the society and one would witness less number of such occurrences.

But the point here is will this be sufficient to bring an end to this practice. Will the bill alone be sufficient in curbing such a practice of witch hunting and witch killing? The recent incident of killing of a BA student in Kokrajhar in April 2016, brings in light that the society or the community are still not under a threat by law for doing such a crime.

The Bodo Social Life: the socio-cultural belief systems of the Bodos

K Brahma has made an observation that due to much simplicity, open heartedness, frankness and due to lack of education the Bodo women become easy victims of the anti social elements. Witch hunting is one such anti social element present in today's time. Education is the sharpest weapon of all to protect themselves from the social enemies and to maintain their position in the civilized human society as always high, so that womenfolk also can contribute a lot to the nation. The use of the country made liquor is deep rooted in the Bodo society and this ill habit destroys many Bodo families. Many a times it is noticed that the occurrence of the witch trail takes place when the villagers are intoxicated and after a fusion this seems to be kind of a feast and thrill for the villagers. Chaudhuri has ascribed the role played by *Haria*(**local liquor**) in her brilliant account of witch hunting in Chandmoni Tea estate in West Bengal. Frustration over the continuing epidemics, anger and under the influence of Alcohol (*haria*) and miscreants are some of the reasons behind the support for the hunts.

There are few mystic elements found in the Bodo culture, which plays a significant role in their lifes. The role of **Deodhani (the possessed women) in Kherai Puja** brings out the mystic element in the traditional religious beliefs of the Bodos. The world of the Bodos is crowned with Gods and Goddesses. Disease of men and catastrophes of the world are traced to angry spirits. Spells and incarnations are used. All these require specially qualified persons like *deoris, deodhais*and*deodhanis.* Sacrifice and prayer form an important element of their culture.

It is commonly believed that the witch can cause harm to animals, children, men, and women—and even make them fatally ill. The witch can cause illness ranging from diarrhea, malaria, and tuberculosis to the common fever and stomach ailments. Sometimes she may cause barrenness or infertility. The witch's evil eye operates through *ban-mara.* It is through the use of *ban* that the witch causes illness in her victims. The witch was typically seen as responsible for causing illness or death in small children, spouses, infants, or domestic animals. She had the power to interfere with nature. She was capable of causing barrenness, miscarriages, or deformed birth. The witch, thus, symbolizes evil and can harm to anyone around her. However, even though the witch's power could bring harm to anyone, her victims tended to be close neighbours, relatives, and people who knew her well enough to anger her. The fear of the witch is deep rooted in the psyche of the people, and the community blame any event or development that is not —normal on the witch. With such a belief the people of the village get together to discuss the matter and then a **calculated attack is planned**. Many of the incidents reported are calculated attacks which mainly are because of personal rivalry or property disputes resulting in killing the victim as a witch.

Rev Sidney Endle in his historic book the Kacharis states that the religion of the Kachari race is distincly of the type commonly known as "animistic" and its underlying principle is characteristically one of fear or dread.

Superstition alone does not appear to be a sufficient reason- as in most of the cases the victim shares the belief system and has concrete inter personal reasons that motivate her victimization. No matter what the belief in the existence of witches and witchcraft is very much prevalent amongst the victims as well as the instigators. Witchcraft as a belief system is very much predominant in the village life.

Witch hunting is a gender-neutral crime against the society mainly due to property grudge, failure in relationships, village rivalry, and mutual jealousy. It is a killing of mankind, not just men or women. In order to prevent the crime it should be a systematized approach from all cultures and people from all walks of life. The Constitution (Eighty-sixth Amendment) Act, 2002-inserted Article 21-A in the Constitution of India to provide free and compulsory education of all children in the age group of six to fourteen years as a Fundamental Right in such a manner as the State may, by law, determine. Education is a constitutional right given to the citizens of our country but many people even now ignore this right to education.

In a recent report on Witch hunting in Assam brought out by NEN and Assam MahilaSamatha Society, it has been reflected that the victims knew the instigators and perpetrators. They were either physically proximate to the victims or with family ties to the victims. The study shows a high rate of involvement of neighbors as instigators, followed by relatives and co-workers.

How does the witchcraft accusations start? One can refer Chaudhurihere who has stated that there are two kinds of attacks: Random attack and calculated attack. It can be said to take place in the local settings too- in a calculated attack, witch-hunts are preceded by clear motives on the part of the accusers based on what the accusers claim to be instigation from the accused. The motives on the part of the accusers can be almost anything, including maligning the reputation of the accused woman, serving personal motives, seeking revenge to settle disputes over property, or explaining why illnesses or diseases happen. In cases in which witch-hunts serve the purpose of revenge over personal conflicts, disease or ailments play a major role in instigating the hunt. In cases of *surprise or random attacks*, the women victims and their families were, prior to the attack, were or claimed to be unaware of the accusations against them. The attack happened without any instigation in the form of prior conflict or any history of witchcraft accusation against the accused witch. Even in cases of surprise attacks in which there were no prior warning signals that an accusation was taking place, some immediate cause prompted the attack. In most cases, the cause was an ailment, but in a few cases it was a petty brawl or verbal exchange that preceded the attack.

Verbal taunts and slurs, through local terms denoting 'witch' as well as other abuses aimed at demonizing and isolating the victim and her family, often accompanied by minor to grave physical violence and a small fraction of cases resulting in murder.

RESULTS: Why is such a practice still prevalent?

Why is such a practice still prevalent? Be it the Bodos of Kokrajhar or the tea plantation workers of Chandmoni Tea estate in West Bengal (Chaudhuri). One can see that in most of the cases it is the tribal population and not the people belonging to the mainstream. Even after an array of development projects and initiatives undertaken tribals are still under the threat of such atrocities. Who is to be blamed for such underdevelopment of the people? It is the government or the local authorities or the people themselves?

The struggle over land inheritance, epidemics has been one of the primary causes for witchcraft accusations in the region. The point to be noted here is that such attacks are against the law. Murder of someone as a suspect witch is a crime. Most of the cases involved accusations that the woman attacked had caused illness, disease or death. Scapegoating, village rivalries, inheritance, conflicts and female threats to patriarchy are introduced in explanations of early modern hunts and similar theories are raised to explain attacks on witches in contemporary India.

As Nathan observes that the indigenous peoples have their own ways of suppressing women, often involving violence. Whether as dain, tonhi, or in some other form there is an ongoing violence against women, as part of the process of establishing or strengthening forms of patriarchy. Opposing such culturally-bound forms of oppression and violence is part of the process of further democratizing indigenous communities themselves (Dev Nathan).A remarkable note to be made here is that recent trends and data shows that witch-hunting is not only restricted to women but also significant number of men are targeted.

The major reasons behind such killings

On being perceived the economic backwardness as to be the vital factor behind this social problem, the government over the years has been launching many developmental schemes for rural areas. But its slow impact on rural mass still forcing the society to engulf with this perennial adversity.

An important reason instrumental behind the witch killings in the Kokrajhar is **illiteracy and inequality**. Knowledge is power that saves us from ignominy and exploitation by unscrupulous persons. Literacy dispels the darkness of ignorance, hunger and backwardness. The state has been spending millions to educate the vast army of illiterates, but the goal of achieving 100% literacy still remains elusive, a rosy and distant dream. Education, according to Human Rights Commission, is man's basic right. It is the only courses, which make man self-reliant. No one likes to remain ignorant and illiterate in this electronic age. The literacy rate in the district of Kokrajhar is 65.55% of which female literacy is 58.27% as per 2011 census.

The rural areas of Assam are very much underdeveloped and this results in **poverty**. Rapid progress in GDP growth and globalization in the last decade has primarily impacted the urban economy. While software exports, business process outsourcing, etc, have helped urban economic growth, it has done relatively little for the rural economy. Rural India is caught in what is called a development trap. Because of lack of economic opportunities, incomes are low. Therefore they are unable to pay for goods and services that would enable them to increase their incomes.

Right over property is a very important reason behind such killings. In a substantial number of reported cases, witch-hunting is resorted to, so as to rob the men or women of her property rights. Efforts to exercise those rights are thwarted by the method of declaring the men or woman a witch and so rob them of their right to the land. And it is not always the woman's family, which is necessarily involved. Particularly where the woman is unprotected, a widow or a single woman, there is no dearth of others who have an eye on the land, would use the services of the ojhas. For example, there are cases where such identification has been made when upper castes want to grab the land distributed to the poor tribal communities. Agarwal (1994) gives a brief elaboration about the pattern she finds in South Asia. Agarwal argues that the single most important economic factor affecting women's situation is the gender gap in command over property. In rural South Asia, the most significant form of property is arable land, a critical determinant of economic well being, social status, and empowerment. But few women own land; fewer control it. "In communities where women never held land, such rights tend to generate hostility - divorces, accusations of witchcraft, threats, attacks, torture, even murder". Thus witchcraft is also a result of disputes over property and land and it is this gender relation, which plays a detrimental role in such accusations.

Further when the 'jadutona' of the witch doctor fails to cure the patient, a scapegoat has to be found and mostly it is the poorest and most vulnerable in the society is sacrificed. The target chosen in such cases usually has little social support. Women in non-stereotypical situations, lacking protection or support, single women, women without children, widows and the disabled, are the most vulnerable. The hunt is usually accompanied by a mob, whipped into hysteria by the ojha. Such incidents also reinforce the fear and power of the ojha, which suits the vested interests.

Shortage of doctors, nurses and the Primary Health Centre or Public Health Centre (PHC) in remote or rural areas compel the tribal clans to rely or trust on Kabiraj (that is, exorcist or sorcerer, locally called Ojha or Baiga) and also the quack, who on failure to cure serious diseases, put the blame on witch-craft and numbers of Tonhi or witch. Proper medical facilities should be provided to the remote villages so as to curb such dangerous outcomes.

Looting money and Excessive intake of alcohol. In few cases it has been seen that victims are killed and attacked only to loot money. In one such incident the accuser killed a victim in the name of witch but he was under the influence of alcohol and in the morning when he was in a normal state he confessed and gave a statement that it was due to alcohol that he committed such a crime.

From the incidences following are the observations to be made:

- It occurs mostly in the Tribal areas.
- It occurs mostly in the rural areas.
- Males and Females both are targeted. It is a gender-neutral crime. (In a written reply to a query by BJP MLA PrasantaPhukan, Parliamentary Affairs Minister RockybulHussain said a total of 77 persons, including 35 women, were murdered due to the superstition between 2010 and February 2015. Of the injured 60 people, 46 were women)
- Mostly it is prevalent amongst the uneducated and illiterates.

Having taken into consideration the above factors one notice that witch-hunting is a very real phenomenon and such a practice is very prominent in Assam at the present time.

Past history and the data referred indicates the following reasons to be instrumental behind the whole practice of witch killing in the district:

(1) Superstition and influence of sorcerers.
(2) Illiteracy and inequality.
(3) Lack of economic development in rural areas and poverty.
(4) Land rights, inheritance and property dispute.
(5) Weak health care services.
(6) Increasing intolerance, jealousy and old enmity.
(7) Looting money and Excessive intake of alcohol

The centers of witchcraft accusations within the adivasi worker group as pointed by Chaudhuri are the illness and misfortune in the community that are blamed. Lack of healthcare, sanitation and irregularity of payment, health issues and starvation are considered to be major problems in the *adivasi*regions and witchcraft is given as the most common explanation. Similar factors can be attributed to the Bodos in Kokrajhar where people are still relying on Ojhas as there is lack of proper medical facilities. Local politics, personal conflicts and the gendered nature of violence play a huge role. Rumors, gossip and conspiracies play a crucial role during witch-hunts by displacing reality in the mind of the community. There is a power play involved in the displacement and replacement of reality and in its construction. Primarily the men in the community, who manipulate it for a motive that is profitable to some, hold this power; the women are mere passive participants or victims in the hunt.

Conclusion

The Assam Police are doing their best by reviving a targeted education campaign called Project Parhari, which aims to disabuse villagers of the notion that malicious sorcery is real.

Educating the people and framing laws for the protection of women and people belonging to the 'lower' classes of the society who also constitute another target group of such witch hunts is important. Until then, such beliefs in the existence of black magic and 'dainis' will prevail along with the prevalence of 'ojhas' who have a very big influence in village life.

The above facts transpire a very perplexing approach towards the problem. Therefore, all likeminded individuals, social organizations including government shall join hands to form a new mindset with a view to evolve a new mechanism, which will pave the way for a logical and permanent solution to this social problem. However, an analytical study on the past incidences of witch killing in different parts of this district transpires the fact that superstition, lack of economic development and illiteracy cannot merely be the causes of witch-hunt. The argument behind is that the current rate of literacy, per capita income and health care facilities are much more high in comparison to the beginning of this century. Therefore, our focus needs to be concentrated on certain other realities and which perhaps requires serious attention at this moment of time.

Development as a concept is touching every nook and corner of the world, but even then the identity of the tribal is lost? Proper utilization of the development initiatives and implementation is required. We need well planned more effective schemes to contribute to the welfare of the people. Tribal communities traditionally brew liquor from rice or other food grains for their consumption and this has started impoverishing of the tribal population leading them to suffer from indebtedness and exploitation.

With special reference to the Bodo Community, it will develop only when the women empower themselves to fight for their rights and lives. Men and women should not be differentiated and everyone should be treated equally in society. Only then can such a practice be eliminated with initiatives from the government

The belief in witches among the indigenous communities of Assam gets perpetuated through a vicious combination of government apathy and ignorance of the people. The communities, which are otherwise deprived of resources probably, express their frustration through the acts of witch-hunting. The women within these communities become vulnerable owing to a lack of support system within the family or community; for not being economically self reliant and for lack of information about better opportunities.

Gender violence is a multifunctional phenomenon containing political, social, cultural and interpersonal conflicts. It is partly a result of gender relations that assume men to be superior to women. But as per the latest records we see that men and women are equal targets and hence power inequalities or gender violence cannot be an appropriate reason behind such killings.

Chaudhuri says violence is often used as a mean to disrupt order (riots, genocides) and it is often the beginning of Anomie. Anomie is the state of normlessness in society. Here the Durkhiemian notion of Anomie comes into existence. In a state of Anomie no development can ever take place in a true sense.

Law alone cannot diminish the problem. Rigid and severe laws are essential part to deal with the problem but society must be more gender sensitive and discard prejudicebased on irrational beliefs. Social biases or any kind of dogma should be done away with. Justice is something, which is granted by law, and it cannot be taken in one's own hands, which is illegal. The villagers should be educated so as to not take laws in their own hands. Focus should be on shifting attitudes of the general people and initiatives should be taken to broaden their outlook towards the society. This is important because violence against women is related to development outcomes. Sustained focus from government, donors, international organizations, civil society and research community are essential.

Despite the fact that many social organizations as well as NGO's are making continuous campaigns for generating awareness against witch- hunting, this phenomenon has still persisted in the tribal societies, causing innumerable loss of lives of innocent villagers. So, it is assumed that such kind of awareness campaign has not reached the minds of those, who indulge into such evil acts. Now, it is a high time for all of us to evolve a new mechanism having more realistic and sensible approach, which can possibly help the society in getting rid of this modern scourge.

It is the interplay of religion, power relations, social and cultural life, economic backwardness and lack of medical facilities, which are in existence for such a continued practice of Witch hunting in the region. Development of the Bodos and the identity of the tribe can only be retained if a new mechanism is evolved with a gender sensitive approach, stringent laws, tribal empowerment and good quality education.

Killing of women in the name of witches is just not a simple crime. It is the entire feminity that is at stake. The enormous pain and torture, which a women or a family undergoes, might not be described in words. The throwing out of village, the resettlement, the mental trauma undergone puts them into too much agony and oppression. Here empowerment is a big responsibility and awareness is one of the most potent solutions to this problem. Even when there are various steps taken by the government but they can only spend so much time in each settlement, spreading their message of reason. Perhaps the better long-term solution is to provide villagers with better means of dispute resolution and to ensure that justice is swift and certain when killings do occur, even if it means carting off every single participant.

Witches are humans. They belong to the society – a disguised enemy within. They are the other and yet they are also us i.e. the self. To quote Gail Omvedt in one of her keynote speech "The end of identities of self and other playing the role of obstacles in the road to liberated humanity, could be removed only by creating a healthy democratic space for a non-domineering identities of various self's and others."

References:

Agarwal, Bina. 1994, *A Field of one's own: Gender and Land Rights in South Asia*. Cambridge: Cambridge University Press.

Anderson, Perry. 1990. Witchcraft. *London review of books*.Vol. 12 No.21. pp-6 11.

Bailey, F.G. 1997. A *Witch-Hunt in an Indian village or a triumph of Morality*. Delhi: Oxford University Press.

Bergesen, Albert James. 1978. 'A Durkheimian Theory of "Witch-hunts" with the Chinese Cultural Revolution of 1966-1969 as an Example', *Journal for the scientific Study of religion*, 17 (1): 19-29

Bose, M.L. Social History of Assam. 1989. Concept publishing company. New Delhi.

BosuMullick, Samar. Gender relations and witches among the indigenous communities of Jharkhand, India p. 119-146 IN Gender relations in forest societies in Asia: patriarchy at odds/ed. by GovindKelkar, Dev Nathan and Pierre Walter. - New Delhi: Sage,2003.

Brahma, K. 1992. A study of Socio-Religious Beliefs practices and ceremonies of the Bodos.Calcutta:PunthiPustak.

Butler, Judith. 1999. *Gender Trouble*. Routledge.

Chakraborty, J & Borah, A. Jul-Dec. 2013.Journal of Nort east Indian Studies. Vol 3(2), pp. 15-24.

Chakravarty, A &Chaudhuri, S. 2012. Strategic Framing Work(s); How Micro-credit loans facilitate Anti- Witch Hunt Movements. Mobilization. Vol. 17(2) pp. 175-194

Chakraveti, Ipsita Roy. 2003.*Beloved Witchan Autobiography*. India: Harper

Chaterjee M. Violence, silence and memory of witches in Violence against women.Avnishkar publishers, Jaipur, 2006

ChatterjiJyotsna. 2002.Challenging Witchcraft and cultural and customary practices IN living death, trauma of widowhood in India edited by V.MohiniGiri. Gyan Publishing, New Delhi.

Chaudhuri Soma. 2013. Women, Tea Plantations and Lives of Migrant Laborers in India. Cambridge University Press India Pvt Ltd.

Chaudhuri, Soma. 2012.Women as easy Scapegoats: Witchcraft Accusations and women as Targets in Tea plantations of India. *Violence against women 18, no. 10 (October 2012): 1213-1234.*

Chaudhuri, Soma. March 2013. Extending the Logic of Functional Explanations: A theoretical model to explain the Victimization Process during an Indian Witch Hunt in Global Criminology: Crime and Victimization in a globalized era edited by K. Jaishankar&NattiRonel. CRC press.

Chaudhuri, Sucheta Sen. 2004.The Bodo movement and women participation. Mittal Publications.New Delhi.

Choudhari, A.B. 1984.*Witch Killings amongst Santals.*New Delhi: Ashish Publishing house.

Das, Jogesh. 2012. *Folklore of Assam*. National Book Trust, India.

Devi, M. Tineshowri. January 2013.Women Status in Assam.Journal of Business Management and Social Sciences Research.Vol. 2, No.1.

Devi, Premalata. 1998. Social and Religious institutions of the Bodos. Geophil Publishing House, Guwahati.

Douglas, Mary. 1966. *Purity and Danger*. London: Routledge and Kegan Paul.

Durkheim, Emile.2001 [1912]*The elementary forms of religious life*. London: Oxford University Press.

Endle, Rev Sidney.2010 [1911]. *The Kacharis(Bodo)*. Delhi: Low Price Publications

Federici, Silvia. 2013. *Caliban and the Witch: Women, the Body and Primitive Accumulation*. Phoneme Publishers and Distributors Pvt Ltd, New Delhi.

Gaskill, Malcolm. 2010. *Witchcraft a very short introduction*. Oxford University Press.

Geschiere, Peter. 2003. 'Witchcraft as the Dark Side of Kinship: Dilemmas of Social Security in New Contexts', *Ethnofloor,* 16(1):43-61.

Gohain, Hiren.1989. 'Bodo stir in perspective', *Economic and political weekly,* 24(25):1377-1379

Kelkar, Govind. 1985. 'Women and Structural Violence in India', *Women's Studies Quarterly,* 13(¾):16-18

Kumar, Radha. 2000. *The History of Doing: An illustrated account of movements for women's rights and feminism in India. Zubaan Books.*

Larner, Christina. 1984. *Witchcraft and Religion: The Politics of Popular Belief.* New York: Basil Blackwell.

Larner, Christina.1981.Enemies *of God: Witch Hunt in Scotland*. Maryland: John Hopkins University Press

Majumdar, Maya.2001. *Protecting our Women, Victimised women: Repression and Social Response*. New Delhi: Dominant Publishers and Distributors.

Malinowski, Bronislaw. 1954[1925] *Magic, Science and Religion and other essays.* New York: Free Press Publishers.

Mallick Atta, Sept 27- Oct 3 2008, Witch Hunting in 1857, Economic and Political Weekly, Vol. 43, No 39, pp. 118-119, New Delhi

Miguel, Edward. Oct 2005. 'Poverty and Witch Killing', *The review of economic studies,* 72(4):1152-1172.

Nathan, D and Kelkar, G, &Xiaogang, X 1998. 'Women as Witches and Keepers of Demons: Cross-Cultural Analysis of Struggles to change Gender Relations', *Economic and Political Weekly,* Vol.33 pp. 58-69

Nelson, Mary. 1975. 'Why Witches Were Women', *Women: A Feminist Perspective,* CA: Mayfield. 335–50

Oldridge, Darren.2008.*The Witchcraft Reader* (Routledge Readers in History). London: Routledge; 2 edition

Pritchard, E.E. Evans. 1935. 'Witchcraft', *Africa: Journal of International African Institute,* 8(4): 417-422

Pritchard, E.E. Evans.1976 [1937].*Witchcraft, Oracles and Magic among the Azande.*London: Oxford University Press.

Purkiss, Diane.1996. *The Witch in History: Early Modern and Twentieth-Century Representations.* London: Routledge; First edition

Schoeneman, Thomas J. 1975. 'The witch hunts as a cultural change phenomenon source', *Ethos,* 3(4): 529-554

Singh, Rakesh K. January-march 2011. Witch-Hunting: Alive and Kicking. Crime against women. Vol. 17 No 1.

Sinha, Shashank. May 12(2007), Witch-Hunts, Adivasi and the uprising in Chota Nagpur, Economic and Political weekly, New Delhi, Vol. 42, no 19, pp. 1672-1676

Skaria, Ajay. 1997. 'Women, Witchcraft and Gratuitous Violence in Colonial Western India', *Past & Present,* 155:109-141

*Support services to counter violence against women in Assam: A Resource Directory.*2003.Assam: North East Network.

Tiwari, Siv Kumar. 1994. *Encyclopedia of Indian Tribals 1.*New Delhi: Rahul Publishing House.

Toivo, Raisa Maria.2005. 'Women's History Revisited'.*Historiographical Reflections on Women and Gender in a Global Context.* The 20th International Congress of Historical Sciences, University of New South Wales, Sydney, Australia.

Turner, Paul R. 1970. 'Witchcraft as Negative Charisma', *Ethnology*, 9 (4): 366-372.

Turner, Victor W.1964.*Witchcraft and Sorcery: Taxonomy versus Dynamics.* Africa: 3(4): 314-324

Turner, Victor. 1980. *Social dramas and stories about them.* Critical Inquiry 7(4): 141-168

Versnel H.S. 1991. 'Some Reflections on the Relationship Magic-Religion', *Numen*, 38:177-197

Wilson, Jennifer M. 2005.*Witch.* Bloomington: Authorhouse.

Internet Sources:

http://www.sociologydiscussion.com/society/types-of-society-tribal-agrarian-and-industrial-society/2190

http://www.telegraphindia.com/1150409/jsp/northeast/story_13497.jsp#.VS4sgKYxGRY

http://zeenews.india.com/news/assam/77-killed-in-witch-hunting-incidents-since-2010-in-assam_1566297.html

Customary Law and Gender Relations: A Study of its Impact on the Women in North-east India

Bhanuprabha Brahma

Introduction:

The Indian state presents itself as the quintessential post-colonial state which is continuously imagining and re-imagining its nature at the scope of the interface of tradition and modernity. One of the major zones of this kind of negotiation occurs in the legal framework where various components like democratic constitutional law, community based law and religious personal laws are engaging and negotiating with each other within the framework of the universal modern state structure. This universality is sought to be achieved through a process of accommodation and representation of different ethnic groups, indigenous communities, caste and gender. There are many indigenous communities in India which have their own customary laws along with community values. These laws in tandem with the particular values operate in a complex terrain of the social, political and economic structure. This paper is an attempt to engage particularly with the experience of the gendered citizen who is at the intersection of the modern law with the community based customary law. In India there are many indigenous communities of which the largest live in North-east. The people in northeast have their own particular culture which governs them in all aspects of public and private life. The modern state also has its set of universal laws which deals with the issues of rights and access to resources. It will be interesting to examine the convergence and divergence of customary law and modern law particularly in their engagement with women's issue.

Combined allegiance and diversified access towards many legal systems in many tribal societies had gendered impact on its women. Walter Fernandes and Sanjay Barbora (2002) in their work "Modernisation and Changing Women's Status in the Northeast" has indicated that when tribal societies encountered modernisation without preparation and without being able to counter its ill effects this can result in class formation and can reinforce patriarchy. However it does not mean that modernisation is bad in every aspect of a tribe's aspect but only that it has many negative aspects of modernisation that have to be countered. When delving with the tribal customary law and formal law one has to be prepared to deal with the negative effects (Baruah 2002).

The interface between customary law and formal law results in certain change in the status of women. Tradition-modernity interface is a crucial component to study the impact it had on women. It has implications both from a gender and a class perspective and thus it forms the basis of this study. Therefore this paper, based on the secondary sources aims to study the condition of women beyond this spurious notion of liberation in conflict ridden societies of Assam which in turn prevent the women to exercise their basic democratic rights and the gender inequality remains pervasive. This paper is basically divided into three sections. The first section deals with the term 'Legal Pluralism' and the meaning of customary law while the second section deals with interface of customary and the formal law and how the gender relations get impacted. The third part depicts the forms of patriarchy within customary law.

Legal Pluralism and the Meaning of Customary Law-

India has a robust history of diversity and pluralism. Symbiotic co-existence of diverse forms of life, as a given, immutable fact associated with human existence, grounds every sphere of life, religious, legal, cultural, social, etc. The mutual co-existence of varying groups ensured that different social groups or communities enjoy, to the maximum extent, freedom to nurture diverse methods or ways for organising, sustaining and perpetuating their particular forms of living including ways of regulating their life. The legal system is based on different understandings of law, such as official law, state law, modern law, unofficial law, folk law, people's law, tribal law, indigenous law, non-state law, customary law, received law, imposed law. Increasing deployment of the concept of legal pluralism in scientific, scholarly works along with constant rethinking of the epistemological framework for understanding legal phenomena in different societies indicate that the socio-legal world is realising the futility and impossibility of delimiting life spheres into distinct autonomous domains, such as law, religion, morality and politics.

Feminist legal theory is reactive to legal centralism and by merely being a critique of it, paradoxically affirms the paradigms that it seeks to contest. In searching for ways to correct the imbalance in power relations between men and women, feminism has either given prominence to the state as the medium through which to achieve change or expressed doubts about the likelihood of success through law. In both cases, feminists have conformed chiefly to legal centralism, that is, the view that the state is the sole source of law. There has been little feminist theory which has deliberated on enduring structures of power embedded in other normative orders – such as the lineage, the clan or groups engaged in the informal sector of the economy – which legal centralism refuses to characterise as law. In consequence, other sources which generate law, the ways in which they secure compliance and their effects have been neglected.

Legal pluralism has served as a general tool to understand law in all its complexity. There has been immense debate on the definition of law and the concept of legal pluralism complicates this issue further. Realisation about the inadequacy of hitherto accepted terms such as 'customary law' to denote the legal phenomena of the "indigenous" societies are reflected in the on-going attempts to find labels for identifying legal systems based on different understandings of law. Customary laws very usually become an essential part of a people's culture. The origin of customary laws lies in the habitual practice of people as it usually becomes a custom. In traditional societies that did not have written laws, the customary law maintained social order, prescribed rules of conduct to individuals and regulated human behaviour. The tribe cherished its laws as intrinsic to its identity. The customary law thus provided some formal rules of behaviour, enforcement procedures and punishment for violation, thus turning it into a guardian of its values and norms (Singh 1993: 17). Beker has defined Customary Law to be an established system of immemorial rules which evolved from the way of life and natural wants of the people, the general context of which was a common knowledge, coupled with precedents applying to special cases, which were retained in the memories of the chief and his counsellors, their sons and their son's son, until forgotten, or until they became part of the immemorial rules' (1989: 11). Customary law has always been cherished and it remains inherent to their uniqueness and culture of the distinct tribes. Therefore the existing practice of customary laws acts as a powerful tool to define the roles of men and women that dictates acceptable standards of behaviour. Some of the provisions that gave customary laws a secured place in society includes *Scheduled District Act of 1874* recognised by the British administration, *the Assam General Clauses Act, 1915* that protected tribal customs and practices by restricting the application of provincial laws in the hill areas. The 1930 Indian Statutory (Simon) Commission recommended that tribal customary rights be protected. *The Government of India Act 1935* accepted it and divided the hill areas into Excluded and Partially Excluded and stipulated that no Act of the Central or Provincial Legislatures would apply to them unless the Governor in his discretion so decided. It empowered him to make regulations for peace and good government in these areas (Goswami 1985: xii). The Sixth Schedule is a medium that keeps an ongoing relation between customary laws and the formal system represented by the Indian State. The former was based on the community control over their livelihood of land, forests and water sources and the latter on individual ownership. However, an exception is made in the case of the Sixth Schedule areas. While in India as a whole, land laws are based on individual ownership alone, in the Sixth Schedule areas community ownership is recognised (Barooah 2002). However, the administrative systems dealing with it are based on the individual ethos which creates a contradiction between the two systems.

In the case of most of the states in the North- eastern part of India like that of Nagaland and Mizoram, the customary laws are recognised by the state law and provide them with special status and grant them additional administrative powers in the form of Autonomous District Councils(ADCs). Moreover they constitute the integral part of modern legal system. The state courts often examine and try to understand customary law in order to make determinative judicial decisions. Leon Shaksolsky(2000) notes that customary laws are as imperative like any other law in the judicial framework. She further evokes that this process is marked when customary courts are set up by law, thereby giving certain validity to customary law (Sheleff 2000).

Interface with the Formal law and Gender issue-

The Northeast is known by the rest of India mainly for its conflicts. One cannot deny that this region, inhabited by many ethnic groups and tribes, has for more than five decades witnessed armed conflicts that are integral to its people's search for a new identity amid the economic and cultural crises they face. The dichotomy between modernisation and tradition has had an adverse impact on many tribes. Visto claims customary law as the habitual course of conduct of a society that contains do's and don'ts based on its norms, practices and usages, mechanisms such as taboos, sanctions, social rituals, culture, public posture and ethics of each individual which restrain their pattern of behaviour and regulate the social, cultural and religious aspects of the individual and the family (2003). The essential point about the customary law is its approval by the community and the way it becomes basic to its identity. If the folk, basically the male leaders feel that a particular practice or behaviour would have a positive effect on the society, it is adopted as a custom which is gradually acknowledged by the rest of the community and in course of time becomes law. While the difference between customary law and customs is that the former are mandatory and enforceable by the tribal chiefs while a custom is not enforceable (Narwani 2004: 31). Basically customary law includes rules and regulations governing marriage, property rights and other social relations expressed in the form of laws giving them a concrete form. The main features of a tribe's culture are community ownership, equity and a relatively high status (but not equality) of women. The problem arises when these laws being intrinsic to a tribe's identity and culture have to face the changing trends of modernity. This interface with the formal law affects the functioning of customary law. As Milner and Browitt (2003: 25-26) are of the view that in this interface a community both interprets other forms according to its own worldview and changes its own systems. Elements of the customary law change because the stronger "modern" culture imposes itself on their tradition (Fernandes and Barbora 2002: 85-86).

Since customary law is among the most distinctive features of the tribes, when they are subjected to economic, social, political and religious pressures it erodes many of their systems. Other provisions are made through the Sixth

Schedule that applies to the whole of Meghalaya and the Karbi Anglong and N. C. Hills districts of Assam. Some other tribes of Assam and Tripura have district autonomous councils (DAC) without the Sixth Schedule. Some elements that are specific to the Sixth Schedule, such as the precedence of customary law, have not been granted to the DACs outside the Sixth Schedule areas while the DACs in the Sixth Schedule areas have transferred to themselves powers such as control over land, forests and other natural resources. Under their customary law they belong to the village council. Though most states continue to retain their customary law to which the State has accorded constitutional recognition in Nagaland and Mizoram, others like Assam, Manipur and Arunachal Pradesh live according to it without formal recognition but want the State to grant them constitutional recognition. The Manipur tribes have some protective mechanisms while the Arunachal Pradesh tribes only have the administrative rules framed in the colonial age that cannot be called protective mechanisms (Barooah 2002: 69).

Customary laws often become a tool for the tribes in North-east to re-assert their identity through their customary law. Those progressions that modernisation presented around those tribes is the legal system. Any attempt to define law will fall into one of the two categories: Law as concrete patterns of behaviour within social groups or law as institutionalised norm enforcement. In the first category, the focus is on the norms and mechanisms embodied within ordered behaviour itself, and in the second category the focus is on institutional responses to the disruption of ordered behaviour, but we see that both categories revolve around the maintenance of social order. The vast majority tribes of the north-east consolidate fidelity to the formal legal system of the Indian constitution. They also adhere to their customary law which remains intact to their social life. Due to those twofold allegiances, there are conflicts of opinions. A section of people feel that these transformations have been forcibly imposed upon them and they demand self-governance or self-determination. Many consider their customary law innate to their existence and there are also fundamentalist interpretations, particularly on the gender issue. These tradition-modernity interfaces are usually poised to be against women. Since men have an upper hand in society, women being charge of the family hardly matters.

Hence an analysis needs to focus on the gender relations of the tribal which constructs inequality. The position of tribal women whether customary laws have benefited tribal them equally or not need to be looked upon. It is often seen that informal laws fortifies patriarchy by shoving them to the provincial coliseum instead of directing, including them in the decision making process toward societal forums. Community ownership of their livelihood (CPRs) needs to be mentioned here as in the context of the higher status that most tribal women have enjoyed in their tradition, without being equal to men being based on CPR.As long as their land, forest and water resources were community owned, women, being in charge of the family economy had some say in their management (Menon 1995). Modernisation to need emphasized on to bring gender equality yet the inverse appears to be with their interface with those formal frameworks. In this way those tradition-modernity interface is a significant part to examine those effect on women. The present paper will try to understand this interface and see in what manner it has affected the basics of their culture and identity especially class and gender relations. Modernity has both positive and negative impacts so it cannot and should not be stopped but it cannot be imposed either on the traditional communities without measures to counter its ill effects. Otherwise, the changes it introduces far from benefiting the tribe in general and women in particular, can result in the deterioration of their status. Changes in the land laws that began in the colonial age were based on the concept of individual ownership. They clearly states that what does not belong to the individual is State property. This resulted in the reduction in the little power that women had in their communities as it transferred power from the community to a few individual men belonging to an elite among them. Class formation and stronger patriarchy are its results (Fernandes and Barbora 2002: 103-105). These changes have affected also the family sphere. Traditional ideas cling to the belief that girls should be brought up to be good daughters and later dutiful and submissive wives. Docility has become an appreciated and rewarded attribute for Indian women. The most accepted belief about women is that if women move away from social norms dictated by the society they bring shame both upon their family and community. This then should be responded by punishment, often employing violence as a means of social control. These social norms that assign a particular role for women can be seen from mythological Hindu epics such as the Ramayana to Indian cinema. A look at child upbringing showed that money has become the interface between the family and society.

Though most of the customary laws have undergone changes in terms of their elucidation and enforcement, they can also stagnate if their social base has changed. The Adivasi women still continue to herbal and other medicines extracted from the fields and forests in and around the village though most have switched over to allopathic medicine or combine religious rites. A community at times easily justify their continuance or avoidance by stating that its forefathers have ordained them. In Nagaland though women have made inroads into spheres such as education and politics but men resist this change on the basis of tradition. Modernity alters the meaning of the public and a private space. That modernisation of their tradition goes against women was clear from decisions concerning education. It was an interface with society already in their tradition. The woman was involved in the child's socialisation but the training of boys into adulthood was the man's domain. Modern education involves money which some like the Angami and Dimasa earn by growing commercial crops. When children reached the college going age, the Angami who had preserved their forests when their neighbours were destroying them, began to cut them in order to earn money for it (D'Souza 2001: 50-51). In a limited choice to spend money many tribes discriminate against their own children in higher education. They invest it in boys because according to the *Adivasi*, they will contribute to the family since they remain at home while girls go away after their marriage. Those who afford to give education to their girls at the higher education level claim that, education a gift they give to the daughters, it becomes their personal property which they take with them to their husband's house, so they should not demand inheritance rights. Exclusion of heterogeneous from of everyday practice and thought is reflected in the construction of the modern nation-state which has been brutal in order to construct further the ideas of masculinity and patriarchy.

Forms of Patriarchy within Customary Law-

The space created by the society is always shaped by social and power relation. This space can never maintain impartiality. Power relations too have become cultural constructs defining citizen's identities and rights. Enforcement of cultural symbols on the women in Assam always leads to the cases of moral policing resulting in humiliating existence. The presence of a bogus union amid culture and violence justifies such violence that makes women's life difficult to sustain in society. There are instances of moral policing where women are harmed by the community dictates exercised through the village heads that stands above the dictates of family. For instance, in a village of

Assam a Hindu woman was stripped and paraded as she was convicted of eloping with a Muslim man. There was not a single person in defence of the woman which depicts the power of societal norms that makes people its silent spectators. The 'sindur' (vermilion) is a compulsory cultural constructs to be worn by the Hindu women in Assam on their forehead after marriage that enforce certain limits to their life so that they remain apart from the influence of modern constructs submitting themselves in the pleasure of their husband. A kind of joint patriarchal supervision between the individuals linked to state organization and the community leaders allows the perpetrators of violence to go scot free. This joint patriarchal supervision is one of the main reasons that creates gender riots in societies of Assam and sets a wave of ideological belief and practices legalizing the action, reinforcing the cultural codes.

It would be of great importance to discuss the customs of adivasi as they have so much of customary laws attached to it. Adivasi belong to different tribes and live in different areas their customs vary. So the forms of patriarchy may also vary. Discrimination against women is seen in the form of denial of land rights and their restricted role in community public activity and religious worship. Witch hunting, polygamy and liquor consumption are the unimaginable ways that patriarchy manifest itself. The Birhors of Jharkhand hunting wild animals and deep forests are taboo for women. During menstruation women are not allowed to enter the temples and touch anything and remain confined to room in Assam. Men hardly participate in the domestic labour of cleaning, cooking and childcare. They do these jobs only if the woman is ill or otherwise unable to tackle them. Among the Ho and Munda a woman must not even touch the plough while among the Santhal, Oraon and Khasia they can't carry it on their shoulders. Santhal and other tribal women cannot thatch a roof or use a leveler. They may not shoot arrows, use a razor, chisel holes, and strike an axe or fish with line and hook. They cannot weave cloth or string a cot. The absence of women's rights over land and other productive resources, the practise of polygamy and the incident of migration have all combined to create an environment where deserting of women by their husbands is extremely common. Access to land, that is, in combination to other forces is much more than a mere economic factor affecting adivasi women but has strong social implications. Santhali customary law permits a man to have five wives at a time. He can easily leave her and with no land in her name, this leaves her in a particularly vulnerable position. Their rights to their children are also not absolute. In some tribes if a woman remarries she may not take her children with her.

Witch-hunt on the other hand is one of the brutal acts which often take place in certain parts of Assam where many women being accused of witchery face inhuman torture and deaths. Illiteracy and superstition are often thought to be the reasons behind belief in witchery. But the force of nativity that appears in the defence of culture and tradition to inflict harm on women always remains unnoticed. Culture has always been linked with women and at the same time been a tool to oppress women. There are many incidents of violence in the name of tradition and culture. There is an urgent need to look up these vital issues of violence on a larger scale. Customary laws and practices have been the biggest stumbling block for women's empowerment, both politically and socially, in Nagaland. "Women in Nagaland do not enjoy equal social and political status with men. They do not enjoy land, property or inheritance rights as per the customary laws. In sharp contrast with the Hindu Succession Act and the Muslim Personal Law, the Naga customary laws do not recognise inheritance or property rights even if you are the only child or daughter. So, when a man, who doesn't have a son, dies, the property and land will be inherited by a male relative who may be five or six cousins away in family line," men always use the customary laws and practices as an excuse to exclude women in all spheres thereby violating their rights. The biggest tragedy of women in Nagaland is that there has not been the slightest change in their position in the society over the years. The customary laws in matters of marriage and divorce also are far from favourable to women. Among many of the tribes in northeast India, women are treated as mere commodities which can be seen in their custom of bride price. Bride-price prevails among the various communities in northeast India where the bridegroom has to pay certain amount of money to the girl's parent. This custom of bride-price which is practiced among the tribes is based on the recognition of the importance of women's role in the economic sphere. It is the 'reflection of the fact that women area productive worker in the economy of the tribe' (Nembiakkim, 2008:13). The payment of bride price did not protect women against exploitation within the family (Krishna, 2005) rather it creates limitation on women's right to initiate divorce as it 'entails the obligation to return the bride price to the husband. So women prefer to suffer in silence even if she is ill-treated rather than take recourse to divorce' (Nongbri, 1998: 22-23). In most of the communities of the northeast, the customary laws are constituted and interpreted by male alone. Women have no role indecision-making. Due to their customary laws, they aren't allowed to share their ideas in village decision-making (Fernandes and Gita, 2009).Women are excluded from participating in all the important decision making institutions (Ao, 2010). Almost all the communities in northeast India are patrilineal society where descent is traced from father to son except for the state of Meghalaya, where the Khasis and the Garos follow the matrilineal system where descent is traced from mother to the daughter. Yet what remains similar is that patriarchy rules in all these societies. Women were never allowed to represent the family or the kin group at the community level. Moreover, they are neither being given any authority at the social level. Thus, even though women have property rights in the matrilineal society, but when it comes to decision making whether it is in matrilineal or patrilineal societies, it is regarded as the domain of men (Gneezy, 2009; Krishna, 2005). The women in north-east appears to be living around an environment free of certain evil practises like dowry, female infanticide but in reality it erects a false notion of gender emancipation as women are still the victims of gender based violence in Assam. Enforcement of cultural symbols becomes one of the basic ways to assert the identity of different cultural groups which always targets women and leads to the incidence of moral policing resulting in humiliating existence of women and the creation of gendered forbidden place. Therefore this paper aimed at studying the condition of women beyond this spurious notion of liberation in conflict ridden societies of north-east which in turn prevent the women to exercise their basic democratic rights and the gender inequality remains pervasive.

Concluding Remarks

People generally avoid being accused of essentialism in this age of postmodernism and try to maintain a silence over issues of tremendous social relevance. Fundamentalism and identity politics centre on women as both their victims and their constituency. The pattern of socio -physical spaces of women depends upon the social construction of that particular society. Despite decades of development the fact remains that women in Assam, are still categorized as deprived sections of society. The paper has indicated that modernization superimposed on the tradition of the tribals without protective mechanisms can go against women and can lead to uneven economic growth. It pointed out that the interface of customary tribal law with modern administrative and legal systems in North East India has led to lopsided development in the form of sidelining the women power and ushering in an era of class struggle.

In the name of preserving traditional customs and tribal identities, very often individual and gender choices get foreclosed and women are relegated to the lower status. The customary laws and practices among most of the tribal societies in northeast India treat women as 'second sex'. Such practices overlap with gender equity, women's liberation and their empowerment. The customary law of all the community needs to be grounded on equality and human rights such that both men and women are given equal rights. North-east needs to make a positive contribution to prepare the tribal communities in its encounter with the modern systems. For all the communities to get the benefits of development, social processes and economic investment should be tools in giving the subalterns hope in their future. State apparatus should respond to the community-based ethos of this region to go beyond a relatively high status of women to gender equality. What is needed at this moment is a cautious approach to development that takes tribal values and ethos as the starting point without internalising an ideology of stronger patriarch and class based hierarchy.

References

Barbora, Sanjay and Walter Fernandes. 2002. "Modernisation and Tribal Women's Status in Northeast India," in Walter Fernandes and Sanjay Barbora (eds). *Changing Women's Status in India: Focus on the Northeast.* Guwahati: North Eastern Social Research Centre, pp. 114-138.

Barbora, Sanjay. 2002. "Ethnic Politics and Land Use: Genesis of Conflicts in India's North-East," *Economic and Political Weekly,* 37 (n. 13, March 30-April 5), pp. 1285-1292.

Barooah, Jeuti. 2002. "Property and Women's Inheritance Rights in the Tribal Areas of the Northeast," in Walter Fernandes and Sanjay Barbora (eds). Op. cit. pp. 99-113.

Changkija, Monalisa. 2004."Right to Choose One's Destiny," *Telegraph,* 19th March, p. 16.

Chaudhuri, Buddhadeb. 1997. "Nehru and Tribal Development in Inida," in J. S. Bhandari & S. B. Channa (eds). *Tribes and Governement Policies.* New Delhi: Cosmo Publications, pp.139-157.

Datta, Brijendranath. 1990. "Ethnicity, Nationalism and Sub-Nationalism, With Special Reference to North-East India," in B. Pakem (ed). *Nationality Ethnicity and Cultural Identity in North East India.* New Delhi: Omsons Publications, pp. 36-44.

Dreze, Jean and Amartya Sen. 1989. *Hunger and Public Action.* Oxford: Clarendon Press.

Eckert, Julia. "Urban Governance and Emergent Forms of Legal Pluralism in Mumbai." *Journal of Legal Pluralism,* 2004

Fernandes, Walter and Sanjay Barbora. 2002a. *The Socio-Economic Situation of Nagaon District: A Study of Its Economy, Demography and Immigration.* Guwahati: North Eastern Social Research Centre (mimeo).

Fernandes, Walter and Sanjay Barbora. 2002b. *Modernisation and Women's Status in North Eastern India: A Comparative Study of Six Tribes.* Guwahati: North Eastern Social Research Centre.

Fernandes, Barbora & Gita. 2003. Primary Education of Plantation Labourer's Children in Assam: Draft Report, Guwahati: North Eastern Social Research Centre (mimeo).

Fernandes, Walter. 1999. "Conflict in North-East: A Historical Perspective," *Economic and Political Weekly,* 34 (no. 51, Dec. 18-24), pp. 3579-3582.

Goswami M. C. (ed) 1981. *The Customary Laws and Practices of the Ao of Nagalnd,* Guwahati: The Law Research Institute, Eastern Region, Gauhati High Court.

Goswami, M. C. (ed). 1985. *Customary Laws and Practices of the Angami Nagas of Nagaland.* Guwahati: The Law research Institute, Guwahati High Court.

Griffiths, John. "What is Legal Pluralism." *Journal of Legal Pluralism,* 1986: 1-55.

Mann, Michael (ed). 1987. *Macmillan Student Encyclopedia of Sociology.* London and Basingstoke: Macmillan & Co

Marak, Caroline. 1992, "Status of women in Garo Culture" in, Soumen Sen (ed), Women in Meghalaya, New Delhi, Daya Publishing House.

Marak, K. R. 1997. Traditions and Modernity in Matrilineal Tribal Society, New Delhi: Inter-India Publications.

Mathur H.M. (ed). *Anthroplogy in Development Process.* New Delhi: Vikas Publishing House.

Menon, Geeta. "The impact of Migration on the work and tribal Women's status." In *Women and seasonal labour migration,* by Loes Schenken Sandbergen, 79-154. New Delhi: Sage, 1995.

Menon, Manju et al. 2003. "Large Dams in the Northeast," *The Ecologist,* Vol.11, N0. 1, pp. 3-8.

Menon, Nivedita. "Tarshi." *Nivedita Menon: Feminism And Feminist Conundrums.* 1 March 2015. http://www.tarshi.net/blog/interview-nivedita-menon/ (accessed March 10, 2015).

Merry, Sally Engel. "Legal Pluralism." *Law & Society Review* 22, no. 5 (January 1988): 869-896.

Moore, Erin. ""Gender, Power, and Legal Pluralism: Rajasthan, India." *American Ethnologist* 20, no. 3 (August 1993): 522-542.

Qureshi. Muniruddin (ed) 2003. *Social Status of Indian Women, Vol.1, Emancipation.* New Delhi: Anmol Publications Pvt. Ltd.

Ramanathan, Usha. 1999. "Public Purpose: Points for Discussion," in Walter Fernandes (ed). *The Land Acquisition (Amendment) Bill 1998: For Liberalisation or for the Poor?* New Delhi: Indian Social Institute, pp. 19-24.

Roy, Ajay. 1995. *The Boro Imbroglio.* Guwahati: Spectrum Publishers.

Schumacher E. F., 1977. *Small is Beautiful.* Radhakrishna.

Singh. K. S. (ed), 1993. Tribal Ethnography Customary Law and Change, Concept Publishing Company, New Delhi.

Tripathi, C. B. 1997. "Approaches to Tribal Development and Experience," in J. S. Bhandari & S. B. Channa (eds). *Tribes and Governement Policies.* New Delhi: Cosmo Publications, pp.111-138.

Vitso. Adino. 2003. *Customary Law and Women. The Chakhesang Nagas,* New Delhi: Regency Publications.

Correlating Magic and Witchcraft with the divine: A Study of Paulo Coelho's Works

Gitanjali Baro

Women have made tremendous advancement through the ages and now enjoy liberty and freedom. However a glimpse into the past exposes a narration of discrimination against the woman which still remains. One of the issues which ignite the discrimination against women is the concept of witchcraft associated with black magic. This proposition of women as witches still lingers across the corners of the world. The theoretical works like *TheMalleus Maleficarum (Hammer of the Witches)*(1487) and many other official authorizations in the past had uplifted the perception of witchcraft. *TheMalleus Maleficarum (Hammer of the Witches)*by Heinrich Kramer and Jacob Sprengeris divided into three sections; the first section analyses the concept of witchcraft theoretically, the second discusses the power of the witches and the third deals with the legal procedures to execute the witches. According to the authors the art of witchcraft exists as the Devil exists. They further advocate that witches enter into a treaty with the Satan to gain power to accomplish heinous supernatural activities and that whenever a woman did not shed tears in the course of their trial was inevitably assumed to be a witch. In *The Second Sex* (1949), Simone De Beauvoir advocates that men primarilysubjugatewomen by portraying them as the 'Other' on every level denying their humanity, in opposition to men. She states that "One is not born, but rather becomes a woman". She is defined and differentiated with reference to man and not he with reference to her; she is the incidental, the inessential as opposed to the essential (sic) (Beauvoir 26). He is the Subject, he is the Absolute – she is the Other (ibid.). The insight of women as the 'Other' expounded by Beauvoir encourages the paradigm of women as witches and it has led to heinous act like The Salem Witch Trials in Massachusetts[1]. In the book *The Salem Witch Trials*, the author Lori Lee Wilson illustrates the horrifying episode of the Salem throwing light on the various perspectives which led to the executions of twenty women accused of witchcraft in colonial Massachusettsbetween February 1692 and May 1693. She also highlights the viewpoints of the different historians on the Salem episode. In the section "Feminists and Witchcraft", Lee connotes that the feminist historians emphasize property law-suits between men and women as one of the causes leading to witch-hunt in Salem. In interpreting witchcraft at Salem, feminist historians seek in part to understand the origin of some male prejudices women still face (sic) (Wilson 77).

During the first half of the 20th centurya contemporary Pagan new religious movement known as pagan Witchcraft or Wicca was established[2].*Witchcraft Today* (1954), a book by Gerald Gardner boosted the pagan Witchcraft. Dr Gardner has shown in his book how much of the so-called "witchcraft" is descended from ancient rituals, and has nothing to do with spell-casting and other evil practices (sic) (Murray 6). In *Enchanted Feminism: The Reclaiming Witches of San Francisco*(2002), JoneSalomonsenrepresents an anthropological study of the pagan Witchcraft. This book represents an in-depth study of how contemporary Witchesin the Reclaiming community of San Francisco attempt to construct new cultural visions and new religious agency and identity by means of nature-oriented goddess worship and magical, ritual performance (sic) (Salomonsen 1). Salomonsenindicates the growing interest in the spirituality and ritual practices of shamanism and ancient paganism. She further highlights that the Reclaiming community of feminist Witches was formed in 1979 by two Jewish women Starhawk and Diane Baker. Twenty years later, Reclaiming has grown into a large, with sister communities all over US, Canada and western Europe (sic) (Salomonsen 1).The feminist Witches embrace ancient paganism and goddess worship in order to heal experiences of estrangement prompted by patriarchal biblical religions. They assent to the significant nature of reality: (divine) immanence, ecological (interdependence) and the sexed nature of the elemental birthing power (female Creatix).*The Spiral Dance:*

A Rebirth of the Ancient Religion of the Great Goddess (1979) by Starhawk is about the contemporary pagan belief and its practices. Starhawk connotes that the Witchcraft is the oldest religion extant in the West. It existed even before Christianity, Judaism, Islam, Buddhism and Hinduism. She indicates that Witchcraft takes its teaching from nature and reads inspiration in the movements of the sun, moon and the stars, the flight of birds, the slow growth of trees and the cycles of the seasons (sic) (Starhawk 2-3). She also points out that the spiral dance is an eminent part of the witchcraft. Her book emphasizes mysticism and ecstatic experience. Her book also focuses the Goddess worship. Paulo Coelho, a renowned Brazilian novelist expounds the pagan Witchcraft in his works. In his novels, he amalgamates the mysteries of the transcendental world with the mundane. He uses Magical Realism as a narrative mode where there is a co-existence between real and magical events. In most of his books, he writes about the prejudices revolving around the concept of "witch" in the contemporary society. According to him:

> "a witch is a woman who is capable of letting her intuition takes hold of her actions, who communes with her environment, who isn't afraid of facing challenges".

He associates magical elements with women and elevates the feminine side of divinity and therefore, some of his novels highlight the concept of contemporary paganism. This paper attempts to study the select novels of Paulo Coelho and exemplify that unlike the conventional notion of witches which associates magic with dark, devil and evil, Coelho correlates witches and magic with the feminine side of divinity, shaman, purity and miracle.

Coelho's *The Witch of Portobello* (2007) is a provocative book that asserts the primacy of the spiritual and transcendental over the material and empirical. The novel revolves around the life of the protagonist Sherine Khalil who renames herself Athena, and who is ultimately known as "the witch of Portobello".In one of the interviews the author points out that the book deals with the feminine side of divinity:

> "...in The Witch of Portobello I wanted to explorethe feminine divinity, I wanted to plunge into the heart of the Great Mother. I felt the need of question why society had tried to lock away the feminine side of God."

He works through the theme of "the feminine divinity" throwing light on the notions of the feminist Witches. He highlights the concept of neo-paganism in the novel. The central character Athena is nothing but a Coelho's witch. Coelho emphasizes that society is all about being completely transparent not only to the world but to us; it is about the misconception that all is explainable. Coelho endorses shamanism, ancient paganism and goddess worship. The central character Athena is Coelho's way to unveil the mystery engulfing the concept of witchcraft and its association with black magic. Athena was a "dare devil", ever ready to face the challenges of the mundane world by her own. She startedto have visions of saints and angels since her childhood and her wistful nature develops fully later in her life. Athena was a priestess who could understand the forces of nature. Athena left education and married her ex-husband Lukas at the age of nineteen and divorced him after their son Viorel's birth. When Lukas asked her to give a thought before taking a radical step to leave university, she quoted Robert Frost:

> "Two roads diverged in a wood, and I-
> I took the one less traveled by,
> And that has made all the difference."(TWoP 35)

And that was the path she took her entire life until she was condemned for blasphemy and witchcraft. Father Fontana mentions that Athena left the Church, after it forbade her from receiving sacrament as she was a divorcee. She swore never to set foot in a Church ever again. Athena dared to choose to respect the words on which the religious institution was based rather than the institution. Athena, thus, embraced the pagan Witchcraft in order to heal the experiences of estrangement prompted by patriarchal biblical religion. From Beirut she migrated to England where she discovered Vertex through trance dancing and calligraphy:

> "When I dance, I'm a free woman or rathera free spirit who can travel through the universe, contemplate the present, divinethe future, and be transformed into pure energy." (TWoP 61)

In London from PavelPodtielski Athena learnt that "in life Vertex is the culminating point, the goal of all those who, like everyone else, make mistakes, but who, even in their darkest moments, never lose sight of the light emanating from their hearts. The Vertex is hidden inside us, and we can reach it if we accept it and recognize it". And in the Middle East from NatilAlaihishe learnt that calligraphy is the search for perfect meaning of each word through writing. A single letter requires us to distil in it all the energy it contains, as if were carving out its meaning. They contain the soul of the man making the lines to spread them throughout the world. The art of calligraphy is all about objectivity, patience, respect, elegance and mastering the blank spaces. She returns to Romania and from her biological mother she realized the existence of blank spaces in her life. She learnt that there are blank spaces in everyone's life, one needs to understand these blank spaces to make one's soul composed and calm and that these blank spaces, pauses give meaning to a life just as they giving meaning to sentences and music. Athena preached and rejuvenated people around her through the beauty and wisdom of these knowledges.

Finally she became a controversial spiritual leader in London preaching the pagan Witchcraft. She used to go to the state of ecstasy while trance dancing and spoke to others as the spirit of omniscient Goddess, Hagia Sofia. She was a woman of twenty-second century living in the twenty-first, and making no secret of the fact either. Athena had chosen the Portobello Road in London as her worship meeting point for her followers which was disrupted by a Protestant protest and which ultimately led her to achieve the title, "the Witch of Portobello". She went to teach people the manifestation of what the people call 'the Great Mother', the Goddess of Creation. She was bringing to the surface, the immensely rich world we carry in our souls, without realizing that people are not yet ready to accept their own powers. That became her biggest problem which led her to her ultimate doom.

In *The Second Sex*, Beauvoirmentions that Christian ideology played no little role in women's oppression. Saint Paul commands self-effacement and reserve from women; he bases the principle of subordination of women to man on the Old and New Testaments (Beauvoir 133). "The man is not of the woman; but the woman of the man"; and "Neither was man created for the woman; but the woman for the man" (ibid.). She depicts that fear of the other sex is assumed by the anguish of man's uneasy conscience. In a religion where the flesh is cursed, the woman becomes the devil's most fearsome temptation (Beauvoir 133). Tertullian writes: "Woman! You are the devil's gateway" (ibid). Further the idea that Eve led Adam to sin is also constructed by the orthodox religious preachers. Joan of Arc was put to trial and later executed by burning in the Middle Ages just because she did not conform to the laws framed by the orthodox religious preachers.

She became "the Other" and was condemned for heresy and blasphemy. Just like her, Athena was alsoconvicted for blasphemy and witchcraft practice by the Protestants. At the height of her popularity she was compelled to fake her own death in order to avoid an inevitably undesirable and chaotic situation.

Coelho's *Aleph* focuses on the concept of the Aleph, the first letter of the alphabet in Hebrew, Arabic and Aramaic and which according to the "magical tradition" is a form of "Divine Energy"[3]. In the chapter "Sharing Souls", a Turkish woman named Hilal who is a violin virtuoso is introduced. Coelho and Hilal experience the Aleph. Coelho gradually realizes that Hilal can unlock the secrets of a parallel spiritual universe and thus he travels back through time and space and realises that Hilal is the woman whom he loved and betrayed five hundred years ago in different incarnation. Initially Coelho does not have the idea about the consequences which made him betray her, but as the story proceeds he ultimately seeks the answer. In the year 1492, eight girls were condemned for practising witchcraft by the Church. Hilal was one of them. Coelho loved her before entering the Dominican Order. Coelho was not able to save any of the girls and they were tortured and burnt to death. Coelho mentions that he has met the four girls out of the eight in the present incarnation and that Hilal is the fifth one. He seeks for her forgiveness. He also becomes aware of the fact that he loves Hilal, that they have always loved each other. In the chapter "The Eagle of Baikal", Coelho talks about the forgotten feminine side of divinity. Coelho explains vividly the role of the shaman as he had read in the history of civilization. Coelho explains how the first shamans of humanity were women. To quote Coelho:

> "Along with the birth of love came a need to find an answer to the mystery of existence. The first shamans were women." (*Aleph*240)

However at some undefined moment in history, the female gift was usurped by men. And the natural gifts of women were ignored as only the power of the men mattered. Thus, male entered to organise shamanism into a social structure. Then the religions were introduced. When the women started demanding back their role as shamans they were treated as heretics and prostitutes. They were punished with burnings, stoning and, in milder instances, exile. And in this way the female religions were erased from the history of civilisation. Likewise Coelho's *Brida*is a tale of a young Irish girl named Brida and her quest for knowledge. The novel deals with the concept of the contemporary paganism through which Brida attains enlightenment. Brida encounters a practitioner of the craft Wicca. Wicca who follows the tradition of the Moon accepts Brida as her student and she becomes the sorcerer's apprentice. Brida, thus begins her journey toward becoming a witch. Wicca teaches her trance dancing, to dance to the music of the world, aboutthe tarot cards and story of cards, and the procedure to worship the moon. Through the Wiccan knowledge Bridamakes her own voyage of discovery, explores life, discovers divinity, magic, spirituality and learns to connect with her truest self.

Paulo Coelho, thus, in his novels correlates magical elements with women, elevates the feminine side of divinity and throws light on the pagan Witchcraft associating it with shamanism, purity and miracle. He emphasizes the Goddess worship relating it to mysticism, ecstatic experiences and merges the mysteries of the transcendental world with the mundane.

NOTES

1. The Salem Witch Trials in colonial Massachusetts were sequences of hearings and trials of those women accused of witchcraft. It took place between February 1692 and May 1693. Following the prosecutionstwenty women were executed.
2. Wicca also known as Contemporary Paganism and Neo-paganism is a new religious movement. Influenced by the various historical pagan beliefs of pre-modern Europe. It includes worshipping of Goddess and God. They are traditionally viewed as the Moon Goddess and the Horned God.
3. Coelho describes Aleph as the first point in the universe that contains all other points, present and past, large and small. He further illustrates that the great Aleph occurs when two or more people with a very strong affinity happen to find themselves in the small Aleph. Their energies complete each other and provoke chain reaction.

WORKS CITED

Beauvoir, Simone De. *The Second Sex*. Paris: Editions Gallimard, 1949. Print. Trans.

Constance Borde and Sheila Malovany-Chevallier. New York: Vintage Books, 2009.

Coelho, Paulo. *Aleph*. London: HarperCollins*Publishers*, 2011. Print. All subsequent references of the bookare from the same edition. In all cases, page numbers have been given immediately afterthe quotations in parenthesis with *Aleph*.

----. *Brida*. London: HarperCollins*Publishers*, 1990. Print.

----. *The Witch of Portobello*. London: HarperCollins*Publishers*, 2007. Print. All subsequent references of the book are from the same edition. In all cases, page numbers have been given immediately after the quotations in parenthesis withabbreviation T WoP.,

Gardner, Gerald.*Witchcraft Today with an introduction by Dr. Margaret Murray*. London: Various, 1954. Print.

Kramer, Heinrich and Jacob Sprenger. *The Malleus Maleficarum (Hammer of the Witches)*.Germany, 1487. Trans. Christopher S. Mackay. Cambridge: Cambridge University Press, 2009. Print.

Salomonsen, Jone. *Enchanted Feminism: The Reclaiming Witches of San Francisco*. London:

Routledge, 2002. Print.

Starhawk. *The Spiral Dance: A Rebirth of the Ancient Religion of the Great Goddess*.

San Francisco: Harper and Row Publishers, 1979. Print.

Wilson, Lori Lee. *The Salem Witch Trials*. Minnesota: Lerner Publications Company, 1997. Print.

Traditional World-view of the Adi Tribes of Arunachal Pradesh and the Poetry of Mamang Dai: a Parallel Reading

Farina Basumatary

"A world view is a coherent collection of concepts and theorems that must allow us to construct a global image of the world, and in this way to understand as many elements of our experience as possible" (Aerts et al., 8). Going by this definition, this paper aims at studying the Adi conception of God, spirituality, the positioning of humans in the ecosystem, the human relationship with non-human nature, evolution of humankind and other creatures, life after death, and social, cultural, and moral obligations in the Adi context.

The Adi are a people belonging to Arunachal Pradesh in North East India. They are a patriarchal ethnic group. They have their own unique concepts of governance, rituals, and God; the aspects of life which "modern" society terms, politics, philosophy, science, religion, and ethics, etc.. The Adi world view has for long remained isolated from influences from external world views like the western conceptions, or that of Hinduism. But the penetration of these 'widely influential' systems produced a certain resistance to as well as trends of assimilation with these new systems of understanding the world. The influx of missionaries during the colonial era, and that of the plainspeople in

Arunachal Pradesh, account for shifts in the belief systems of the indigenous people, as well as efforts to resurrect their uniqueness as upholders of different world views in the face of being confronted with alien philosophies. This has projected into struggles to reassert their identity through poetry, as is seen in Mamang Dai's works.

Evident in the poetry of Mamang Dai are popular concerns regarding the male-female divide, the human-nature divide, etc., which are viewed differently from different world views and perspectives. Contemporary trends of globalization pose as a threat to indigenous world views. The traditional Adi conception is that humans are kith and kin to non-human nature. Consequently, inter personal and inter species relationships are perceived in a way that stands in contrast to Western capitalistic outlook towards 'otherized' beings and species. In the Adi worldview, social, religious, moral and ethical beliefs and obligations overlap. For most of the Adi beliefs, what is religious extends to the realm of what is social and cultural, and vice versa. Central to all socio-religious beliefs and rituals is their concept of soul, spirits, God, and their oral tradition.

Concept of God.

Philippe Ramirez differentiates the types of invisible beings supposedly known to the Adi people. There are very few overwhelming, omnipresent and omnipotent deities, like the Donyi Polo (sun-moon). "*Donyi* and *polo* literally mean "sun" and "moon," which the Tani group of tribes in Arunachal Pradesh, such as the Adi, Nyishi, Apatani, Tagin, and the Galo, worship for prosperity, fertility, and protection from calamities (Chaudhuri, 263)". The second category of 'special' entities are the *wiyu* (pronounced as *uyu* by the Adis), or "spirits". These spirits, according to Ramirez, may evolve in specific marks of the landscape like mountains, rivers, or air; no spirit is strictly benevolent or malevolent; but the spirits of the wild are more feared than those residing in human settlements. According to the Adi indigenous religion, there is a supreme God, whose agents are manifest in different forces in nature. These are spirits. These spirits have human-like character. They may be malevolent, or benevolent. Like an officer in-charge of a department, the Adi people have a spirit-in-charge of different things that matter to the Adi people. "It seems that the societies of central Arunachal-Pradesh conceive their relationships with the supernatural in the terms of a power balance, and by no means in those of a submission to a sovereign or higher authority. If the spirit attacks, one does not bow down, one defends oneself; if it remains deaf to a request, one gets rid of it. . . The attacking spirit is not the enforcer of a punishment, it is indeed an enemy, and thus in a way a similar being, with which one has to fight on an equal basis"(Ramirez, 8). The worshippers of the Donyi Polo religion give an imaginary figure to different forms of gods and goddesses they worship in order that their faith may not waver. The different forms given to Doying Bote, Kine Naane, etc., are manifestations of the different aspects of the central gods, Donyi and Polo.

The Adi people have come to associate the sun and the moon with good qualities as good omen. Mamang Dai too uses these stereotyped symbols to resuscitate the belief systems of the persona in some of her poems. For example, in "A prologue", a Mrs X is spiteful about the unstable love life of the poet persona, which seemed as though destined to end. Nonetheless, a full and round moon appeared. She finds that the full moon has belied her expectations. The full moon symbolizes hope, and good tidings. This imagery is congruent with the religious belief system of the Adi people, who believe in the Sun and the Moon being constant bearers of truth, and provider of hope. In the poem, "Green in the time of flood", Dai writes: "I stake my claim to peppermint and green fruit,/ and a slice of moon across the world,/ where the bank slips away/ and a new boundary marks our night and days" (*Midsummer Survival Lyrics*, 5). A slice of moon here, again, signifies a mighty and protective power overlooking the poet persona's world.

According to the Adi worldview, death is not the end of life. In fact, for the Adi people, the cosmos is one big jumble of beings we have come to call God, humans, animals, spirits, etc.. Dead people also live as spirits. At times, the spirits of dead people hover about their previous dwelling places in case of unnatural deaths, or in case of people who did not receive proper funeral rites. These people seemingly become evil spirits. They are called *Urams*. In her poem, "Dotgang", Dai writes about the performance of a ceremony the Adi people perform in order to appease the dead. The ceremony is called *Dotgang*. To quote Gibji Nimasow: "*Dotgang* is a form of sacrifice of *mithun* at the time of death of a person. It is believed by Adis that if such sacrifice is made, it appease[s] the soul of the dead and keep[s] the soul away from hovering around restlessly (Nimasow,)". In "Dotgang", Dai describes a grave decorated with seeds, fruits, birds, squirrel, skulls of the *mithun*, Bos frontalis, fish, and a little soup. Offerings had continued for a year. Presently, the grave is ready to be closed. According to Dai, this farewell is "Death, and the beginning of another life. Letting go, on both sides (*Midsummer Survival Lyrics*, 21)". As the poem makes one understand, death is not the end of life. It is a kind of change of form of existence.

Other Lives

Oral narrations help the people identify themselves in relation to their environment. The creation story of the Adi people goes thus: In the beginning there was only *Keyum*, nothingness. Out of it, came cloud and mist. From it came *Khupning-Knam*, Cloud Woman. Cloud Woman gave birth to snow. From the snow was born a girl, *Inga* or earth; and a son, *Mu* or sky. *Inga* and *Mu* gave birth to *Imbung*, the wind. *Imbung* blew very hard and separated his parents, *Inga* and *Mu*. Hence, came to existence, heaven and earth. And henceforth, all creations came into being. The concept of creation, and of the idea of life after death is a serious point in which the Western and the Adi views collide. According to Christian theology, humans were assigned stewardship over every other creature in the world by God Himself. But the Adi people believe that there is no hierarchy of beings; that humans are brothers to the bat, the snake, and the tiger. Dai reiterates the same view in her poem "Birthplace". To quote from the poem: "We are the children of the rain/ of the cloud woman,/ brother to the stone and bat" (*River Poems*, 79). Since every form of creation traces their origin to Cloud Woman, therefore, every creature on earth are siblings.

Also, in Dai's poems, "Man and tiger" and "Man and tiger (2)", Dai endorses the Adi view that the tiger and man were born brothers. To quote from the poem, "Man and brother":

> The tiger runs swiftly from my father's house
> calling my name.
> Brother: Man brother!
> Have mercy for our destiny! (*Midsummer Survival Lyrics*, 49).

On being hunted, the tiger calls out to the human hunter to be saved, addressing him as 'brother'.

The history of ancestry of the humans with the tiger has been told by women from generations, as suggested in the lines quoted below, from another poem, "Man and brother (2)":

Deep into the night the women tell stories.
In the incestuous hunger of birth and creation, they say;
we tumbled down the same stairway
of stars, fire and salt. (51)

Women are the harbingers of stories and knowledge from the past to
the present. Among the Adi people, women are usually assigned the role
of storytellers. Apparently, it came down through stories that humans and
the tiger tumbled down into the sea of existence from the same stairs, and
therefore, are equal.

In "The days in our hands", Dai argues that probably the clouds, the trees,
and the sun have a language too. Only it is different from that of humans. But
humans do not care to acknowledge this fact. To quote Dai:

Who would say
look, the rainclouds are swollen
because they cannot speak.

Who would say,
the loveliness of trees has failed this year,
they wait in vain;
because the sun is tight-lipped
about time and distance. (54)

The section, "Other Lives" in *Midsummer Survival Lyrics* contains forty
one poems. Most of the poems in this section echo Dai's conception that forms
of life other than humans need considerable attention and care. Survival means
something composite. And like the Adi view suggests, humans are just one of
the innumerable forms of life on the planet, and not the most important one.
To quote from Dai's prosaic poem "Other lives":

The land is a being just like us. We live the weather, share food,
rice, water, salt. We go to war, kill each other with our weapons and are
killed by a drowning river or an avalanche of rocks. It is a bond both
cruel and kind; like brothers claiming territory. Since both are equal
to the other it is a state of mutual regard, a state of kinship.
(*Midsummer Survival Lyrics*, 44)

According to Dai, not only is the belief in the equality of all forms of life a traditional theory. It is true from a logical viewpoint too. Human beings, and the land, and other beings on it fight for survival. And that fight can be likened to the struggle between two brothers claiming territory. The struggle is inevitable, but the relationship between the struggling parties is that of kinship and not that of 'steward' and 'resources'.

Perception of history

Oral tradition of the Adi people influence a large part of their belief systems including their idea of their history. "The history of what is now known as the North-East Frontier Agency ascends for hundreds of years into the mists of tradition and mythology. (Discovery of North-East India. Vol 2. NEFA, Verrier Elwin, 1)". The people of Arunachal Pradesh have not had a script since early on. For them, history and mythology have fused into one. Therefore, what is known of the history of the people is what has been handed down orally. These oral transmissions may be in the form of stories, rituals, or customs, and belief systems, also superstitions.

In the poem, "The Missing Link", the poet talks about a "great river that turned, turning/ with the fire of the first sun, (*River Poems*, 11)". In the footnote to the same poem, Dai suggests that the river being referred to is the Siang. The Siang was supposed to be the 'missing link' between the rivers, Tsangpo, and the Brahmaputra. The persona remembers the river to be a landmark in their journey southwards from "the old land of red-robed men" (*River Poems*, 11). This comes parallel to the theory of migration of the Adi people to present day Arunachal Pradesh from Tibet. According to Stuart Blackburn, there are two theories as to where the central Arunachali tribes have migrated from: the "Tibet" hypothesis, and the "Burma/ China" hypothesis. The Tibet hypothesis assumes the central Arunachali tribes migrated to their present abode from Tibet. Blackburn also argues that he tribes probably migrated in patches and installments. Mamang Dai's "The Missing Link" refers to the story of the southward migration of the Adi people from Tibet, which is congruent to Blackburn's "Tibet" hypothesis. "In sum, migration legends are less like orally transmitted narratives and more like memorised historical records"(Stuart Blackburn, 17). Dai's account of how the 'missing link' helps her people identify themselves in relation to the landscape around them is entirely based on memory. The line, "I will remember then" has been used as repetition to intensify the effect of memory. Everything that they 'know' about the past of their people is through memory and stories.

Women

That womanhood is a socially constructed state of being has been asserted by feminists like Simone de Beauvoir. In this regard, Beauvoir has this remark to make: ". . . 'the division' of humanity into two classes of individuals- is a static myth. . . To pose Woman is to pose the absolute Other, without reciprocity, denying against all experience that she is a subject, a fellow human being (1407, Beauvoir)". Feminist critics like Beauvoir strongly oppose the classification of the human race to Man and Woman. The word, 'Woman' seems to be a derivation from the word, Man, implying that Man is central, and Woman is something different from the man, and thus the peripheral. According to Beauvoir, such a perceived difference is a myth that wrongly justifies all privileges men enjoy in society, and authorizes the abusive stand they may take towards women. (Beauvoir, 1409). In line with this thought goes the stereotyped roles assigned to men and to women. Several of these result in suppressing the natural urges of women to fight for honor, chase a career, etc., and restricting women to domestic roles. Therefore, a Woman perceived as a 'wife', a 'daughter', a 'daughter-in-law', etc. has dangerous connotations. Such terms used for women hold within them the prescribed gender roles that hold that women should do certain tasks men do not want to do. Men are a pressurized lot too. But gender roles assigned to men lie in the social sphere. Everything they do earns them a social status. Whereas, women do everything without much returns.

In North Eastern India, and also in Arunachal Pradesh, there is relative absence of cases of dowry, female infanticide, sex determination, *purdah*, or *sati*. However, preference for sons over daughters does exist. Some ethnic populations follow the practice of paying bride price. Bride price, in the Adi context, is the price in the form of *mithun,* pigs, or jewellery, the groom pays the family of the bride as he is taking away a working hand (the bride) from her previous family. However, just as observed by Z Khiangte, the institution of bride price is also a kind of commodification of women. The Adi people follow patrilineality. The women look after the household, and also perform functions in the field like, sowing, weeding, and transplanting. The men are in-charge of social activities. They also take part in activities relating to cultivation. However, it can be seen that women and men do perform stereotyped gender roles even in Adi society.

Gender-issue is not a very prominent aspect of Mamang Dai's themes as a writer. But Dai certainly writes from a feminine point of view when she writes about the "sorrow of women". Mamang Dai through the poet persona in "The sorrow of women" describes the helplessness women feel on being denied a share in discussing the larger social problems like war, escape, and liberty. To quote from the poem:

> My love, what shall I do?
> I am thinking how I may lose you
> to war and big issues;
> more important than me. (*Midsummer Survival Lyrics*, 9)

Dai throws the point across that it is lamentable that women are reduced to mere issues in men's lives. Other issues, one of which is war, are considered 'bigger' than women being in men's lives.

Women are the teachers at home. It is generally women who tell the children of the tribe stories about migration, as can be gathered from "The Missing Link": "I will remember then the fading voices/ of deaf women framing the root of light/ in the first stories to the children of the tribe" (*River Poems*, 11). Indirectly, women are responsible for educating in the informal way. In "Let No Tear", women are referred to as storytellers: storytellers that emerge as historians after any remarkable event that affects the tribe.

In "Sky Song", the children play, the women talk, and the men predict harvests one summer morning. This trail of images is part of the landscape, where men and women perform stereotypical functions. To quote Dai:

> We left the children playing.
> We left the women talking
> and men were predicting
> good harvests or bad, (*River Poems*, 22).

In the poem, "Images", the earth and the sky are projected as woman and man respectively. This form of projection draws inspiration from mythology of the Adi people. The Adi people believe that the earth is a female. It once rose to meet its lover, the sky. In the process, parts of the earth rose and are forever shaped as mountains since then.

> The mountain is a disguise of earth woman rising to meet her sky lover. (*River Poems*, 31)

In Mamang Dai's poetry, women occur in their stereotypical forms. Women occur as people performing gendered roles.

Conclusion

The conception of the Adi people regarding life, God, "nature", relationships, etc. starkly contrasts popular conceptions. In a world where globalization and capitalism is the norm, the Adi emphasis on mutual regard for survival instead of survival of the fittest, deserves consideration at least from the point of view of ecological conservation. Harris and Wasilewski share this opinion when they say: "We believe that an articulation of Indigenous perspectives, of the concept of Indigeneity, with its inclusive management of diversity, constitutes a contribution to global discourse which has the potential of positively transforming the relationship dynamics of the 21st-century world, politically, socially, economically and spiritually (Harris & Wasilewski, 2)".

REFERENCES:

Aerts, Diederik. Apostel, Leo. Belle, Hubert Van. Hellemans, Staf. Maex, Aedel. Moor, Bart De.

Veken, Jan Van der. *Worldviews: From fragmentation to intergration.* (VUB Press, Brussels,

1994). 2007. Internet Edition.

Beauvoir, Simone de. From *The Second Sex. The Norton Anthology: Theory and Criticism.* Eds.

Vincent B. Leitch, William E. Cain, Laurie Finke, Barbara Johnson, John McGowan and

Jeffrey J. Williams. New York: W.W. Norton & Company, Inc., 2001. Print.

Blackburn, Stuart. "Memories of Migration: Notes on legends and beads in Arunachal Pradesh,

India". *European Bulletin of Himalayan Research* 25/26 (2003/2004): 15-60.

Chakravarti, B. *A Cultural History of the North-East India (Assam).* Calcutta: Self Employment

Bureau Publications, 2000. Print.

Chaudhuri, Sarit Kumar. "The Institutionalization of Tribal Religion: Recasting the *Donyi-Polo* Movement in Arunachal Pradesh". *Asian Ethnology* 72.2 (2013): 259- 277.

Dai, Mamang. *Once Upon a Moontime.* New Delhi: Katha, 2005. Print.

Elwin, Verrier. "The North-East Frontier Agency". *Discovery of North-East India: Geography History Culture Religion Politics Sociology Science Education and Economy.* Ed. Sk Sharma and Usha Sharma. Volume 2. New Delhi: Mittal Publications,. Print.

Khiangte, Zothanchhingi. "Gender Equity in North-east India: The Paradox Within". Journal of North-East Region 2 (2014): 191-196. Print.

Nimasow, Gibji. "Socio-economic Importance of Mithun (*Bos Frontalis*) Among the Adi Tribes of Arunachal Pradesh, India". *Science and Culture* 81 (7-8) (2015): 200-205.

Puthenpurakal, Joseph. Puykunnel, Shaji Joseph. Subba, T.B., Eds. *Christianity and Change in Northeast India.* New Delhi: Concept Publishing Company, 2009. Print.

Ramirez, Philippe. "Enemy spirits, Allied Spirits: the Political Cosmology of Arunachal Pradesh Societies". *NEHU Journal,* January 2005. Vol- 3(1). Pp. 1-28

Sharma, S.K.. Sharma, Usha. Eds. *Discovery of North-East India: Geography History Culture Religion Politics Sociology Science Education and Economy.* Volume 1. New Delhi: Mittal Publications, 2005. Print.

The African World and the Continuum of Conquest: An Analysis of *Things Fall Apart* and *A Grain of Wheat.*

Debojyoti Biswas

And slowly answer'd Arthur from the barge:
"The old order changeth, yielding place to new,
And God fulfils himself in many ways,
Lest one good custom should corrupt the world.
Comfort thyself: what comfort is in me?
(from *The Passing of Arthur* by Alfred Tennyson)

Africa, by the European consciousness, has always been projected as a 'Dark Continent[1]' inhabited by savage races, a foil and an "antithesis to Europe[2]". Their existence depended only on the discovery[3] made by the European colonizers, hence when the unchartered world had been drawn on the maps[4], it fascinated the minds of the European explorers which eventually led to the imminent expeditions in search of immense wealth to be discovered in those places as pointed out by David Arnold (Arnold, 2002, p. 11); and in doing so the explorers often came into direct confrontation with the indigenous people inhabiting those lands. These explorers had maintained in their travelogues, diaries, memoirs and reports that these tribal were immensely savage and incomprehensible to a civilized world. As Donald H. Matthews puts it, "the travel diaries and reports of early European explorers on West African civilizations are replete with a sense of awe and fear of a world that was the same and yet different from their own" (Matthews, 1998, p. 5). Therefore, along with the expansion of trade and territories, there also entailed the hydra-headed civilizing missions at certain areas which otherwise resulted in annihilation of a huge chunk of aboriginal tribes, as in the case of Australia[5] and the domination of the African nations. Whereas, writers like Rudyard Kipling, E.M. Forster and Joseph Conrad had given pictures of the 'savage world' from their Eurocentric imagination- those glossed over the rich and intricate structure of the tribal societies of the Orient and the Africa; Writers like Ngugi wa Thiong'o and Chinua Achebe rebutted this and exposed the Eurocentric biasness through their works. The novels *Things Fall Apart* and *A Grain of Wheat* recounted the coming of the colonizers which had resulted into the disintegration of the African tribes that led to the colonization of the place and people; and the eventual departure of the colonizers from the colonies leaving a trail of complete chaos and spread of European vices like corruption and power politics. Eminent Ghanaian historian also had a similar view as cited by Ode Ogede: "But aside from its obvious brutality, colonization also unleashed other far-reaching, long term traumatic consequences: it altered dramatically the cultural, economic, social and political climate of the continent" (Ogede, 2008, p. 2) Although Africa had been colonized by different nations at different times, the British colonialism in Kenya and Nigeria was greatly coercive to the indigenous cultures. As Julius cites Bade Onimode,

> "the mechanisms of colonialism in Nigeria centered round the colonial state and economy. They included military conquests and political coercion through British monopoly of the colonial state apparatus, the manipulation of this political power for unequal trade, capital import, cultural penetration, through Christianity and colonial education as well as the dissemination of the British illusion of colonial epoch" (Ihonvbere, 1994, p. 12).

Both the novels mentioned above can be seen as complementary to each other as they are seminal in understanding the rise of the colonial powers and the fall of the tribal communities in those nations. The theory that can be formulated on the basis of this understanding - the gradual conquest of the tribal communities/territories by the British power- will help in understanding the overall colonization process of the British Empire elsewhere too. In dealing with the writers' point of view about the cultural richness of Africa and the corruption of this rich heritage by colonial intervention, the paper will attempt to establish the hypothesis that the disintegration of the African tribes and their eventual colonization was not solely caused by the clever tactic of the masquerading exploiter/colonizers; but that the fault lied within the society which resulted in its disintegration and its subjugation to colonial powers.

When the novel begins, one finds Achebe presenting the culture and tradition of the Igbo tribal society on which it hinges. The society, a repository of cultural values and the individual as the vanguard of these values exist in binding reciprocity. The society is held together by the faith of the individual into the social codes. As one of the oldest members of the 'umunna'[6] of Okonkow's mother's clan at Mbanta observed during the feast offered by Okonkwo before his departure:

> A man who calls his kinsmen to a feast does not do so to save him from starving...we come together because it is good for kinsmen to do so...But I fear for you young people because you do not understand how strong is the bond of kinship. You do not know what it is to speak with one voice. And what is the result? An abominable religion has settled among you. A man can now leave his father and his brothers. (Achebe, *Things Fall Apart*, 1975, p. 152)

Vernantius Emeka Ndukaihe points out that 'to belong is well emphasized" in Igbo society (Ethics, 2006, p. 204). The Igbo community also had a structured society: they followed multiple cropping; they had a town-crier, who delivered messages; there were rules to settle disputes with neighboring villages; a hierarchy in social status was followed; social custom like 'week of peace' was observed; strict social laws were enforced with severity and the defaulters were punished according to the tribal law; justice and equality existed; customs and rituals related to the rites of passage were honoured; marriage and burial rituals were followed; a village playground existed where important functions and meetings were held; cultural tolerance and mutual respect were visibly present. The Igbo community was also rich in oral tradition as evinced from their use of folktales and proverbs: "Proverbs are the palm-oil with which words are eaten" (Achebe, Things Fall Apart, 1975, p. 6). They not only had respect for society as a whole but also for individuals' personal achievements. Okonkwo remained the undisputed warrior who rose to prominence by dint of his hard labour, strength and valor. He had not only won three of the four titles in the clan, but was also a great warrior and a successful cultivator. He was a sharp contrast to his father Unoka. Okonkwo had also equally contributed towards his social responsibility by being an emissary for the clan in settling disputes with neighboring villages, and as an 'egwugwu'[7] in dispensing justice to the clansmen. Okonkwo's multiple role within this structured society pointed to the fact that the society was still at a rudimentary stage with the sign of a simple society. As Herbert Spenser had said: "While rudimentary, a society is all warrior, all hunter, all hut-builder, all toolmaker: every part fulfills for itself all needs (Spencer, 1967, pp. 4-5)."

As the society evolves, the community refines its qualities and progresses towards a better position. This is a natural process. As Achebe believes that human values, like that of the society to which one belongs, are never "fixed and eternal… values are relative and in a constant state of flux."[8] But when one culture comes into contact with another dominant culture and the latter forces the former into accepting their culture through coercive techniques, the host culture is not able to fully reconcile with the new culture naturally. There is no exchange of culture, as a consequence, but only a colonization of culture takes place. This results into the unintelligibility of the cultures. Neither Nwoye understands the "mad logic of the Trinity" (Achebe, Things Fall Apart, 1975, p. 134), nor does Reverend James Smith understand the 'irrational' customs of the Igbo community (Achebe, Things Fall Apart, 1975, p. 167). The result is not enriching as there had been no cultural exchange or transmission but cultural conflict and cultural subordination. Ogede observes that "the attempt by the colonialists to turn Igbos into imitation whites caused major realignments of values, leading to no small consternation and cultural confusion" (Ogede, 2008, p. 3). As a result this has led to the abhorrence and condemnation of the Igbo culture by the British. However, while despising and looking down upon the African culture, the Europeans overlooked and downplayed the 'rites of passage' that every civilization must pass through. Chinua Achebe rightly comments on the European biasness of the African world:

> For the Thames too "has been one of the dark places of the earth."
> It conquered its darkness, of course, and is now in daylight and at

peace. But if it were to visit its primordial relative, the Congo, it would run the terrible risk of hearing grotesque echoes of its own forgotten darkness, and falling victim to an avenging recrudescence of the mindless frenzy of the first beginnings. (Achebe, An Image of Africa: Racism in Conrad's 'Heart of Darkness', 1988, p. 2)

The European nations in general, and England in particular (symbolized by Thames, River is also a symbol of progress and movement of time) had been through the various stages of evolution, and have done away with the primitive rituals of superstitious world to a great extent. Advancement of knowledge, science and society had worked as a sieve to remove the ignoble from the sublime. Whereas Europe had its own history and course of evolution that culminated into its present position, the Africans were also following its natural course but with the European intervention it passed through a violent phase.

The contact of the Africans with other civilizations was evident from the use of the gun by Okonkwo. It was an old and rusty gun made by a clever blacksmith who came to live in the village. Gun became a symbol of an invasion by an alien culture into the Igbo society. The community was too young to know its use, as it was still in the primitive form and was only evolving at a natural pace. Therefore, the gun could only create destruction when not handled properly, and the community was yet to learn its use. Okonkwo had never haunted any animal with the gun; moreover on one occasion he nearly shot his wife, had he not missed his aim. The Igbo Community in general and Okonkwo in particular lived in a society which believed that physical might and strength only existed in manliness. Not only men but also women and the society as a whole admired the manliness unanimously which was exhibited through the wrestling match, one of their chief annual events. This show of manliness had become a thing of past in European societies, which had started using gun as the most potential weapon for modern warfare; whereas, the tribal societies still used the old and traditional style of warfare. This modernization of techniques in wielding strength and power (As Power comes through the barrel of the gun) has rendered the Igbo community obsolete. The modern society was sophisticated and Okonkwo's simplicity could not comprehend the subtleties hidden behind the Imperial power. This is why he could not know the proper handling of his 'rusty' gun, and it also becomes the cause of his doom: "Okonkwo's gun had exploded and a piece of iron had pierced the boy's heart." (Achebe, Things Fall Apart, 1975, p. 112) According to the rule of the

Igbo society, Okonkwo was forced to go on an exile for seven years. Okonkwo was resilient to the changes and eventually had to meet with the turbulent current of changes. He could not tolerate the "womanish" Christian religion and the inaction of his community (He knew that Umuofia would not go to war (Achebe, Things Fall Apart, 1975, p. 184)) which was taking the path of his son Nwoye, so he killed himself. What Unoka said to Okonkwo in the beginning of the novel became true: "You have a manly and a proud heart. A proud heart can survive a general failure because such a failure does not prick its pride. It is more difficult and more bitter when a man fails alone." (Achebe, Things Fall Apart, 1975, p. 23)

It so appear that Achebe had already calculated the death of Okonkwo, because the end of Okonkwo was symbolic of the death of Igbo community. As Okonkwo observed about his son Nwoye that "Living fire begets cold, impotent ash" (ibid 140), the new religion had made the Igbo community effeminate and inactive. The evolution of Igbo society seems to be unnatural.

Lewis A. Coser cites Comte to describe the evolution of the societies:

> The passage from one social system to another can never be continuous and direct. In fact, human history is marked by alternative "organic" and "critical" periods. In organic periods, social stability and intellectual harmony prevail, and the various parts of the body social are in equilibrium. In critical periods, in contrast, old certainties are upset, traditions are undermined, and the body social are in disequilibrium. (Coser, 2011, p. 8)

In case of the Igbo society, it was certainly the "critical period". The British had already passed this stage of evolution through a natural process. However, in the case of the Africans there had been an imposition of a culture and a religion which was foreign to them. How was the imposition possible then? Jabbi writes, "Culture, like life itself, is a dynamic or continuing process; and its quality often depends upon a people's responses to evolutionary pressures from within or to stresses generated from outside through friction with new sets of values and institutional structures." (Jabbi, 2003, p. 201) Despite of having a structured and strong society, what had led to its disintegration was the pertinent question posed by Okonkwo towards the end of the novel. Obierika, Okonkwo's friend, blamed the white man for this disintegration:

The white man is very clever. He came quietly and peaceably with his religion. We were amused at his foolishness and allowed him to stay. Now he has won our brothers, and our clan can no longer act like one. He has put a knife on the things that held us together and we have fallen apart. (Achebe, Things Fall Apart, 1975, p. 160)

In Ngugi's *A Grain of Wheat,* Kihika cited the Swahili proverb to his tribesmen: "'Watch ye and pray…Kikulacho kimo nguoni mwako." (Thiong'o, 2002, p. 15) That means what eats you is within you. Things fell apart not because of the Colonizer's exploitation; but because of the fear that lurked within the tribal society. The society had become weak because of the defects that it had within itself. According to Jabbi, the problem lied in "cultural weakness" and "the streaks of violence and destructiveness" which were "finely ingrained in the traditional philosophy and institutions" of the Igbo people. "These weaknesses" played "an important part in the acceptance and spread of Christianity among the people" in the Igbo community (Jabbi, 2003, p. 207). If faults are not identified and repaired on time; if the society does not change with the demands of time, when the world around is changing; then external influences sweeps such society off the feet.

A meticulous inspection of the novel will reveal interesting facts. More than love and respect, it is the fear which has held the clan together. A family is the smallest unit in the society. The society is held together by the unanimous faith reposed by the people on that culture, tradition and religion. But fear creates fissures in faith. If those fissures are not mended, it gives way to the changes. Okonkwo was afraid of many things. He feared that if he displayed emotion, people would count it as weakness. He did not want people to call him 'agbala', an effeminate, like his father.

…his whole life was dominated by fear, the fear of failure and of weakness. It was deeper and more intimate than the fear of evil and capricious gods and of magic, the fear of the forest, and the forces of nature, malevolent, red in tooth and claw. Okonkwo's fear was greater than these. It was not external but lay deep within himself. It was the fear of himself, lest he should be found to resemble his father. (Achebe, Things Fall Apart, 1975, p. 13)

This is also the reason why he killed Ikemefuena. He did not show any sympathy towards him nor did he protect him even though he liked the boy who was like a son to him and lived with him for three years. He was afraid to show love, sympathy or emotion: "He heard Ikemefuena cry, "My father, they have killed me!" as he ran towards him. Dazed with fear, Okonkwo drew his matchet and cut him down. He was afraid of being thought weak (Achebe, Things Fall Apart, 1975, p. 55)". Ikemefuena's whimper would have moved any soul to pity but Okonkwo's. Apart from that Okonkwo was also resistant to changes. Okonkwo's son Nwoye was totally devastated after the murder of Ikemefuena. The gap between the father and the son further widened, but he was afraid of Okonkwo so he could not protest openly. The Igbo society had many superstitious beliefs that resulted into the sacrifice of many lives on the altar of religion. Twin babies were left to rot in forest; people suffering from certain diseases were left to die in the "Evil forest". There were social outcasts who lived lives of predestined isolation generation after generation. However this ubiquitous culture and tradition was honored unanimously by each and every member of the society. Bestman writes, "In telling his own story in order to refute the white man's perception of Africa, Achebe depicts the Igbo society of that period and it was a well-structured society with its traditions and taboos., its strengths and weaknesses. Part of the strength of *Things Fall Apart,* lies in Achebe's ability to objectively portray both the positive and negative sides of his people's culture" (Bestman, 2012, p. 158). Although brows have been raised on the preposterousness of certain traditions, no one had openly dared to challenge it:

> "I cannot understand why you refused to come with us to kill that boy," he asked Obierika.
> "Because I did not want to," Obierika replied sharply. "I had something better to do."
> "You sound as if you question the authority and the decision of the Oracle, who said he should die." (Achebe, Things Fall Apart, 1975, p. 60)

All these misgivings created fissures internally within the society, and the winds of change brought about by the 'new religion' targeted the weaker joints in the chain. Therefore it was not surprising that the mother of the twin-babies, the outcasts and Nwoye were the first to be converted to Christianity in Umuofia. These people were converted and empowered and made to stand against their own people. The first desecration of the sacred places was done by these overzealous new converts. Whereas in *Things fall Apart,* Enoch not only kills the sacred python, but also unmask the 'egwugwu' (Achebe, Things Fall Apart, 1975, p. 161); and in *A Grain of Wheat,* "The few who were converted, started speaking a faith foreign to the ways of the land. They trod on sacred places to show that no harm could reach those protected by the hand of the Lord" (Thiong'o, 2002, p. 11). Ogede is of the opinion that

> "Ironically, while the Igbo societies' rejection of some of their members as equal human beings caused a separation between them, forcing those consigned to the sphere of the inferior to seek social uplift though pacts with the European occupation forces, what these renegade groups could not suspect was that meaningful integration (or structural assimilation) was not a realizable goal due to the fact that compititiveness would, in turn, force the dominant group to seek to preserve to its advantage by depriving the conquered community of the ability to compete effectively as one unit" (Ogede, 2008, p. 4)

The Africans could not discern this and the colonizers took the advantage of this internal social disparity. Gradually the power of the colonizers started looming large and the once powerful community dwarfed into colonial subjugation. At the end when Okonkwo realized that the society of Umuofia had transformed and the people would not go to war, he ended his life. Change was inevitable, but Okonkwo would not change. Okonkwo, 'the roaring flame' (Achebe, Things Fall Apart, 1975, p. 139), preferred death than change. *Things Fall Apart* only deals with the coming of the British; whereas, *A Grain of Wheat* deals with the resistance of the Africans and their subsequent freedom from colonization. The revolution in *A Grain of Wheat* was spawned with the blood of fighters who laid down their lives: Waiyaki, Harry Thuku and Kihika. Kihika, called the 'burning Spear' in the novel *A Grain of Wheat,* is a reincarnate of the counterpart Okonkwo, 'the roaring flame'. The fight which was incomplete in one was taken ahead in the other. Towards the end of the novel *Things Fall Apart,* the readers witness the coming of corruption in the Igbo community. On the other hand, Ngugi gives a full exposition of the corrupt and debauched life in *A Grain of Wheat.* The British officers and their wives lived a lewd, immoral, corrupted and debauched life which had not left the Kenyans untouched. Along with the moral degradation there was all round change in the Kenyan society. The end of colonialism marked the beginning of neo-colonialism in Africa. As power was transferred from the Whites to the Black Administrators, the latter (only a selected few) continued with the exploitation as they had witnessed in their colonial masters. This becomes apparent when the MP fools Gikonyo. Instead of helping Gikonyo as promised, he buys the Estate of Richard Burton.

These two novels are the two beginnings in African history. Whereas, *Things Fall Apart* (1958) marks the beginning of Colonial rule, *A Grain of Wheat* (1967) marks the beginning of Colonial end. The date of publication of the two novels and the year of Independence gained by the countries[9] which produced them is relative and symptomatic in understanding the politics of the decolonization process. Achebe wrote the novel before Nigeria's Independence and Ngugi wrote his novel after independence. Achebe's aim was to establish the cultural richness of an African community which the Europe overlooked; and Ngugi's aim was to expose the evils of the British colonialism that had corrupted the rich heritage of an African community. Both the texts are a new discourse in the trajectory of the African literature, but counter-discursive in western context. As Helen Tiffin puts it, that such texts are set on a counter-discursive pattern to the then existent notions and their primary objective is to subvert the colonial image of the African colonies[10]. Whereas, Achebe's text is an exposition of the rich and intricate Ibo social structure; Ngugi's text is a blatant attack on the Pandora's Box unleashed by the British administration in Kenya that has pushed the nation to a decadent future. The only excuse given by the British for this plunder had been that they were on a civilizing mission.

The African continent had often been projected as a 'dark continent' and the people were referred to as the 'savages'. The British took the onus of 'civilizing' these 'savages' on themselves thereby embarking on the perilous journey of civilizing missions throughout the world. This had not only led to the mutilation of indigenous culture and tradition, but also had created a complete chaotic situation once they left. Between this coming-and-leaving there was the equation of loss and gain: The loss of culture by the Africans, and the gain of wealth by the British. The mirage of civilizing mission had been created to camouflage the colonial mission of economic exploitation of other nations: "...a forest research station was set up in the area...as part of a new colonial development plan. Soon Githima Forestry and Agricultural Research Station teemed with European scientists and administrators." (Thiong'o, 2002,

p. 33) The initial project of civilizing the Africans was seen to be carried by such zealous missionaries like Mr. Brown and John Thompson, who after coming to Africa got disillusioned by Cartierism, and then resorted to the violent ways. John Thompson too had 'moral vision and optimism' when he first arrived to Kenya. But in transforming the 'colonised', he underwent a moral transformation himself. (Thiong'o, 2002, p. 48).

The life and journey of John Thompson seemed to be an irony when juxtaposed with his early ambitious zeal to execute the 'white man's burden' and his eventual transformation into a 'savage' under the ulterior motive of British's exploitation of the African hinterlands. The reference to Rudyard Kipling's poem and its influence on John Thompson was undoubtedly the hint to 'white man's burden' which had inspired him to embark on the mission. After meeting the two Africans who have come from the family of Chiefs from Gold coast to be educated at Oxford, he had been convinced that "here are two Africans who in dress, in speech and in intellectual power were no different from the British. Where was the irrationality, inconsistency and superstition so characteristic of the African and Oriental races? (Thiong'o, 2002, p. 52)" Therefore even before coming to Africa on this last mission, he had been indoctrinated with the European prejudice of African savagery on one hand, and the possibility of removing that darkness with the light of Christianity. He believed in three things: the principle of Reason, of Order, and of Measure. He was happy to see the two Africans to be proud of their British heritage and tradition, which they had newly acquired by abandoning their indigenous ways. Thompson clearly saw that his next mission would be to "lead to the creation of one British nation, embracing peoples of all colours and creeds, based on the just proposition that all men were created equal." (Thiong'o, 2002, pp. 52-53). He once believed in administering the soul of the people; however illusion soon gave way to reality. Once landed in Africa to transform the lives of the savages, and invested with the double ambition of the British imperialism: exploitation of resources and civilizing mission, Thompson underwent the transformation himself. He wrote in his note book:

"what is this thing called Mau Mau?

Dr Albert Schweitzer says 'the Negro is a child, and with children nothing can be done without the use of authority.' I've now woked in Nyeri, Githima, Kisuu, Ngong. I agree…

Colonel Robson, a Senior District officer in Rung'ei, Kiambu, was savagely murdered. I am replacing im at Rung'ei. One must use a stick. No government can tolerate anarchy, no civilization can be built on Violence and savagery.' (Thiong'o, 2002, p. 54)

No doubt the British had built schools, hospitals and railway infrastructure in the colonies, but it was not for philanthropic purposes, it was a temporary means to appease the local uprisings, the tactic which the British applied in most of the colonies as pointed out by Fanon:

> Today we know that in the first phase of the national struggle colonialism tries to disarm national demands by putting forward economic doctrines. As soon as the first demands are set out, colonialism pretends to consider them, recognizing with ostentatious humility that the territory is suffering from serious under development which necessitates a great economic and social effort. And, in fact, it so happens that certain spectacular measures (centers of work for the unemployed which are opened here and there, for example) delay the crystallization of national consciousness for a few years. (Fanon, 2001, p. 167).

The British posited themselves as the savior of other 'races' and their position was 'axiomatic' (to use the word of Helen Tiffin). This is why we see that Thompson's idea of writing a book, in the novel *A Grain of Wheat*, called 'Prospero in Africa' highlights his own subject position as a 'Prospero' who is in control of the lives of the 'Caliban'. On the other hand, The District Commissioner's idea of writing a book entitled "The pacification of the primitive Tribes of the Lower Niger" is a farce on the tribal communities which dehumanize the entire tribe into an anthropological object.

From the above discussion it can be surmised that every society evolves at its own pace depending on the geo-demographical necessity. Whereas European nations felt the necessity to flex its powers beyond their small geographical locations in order to meet the rising demands of its growing population in conjunction to its scientific advancement, putting the latter into use to achieve the former; the African tribes had less pressing needs in matter of population or territory. Therefore, along with the changing needs of a society in consonance with the changing time, new tactics have been put to use to pursue old needs. Whereas the older generation, usually during the nascent period of societies, believed in frontal attack; the new civilization applied more sophisticated techniques. It was one good custom to which they religiously adhered: the show of manliness by bringing home human heads. Okonkwo was the emblematic of tribal strength and valor and believed in direct confrontation. Any other tactic of war was unthinkable of and was considered as profane. Thus the entire tribal population was mesmerized by the 'sugar coated tongue' of the missionaries. But behind those missionaries stood the people in 'red dress'. The missionary acted as an emissary and an important piece in the colonization process. This is why Mr. Brown "came to the conclusion that a frontal attack" on the clan "would not succeed" (Achebe, Things Fall Apart, 1975, p. 163). In Ngugi's *A Grain of Wheat* one sees similar repetition of the British strategy:

The few who were converted, started speaking a faith foreign to the ways of the land. They trod on sacred places to show that no harm could reach those protected by the hands of the Lord. Soon people saw the white man had imperceptibly acquired more land to meet the growing needs of his position. They looked beyond the laughing face of the whiteman and suddenly saw a long line of other red strangers who carried, not the bible, but the sword. (Thiong'o, 2002, pp. 11-12)

A quick glance on the history of the world will at once reveal the different tactics used by one nation on another since antiquity to extract the resources: At first it was the simple and direct war, a form of conquest. Then a direct confrontation seemed obsolete and in order to avoid causalities by the invading nations, war was replaced by colonization. The third from of the conquest is the spread of cultural imperialism and the last and present day stage is the conquest by means of globalization.

Whereas the evolutionary process of conquering nations had shaped the colonization process, and new tactics and requirements are being incorporated into it; the Igbo society was still at its primitive stage which naively followed the old tactics. Okonkwo and his fellow villagers could not fathom the stratagem employed by the District Commissioner (A Symbol of Imperial power) and fell victim to his designs:

"Three days later the District Commissioner sent his sweet-tongued messenger to the leaders of Umuofia asking them to meet him in his headquarters. That also was not strange. He often asked them to hold such palavers, as he called them. Okonkhwo was among the six leaders he invited...

It happened so quickly that the six men did not see it coming. There was only a brief scuffle, too brief to allow the drawing of a sheathed matchet. The six men were handcuffed and led into the guardroom." (Achebe, Things Fall Apart, 1975, pp. 173-175)

Unlike the Igbo community, the British showed no respect to the people of another community. The love and faith which the Christian missionaries talked about proved to be falsified by the act of the District commissioner in *Things Fall Apart*. The British, who preached the greatness of the religion, turned a deaf ear to the gospels themselves in *A Grain of Wheat*: "come unto me all ye that are hungry and thirsty and I will give you rest" (Thiong'o, 2002, p. 39).

There was only deceit and cunning. Thus the death of Okonkwo was inevitable, so also the disintegration of the Igbo community owing to the inherent retardation of the community to evolve a defense mechanism required in countering the new tactics of the fast growing nations around the world. The Igbo community could not build the anti-body in order to resist the invasion of a foreign particle owing to its rigidity and adherence to old customs blindly. The community lacked the introspective quality to detect and do away with harmful and detrimental practices. It held sway into the hearts of the tribesmen as a fixture invoking fear and awe. The new religion just took the advantage of this weakness and planted its roots by conquering them in the form of colonization. The naivety of Okonkwo (Igbo Society) could not comprehend the shrewdness of the colonial masters until they came into contact with each other. However, very fast they started learning the corruption, deceit and cunning of the new colonial masters, emulating them gradually.

The world is constantly changing, and yet there is always a resistance to change. The waning of an old culture and the emergence of a new culture due to this change can either be perceptible or imperceptible. When it is perceptible, it comes into direct confrontation with those who try to adhere to the old customs. In other case, if it is imperceptible, then it does not come into direct conflict, because it cannot find the object of conflict, and by the time they detect the variation in the continuum, it already becomes so deeply rooted within the existent culture that it becomes impossible to regress to restoration-point-in-the-past from the present vantage point. In this connection, the post-colonial Indian condition[11] is an instance. The communities or forces which carry the culture, often enforce their culture on the ones whom they conquer, but in exceptional cases, they affect and also get affected with the culture that they are invading, as in the case of the Ahoms and Mughals in India, and the Norman-French in Britain. They acculturate themselves with the existing culture of the place they invade, and also influence the receptive culture. However, when the culture is imposed and the changes become perceptible from the very beginning, it often meets with steep resistance. And this is true of the colonial enterprise, unlike the invaders settling down. The British colonialism in Africa is one such instance.

Notes

1   Ode Ogede in his book *Achebe's Things Fall Apart* explains how the European powers projected Africa as the Dark Continent.

2   Chinua Achebe uses this phrase in his essay *An Image of Africa: Racism in Conrad's 'Heart of Darkness'*

3   The prejudice had prevailed until mid twentieth century that the Africans cannot have a history as pointed out by Chinua Achebe: "For did not that erudite British historian and Regius Professor at Oxford, Hugh Trevor Roper, also pronounce that African history did not exist?" (Achebe 251)

4   "The Map of the world is not merely an objective outline of discovered continents, but an 'ideological or mythological reification of space' which opens up the territories of the world to domination and appropriation. 'The world' only acquired spatial meaning after different regions had been inscribed by Europeans, and this inscription, apart from locating Europe at the top of the globe or map, established an ideological figuration, through the accompanying texts and illustrations, which firmly centralized Europe as the source and arbitrar of spatial and cultural meaning" (Bill Ashcroft, 2000, p. 91)

5   Ken Goodwin writes about the various experiences as narrated by the explorers: "The people seemed entirely alien and even dangerous. In 1623, Jan Carstensz, having landed on a Cape York beach, became alarmed by the behavior of Aborigines and fired on them, killing some. (Goodwin 9)

6   A wide group of Kinsmen (Achebe, Things Fall Apart 191)

7   A Masquerader who impersonates one of the ancestral spirits of the village (Achebe, Things Fall Apart 189). There were nine egwugwus in Umuofia.

8   Quoted from Bu-Buakei Jabbi's *Fire and Transition in Things Fall Apart.*

9   Nigeria and Kenya gained independence from the British on 1st October 1960 and 12th December 1963 respectively.

10   Helen Tiffin writes, "Decolonization is a process, not arrival; it invokes an ongoing dialectic between hegemonic centrist systems and peripheral subversion of them; between European or British discourses and their post-colonial dis/mantling. Since it is not possible to create or recreate national or regional formations independent of their historical implication in the European colonial enterprise, it has been the project of post-colonial writing to interrogate European discourses and discursive strategies from a privileged position within (and between) two worlds, to investigate the means by which Europe imposed and maintained its codes in the colonial domination of so much of the rest of the world… Post-colonial literatures/ cultures are thus constituted in counter-discursive rather than homologous practices, and they offer 'fields' of counter-discursive strategies to the dominant discourse." (Tiffin 99)

11   One cannot undo the transformations brought about during the colonial times. Although efforts are underway, externally, an internal cleansing process is not possible because people have not only been physically conquered, but also have been mentally conquered. This is on an average the post-colonial Indian condition. But within the geographical boundaries of India, there are some pockets which have been mostly untouched by the colonial factors, or the post-colonial Indian factors. These are the tribal areas; and post-independence, when there had been a dialogue to bring these communities, living aloof in wilderness, into the mainstream India, Verrier Elwin very rightly remarked that they should be allowed a natural course; or else the enforcing of modernization on these tribes will be of severe consequences (Elwin).

Works Cited

Achebe, C. (1988). An Image of Africa: Racism in Conrad's 'Heart of Darkness'. In R. Kimbrough (Ed.), *Massachusetts Review* (Third ed., pp. 251-261). London: W. W Norton and Co.

Achebe, C. (1975). *Things Fall Apart.* New Delhi: Arnold Associates.

Arnold, D. (2002). *The Age of Discovery, 1400-1600* (2nd ed.). New York: Routledge.

Bestman, A. M. (2012). Reading Chinua Achebe's Things Fall Apart through Womanist lens: The Imperative of Female Principle. In K. A. Chima Anyadike (Ed.), *Blazing the Path: Fifty Years of Things Fall Apart* (pp. 155-173). Ibadan: HEBN Publishers Plc.

Bill Ashcroft, G. G. (2000). *Post-Colonial Studies*. New York: Routledge.

Coser, L. A. (2011). *Masters of Sociological Thought* (Second ed.). (R. K. Merton, Ed.) Jaipur: Rawat Publications.

Elwin, V. (1964). *The Tribal World of Verrier Elwin*. Bombay: Oxford University Press.

Ethics, A. a. (2006). *Vernantius Emeka Ndukaihe*. Berlin: Lit Verlag.

Fanon, F. (2001). *The Wretched of the Earth*. (C. Farrington, Trans.) London, England: Penguin Books Ltd.

Goodwin, K. (1986). The First Hundred Years of Colonization. In K. Goodwin, *A History of Australian Literature* (pp. 8-35). Hampshire: Macmillan.

Ihonvbere, J. O. (1994). *Nigeria: The Politics of Adjustment and Democracy*. New Jersey: Transaction Publishers.

Jabbi, B.-B. (2003). Fire and Transition in Things Fall Apart. In *Chinua Achebe's Things Fall Apart (A Casebook)* (pp. 201-220). New York: Oxford University Press.

Matthews, D. H. (1998). *Honoring the Ancestors: An African Cultural Interpretation of Black Religion and Litarature*. New York: Oxford University Press.

Ogede, O. (2008). *Achebe's Things Fall Apart*. London: Continuum.

Spencer, H. (1967). *The Evolution of Society: Selections from Herbert Spencer's Principles of Sociology*. (R. L. Carneiro, Ed.) Chicago: The University of Chicago Press.

Thiong'o, N. W. (2002). *A Grain of Wheat*. London: Penguin Books Ltd.

Tiffin, H. Post-colonial Literatures and Counter-discourse. In G. G. Bill Ashcroft (Ed.), *The Post-Colonial Studies Reader* (Second ed., pp. 99-101). Oxford: Routledge.

Exploring Gender-relations In The Post-partition Women-narratives of Bengal (1947-'57)

Debarati Chakraborty

On February 20, 1947, British Prime Minister Clement Richard Attlee had announced in the House Of Commons that Britain was ready to take legal actions for transferring power to Indian indigenous leadership by June 1948 and soon after this proclamation British parliament passed the 'Indian Independence Act' in July 1947, in which the concept of 'fragmented' independence of India, i.e., the 'partition' creating sovereign dominions of India and Pakistan was officially declared. The colonial power during their despotic reign had always tried to disturb India's religious-communal unity, specifically, the long-standing bonding of Hindu and Muslim was always at stake as the British injected the 'Muslim Tyranny' theory in the blood of Hinduism. In 1905, Lord Curzon's announcement of Bengal Partition was the earliest step to break Bengal's sectarian harmony. The anti-partition movement of 1905-'11 had yielded the British government to call off the partition but simultaneously that imperial politics had initiated the socio-political alienation among Muslim community which ultimately resulted in the growth of Muslim Nationalism and Muslim league in1909. The political dilemmas of Indian National Congress at the second half of twentieth century had deepened the

breach of these two salient nationalist entities and from 1940's Muslim League
had decided to raise voice for sovereign Pakistan state. The partition of 1947
was therefore not only a colonial-political 'trickery', but it also was a failure of
our national integrity.

The 1905-anti-partition movement was constructive in every way as
it initiated indigenous enterprises in industry and agriculture, encouraged
patriotic literature and most importantly improved the relationship between
Hindu and Muslim. On the contrary, the partition 1947 had devastated the
nation, burnt the dreams of much-awaited freedom from colonial domination
and most terribly the partition-aftermath had thrashed the women of the
nation with unprecedented violence and assault. In the nationalist discourse
of mother-centric patriotism, 'Woman' as a 'body' and 'existence' was solely
conceptualized as a sexless, voiceless divine legacy of purity, chastity and
traditional womanhood of India and so was equated with the captive-colonized
motherland. Quite sarcastically when India won independence from the
colonial hegemony of two hundred years, the mothers and daughters who once
symbolized the austerity and veneration of colonized nation, were brutally paid
back by their own coins of 'sexuality' in the new independent nation-states---
India and Pakistan. The consequences of partition not only changed the lives
of thousands of women across the border but also greatly affected the gender-
relations and the agential shifts of women-perspectives. In the meanwhile the
advent of Marxist politics together with the uproars of peasant movements
commenced a brand-new political era in Bengal politics. The egalitarian
culture of Marxist socialism defied the established power-structure in society
and politics both. The communist call of class-struggle to demolish despotic
feudalism not only awakened the deprived peasant class but it also aroused the
tortured souls of marginalized, victimized women of this disastrous age. The
post-partition women-narratives have enveloped the socio-political relocation
related to the changes of women—role in family, society and gender-perspective
along with the problems of rehabilitations of persecuted refugee women.

In the present paper I intend to analyze the views of the leading female
fiction writers of post-partition period (1947-'57) to review the aftermath of
partition and its impact on female survivors which led to their changing views
on gender-relations.

Sabitri Roy(1918-'85) and Jyotirmoyee Devi(1894-1988)are the most
courageous writers of post-partition period as far as mainstream politics and
political feminism are concerned. Whereas the catastrophic partition and

its aftermath have weighed down the pages of Jotirmoyee Devi's narratives, the post-partition scenario of gender politics and gendered politics have been severely criticized by Sabitri Roy's diction. In both of these duo's compositions the stereotypes of gender-distribution and power-structures of neo-patriarchy are always been probed. Motherhood, widowhood, singlehood, extra-marital relationship, romantic courtship free from marital vows have often been posed as 'problematic' in Roy's and Jyotirmoyee's texts as well. In her first published novei *'Baisakher Niruddesh Megh'*(The Vanished Cloud Of Baisakh 1948) Jyotirmoyee has portrayed woman –charactersof different backgrounds, provinces and cultures. Nitish, the hero of this novel being an orphan finds difficulties and apathy of his relatives after the decline of their large joint family. Through his journey of self-recognition and establishment he is introduced to the woman-protagonist of the narrative Bina and another important lady Ruth. Bina being a lady of dark complexion faced complexities for marriage in her society but except cursing her fortune she not only moved to a successful academic career and became a professor but also participated in the Dandi-march to rewrite her new socio-political identity. Ruth on the other hand a modern woman in every sense, revolted against her family and denied to marry both of Nitish for whom Ruth had an embedded feeling and Siunarayan who was attracted to Ruth. For this upright decision Ruth's reason was quite impressive;- "The new-age women have changed their mind too. It is as tough to marry someone does not love me as to a person I do not love. After all a worthless marriage does not make any sense."(CW 1,p-69) When Ruth was redefining love, romance and marriage in her own terms of self-consciousness, then Bina the 'black' lady of the narrative was searching the existence and significance of woman's own;-"The identity of woman is either all about a history of her relationship to anyone or a nameless, relation-less fiery story of scorching or getting scorched in lustrous sensation. Except this she has no other identity, no entity of human-being she owns in the history of human-civilization...They are either in the side of Sati, Sita, Sabitri, or they crowd the team of Urvasi, Basantsena or Cleopetra. But in this generation that past legacy is supposed to be come to an end and right there the journey of the women like Bina starts, who are modern and apprehensive to find their own self."(1,50)

Jyotirmoyee thus has continuously hammered the pigeonholes of socially constructed gender-roles and advocated for more space, parity, honor and freedom for women. In her second novel 'Epar Ganga Opar Ganga'(The River Churning 1968) she sketched the character of Sutara, who was a partition-survivor, had lost her family, fortune and social honor in that apocalypse but in spite of giving up hopes she took her arms against the 'slings and arrows of outrageous' society engrafting her own identity as a history-professor in yangaseni College, Delhi. Sutara not only witnessed the rupture and its aftermath but through her stormy journey she recollected and revised the unheard 'her-story' of women;- "Sutara is now aged-as if centuries and millenniums have been blended in her blood, body and mind. In the history of all ages and era-Satya, Treta, Dwapar, Kali- her age has been churned. As if she is becoming the representative of arbitrarily humiliated, tormented, disregarded and abandoned women of all ages." The remarkable feature of Jyotirmoyee's reflection is, the hitherto unexplored women-history, dominated and suppressed by patriarchal tyranny, in this narrative has been recognized and revisited by the male-protagonist Promod when he compares the uprooted, homeless and assaulted refugee women with the exploitation of Sita;- "Sita was abducted. Ram and Ravan had a terrific face off. Then Vivishan and Ram owned the thrones of Lanka and Ayodhya respectively. But the exile and self-sacrifice of Sita and her community was never come to an end. Ram and the subjects of Ramrajya have always rejoiced the power, pleasure and luxuries of royal court. Rama's banishment was persevered by Sita too, but Ram didn't accompany Sita in her exile."(1,177) In Jyotirmoyee's composition thus a male- gaze is developed to scrutinize the 'tradition' of abusing woman-resources. Jyotirmoye Devi has always persuaded a free, unconventional and unprejudiced social mobility between men and women. In her first novel *'Baisakhe Niruddesh Megh'* Jyotirmoyee has reviewed the problems of middle and lower-middleclass women from different socio-economical array. Bina and Ruth – the dreamt characters of Jyotirmoyee didn't at all represent the crisis of majority of Bengali middleclass girls. Therefore Jyotirmoyee has portrayed the characters of, Tulu-Bulu-Ila-Bela-Sumitra-Urmilla—who irrespective of their financial class and educational qualification share the same kinds of agony and anxiety resulting from frustrating relationship, forceful marriage, suppressed envy and sorrow. Therefore when Tulu's marriage-proposal was rejected by Nitish,;- "Bulu sympathized her. She is now newly married. Forget love. At least she is now settled. After all, marriage of woman is not mere marriage. Now she doesn't need to flow haphazardly like moss.

Ila also pities Tulu. She wants to inform her that, she knew, Nituda would not marry Tulu at any case. Their sister-in-law becomes happy unnecessarily. She criticizes Nitish casually.

Sumitra is either happy or not. She has also died so many times. In every crude night, in every dreamy day she has breathed her last. In a well-furnished, luxurious room when she received well-dressed people, discussed art and literature, sang trained songs in womanly tune, when an audacious smile of her attractiveness and adoration showered from her lips, in those moments she somehow felt that she is also as deprived, unhappy and exploited like Tulu."(1,35). Thus 'marriage' in Jyotirmoyee Devi's literary canon has always been a dubious institution for women-integrity and emancipation. In her first novel when she has contested and encouraged the gender-relation in the terms of comradeship and friendly convention free from marital vows, likewise, in her second novel 'Epar Ganga Opar Ganga' Jyotirmoyee advocated for inter-caste and inter –racial marriage, more specifically she emphasized the romantic bonding in marital relationship. The new-age educated, self-dependent characters of Jyotirmoyee's narratives Sutara-Promod, Bina-Nitish-Ruth not only shared their misery, stress, exploitations but breaking the norms of patriarchal power-relations they became the triumphant as they re-captured their own 'root', own 'land' of freedom, love and comradeship.

The marital dilemma, anxiety of fidelity, trust and devotion in marital relationship have always distressed the heroines of Sabitri Roy. The gradual growth of communist culture and its intrinsic predicaments in the socio-political fabric of Bengal at the post-partition period have been intertwined with the emerging confusions of feminist politics in Sabitri Roy's discourse. In her earlier works 'Srijon'(The Creation 1946), Trisrota(The Tri –streamed 1950), Swaralipi(The Notation 1952) she has fraught the partition-aftermath and its impact on the changing gender-roles. The heap of broken images, the screams of divided souls, the fragmented- uprooted entities of nation have crowded the 'memory' of Roy's texts and simultaneously from that apocalyptic rupture a dream and desire of reconciliation in a more liberal and egalitarian society was envisaged by the communist men and women protagonists of her narratives.

Roy's first novel 'Srijon' is a reflection of Roy's own personal experience and psychological crisis resulting from the confusions of implementing communist ideology in the domains public and private. Biswajeet, the protagonist of this novel despite being a Marxist could not confront the feudalist structure of his family and fails to accompany his wife against his mother's unreasonable and tormenting summons relating his wife Jaya's pregnancy, motherhood and access to public life. Jaya, the heroine of 'Srijon' had to sacrifice her political career and social life for family-responsibilities. On the contrary, Padma, the heroine of Roy's second novel 'Trisrota' did not compromise with her socio-political identity. As being a witness of partition-- the trauma, trouble, hunger, violence, famine along with the suspension and other socio-political restraints that impeded the growth of communist politics in Bengal—all of these anxieties have shattered Padma's experience, consciousness and journey of her life. She was not a political activist like Bipasha, her friend, who had dedicated her life to party-politics and to ameliorate the situation of deprived class. But Padma stands alone at the age of multi-layered conflicts between family-relationship-politics and social struggles. She is a wife, a mother, a friend, a comrade. When she attends meeting her breast flows for her little child, but she does not confine herself in narrow domestic space, she moves from lane to lane with her friends to promote women-franchise. Sabitri Roy thus portrays a new –age woman of her own political culture who antagonizes the 'nationalist' projection of mother-centric womanhood and breaks the ice between home/world dichotomy. Padma is a sublime rebel who nourishes her love and affection to her husband and child but never hesitates to accept her deep-rooted feeling for Biswarup, her husband's colleague;- "Padma could not forget Biswarup. A deep-rooted empathetic agony she feels for him in her every vein. Arunabha and Biswarup-both of them simultaneously has occupied her romantic reverie. A delightful feeling for both of these personalities silently is streaming in her."

Padma and Jaya the two protagonists of Roy's earlier narratives have redefined motherhood and marital relationship in such a semi-feudal ambience where the new social currents of communist ideology was intervening the traditional past and nationalist imposition of womanhood. Although the leftist concept of gender and feminism was also quite vague and disputable at this age. Biswajeet and Arunabha in the respective novels 'Srijon' and 'Trisrota' never allowed their partners to join hardcore politics. Padma and Jaya's sighs of frustrations for being secluded and enclosed in their demarcated 'home' and 'feminine' responsibilities have weighed down the pages of Roy's compositions. The dualism of leftist sociology that refused feminism and gender-war as a political collective and the 'second sex' as a true comrade is quite visible in the inhibitions and anxieties of Biswajeet and Arunabha's attitude. In her third novel 'Swaralipi' Sabitri Roy confronted this deep- rooted patriarchal contradictions of communist politics. Swarlipi is therefore a rebellious text in many senses Here Roy not only evokes the woman-power in socio-political activism, but Sita and Sagari the two political activists breaking the norms of feudal-patriarchal concept of femininity became the first political 'prisoner' and martyr' respectively. Being a partition-text 'Swaralipi' has enveloped the trauma and violence of partition, together with the post-partition political corruptions, political murder and rape, sexual exploitations of refugee and marginal women. In a vast canvas of partition, power-politics, communist ideological dilemma Sabitri Roy projects the 'women as 'problematic', as a 'struggling' class in the new-born nation-state. The term 'struggle' here is not coined in 'Marxist' thought, rather it signifies the feminist creed to defy marriage-institution- widowhood-motherhood-love-romance-sexuality of women according to their own experience and choice. Shita, the protagonist, once refused by Prithwi, the hero, married Debojyoti but could not forget her first love. After her husband's demise she was stuck by the 'motherly' responsibilities and lived her widowhood as a penance as she had a guilt-feeling for being reluctant to her husband and marital ethics. But Prithwi's return as a vibrant political activist broke the silence of Shita. Unshackling herself from her demarcated patriarchal boundaries Shita accompanied Prithwi and at the end of the story she bravely embraced her imprisonment for providing shelter to exiled communist party-member. On the other hand Sagari who was married to her beloved Rathi, misled by Nandalal, the corrupt leftist when found himself to be a 'prey' of Nandalal's sexual lust, she left the party-line and in the guise of Jaba she diligently worked for the exploited 'Tebhaga' peasants and ultimately sacrificed her life in police-firing. Shita and Sagarari's journey started from two different points of gender-relations. Shita did not face the violence of partition or never became a victim of physical assault or political exploitation. She chose her own way of fulfillment accepting her love and dedication for Prithwi. Although there remains an unsolved suspense at the end of the story about her post-arrest assault and torture in police-custody. On the other hand, Sagari found it difficult and unethical to combine personal relationship of romance, marriage or motherhood with the political dedication that demands celibacy and sacrifice;- "A delicate desire of motherhood excites her thought-she wants to give birth Rathi's child.

But suddenly the headlines of today's newspaper flashes upon her inward eyes. In a fraction of moment both of them regain their consciousness of social responsibility. An ominous announcement from a remote sea is resonating on the heart of this night. Restraining their weak senses Sagari withdraws herself and takes herself away. The respite of conceiving their child is yet to come.

Before that they have to secure the desire of designing a playhouse of their dreamy children by their staunch, united commitment."(Roy 1,380)

----Sagari compromised her dream for her social commitment but could not justify Rathi's love and political company as she was trapped in a conspiracy. She therefore penalized herself through her martyrdom. When Sagari dedicated her dream of motherhood then Shita being a mother of a girl-child redefined motherhood as she listened her little child's helpless cry churning with the screams of universal revolutionary souls;- "Shita cannot tolerate the heart-rending laments of her child. Assembling all the strength in her grip she restively told in her mind-Mithu do not weaken me. Give me more power, more strength-Prithwi! Falgu! O my revolutionary friends of World!".

'Swaralipi' thus becomes a 'notation' of rebel souls of the exploited, expatriated, exhorted mass irrespective of class, creed and gender who encumbers the pre-established male/female, private/public, home/world, power/knowledge dichotomy to evoke a brand- new fabric of gender-role, class- identity and social relationship.

Ashapurna Devi(1909-'95) and Mahasweta Devi(1926) the two most eminent fictionists of post-independence period have been encompassed in the streams of Bengali narratives for their remarkable contributions in envisaging domestic and sub-altern politics respectively. It is although quite surprising that the apocalyptic 'partition' has never touched the periphery of their contemplations. Mahasweta's first novel *'Jhansir Rani'*(Queen Of Jhansi 1956) in her words;- " ...is not a novel, It's an unskilled attempt to scribble a history-centric biography by a novice English-literature graduate who is often ignored by learned class,"(Granthaprasanga, Rachanasamagra,1, p-515). For Mahasweta 'history' is not mere recorded, chronological descriptions, but it is flowing through the oral tradition and mass-culture, as a subjective and as a 'chronotope' 'history' is transitional;- "..history is written precisely when the historian's vision of the past is illuminated by insight into the problems of present"(Preface, Amritasanchay). This historicity that constructs Mahasweta's compositional world therefore simultaneously conjugates her nostalgic journey to her dilapidated present—the 'present' of post-partition period which was in Mahasweta's experience;- "War after war—August Movement-famine-Naval Revolt-Azad Hind Fauz-official inauguration of communist party—People Theatre Association's drama, songs-riot-independence-partition-assassination of Gandhi-Tebhaga Movement-ban on communist party-(chronologies are not maintained, please arrange it)-such things were happening at that time--that tumultuous time was the earlier ages of my adolescences and youth. Can anyone discard the debts of such a time?"-Mahasweta therefore could not erase her 'present' of a violent catastrophe from her personal or narrative memory. Rewriting the history of 'Laxmibai' she not only reconstructed the suppressed, oblivious pages of woman-history but also through this feminist approach of historiography she represented century-old freedom-struggle for land, right, justice and integrity of a nation and a woman. From a distant past when she re-discovers the voice of 'Laxmibai'—'Meri Jhansi dungi nahi'—(I will not sacrifice my Jhansi) then the 'voice' somewhere merges with the reality of Mahasweta's own 'present' and echoes the 'polyphony' of homeless, expatriated souls of partitioned Bengal. In this biographical narrative Mahasweta documented the unexplored pages of nineteenth- century social history of peasant's exploitations, feudal authority and imperial hegemony which infuriated the insurrection of 1857. Her second novel 'Nati' was posed in he same historical milieu, but this time a romantic love-story of Moti and Khudabaksh led the story-line. Moti, a dancer and Khudabaks a soldier loved each other, but their individual love did not surpass their burning patriotism. They sacrificed their lives at the battle-field and immortalized their love-story. Moti's mother Roshan was also a dancer who was exploited by a feudal lord. Moti could not avoid her fate to be a dancer, but her love for her partner and motherland protected her from utter humiliation and sexual exploitation. Thus Moti reconstructed her identity from a 'Nati' to a martyr.

Ashapurna Devi—an impressive story-teller of Bengali household has delineated the untold pains, frustrations, agony and conflicts of middle-class Bengali women in a broad canvas of declining feudal and joint family structure. In her earlier texts 'Unmochon'(The Exposition 1957), Balaigrash(The Annular Eclipse 1955), Jog Biog(Plus-minus 1953), Nirjan Prithibi(The Lone World 1955) she confronts the predicaments of romantic and marital relationship from a woman's changing perspectivs. Ashapurna could not afford institutional education neither she had access to public or political life, still she received the currents of the emerging socio-political polemic. Ashapurna's heroines have always revolted against the social pigeon-holes of forceful marriage, motherhood, widowhood and the expected surrender to unquestionable marital laws of chastity, care and subordination to male-authority. Ashapurna has enlightened the unexplored and buried thoughts of women-psychology –the unsatisfied desires, dreams; confusions and anxieties-unrevealed; conflicts of perceptions. In her earlier phases of narratives we often find a woman surrounded by critical situations is grappling to discover an identity of her own. In 'Balaigrash', Tuni, the protagonist was rejected and abandoned by her own parents as she was a child of unmarried relationship. After her birth Mahalaxmi her grandmother threw her to a servant's responsibility' neither her mother Lila nor her father Jyotiprakash provided her identity and shelter. Tuni had to leave her last address, servant Bindu's home who was prozected as her mother. She fled from one place to another in search of her own space, protecting herself from the lust and greed of unjust male-dominated society. With the journey of her life she grew young and finally when she found her parents eager to get her back in their newly married life, she did not support this easy resolution, rather she appeared with a staunch objection to recognize Lila and Jyotiprakash as her parents. The protest of an agonized self thus grimed the ambience of the narrative. In 'Nirjan Prithibi' an another aspect of woman's agential subjectivity has been envisaged. Nirupa, the protagonist of the story had taken a rebellious decision to marry Animesh, her love, going against her family. But all her dreams were crushed when she failed to find her expected life- partner in the feudal milieu of her in-law's household and retrogressive attitude of Animesh. Nirupa did not indulge her senses to weaken her self-respect, because she knew;- " The magical intoxications of this perilous night have always impeded the emancipating progress of human-beings, have made them slaves.

When this night passes away, the daylight is brightened, then they again retrieves themselves....

That is why from time immemorial, men and women are engaged in an incessant battle! It is the reason that they have envied themselves, hated and mistrusted themselves! They have not hesitated to ruin themselves in the shameless effort to dominate each other."(1,239)

----Nirupa knew this truth. So she never compromised with her dream. Despite Animesh's love and possessiveness she decided to leave him and to start her own vocation with medical study. Animesh on other side also realized that the physical needs care and subordination he expects from a wife Nirupa is not only unable to provide that but she actually stays in a world of higher reality where materialist hedonism has no place. Still Animesh cannot falsify his love for Nirupa;-- "If any day Animesh feels tired of his daily monotonous trivialities, feels suffocated for dearth of air, then he would find respite from this elevated firmament."(1,270)

In Ashapurna's literary canon thus the gender-relations have been detected from a very meticulous and moderate point of view. Although it is also true that the gender roles and relations Ashapurna had visualized was hypothetical and time's ahead. As for example she has sketched a mother character in this novel 'Nirjan Prithibi', Anurupa, who did not want her daughter Nirupa to get married earlier rejecting her career, as she felt;- "A complete woman, Nirupa and she is her daughter, Nirupa has deprived her from this glorious thought."(1,270). Ashapurna's mother –characters have always defied the social stereotypes of maternity or motherhood. In our next discussable novel 'Unmochon' Ashapurna sketches the protagonist Manasi, a wife, a mother who refuses to perform her expected gender-role as a widow and a mother. Discarding the social norms of widow-celibacy she left her arrogant son and hollow 'home' to accompany the love of her life--- Professor Sen. She wanted to get rid of her social identity of 'Fultuser Ma'(The mother of Fultus) and stretched her feathers to explore a relation of her own, she was then a forty-crossed widow;- "At the shore of this endless, timeless sea I have achieved the power to realize the real truth from this baritone roar. I will never commit wrong, Now come with me!" (Unmochon,195)

Ashapurna realized the thirst of a woman, her basic appetite and craving for life. But there was another important woman fictionist who not only recognized the physical entity of a woman but also narrated her sexual expressions and somatic experiences through her feminist lance. Bani Roy(1918) in most of her narratives—'Chokkhe Amar Trishna'(Thirst In My Eyes 1962), 'Sreelata O Shampa(1948)',' Promotto Prohor'(The Intoxicated Night 1962) has explored the repressed genre of woman-sexuality. In Bani Roy's fiction on the contrary, the taboos of somatic manifestations have been subdued with an unprecedented conviction. In her first novel 'Chokkhe Amar Trishna' Bani Roy pens the character of a twenty-one years young girl who was married to a fifty years old but rich and eminent leader by her own choice but could not find satisfaction in her conjugal life. She expected a lavish and luxurious life out of this marriage which she indeed achieved but simultaneously she realized that her happiness, opulence, social status—everything was an outcome of her husband's lawful, unrestrained right on her body and mind;- "In reality he can use me however he wishes. Society, religion has granted him that claim, that right. I can rejoice all of his affluences only after offering my body to his gratification."(Roy,1,66) Throughout this journey of the unnamed girl numerous moments have been created to depict her sexual needs and frustrations of dissatisfactions. She quite naturally fell in love with her husband's nephew Niranjan. But, again the 'control' of that young chap not only let her down but the rejection and her fruitless life provoked her to commit suicide in just twenty-three. But before parting, she threw some fiery questions to this hypocrite, unjust society;-- - "All the vacuum has been crammed by images----Ahalya, reeda, Tara, Helen, Salome, Kunti, Saffo and so many. All of hem are the heroines of unlawful love. Have we all not loved? If love is the greatest manifestation of mind, then why our love go in vain? The air gets suffocated with suppressed cries.."(Roy,239). Physical beauty and seduction of women have become pivotal in Bani Roy's narratives. In her very first novel *'Prem'*(Love 1942) the protagonist Rupali had developed physical relations with her partners ignoring her unmarried status. But at end of the day she also had to welcome marital tie compromising the love of her life. In 'Sreelata o Sampa' the crisis came from the fruitless pride of declining feudal family and inner conflicts of the two sisters Sreelata and Sampa. Sreelata disappointed her lover Deepankar as she could not challenge the feudal power- structure of her family, likewise Sampa too in spite of stimulating Goutam's senses and inviting him in a bold relationship could not reconcile her love due to that shackles of Roy family's tyrant conventions. On the other hand the love of the protagonist of 'Pramatto Prahar' remained futile only because of her dearth of bodily fairness. Thus we can see in Bani Roy's narrative canon woman-body has become a demarcated polemic and in search of sexual satisfaction and emancipation the revolting characters of Roy have become the prey of their own frustrations and obligations. Although it cannot be denied that Bani Roy and her heroines breaking the norms of women-passivity in male-dominated hetero-sexual power- structure, initiated the woman-voice, choice and activity which always had gone unrecognized.

---------- On this context we can remember Sabitri Roy once again. In Sabitri's narratives we have also found the emancipating women who also defied the social stereotypes of marital subjugation. Alike Padma(Trisrota), Jaya(Srijon) and shita(Swaralipi) the leading character of 'Malosree'(Malosree-The Nocturnal Tune 1954) --Rakhi also discovered her love in Soumitra and Diganto both, it was not her shame, rather she realized the joy of sharing the colors of love. But Sabitri Roy despite being a radical woman-fictionist never indulged unrestrained sexuality or its depiction in literature either. Rakhi- the protagonist of 'Malosree' being a writer criticized the sexual representation of women in masculine literary trends;- " O! Writer your admiring insight still is confined beneath the female part. But the heart that has nestled itself down the woman-bosom is not mere feminine sex. Its rather the origin of your soul."(Roy, Malosree 186)

In a 1988-essay Gayatri Chakraborty Spivak commented;- "Between patriarchy and imperialism, subject-constitution and object-formation, the figure of the women disappears, not into a pristine nothingness, but a violent shuttling which is the displaced figuration of the 'third world woman' caught between tradition and modernization." (306) The otherness and silence of marginalized women of third-world women was always a problematic in feminist politics and culture as the Asian despotic society has often suppressed their voice or has forced them to speak for the sake of existing patriarchal power-structure. In the post-independence era the other side of silence was raising its existence. Confronting both tradition and forced modernity they were articulating their own space and choice of social and gender relations along with their own language of sexuality. Love and sex which are conceived as institutional power-relations in heterosexual patriarchal politics according to western post-modern theories, have also been confronted in post-partition women- literature of Bengal. Moreover the partition-aftermath has deepened the tension of socio-cultural and sexual relationship in these narratives. Thus a political catastrophe not only changed a national boundary but expatriating thousands of people from their root, culture, land and legacy it emanated a new social and cultural revolution with some new dreams, desires and deconstruction of tradition and relationship.

Works Cited

Ashapurna Devi, *Saptasindhu Dus Diganta*. Prima Publication.calcutta.1977
Ashapurna Devi'*Rachanabali*, vol 1 Mitra and Ghosh Publishers Calcutta.2011
Bani Roy, *Granthasankalan*. Vl 1.Sarat Book House.Calcutta.1986
Jyotirmoyee Devi. *Rachana Sankalan*, vol 1, Dey's Publishing & School Of Women Studies Jadavpur.2011.
Mahsweta Devi.*Rachanasamagra* vol 1.Dey's Publishing. Calcutta 2001.
Sabitri Roy. *Rachanasamagra*.vol 1. Granthalaya Pvt. Ltd, Calcutta.2005

Reference

Gayatri Chakraborty Spivak. Can The Sub-altern Speak? Marxist Interpretation Of Culture. Ed Cary Nealson&Lawrence Grossberg.Macmillan. London.1988.
Sudakshina Ghosh. Meder Uponyase Meder Katha.Dey's Publishing. Calcutta.2008.
NOTE-----Translations of the Bengali novels are all mine.

Status of Khasi Women in Khasi Traditional System: Its Continuity and Change

Armstrong Swer

Introduction

The Khasis are the indigenous tribes of Hill Ranges of present day Meghalaya. Khasi Hill Ranges are situated in between the two great valleys[1] i.e. in the north the Brahmaputra Valley and in the south the Surma Valley. These tribes have lived in relative isolation in the sense that not much contact with the outside world except through raids and plunders of the villages in the neighbouring plain areas[2]. However towards the later parts of the Ahom rule, regular economic relations has emerged between the people of the hills and plain areas particularly in the border markets adjoining the plain areas. Apparently close relations between the people of Khasi hills and plains areas especially with erstwhile Bengal (present day Sylhet District of Bangladesh) has emerged as a result of economic interdependence between these areas. Border markets along the foothills of Khasi Hills have appeared as the places where the Khasis have exposed to the technologies and cultures of inhabitants of plain areas of Bengal as well as Ahom Kingdom (present day Assam). Trade relations with the people of plain areas of Bengal in particular did provide important avenues for cultural exchange. However in spite of contact and exposure to the cultures and languages of the people of plain areas particularly of erstwhile Bengal, the Khasis have maintained a distinct cultural identity of their own.

Prior to the advent of the British, the Khasis did not have their own script as a result there was no literary works in Khasi language. In its absence, the Khasis used oral tradition to transmit traditional knowledge and ideas from one generation to another. The oral tradition found expression in the form of folk tales, stories, fables and rhymed couplets. The acquaintance of knowledge through oral tradition has sustained all the way till the development of literature in the early parts of the 20th century. The Khasis have a number of folk stories about their origin, gods, migration, customs, wars, matrilineal system and their contact and relations with the foreigners.

Like most tribal of North East India, the Khasis are famous hunters, fighters and raiders[3]. In fact the Khasi *Hima* (states) have no standing army and all healthy men of the tribes are expected to protect their territorial integrity from any kind of incursion or threat of war. At the same time men are responsible to protect the honour and prestige of women and children. However due to constant fighting with the neighbouring enemies, raids as well as plunders of the villages adjoining the plain areas are responsible for long absent of men folks from their hearth and home. Men folks used to venture also to faraway places in order to carry on trade and commercial transactions with the people of neigbouring countries. Their jobs and duties are in the spheres outside their own houses. Presumably due to such state of affairs that have obliged men folks to entrust and authorize women folks with the task of managing all the family responsibilities.

Status of Khasi Women in traditional system

Before we proceed with the study of the status of Khasi women in the traditional system it would be worthwhile to examine within the context of the matrilineal system as being practiced by the Khasis. Matrilineal system is the most distinct feature and uniqueness of the Khasi society[4]. Descent is traced from the mother's side, and kinship is closer to the maternal or matrikin (ki kur ki jait) than to the paternal side (Ki kha ki man)[5]. The offspring take the surname of their mother. The youngest daughter (khadduh) remains in her parents' house and inherits the ancestral property[6]. It must be mentioned here that in Khasi matrilineal system there is a close and intimate relations between the members of the *ing* (family) and sub-clan. Thus a woman is a mother not only to her children but also to her sisters' children. Traditionally the clans are bounded together by the stringent decree of religion, ancestor worship and funeral rites[7]. Some specific clans have been selected with religious responsibility.

The ancestral father of the Khasis too occupies a significant position. Apparently due to that reason the forefathers have supported the notion of *kur* (maternal clan) and *kha* (paternal clan)[8]. The notion of *Kur* and *Kha* was one of the basic and cardinal principles of the Khasi society, culture and religion[9]. Thus, *Tip kur Tip Kha* (to know maternal relations and to know paternal relations)[10] became a part and parcel of the Khasi societ. It used to be the common belief among them that all Khasis are *Ki kur ki kha* (clan from mother's side as well as father's side). For that reason, there is no upper or lower caste or any kind of class discrimination or class-consciousness.

In the Khasi society, there are two types of property such as *nongtymmen* or the ancestral property which include a house and other goods which are inherited from predecessors. The second type of property is known as *nongkhynraw* or property acquired by the members of the family. The property and wealth of the Khasis include land holdings, jewels, ornaments, gold, money, attire, livestock, etc. According to the Khasi custom, an ancestral property of the family goes to the youngest daughter (Ka Khadduh) of the family. The only exception to this custom is the *war*[11] people who grant equal property right to both male and female.

The youngest daughter gets the lion's share of the property. The other daughters of the family also obtain a small share of the family property in the form of kitchen wares, ornaments, etc in case they belong to a well to do family. However, in spite of the fact that the ancestral property goes to the youngest daughter of the family, she cannot dispose or mortgage or sell the ancestral property as she likes, it must be consented by her maternal uncle, brothers and sisters.

Traditionally men in Khasi matrilineal system cannot own any property. A father who should play a leading role in the family becomes less important in his own house because of his role as a maternal uncle (U Kni). As a maternal uncle in the Khasi society, he used to occupy a very high position in a family or a kinship group. He is the centre of authority[12] over the whole clan or any particular family and his sisters cannot do anything without his knowledge. He exercised control over the management of the family property- movable and immovable. It is imperative to state here that the maternal uncle and the youngest daughter are responsible for all religious and economic activities of the family[13]. Social obligations of the family also fall on both the shoulders of the youngest daughter and the maternal uncle.

The status of the youngest daughter according to the custom and practice of the Khasis is like the custodian of an ancestral property and keeper of the religion[14]. It is her obligation to maintain and take utmost care of all the family property. Besides, she has to shoulder and accept various responsibilities like performing religious ceremonies, naming ceremonies, looking after parents and dependent or unmarried brothers and sisters of the family, any other related family matters and also bear the expenses of the family functions. There is no doubt that other members of the family also contribute goods or money for family ceremonies and functions but she has to bear the rest of the expenditure. Thus the youngest daughter has no absolute power over the ancestral property due to control of male members such as maternal uncle and brothers, but it is undeniable fact that she and her sisters have the right to use as well as control and manage their own self acquired property.

Though according to the Khasi traditional system woman cannot exercises full control over property, but she occupied an important position in her own family and wield lot of powers particularly when her maternal uncle and her brothers are not in the same village, as her husband has no right over her ancestral property.

Khasi women also participated freely in all sorts of activities in complementing family income. They work side by side with men in the agricultural fields and orchards. In the areas pertaining to her own affairs especially marriage, she is free to choose her own husband although the proposal must come from male's side. If she liked him she must tell the parents and uncle of the desire to marry followed by proper investigations whether there is any connection between the two clans. In case both sides satisfied and no case of incest (sang) existed, marriage could take place. In case of divorce, a man or woman could do so on the grounds of barrenness and adultery with the knowledge of both clans.

In Khasi Hills, despite social and economic status that women are enjoying according to the Khasi custom and practice, they are not permitting to attend traditional *Dorbar*[15]. Traditionally, women in Khasi society cannot participate in the political activities of the state[16], neither do they have the right to contest the election to the office of the Traditional Council nor are they permitted to exercise their franchise. The Traditional Council would consist of only male members and the voting procedure to elect those members are also exercised by the male members. Moreover, women could not become the rulers of the *Himas* (states) except in the case of total absence of male heirs from a particular royal clan (syiem)[17]. Thus, the administration of the *hima* (state) is the prerogative of male members only.

The Present Scenario

As we all know that adaptation to modern culture is evident in every society, the Khasi society too is no exception to it. In the last century, the process of transformation of a small and isolated community has taken place in a steady way due to contact with Christian missionaries[18]. Modern education and exposure to the outside world are also responsible for the changes that have taken place in the Khasi society[19]. In the past, the youngest daughter together with her maternal uncle play crucial role in the family's affairs. They are responsible for the family's management and progress, which we can consider them as the strong pillars of the family. In the context of present day Khasi families where the majority of the Khasis are converted into Christianity, the status and responsibility of both the youngest daughter and maternal uncle is quite different. The youngest daughters' correlation with Khasi religious ceremonies and rituals are vanishing away from the scene. The status of maternal uncle is not powerful as it used to be in the olden day.

Through formal education, the Khasis are exposed to western thoughts and ideas which have a lasting effect on the society as a whole. The development mechanisms have far reaching effect on the simplistic and isolated Khasis society. The advent of the British unified the Khasi *Hima* (states) which are fragmented, isolated and exclusive into a single administration and selected Sohra language as a common language for the whole tribe to be used in schools and churches. All these activities have strong bearing on the Khasi customs and practices. The dealings and approaches of the Christian missionaries toward the Khasi customs and practices was complex, though they have adopted status quo with regards to customs and practices especially the matrilineal system. For the Khasis convert into Christianity, it was taught to renounce entirely the traditional Khasi religion. With the conversion to Christianity, some kinship practices, so closely allied to religion have altered or been forsaken. Moreover, Christianity has not encouraged women leadership even till these days except in the field of education and health service. Thus, it was quite apparent that they still adopting the traditional way of depriving of women leadership rights in all decision making bodies. However, their involvement in strengthening matrilineal system was evident from the fact that they have emphasized more responsibility on the parents rather than maternal uncle. By stressing the need of more responsibility on the parents, it has positive impact on the Khasi matrilineal society.

In the contemporary times, the youngest daughter or maternal uncle is confined themselves in their own respective family. Maternal uncle is more responsible towards his wife and children. All his assets and income goes directly to his wife and children. In fact the sole responsibility for managing and running the present day Khasi family is in the hands of both husband and wife. Some changes have taken place also in the allotment of the family's property especially among the educated and business stratum of the society where the parent gives a due share to all sons and daughters. In the case disposal or mortgage of ancestral property whether movable or immovable, maternal uncles, brothers, sisters have equal say and responsibility as they used to enjoy in the past.

Due to exposure and interaction with different cultures and values of different societies, some sections of the Khasis are using the father's title or clan while others are following bi-lineal pattern i.e. using both their father's and mother's clan name. This is pertinent if a father occupied a higher position in society. While some other sections of the Khasi society have propagated the idea of doing away with matrilineal system. The *Seng Rympei Thymmai* (SRT)[20] a socio-cultural organization was formed in 1990 in order to initiate changes in the Khasi society. The organization was born out of social response and reaction to the inherent and practical problems that matrilineal system is facing in the present context. The members are of the opinion that lineage must be taken from the father sides and the wealth of the family must be distributed among the sons and daughters.

In fact it is essential to mention here that despite adaptation of Christianity as well as following modern life style particularly by the Khasi educated classes and urban dwellers, the majority of the Khasi have not denounced completely the basic customs such as kinship institution, the matrilineal system, the customary right of inheritance of property, the clan durbar and representation in the durbar *Hima* (state). Intra-clan marriage is still prohibited and regarded as a sin of incent or crime by the Christiana as well as non-Christian, the techniques of cultivation and the community life of the Khasis demonstrate the continuation of the long past cultural and social tradition.

It is undeniable fact that in recent time women have faced new challenges which have manifested in different forms as the values and ethics of the people is degrading day by day. Cases of rape, molestation, sexual harassment, etc are the common news headlines in the newspapers. It must be mentioned here also that women who are from low income families of rural or even urban areas are facing poor health and nutrition which are responsible for high mortality rates among young children as well as mother of child bearing age.

Conclusion

Notwithstanding the emergence of new challenges as well as some restrictions by custom on the status of Khasi women, it is important to mention here that woman as a mother is respected as a family goddess[21]. Matrilineal system has given a sense of responsibility for both sexes for the welfare of the family as a whole and woman in particular is at liberty to take up any job she likes such as trade, business, etc. From time immemorial women in Khasi hills are famous traders, together with men they venture to different market places bordering the plain areas of Sylhet (present day Bangladesh) and Assam far and near, for trade and commerce. In Khasi Hills it would seem strange if a woman does not work and it is rare to come across a woman whose only duty is that of house wife. Irrespective of rural and urban background, women are highly self-supportive and have expertise in their respective works and are shouldering together with men in the process of development.

In recent years, Khasi women have come up in every aspect of life whether in education, business, trade, civil services or professional jobs[22]. It is not very uncommon to see many women contractors and traders in Khasi Hills. The society and family component of the Khasis provide greater freedom for both the sexes. The Khasi customs have identified different assignment for both the sexes. Khasi women are treated equally and enjoy a position of respect at home or in society. As a result there is no question of domination and discrimination of one sex by another. Social restraints[23] which are prevalence in other parts of the country such as dowry system, bride burning, caste system, female foeticide, honour killing, etc are unknown things.

Notes:

1. A.C.Mahapatra, 'Locational Pattern of Markets in the Early British Period in North East India' in J.B.Bhattacherjee (ed.), Studies in the Economic History of North East India, Har-Anand Publications, New Delhi,1994, p.164.
2. Passah, Amena N. 'Matriliny in Meghalaya: At the crossroads?-Some insights' in Momin, Mignonette (ed.), 2003, Readings in History and Culture of the Garos, Regency Publications, New Delhi, p.181.
3. Snaitang, O.L, 'The impact of Christianity on the Khasi-Jaintia Matrilineal Society' in Chacko, Priyaram M (ed.), 1998, Matriliny in Meghalaya: Tradition and change, Regency Publications, New Delhi, p.55.
4. Joshi, H.G. (2004), Meghalaya: Past and Present, Mittal Publications, New Delhi, p.288.
5. War, Juanita 'Status of women in traditional khasi Culture' in Sen, Soumen.(ed.), 1992, Women in Meghalaya, Daya Publishing House, New Delhi,p19.
6. Bareh, H. (2001), Encyclopedia of North East India, Vol.IV, Meghalaya, New Delhi, Mittal Publications,pp.12-13.
7. Ibid, pp.254-255.
8. Momin, Nikme Salse C. (2010) Understanding across Cultures of North East India, DVS Publishers, Guwahati, p.50.
9. Chowdhury, J.N. (1996) Ki Khun Khasi Khara (The Khasi People), Jeetraj Publications, Calcutta, p.203.
10. Ibid.
11. War people refer to those Khasis who were inhabiting the southern parts of Khasi Hills adjacent with Bangladesh.
12. Lyngdoh, Sohble Sngi 'The Khasi Matriliny: Its Past and Present' in Chacko, Priyaram M (ed.), Op.cit, pp.32-33.
13. Ibid.
14. Bareh, H. Op.cit, 254.
15. Joshi, H.J, Op.cit,p. 288
16. Ibid.
17. War, Juanita. Op. cit,p19.
18. Lyngdoh, Sohble Sngi, Op.cit. p.40.
19. Ibid, pp.41-42.

20. Syiem, I. M 'Religion and Matriliny in Khasi Society: Some Observations' in Chacko, Priyaram M (ed.), 1998, Matriliny in Meghalaya: Tradition and change, Regency Publications, New Delhi

21. Snaitang, O.L 'Impact of the Christianity on the Khasi-Jantia Matrilineal Family' in Chacko, Priyaram M (ed.), 1998, Ibid, p. 59.

22. Mawlong, Adila 'Some aspect of Change in the Family system of the Khasis' in Chacko, Priyaram M (ed.), 1998, Ibid, p.83.

23. Pala, V (2015), 'Rights and Responsibilities of Tribal women at home and work in rural Meghalaya' Man and Society: A Journal of North East Studies, Vol.VI.

Khasi Megalithic Culture:
A Study from Gender Perspective

Streamlet Dkhar

Meghalaya "the abode of clouds" is a hilly area with natural beauty all around. Beautiful hills, valleys, caves, rivers and waterfalls are available in abundance in and around the state. Meghalaya is also rich in its tradition, folklore and cultural heritage. The uniqueness of its system is because of the matrilineal system they practice where the lineage is traced through the mother. One can also witness the rich topographic deposits of hard-stones. One of the important aspects of the Khasi culture that is worth mentioning is the presence of megalithic culture. These stones structure like monoliths have their connection with the ancestors as a link between the living and the dead. The spirits of the ancestors are concretized in stones through the megalithic monuments.

Monoliths are monumental stones built to remind the next generations (i) of the religious rites of the clan and (ii) to commemorate the great feats achieved by them. In Khasi, monoliths are known as "Mawbynna". The word "Mawbynna" gives the meaning and context as those stones which announce or proclaim or "Pynbna" which means to give an idea of telling something or pronouncing of any event.

The main types of monoliths are:

1. "Mawbynna - Nam" or the commemorative stones
2. "Mawbynna - Niam" or the Religious stones

Other structures of Monoliths are:

"Mawshongthait" or the Rest stones
"Mawkjat" or the Foot stones
"Mawlynti" or the Indicative stones
"Mawbah," or the Clan Cairn or ossuary
"Mawshyieng" or the Bone repository of the clan
"Mawbasa" or the big flat stones in the market for merchandise
"Mawpud" or the boundary stones
and Mawbri same as Mawpud
"Mawbynna - Nam" or the Commemorative stones are erected primarily
to honour:

i.   Any dead member of the clan for his noble deeds
ii. A Syiem (Chief) who governs the Hima (kingdom)
iii. to celebrate any notable event: political or social
iv. Setting up of a market place
v.   And for other reasons

In many occasions these stones are also erected for the historical events such as: The territorial boundaries and for holding of traditional Durbars or assembly. Such stones are erected as structures but they all have their own significances. They are erected in odd numbers like 3, 5, 7, etc. "The common monumental stones consist of three menhirs vary to five or seven or nine more than one dolmen are associated". (H. Bareh, 1967, 19). Most of them are erected on the road side so that people see them.

"Mawbynna-Niam" or the religious stones: They are usually symbolic stones and have their own significance and nomenclature. The Menhirs or upright stones are called "Maw-shynrang" or the male stones. They have such names as "Maw-kñi" for maternal uncle, "Maw-pyrsa" for nephew, "Maw-thawlang" for paternal uncle. "Mawbynna-Niam" or the religious stones have something to do with the religious rites pertaining to the clan who constructs it. These stones are known as "Ka Mawbah"/ clan Cairn or osuary; and the Khasis believe that these monoliths are the stone structures erected by the ancestors, on the occasion of 'Thep Mawbah' or bone repository of the clan or its womb attached with rituals.

"Mawbah" means the Khasi clan's cairn or bones repository of a clan connected with rituals- "Thep Mawbah". "Ka Maw-shyieng" means a bone depository of a womb in the same clan temporary placed before the "Thep Mawbah" ritual and finally placing in the clan's cairn or the "Mawbah".

The monoliths that are found on the sides of the road and on the way to market places are called "Maw-shongthait" or the rest stones where people after walking for miles would stop and sit on the dolmen or the female stone and reclining their back on the male stone to rest and relax for a while. There are also stones of these types known as "Maw-lynti" or "Maw-kdew" or the indicative stones. These stones are found in forest to indicate the way to a certain destination for a place to reach either the market or the place where Dorbar is being held. "Mawkjat" are stones in standing positions with a dolmen at the bottom to indicate that at that place all other clans related to the family by blood connection will go to the family cairn. These stones are strongly integrated in the matrilineal clan organization. They serve the purpose of emphasizing the law of exogamy, social continuity and social order in the society.

Religious monoliths are shorter in height than the Commemorative monoliths. These religious stones can be seen in out of the way placed either deep in forest or far out because the erection of which are connected with religious rites and ceremonies and people are usually not allowed to stamp on them.

Beliefs

The Khasis have their own indigenous religion and beliefs from time immemorial. All aspects of Khasi religion are connected with rituals. The Khasis do not bury the dead but cremate them. So 'ka kpep' or the crematorium has an important connection with those rituals and practices that are performed by the living for the dead body and the departed soul.

After all preparations of the kpep are made, the dead body is taken to the cremation ground where the rituals for the dead will be performed by the maternal uncle. The practice of the Khasis to honour the departed soul show clearly when people come to witness the last rite done for the departed soul and follow the corpse carrying by the relatives in a procession to the cremation ground. All rituals for the dead before cremation are done. When everything was over, bones were collected and were taken to "Mawshyieng" of the particular womb of the clan and then later on to 'Mawbah' or 'Pepbah.' The clan of the dead had to perform all the rites and rituals associated with the dead after cremation in a leadership of the maternal uncle (s).

Nowadays, the ritual of "ka Thep Mawbah" is rarely done by those Khasi clans as in the past. But the rituals and ceremonies for the dead is being done till today with the last and final ritual of ka "Ter-Ïap" after cremation at the cremation ground in a place called "Rsham." "Ter–Ïap" means to christen his / her name that he / she has left the world of the living for his / her reception in the world of the dead.

This is done as the last rite after the cremation of the dead body, by putting the ashes in a kind of small platform and making it at a straight level in such a way that the signs would be able to read in the next morning. This is done because of the principle that the soul never dies but would live with the great ancestress of the clan in the parlour of the Almighty Creator. While from this Rsham the kith and kin of the deceased would be able to interpret the sign and symbol when they thoroughly analyse the signs appeared in the "Rsham".

After a brief information about the Megalithic culture of the Khasis, an interpretation of the positions of stone erection may be done and analyse from the gender perspective.

Gender perspective as seen from erection of monoliths

Since Gender discrimination is the issue of the day, many scholars are enthusiastic in putting questions like: do the Khasis who practice the matrilineal system also face gender discrimination? There are a number of opinions regarding this issue as the practicality of the system does not go in line with the theory that Khasi women are empowered and does not face gender discrimination as women in other patriarchal society. Through the study of monoliths, one can interpret a few aspect of gender discrimination on women in the Khasi society. We begin with a question, how do monoliths reflect as one of the aspects of gender discrimination? By looking at the position of the monoliths structures given in the picture one can interpret the position of men and women in the Khasi society.

Here is the interpretation, the upright stone in the middle is significant of the presence of the maternal uncle called "Maw-suitniakñi" or the "Maw-kñi". To understand the erection of this stone one needs to know the position and the role of a maternal uncle in the Khasi clan. The maternal uncle is the one who has the power to rule all wombs in his clanship. He is always the counsellor who guides the nephews and nieces in all matters related to the clan. He decides everything in his clanship, such as: for the clan's disposal of any ancestral property; he is the priest or the "Lyngdoh niam" in his clan who performs all the rituals, such as: i. Naming Ceremony, ii. Marriage iii. Rituals for disposal of the dead of any member of his clan.

The two menhirs lying on both side of the "Mawkñi" (stone meant for the maternal Uncle) are called "Mawpyrsa" (stone for the Nephews). These stones symbolise the political allegiance of the Khasis as the descendants /inheritors of the rituals and reigning of the Hima (Kingdom). Important point to be noted here is that women have been denied access to their constitutional and political rights to free movement and association as inheritors of the political allegiance of the" longsyiem mansyiem" or the ruling of the hima.

The Dolmen or the Female stone known as "Ka Maw Kynthei", is a stone that is placed at the foot of male stones. This strongly reflects the subordination of a woman to her counterpart. Why the female stone has to be placed at the foot of the male stones? Why it is not placed as upright stone besides the male stones? Answer to these questions is clearly focused on gender bias with the perception that women could not be equal to men.

Understanding Gender

Generally, nature has created two sexes: women and men. Differences between them are the biological functions and reproduction. But when we talk of gender roles and gender differences we must be aware that these are brought by socialisation, historical traditions & customary norms. Gender thus is the object that is being art, a social act and a political tool rather than a natural institution like sex. Therefore gender can be altered, socially engineered and politically reconstructed. In understanding gender one has to first understand the concept of Patriarchy. Patriarchy is the most fundamental concept that forms the basis for understanding many other concepts that deal with women's status. Basically it believes that women are viewed and interpreted in terms of a male dominated society and its interests. That women's lives are governed by a concept of power that controls and subordinates women: their rights, behaviour pattern, physical movement, thinking process, etc. All these control every individual's desires. Having understood the concept of gender one can interpret the position of any society one is familiar with. But to the understanding of a researcher, most things are based on facts rather on hearsay.

Having said so, many non Khasis are of the view that the Khasis practice the Matriarchal system where a woman is the head of the family and the youngest daughter is the sole heir of the ancestral property. This is a wrong opinion and a misconception due to the misinterpretation of the non Khasi writers. In fact the Khasis practice the matrilineal system and she is never the head of the family; the youngest daughter is not the sole heir of the ancestral property; she is only the custodian of the family property and women in the Khasi society are always subordinate to men. Again coming to the political rights, in the Khasi tradition, the children can never be the inheritors of their father's hima even though if their father is a Syiem/Chief. His nephews are the descendants of "Longsyiem mansyiem" or syiemship after the Maternal uncle's death. There is no trace of the syiemship to be given to the niece or daughter. The saying in Khasi maxim, "Haba Kynih ka Iar kynthei ka pyrthei kan sa wai" which means that "when a hen crows the world will come to an end"; is a metaphorical statement that only man can reign and have the power and not a woman. She could never be above man in all respects, nor could she be equal to him. Her being subordinated to man is also proved from the tradition of giving the top most portion of the cooked rice in a pot or "Ja Khlieh khiew" to a father which signifies man as the head of the family.

A woman is considered only to be the ancestral mother who keeps the womb's lineage in all generations. She is the" Ïawbei tynrai"/root ancestral mother and her descendants of the clan continues as long as there are daughters born to the womb of the clan. But in any matter she has to consult the Suitnia-kñi/ the maternal uncle who performs all the rituals and gives the final decision in the clan. Women's participation at the decision making level is only marginal. Whatever decision is to be made is always made either by the maternal uncle at the clan level and by the husband/father at the nuclear family level.

Conclusion

A close analysis of the Monolith structures of the Khasis may reveal certain gender implications in the Khasi society which, though follows a matrilineal system, shows a patriarchal mindset. Subordination of a woman to her counterpart could clearly be interpreted through the erection of monoliths and other aspects of Khasi culture as in a dancing arena of "Ka Shad Suk Mynsiem" and "ka Pomblang Nongkrem". The virgin maidens are to dance inside the arena and men both married and unmarried can dance outside the arena which signifies that women are the keeper of their home and men are the bread winner and supporter of the women and the family.

References:

Bareh, Hamlet. *The History and Culture of the Khasi People*, Shillong: Ri Khasi Press, Second and Revised Enlarged Edition 1985, Print.

Lyngdoh, Homiwell. *Ka Niam Khasi*. Shillong: Don Bosco Press, rpt. 2013. Print.

Status of Garo women of Meghalaya: Its past and present

Mothis M. Sangma

Introduction

Garo Hills Districts of Meghalaya are pre-dominantly inhabited by the indigenous Garo community. The Garos live in the hills and the plains of the Districts alike spreading all parts of North East India as far as West Bengal and Bangladesh as well. Garos are divided into 12 sub dialectical groups each inhabiting a particular area with a distinct dialect.

Garos follow the same tradition and culture, even though they scattered in the sub-continent of Asia. The peculiar, 'matrilineal system' of the Garos is distinct system to the prevailing society of the world, yet the Garo women are relatively better in position as they are the owner of the property in the family according to the customary law of the Garos.

Matrilineal system of the Garos

Garo society being a matrilineal society, the mother/wife can play a very important in the family. She is the link between the husband and the children.

296

In a purely matrilineal and matrilocal society, the position and the status of woman is much better than that in a patrilineal and patrilocal society. Garo social system concentrates power in the **mahari** consisting of a group of matrilineal **Chras** and **paa gachi**. It is they who controls and oversee the welfare of the family of respective **ma'chong** (motherhood).

Forefathers laid the foundation of 'matrilineal system', and strictly adhere to the succeeding generation. The think tank of the primitive society rightly advocates this system as the womenfolk is the physically weaker in the human race and let it be the custodian of property and heirs of the parents. While the menfolk, sent out to fight the enemies and protect the land, as rightly called **"measade do'reng, do'ka, songdu, sagal bilna man'a"**, menfolk is the kite and crock, can fly across the rivers and seas and settle anywhere. As the result, the Garo matrilineal system and traditions are still practicing and prevailing till the present generation.

Rights of Garo Woman (Mother)

The matriarchal system that existed from time immemorial gave the woman, the wife and the mother, a social rather than the personal standing. It is only in their conference, decided to have rectified and reformed the custom that endangered the tribes by giving the full rights and privileges of inheriting the property to woman and never to a son or man. Although there were no written documents to authenticate their oral traditions, the fact remains that even today woman inherits property and not man. The pitch and substance of this arrangement in the matrilineal society is the emphasis of love of mothers to their children and the love of children to their mothers.

Position of Garo Women

The position of Garo women in a matrilineal society is respected but at the same time they are also expected to respect their husbands, 'seko Paako mande ra'a'. Men and women work together for the welfare of the family. A woman cannot divorce or chase away her husband from her own accord. An aggrieved woman first approaches her **Chras** and gets their approval. Her **Chras** considers her complaints in pros and cons before taking or giving final consent and decisions. A woman has to abide by the final decisions of **Chras** either right or wrong. Here the avuncular authority is exercised before giving final verdict on the nature of her complaints. She cannot take any arbitrary decision.

Position of Garo woman in mahari

The word '*Mahari*' means the whole group consisting of all the female members or the relatives of the wife and her husband. In any of the affairs of the *mahari* be it meeting or important decisions, a woman is always consulted and she is at liberty to participate and can air her views. In any of the major and important decisions, women are consulted and they have a final word in such decisions. Of course, their views may be overruled by the decisions of the *chras* or male members who played a dominant role in such decisions.

In the affairs of the *mahari*, women have a little say in decisions making process. Such matters decisions are exclusively taken by the male members or elders. And if the women want to give their opinions, the only alternative left to them was through their husbands. The positions of women in the decision making process of the *mahari* has no value and considered less important. It is the *Chras* and the male elders dominate in such major decisions of settling disputes, marriages, divorces, distribution of property and so on. The reasons of not raising so much against the decisions of her *chras* and elder male members of the *mahari* due to the fact that the women in Garo society considers that all the major and important decisions will be taken for their well being but not against their welfare.

Position of Garo women in village administration and politics

The village administration is usually carried out by the village headman and the women are excluded in the decision making of the village administration and their welfare. A woman can never be the village Headman because the village headman has certain duties to perform such as performing the ceremonial rites which the woman cannot perform. The women in the village administration have no voice at all. Women in the rural areas are seldom consulted and taken into confidence in decisions making even in the matters of the welfare of the village, in social and educational pursuits. But with the introduction of elections, the Garo women take part in the election to Garo

Hills Autonomous District Council and Meghalaya State Legislative Assembly. They also contest in elections.

Garo Women and property

There is no doubt that the property of a family is inherited by woman and not by man as result of which the succession to the family property also falls on woman. The woman who inherited the parental property is known as *'Nokkrom'* (heiress). All the female members of the family are given due share of family property.

Though a woman is a sole owner of family property, but has no right to sale, mortgage or donate any part of the family property either movable or immovable without the prior consent of her *Chras*.

Status of an heiress (Nokrom) daughter

Garos being the matrilineal society, the family property descends through the mother and not through the father under the customary law of inheritance. The entire basic Garo social structure is based on the principle of preservation of wealth and property within the motherhood. It is this principle, the choice of *Nokkrom* (heiress) and the *A'kim* governs the entire tribe. The *Nokkrom* is the absolute mistress of all the family property that she inherits and whatever the property they may earn as husband and wife subsequently. She is given the sole guardian of a family property.

The woman who inherits the family property cannot sale, mortgage and dispose off the property inherited without the prior consent and knowledge of her *chras* and the *mahari*. The property that have earned during the life – time of husband and wife can be disposed off, sale or mortgage in consultation with her children and husband. The *Chras* and the *mahari* will not object to such sale or mortgage of family property for maintenance and welfare of the family. The husband and the wife have dual control over the property earned as husband and wife.

If the man marries another woman, without the consent of the principal wife and the approval of the *Chras,* the second wife shall have no right to claim over the family property. The property either inherited or acquired belongs to the woman in a Garo family, the man cannot sell or mortgage without the knowledge of the wife, children and the *chra*. If any of the family property is sold or mortgage, her *chras*, children and the *mahari* shall have to be consulted first and if no consultations takes place such transactions are invalid.

Thus, in a Garo family, the family property either inherited or earned is indirectly controlled by the *Chras* and the *mahari* from going out of the lineage.

Garo Women and religion

The position of women in a Garo traditional religion known as *'Songsarek'* (paganism) has practically no participation. Garo religion is typically the man's religion. They do not participate in the sacrificial offerings except in worships. Garo deities are practically almost males and few of the females. The priest known as *'Kamal'* is a male and there is no priestess. In all the religious ceremonies males take active part and female do not. For propitiating the evil spirits, the male *'Kamal'* who is conversant with the rituals perform ceremonies.

The women can participate in the religious ceremony is only the *'Gana Nokma'* ceremony along with her husband. But, the women also participate actively in the social part of dancing, singing and merry making after the actual ceremonies are over. Thus, we find that in Garo society the participation of women in religious worship is at the backdrop of religion. Women are to actively participate only in the social part of the ceremonies. However, the situation has changed in recent years especially for those converted Garo women into Christianity; participation in religious ceremonies is increasing. It is a common fact that women's participation in church activities is much higher than man. Even in some Christian denominations women are ordained as pastors or deacons.

Concluding Observations:

The status and position of women in Garo society is carnally appreciable since the system is free-from *purdah* system, **girl child marriage and infanticide**. However, Garo women must not simply satisfied with their position, status, right of succession and inheritance as well as the title of lineage from the mother. The present day scenario is danger for stereo types of culture as the western culture is booming to the indigenous culture and tradition. The indigenous culture of the Garo which is the 'gift of the nature' and that the forefathers have upholding it for the succeeding generation, it is an obligation of every Garo woman to preserve it. If the traditions and cultures are to be preserved for days to come, the forces of the present generation that luring for the twenty first century must stop for linkage. The partial Indianite and the westernize in nature will sabotage our own culture and as a result paralysis the very living of indigenous cultures and traditions. In the case of Garo women, there is every possibility for sea change, so Garo women must be prepared and ready to face the real challenges that lay ahead of them. **Disbanding cross marriage is an urgent task in order to prevent intruding the alien into the indigenous social structure who may also exploit the very foundation of social fabric.** If this present trend continues for several decades, the old aged system of the Garo may decay.

The modification of customary laws and practices by bringing it to statutory provisions with a view to protect and modify the customs to meet the changing scenario is essential. The rights of women need to be protected from the outsiders. And if no suitable laws are enacted in this respect either by the State Government or the District Council, the rights of women even amongst the Garo society may come to a far reaching consequences which will never be brought back to the past glory and practice.

The young generation of 21st century is trying to modernize the system by codifying of customary laws bringing it under the statutory and provisionalise for both man and woman for equal rights in property sharing. The trend is even for switching over from matrilineal system to patrilineal system, due to failure of womenfolk to follow the norms of the customs and traditions and barring to abide the binding principles of **Chras** and **Mahari.** Of course, this emblematical move may or may not see the light of the day but signaling dissatisfaction for the prevailing scenario of the Garo culture. The **seeds of education, civilization, advance of science and technology and economic developments** have penetrated even into the very core of the customary laws, practice and traditions making them difficult to follow and felt the need to change and to adapt to the changing needs of the generations but these trends can still be checked.

a) **Impact of Modernization and Christianity**

Christianity have infringed upon the Customary Laws such as Marriage and Divorce. The system of '**Songsarek**', marriage, which is called '**Do.sia**' have been illusion for the young generation. The religious laws of the Garos are non-performance in the present age. The Authority of **Chras** and Elders in **A'chik mandei** society is not the same like in the pre- modernization period.

A·chik mandei customs and traditions are numerous and intricate but continue to exist in different parts of the state and the customary with minor local adoptions. *A·chik* or Garos could adjust themselves to the challenges of modern civilizations by preserving their basic principles and valuable aspects of customs, traditions and practices. The economic conditions of the people has affected greatly on the customs, traditions, social and cultural activities of the Garos where ever they are. Christianity and spread of education and advances of science and technology have greatly influenced on the life and culture of the Garos.

b) Its importance in the Present day context:

Maintenance and observances of basic principles of Garo customary Laws, practices, traditions, usages amongst the Garo have reached the crucial stage. It is an important for the Garos to abide by their original traditions and cultures, wherever they are, in whatever country or state that they may stay or live, so as to continue to follow and practice their aged old customs, traditions and cultures. If the Garos do not follow and cling to their own customs, traditions and culture then there is every possibility of being lost of identity in the midst of other communities.

Thus in conclusion, the matrilineal system of the Garos, praise the woman and placed the position high in the society, but in practice this system is in vacuum. For instance, *Nok-ma* (mother of the house), land owner, has only titular head, the powers and functions of the *Nok-ma* is run by the husband. Unlike the patrilineal system man/husband is the head of the family and all the property and title goes to the man/husband. In the matrilineal system of the Garo title and the property of the family's inheritance goes to the wife/ woman, but the man/husband still the head of the family.

However, in spite of the above mentioned shortcomings, the status and position of women in Garo society is highly respected. Women work side by side with men in all activities of day to day life and share the burden in family matters. The Garo women occupied a very high position in family and society which is envied by the opposite (patrimonial) system of prevailing customs and traditions of the world.

References:

Books

1. Burling, Robbins, (1963), *Rengsangiri: Family and Kinship in a Garo village,* University of Pynsylvania Press, Philadelphia.
2. Chattopadhaya, S.K., (ed.), 1985, *Tribal Institutions of Meghalaya,* Spectrum Publications, Guwahati.
3. Chocko, Pariyaran. M., (1998), *Matriliny in Meghalaya,* Regency Publications, New Delhi.
4. Costa, Giulio., (1975), *The Garo Code of Law,* Catholic Church, Tura.
5. Goswami M.C. & D. N. Majumdar (1972), *Social Institutions of the Garo of Meghalaya,*
6. Kar, P.C., (1982), *Glimpses of the Garos,* Garo Hills Book Emporium, Tura.
7. Mackenzie, Alexander, (1981), *The North East Frontier of India,* Mittal Publications, Delhi.
8. Marak, Julius L. R., (1999), *The Garo Customary laws and Practices,* Firma Publications, Calcutta.
9. Marak K.R. (1964), *The Garos and their Customary Laws and Usages,* Tura.
10. Marak, Kumie, R., (1997), *Traditions and Modernity in Matrilineal Tribal Society,* Inter-India Publications, New Delhi.
11. Momin, Mignonette., (2003), *Readings in History and Culture of the Garos,* Regency Publications, New Delhi.
12. Playfair, A., (1975), *The Garos,* Spectrum Publications, Guwahati.
13. Rongmuthu, Dewansing, (1978), *Marriage Customs of the Garos,*
14. Sangma M.S. (1981), *History and Culture of the Garos,* Books Today, New Delhi.
15. Sangma, Jangsan (1973), *The Principles of Garo Laws,* Banilekha Press, Calcutta.
16. Sangma, Prabodh M., (2010), *Glimpses of the Garo Heritage and Philosophy,* D.J Publications, Tura.
17. Sangma M.S. (1981), *Political History of the Garos of Goalpara – Kamrup of Assam,* D.J Publications, Tura.

18. Sarma, Siddheswar., (2003), *The Land and Forest*, Bhabari Publications, Guwahati.

Journals

1. Goswami M.C. & D. N. Majumdar (1965), 'A Study of Women's positions among the Garo of Assam', *Man-in –India,* Vol – 45, No.1.
2. Goswami M.C. & D. N. Majumdar (1967), 'Clan organization among the Garo of Assam', *Man-in –India,* Vol – 47, No.4.
3. Majumdar, D.N., (1966), 'Mahari among the Garos of Assam', Jr. of the University of Guahati, Vol. XV, No.2.

Oral Traditions In the Community of The Mizos

Laltluangliana Khiangte

Really, an in depth study of the tribal culture of North-East India is the need of the hour because of the fact that oral tradition predominates the cultural mapping of any tribe and re-reading of the same has to be encouraged in all levels of folklore studies. Before they came to be familiar with the convention of reading and writing all tribes used effectively oral tradition as the main and only source of information and development. When we look at the folk literature of the Mizo tribes as well, it was a non-literate culture and its collection in written form comes at a much later date, say in 1870's.

The compilation and publication of the first book ever written in Mizo language as reduced by the then Lt.Col. T.H.Lewin, in his books, especially in *The Progressive Colloquial Exercises of Dzo (Mizo)* in 1874 ushered a new era for the tribal communities of the present Mizoram. Today, the collection in written form of this oral-practices and various traditions, are an ever enlarging and on-going process where much of the customary laws and practices of the tribe have been recorded along with the languages and literatures of the tribes.

Major genres of Mizo oral traditions are chants, sacred-songs, proverbs, maxims, riddles, traditional sayings and narratives like folk tales, legend, myth and the like. Of these, the chants or songs may be the most meaningful enriching genre. Mizos of Mizoram were and still are today, a singing tribe, who love singing and having different tunes or flows of chants, songs and hymns. The earlier compositions have today, proved to be invaluable sources of oral data of the Mizos while tracing of the history and culture of the tribe. One may say, 'They have no other reliable source except for a few monoliths, tree and stone engravings' since oral tradition proved to be an encouraging scope of research.

After careful examination, songs and chants seem to have been a natural outcome of their poetic and nostalgic nature. The earliest composition seems to have first emerged not out of a conscious effort to compose, but rather out of grief and sorrow. The mourning chants of Ngaiteii's mother, at the lost of her daughter in the great flood (*Tuilet*) was really a spontaneous oveflow, which may be considered as the first one.

> *Oh, Ngaite....Oh, Ngaite.....*(Ngaite is the name of that girl / lady)
> *That you're suffering rough blow of south,*
> *That you're suffering heavy pour of rain,*
> *Oh, Ngaite....Oh, Ngaite.....*

It seems that the first group of expression through songs / chants were really simple and straightforward and words arrangement were not that poetic as well. Believe it or not, according to some writers, the following lines may be one of the earliest songs or chants:

> *That place is visible from this place,*
> *This place is visible from that place.*
> And also, *They say Khawmhma fence bends,*
> *Let it bends as it wishes.*
> (*Khawmhma* is a kind of local fruit bearing-tree.)

So the first group of chants or songs were, in fact dirges expressing grief at the loss of lives brought on by the famine known as *Thingpui tam*. Other songs of this early period include lullabies, *Thuthmun zai, Hlado* (chant) and *Bawhhla* (chant) of hunters and warriors, the first to celebrate slain game and the latter for slain enemies. *Dar-hla* was sung to the accompaniment of gongs on a happy occasion and *Salulam zai* was to celebrate a successful game of hunt.

Just two pieces of *Thuthmun zai* may be highlighted here (Source: Mizo Hla hlui-Mizo Folk Songs, collected by R.L. Thanmawia, Aizawl: 2012) The quality is not nominal but rather impressive as these verse express their real feeling and sufferings.

> *Thalai leh dawn tuai an tliak zo ve,*
> *Chhinglungah mi awm lo, vangkhua zawng ti ula*

Young and dear ones perishes due to calamities, just say there is no one in the village…....

> *Keini riak kan fam lo, mi lai an fam zo ve,*
> *Mi lai an fam zo ve, laikhum a thing reng e.*

Death comes to many, not only our family members, they have departed to make empty beds…..Because of great havoc in the in the land, people suffered and died in numbers. Mourners gathered and recited lamentations. Such kinds of lamentations or chants have been collected by researchers and a good numbers of those have been recorded in book form now.

Then, we may also highlight some of the pieces of *Hlado*, a heroic chant to be chanted by warrior or knight or pasaltha, at the entrance of the village after successful hunting or on the occasion of the celebration in the presence of all other relatives and friends. The modern version can be made as a continuation of oral tradition / folk practices of our forefathers even today in a very meaningful way.

Old but golden in nature, so precious for us now are those songs narrated by some of the older generation. Just one genre may be picked up now. *Lengzem zai* has been considered as one of the earliest compositions of the Mizos, most probably started from the 17 & 18th centuries. One Salvation Army Brig. Ngurliana, in his book ***Pi pute hla*** (1st. Ed. 1981) suggested that it was still very popular even in the 1870's and 1880's. All these are extreme longing and romantic verses like,

1. Kan intiamna khua romei

Thu tin kip te'n kan hrilna,
Kumsul veiah hleite'n a dang leh dawn lo.

(That we have made meaningful promises under the beautiful patches of
cloud above us and I cannot forget it when the next season is approaching)

> 2. *Mut hian ka mu dawn lo,*
> *Tlai khat ka var hlei lo'ng e,*
> *Di kan thenna chung khua rei tawh na reng e.*

(I will not sleep not even one sleepless night for the suffering and loneliness
still persisting afresh)

> 3. *Sum tin tam ka hnawl dawn e,*
> *Ka di val rianga nen chuan*
> *Kan nghak za ang phai zauva nghosai zawng.*

(I will not accept such a huge amount of money for I will wait the time
when my lover attains such a grand success)

> 4. *Ka nu tuan tul ka dawn lo,*
> *Ka zam khua romei angin,*
> *Suihlung a leng kei chu pang-la mai ka lo ni.*

(Mummy I cannot care whether important work to do but I am spreading
my wings just like thin cotton patches)

One of the most important channels for dissemination of useful
knowledge through oral tradition must be the specific hut of the village
blacksmith. In all villages, there will be blacksmith's cabin (pum) where
all the tools for manual workers have to be sharpened for effective use.
Right from morning men will gather there bringing their blunted tools and
apparatus to be made sharper for use in the days to come at their fields. Since
one blacksmith cannot finish all the task at once, of course they have to wait
there waiting first come first basis, except women who may be given priority
there. This is the practice of the days that woman will not be delayed for her

household works and the blacksmith automatically pay attention to her and finish her tools as wanted.

This has been the beautiful practice of the society where women will be given priority in blacksmith's cabin and male will be given priority at public water point (tuikhur). So, there is a clear division of labour and the Mizo society has well defined roles to be played by male and female accordingly.

As the Mizos progressed in dress, food habits and lifestyle, so too did their songs, which again reflected these very factors. Both the festive *Chawngchen zai* and dance note of *Chai zai* were sung by the community and celebratory in nature. *Chai zai* was mostly performed during the *Chapchar Kut* festival when all men and women came together in a clearing to dance, to celebrate the completion of their jhums for rice cultivation. There were separate songs for rituals and religious ceremonies known only to the priests called **sadawt** and **bawlpu**. The latter concentrated more on appeasing evil spirits who caused pain and disease.

The original composers of most of these folk songs like *Thuthmun zai, Dar hla, Salam zai, Hlado* and *Bawhhla* are unidentified, but later, after *Tlangkhaw zai* and *Lumtui zai, Ngente zai* became popular in which songs composed in the same tradition continued to bear their names. Such a practice is rare in other cultures.

Thus we have *Pihmuaki zai, Lalvunga & Lianchia zai, Neihlaia zai, Lianchhiari zai, Hualngo zai, Lallula zai, zopui zai, chhim zai, Laltheri zai, Saikuti zai, Darpawngi zai, Darmani zai, Darlenglehi zai* and so on. So, Pihmuaki was the first known composer and legend has it that the chief and village elders finally had her buried alive for fear she would finish composing all the songs and leave nothing for posterity. Her singing accompanied by her gong was heard for seven days before it finally stilled.

The songs of *Laltheri* and *Darpawngi* may be said to be revolutionary in nature for they were amongst the first to have brought about social change of some significance in Mizo history. Laltheri was the daughter of a *Sailo* Chief who fell in love with, and became pregnant by, a commoner named Chalthanga. He was killed at the order of her father for this was a right they claimed over a layman who dared to be the lover of their women.

In her grief Laltheri stripped herself naked and refused to eat, using her shame and humiliation as weapons to defy her family. She composed songs that spoke of her great sorrow yet defied and mocked the vanity of the Sailo clan of whom it was said that 'they walked between the sun and the moon'- such was their absolute sovereignty in their heyday. Her songs had the desired impact and gradually helped during about a change in the relation between chiefs and their subjects.

To come to the genre of myths, legends and folktales, 66 major tales have been identified and recorded so far in the Folklore series, as collected by the writer of this paper in his *Folktales of Mizoram* (1997) though it is likely that many more remain to be documented. Mizo folk literature is enriched by a unique collection of tales associated with the legendary Chhura who runs the gamut of roles from brother, husband, fool, trickster, to culture hero. Fusion both positive and negative traits, he is in many ways reflective of the various aspects of the native Mizo character itself. There are a group of tales about Chhura and the horn of plenty that reveal his sense of honour and bravery, sagacity and *'tlawmngaihna'* (the Mizo concept of selfless giving of oneself to others in need without expecting returns). Yet there are also numerous tales that tell of his foolishness, revealing him in his most well-known persona, that of the lovable, bumbling fool. These tales reveal, among others, the earthy and often boisterous sense of humour of the Mizos. Yet again, there are a group of tales associated with his trip to *'Mawngping khua'* and the resultant chase by his enemies, that tell us of his wit, resourcefulness, deceit, impudence, sense of humour and lack of his wit, resourcefulness, deceit, impudence, sense of humour and lack of sexual morals. Which is the real Chhura may be a question to preoccupy many a folklorist scholar in the years to come.

To understand the oral tradition in Mizo culture, I have included in this paper a few proverbs, do's and dont's, sayings, idioms and phrases type of oral traditions. I am quite sure that many more are to be documented. These proverbs reveal, among other things, the innate wisdom of a simple tribe that believed in the importance of community life for the common good. It is reflected in sayings like 'Share and survive, eat alone and perish' and 'Even the big boulder cannot survive without the support of the smaller stone'. The status of women may be seen in sayings like 'Women and crabs have no religion' and 'A woman's wisdom does not extend beyond the public water point' and 'As the meat of crab is not a proper meat, so is the opinion of a woman no opinion' and 'Let a woman and a dog bark as it pleases them'.

Some more may be noted here for ready reference:

- **If the shell of a bean is good, the nut it bears is good. If the shell is not good, the nut inside is also poor**. (Kawi pawh a kawm a that leh a rah a tha, a kawm a that loh chuan a rah pawh a tha lo).
- **Those who do not respect their parents never prosper.** (Nu leh pa pawisa lo an ding chhuak tak tak ngai lo).
- **Nothing sticks in the shin of a barking deer nor does self-praise.** (Mahni infak leh sakhi ngalah engmah a bet lo)
- **A man who does not have the courage to help a neighbour in trouble should wear a skirt**. (Thenawm mangang chhan ngam lo chuan pawnfen fen mai tur)
- **A loose woman can spoil the dignity of a whole village.** (Hmeichhe awm tha duh lo pakhatin khua a timualpho thei).
- **Shutting the gate of the bull pen after the bull has escaped is foolishness**. (Se bo hnua se kawngkawr ang - thil atthlak).
- **Finding a husband and a basket full of firewood is not difficult at all.** (Pasal pakhat leh thing phur khat fawm zawng a huphurhawm lo ve)
- **Living together in a same hill and dying together in a vale.** (Dam leh tlang khatah, thih leh ruam khatah)
- **Siblings' narration of a same story could be different.** (Unau thawnthu sawi mah a dang)
- **Liked by a hundred, also disliked by a hundred.** (Duhtu za, duhlotu lah za)
- **Even Liando-a and his younger brother shared a seed of small edible grasshopper**. (Liandova te unau pawhin min fang khat an inphel)
- **Orphans and community co-operate together**. (Fahrah leh vantlang an tang rual)
- **A woman never reprimanded and the edge of a jhum not maintained soon become intolerable.** (Hmeichhe vau leh vau vau loh an pawng tual tual)
- **Do not be blinded by other's kind speech.** (Mi tawngkam tha an um lutuk ngai lo)
- **Men are given priority at the water-point, and women at a village smithy hut.** (Tuikhurah mipa an lal a, pumah hmeichhia an lal ngai e.)

- **The last bull-gayal often gets beaten up**. (Se hnuhnungin vuak an tuar)
- **A person who commits adultery is likely to be bitten by a tiger**. (Uire chu Sakeiin a she duh bik)
- **When a hen griefs, a wild-cat is happy**. (Arpui a lungchhia, sanghar a lung lawm)
- **Unceasing tender care wins the hearts of women and puppies**. (Hmeichhia leh uite chu a chulnel peih peih an ni mai e)

Many thought provoking sayings may be mentioned one after another in this connection. When they say, '*Nu siar nu siar*' in case of women and *pa siar pa siar* in case of men, they mean to say that a daughter will be hopeless as her mother or the son will behave as his father, but not in a positive sense. Parents have offspring of their own type, who are not very much better or worse than the parents.

On the positive side as well, they used to say, 'A beautiful bull-gayal gives another beautiful bull-gayal, and ferocious one gives another ferocious type (*Sial rangin sial rang a hring, sakawlin sakawl a hring*). A beautiful mother would deliver a beautiful daughter and a brave father is succeeded by a brave son. Some may appropriately interpret this as *Like father, like son*.

One who hoards for one self alone will die and those who share with others will survive (Sem sem dam dam, ei bil thi thi) has been the genuine principal philosophy of the Mizos of the past. Sharing with others is the centre of thought and all well to do families would share their treasures at the time of *Khuangchawi* festival by arranging a series of public feast and by distributing different kinds of valuables to the public.

In those days, they did not read the Bible or any other books on moral teaching. They were not instructed to think logically and act wisely. But they were well equipped with unbelievable wisdom that has been handed down orally. It is a pleasant enterprise to note the sayings and proverbs of our forefathers in the present era where documentation of cultural heritage is discussed.

THE DO'S OF MIZO FOREFATHERS:-

- Sharing and giving out is life, eating alone is death.
- Always aware the hints of elders in public activities.

- Always be on the front-line while doing social work.
- Next plot cultivators and next-door neighbours are to be considered as family.
- Always help a weary person on the road.
- Always pass your urine on the lower part of the road and
- Always pass your motion on the upper part of the road.

The DON'TS OF MIZO FOREFATHER:-

- Never refuse what an older person requests you to do.
- Never criticize your parentage or origin.
- Never construct a house by blocking the path of others.
- A house fly does not alight on anything other than a festering sore.
- Cursing and thoughtless talk should not be practised.
- A man should not try to stop two women fighting.
- Never roast a crab in a jhum hut during the season of autumn.
- Never slay a dog in a jhum hut.
- Never use the roots of trees as firewood.
- Never steal a cloth, a hoe or an axe.
- Never ill-treat remaining items of a ritual.
- Never be the first to eat before the elders start.
- Never throw away collected fire-woods in a jungle.
- Never whistle while a strong wind blows.
- They never drink a running river water.
- Never enter a house without making a warning sound.
- They never pollute public drinking water.
- Never block someone's road.
- Never make fun of a handicapped person.

Without any further clarification, the underlying sense may be clear to the reader. I have included just a few proverbs, Do's and Don'ts, sayings, idioms and phrases etc. of oral tradition. I am quite sure that many more are in queue to be documented. These proverbs reveal, among other things, the innate wisdom of a simple tribe that believed in the importance of community life for survival and for the common good.

It is clearly reflected in sayings like *Share and survive or eat alone and perish; Even the big boulder cannot be firm without the support of the smaller stones.*

All these sayings, proverbs, maxims etc. have been used as the guiding moral principle of the Mizos for a long time and it is true to note that they are not inferior to other sayings and proverbs of other great nations.

To conclude, it is a high time for us to think about the presence of numerous tall tales in Mizo oral folk tradition that has yet to be documented in a proper way. These are stories of *Thlanrawkpa Khuangchawi, Tuilet,* life of patriots and chiefs, jhum cultivation and related practices, religious rites and role of priest, festival and other ceremonies, accounts of sacrifices etc. including an interesting tales of *Tualte vanglai.* Tualte is a village in east Mizoram today, but it was believed to have seen better days way back in 1850 to 1856 under the rule of the great chief Vanhnuailiana.

Today, the expression '*tualte vanglai*' is synonymous with any tale of exaggeration and impossibility as contributed together in the blacksmith's hut every morning. These kind of tales and other related narrations are reflective of certain Mizo traits such as the inclination to exaggerate, a humorous and clever way with words and language, and of course, a bawdy sense of humour as well. All tales, accounts, practices are documented accordingly, the richness of the oral tradition of the Mizos may be seen by any reader of Mizo folklore, culture, language and literature.

References:

1. Dokhuma, James. **Hmanlai Mizo Kalphung**, J.D. Press Publication:1992
2. Liangkhaia, Rev. **Mizo Chanchin**, 4th. Edition, Aizawl: 1976.
4. TRI. **Mizo Thawnthu**, Tribal Research Institute, Aizawl:1992.
7. Khiangte, Laltluangliana. **Mizos of North East India**, Aizawl:2008.
8. Khiangte, Laltluangliana. **Mizo Folk Literature**, Indian Literature No.201, Jan-Feb.,2001.
9. *Unpublished Manuscripts & Archival materials* of L.T.L. Library & Archives, B-43, Mission Veng, Aizawl.

(Paper presented by Dr. Laltluangliana Khiangte, Professor & Head, Department of Mizo, Mizoram University, Aizawl in the International Seminar on Orality at Bodoland University, Kohrajar on 26th. May 2016, organized by the Department of English from 25th – 27th, May 2016)

(Paper presented by Dr. Laltluangliana Khiangte, Professor & Dean, School of Education & Humanities, Mizoram University, Aizawl in the International Conference at Assam University Diphu Campus on 5th. January 2012, organized by the Department of English from 4th – 6th, January 2012)

(Abstract)
ORAL TRADITIONS IN MIZO FOLKLORE AND CULTURE
Dr. Laltluangliana Khiangte, Professor & Dean,
School of Education & Humanities, Mizoram University

An in depth study of the tribal culture of North-East India is the need of the hour because of the fact that oral tradition pre-dominates the cultural mapping of any tribe and re-reading of the same has to be encouraged in all levels of folklore studies. Before they came to be familiar with the convention of reading and writing all tribes used effectively oral tradition as the main and only source of information and development. When we look at the folk literature of the Mizo tribes as well, it was a non-literate culture and its collection in written form comes at a much later date, say in 1870's.

The compilation and publication of the first book ever written in Mizo language as reduced by the then Lt.Col. T.H.Lewin, in his books, especially in *The Progressive Colloquial Exercises of Dzo (Mizo)* in 1874 ushered a new era for the tribal communities of the present Mizoram. Today, the collection in written form of this oral-practices and various traditions, are an ever enlarging and on-going process where much of the customary laws and practices of the tribe have been recorded along with the languages and literatures of the tribes.

Major genres of Mizo oral traditions are chants, sacred-songs, proverbs, maxims, riddles, traditional sayings and narratives like folk tales, legend, myth and the like. Of these, the chants or songs may be the most meaningful enriching genre. Mizos of Mizoram were and still are today, a singing tribe, who love singing and having different tunes or flows of chants, songs and hymns. The earlier compositions have today, proved to be invaluable sources of oral data of the Mizos while tracing of the history and culture of the tribe. One may say, 'They have no other reliable source except for a few monoliths, tree and stone engravings' since oral tradition proved to be an encouraging scope of research.

....

1. John Zemke, Professor of Romance Literatures, Director of E-Resource Centre, Editor of Oral Traditions, University of Missouri,

2. Ulo Valk, Professor Eesti ja võrdleva rahvaluule osakond Department of Estonian and Comparative Folklore Tartu Ülikool/ University of Tartu

3. Kailash C. Baral, Pro-Vice Chancellor & Professor of English EFL University, Shillong Campus, Shillong – 793022

4. Maria Inés Palleiro, Buenos Aires University- National Council for Scientific Research, Argentina, e-mail: inespalleiro@gmail.com

5. Salam Irene, Professor of History, Manipur University, Imphal, Manipur

6. Laltluangliana Khiangte, Professor & Head, Department of Mizo, Mizoram University, Aizawl, Mizoram

7. Streamlet Dkhar. Professor &Head. Department of Khasi, North Eastern Hill University, Shillong.

8. Onusa Suwanprest, Head of the Department of Folklore Philosophy and Religion, Faculty of Humanities, Naresuan University, Thailand

9. Dipti Visuddhangkoon, Associate Professor, Mahachulalongkornrajavi dyalaya University
email: dipti.visuddhangkoon@yahoo.com

10. Rashmi Narzary. Author, Columnist and Independent Editor Email: rashmi06narzary@gmail.com

11. Shyamal Prasad Saikia, IPS, Research Scholar, Department of Folklore Research, Gauhati University, Guwahati – 781 014

12. Ksh. Premchandra Singh, Assistant Professor, Dept. of English, *Tripura University* Email: kshprem@gmail.com

13. Deepak Basumatary, Assistant Professor, Dept. of English, Kokrajhar Govt. College, Kokrajhar, Assam.

14. Jeetumoni Basumatary, Assistant Professor, Dept. of English, Cotton College, Guwahati. Assam

15. Jyoti Brahma and BhaskarJyotiGogoi, Ph.D. Research Scholars, EFL University, Shillong Campus, Emails: cactusbr@gmail.com; bhaskargogoi@hotmail.co.in

16. Arnan Basumatary. Independent Researcher, Kokrajhar-783370 arnanb99@gmail.com

17. Tamsin Aftab, PhD Research Scholar, Department of Sociology, JamiaMilliaIslamia, New Delhi

18. Bhanuprabha Brahma, Research Scholar Centre for the Study of Law & Governance, Jawaharlal Nehru University, New Delhi-110067

19. Gitanjali Baro. Research Scholar, Dept. of English, Bodoland University

20. Farina Basumatary. Research Scholar, Dept. of English, Bodoland University

21. Debarati Chakraborty. Lecturer,R.K.S.M Vivekananda Vidyabhavan, Research Scholar, University Of Calcutta. Email-dbarati1985@gmail.com

22. Armstrong Swer. Asst. Professor, Department of Political Science, Mendipathar College, North Garo Hills District,Meghalaya-793112, Email- swerarmstrong123@gmail.com

23. Mothis Sangma. Assistant Professor.Department of Political Science. Mendipathar College, Mendipathar,North Garo Hills, Meghalaya, Email: msangmamothis@gmail.com

24. Debojyoti Biswas, Assistant Professor, Dept. of English, Bodoland University, Kokrajhar, Assam. India.